This is the story of the first Anglo–Spanish campaign again:
War, a previous attempt to launch joint operations during
tion to Iberia having failed before the allies had an opportu

Hardly had the ramifications of Britain's setback in her first Iberian expedition settled before a second was launched, Sir Arthur Wellesley disembarking at Lisbon on 21 April 1809. His primary objective was the liberation of Portugal from what was, at the time, a small but significant French incursion in the north of the country. That achieved, the British commander decided to push the boundaries of his mission, as set by Castlereagh, and enter Spanish territory to link up with Gregorio de la Cuesta's scratch army on the Tagus, his aim being that of pushing Victor's army away from the Portuguese frontier and eventually liberating Madrid.

For all the significance of Wellesley's presence, it could be fair to say that Cuesta was the main protagonist of the Tagus campaign. A somewhat difficult character, he fell foul of Spain's governing *Junta Suprema* in 1808, and was under house arrest pending trial at the time the Spanish armies were being overrun by Napoleon during his winter campaign of 1808–1809.

It was due only to the desperate predicament of Spain that the *Junta* decided to release Cuesta from his incarceration at Mérida and allow him to raise an ad hoc force which he referred to as the Army of Extremadura. It was with this army that he began the daunting task of attempting to prevent the French from crossing to the south bank of the Tagus in early 1809. By then the *Junta* was sitting at Seville, happy to support Cuesta's attempts to halt the French advance on the south, but seeing him as a threat to the continuation of their self-appointed interregnum position as governors of Spain.

When Wellesley entered Spain, the *Junta* saw an opportunity to use the British as partners in a plan to rid them of their troublesome general, their quid pro quo being the appointment of the British general as supreme allied commander. John Hookham Frere, Britain's former plenipotentiary in Spain, was soon eagerly assisting the *Junta* with its intriguing, his friends in Seville appointing him as their chief liaison officer to the British.

So things continued whilst Cuesta was endeavouring to construct a working relationship with Wellesley in the field, but undoubtedly the Spaniard would have heard of the intriguing against him. If so, it may well explain what some writers have referred to as his lack of cooperation with his British allies. However, the Tagus campaign of 1809 may well not have taken place had Cuesta not stood as the only bar to Victor's advance towards the Guadiana and beyond during the first quarter of 1809.

An examination of the Spanish archives affords the reader an opportunity to see just how much of a positive contribution Cuesta made to the Tagus campaign, despite the despicable insubordination of Francisco Venegas and the plotting in London and Seville against him; all of which could have served to extinguish the nascent Anglo-Spanish alliance.

After graduating from the University of Sheffield, John Marsden spent some years teaching Computer Science to sixth form students at Mexborough School, before returning to university to take a postgraduate degree in Control Sytems. A career in IT Systems (defence and telecommunications) was to follow, during which he became a director of a small company offering services to the IT industry. Marriage to his Spanish wife has stimulated an interest in Spanish culture, literature, and history: mainly, though not exclusively, relating to the Peninsular War. His knowledge of Spanish has allowed him to bring to light a number of documents relating to that conflict currently lying in the Spanish military archives. He lives in Hampshire and has two grown up children, Joseph and Teresa. This is his second book, his first being *Napoleon's Stolen Army : How the Royal Navy Rescued a Spanish Army in the Baltic* (Helion, 2021).

The Tagus Campaign of 1809

An Alliance in Jeopardy

John Marsden

 Helion & Company

For my friend, Niall Sloane, whose encouragement provided me
with the motivation to embark upon this project.

Helion & Company Limited
Unit 8 Amherst Business Centre
Budbrooke Road
Warwick
CV34 5WE
England
Tel. 01926 499619
Email: info@helion.co.uk
Website: www.helion.co.uk
Twitter: @helionbooks
Visit our blog at http://blog.helion.co.uk/

Published by Helion & Company 2023
Designed and typeset by Mach 3 Solutions (www.mach3solutions.co.uk)
Cover designed by Paul Hewitt, Battlefield Design (www.battlefield-design.co.uk)

Text © John Marsden 2023
Cover: The meeting of Wellesley and Cuesta at Casas de Miravete, 10 July 1809. Original artwork by
Christa Hook (www.christahook.co.uk) © Helion & Company 2023
Maps by Mark S. Thompson © Helion & Company 2023

ISBN 978-1-804511-90-9

British Library Cataloguing-in-Publication Data.
A catalogue record for this book is available from the British Library.

For details of other military history titles published by Helion & Company Limited, contact the above
address, or visit our website: http://www.helion.co.uk

We always welcome receiving book proposals from prospective authors.

Contents

List of Maps and Illustrations

Acknowledgements

When the Covid-19 pandemic arrived in the UK towards the end of February 2020, the country was ushered into a period of uncertainty about how the new virus might be contained and defeated. Faced with something which was likely to become a prolonged test of mental and physical sanity, many sought out a means to occupy their time and their mind, in an attempt to get themselves through the looming trial. As the authorities, together with the dedicated workers manning the key industries and public services, strained every sinew to bring the country through the crisis, many homebound employees adapted to various ways of remote working as a means of remaining productive. Those who, like myself, had been enjoying an active retirement until Covid struck, turned to hobbies or dormant interests in order to fill their time during the long days of lockdown to come. My own diversion was stimulated during an e-mail exchange with an old friend who was fortunate enough to be able to continue in his cherished métier throughout the course of the pandemic, via a system of remote working introduced by his employers. Impressed by his determination to carry on regardless, I took up his suggestion that it might be time for me to make a start on a second Peninsular War project. Hence this volume, which is intended to shine a light upon the early days of the Anglo-Spanish alliance against Napoleon.

As I began to get down to work, I found that I was able to chase down a lot of primary source material held in the Spanish national archives, via their *Portal de Archivos Españoles* (PARES) – the gateway to a magnificent data store which affords the researcher entirely free access to a veritable treasure of documentation. So, let me begin by acknowledging the work of the technical, archival and curatorial teams of PARES, whose dedication has allowed myself, and no doubt many others around the world, to continue with projects which might otherwise have been suspended due to the pandemic.

Of course, PARES is an overwhelmingly Hispano-centric resource, and as my main aim in this project was to produce a somewhat wider Anglo-Spanish analysis of the Tagus campaign of 1809 than some which have gone before, I was always going to have to consult the relevant British archives in order to complete my work. Thankfully, the British government was able to declare a number of periods of relative freedom between the various lockdown periods, during which I sought and was allowed access to the University of Southampton's Hartley Library collection of Wellington's correspondence, The Wellington Papers. It was during the time I was visiting the university that the archivists were in the midst of a project to create an enhanced, on-line electronic catalogue of the Duke's papers, a beta version of which I was kindly invited to take a look at and comment upon whilst making use of the archive. Once formally available to remote users, I am sure this resource will be a great help to all researchers for whom regular visits to Southampton are either difficult to realise, or all together out of the question. Of course, occasional personal visits to the university will be a continuing necessity for researchers, and during my own appearances at the Hartley Library I was always well received; my pre-ordered documents always being at hand on my arrival. For all of this, and their continuing efforts, I would like to express my thanks to the University of Southampton and their archivists.

I would also like to mention my friend, Dr Arsenio García Fuertes, of Astorga, Spain. A well-known historian of the Peninsular War – or *La Guerra de la Independencia*, as he would prefer to call it, he is always inspiring and quick to offer help and advice whenever I feel the need to consult with him.

Due to the intricacy of the movements made by the various contenders during the 1809 campaign on the Tagus, I felt that the inclusion of a comprehensive set of maps highlighting the dynamics of the contest would help provide the reader with a clear mental picture of what was going on as the contest progressed. As a result, a set of 27 annotated maps have been included in the text; they are not drawn to scale but, in their proportionality, they should give a good indication of the geographical extent and flow of the fighting.

Finally, I should mention my long-time friend and instigator of this project, he of the e-mail exchange mentioned earlier, Mr Niall Sloane, for the example of his indefatigable work ethic and his encouragement of others, via which I found the determination to see this project through.

John Marsden
2023

Introduction

On 27 July 1809, the British army under the command of Sir Arthur Wellesley stood ready to fight its first pitched battle against the French on Spanish soil. The redcoats would not be fighting their old enemy alone, as their Spanish allies, under the command of *Capitán General de Extremadura*, Gregorio de la Cuesta, were standing in rank alongside them on the field of Talavera de la Reina, some 75 miles south-west of Madrid. As the dimming mid-summer sun sank slowly behind them, illuminating the faces of the approaching French columns to their front, the British infantry must have felt confident about their prospects. Just 10 weeks had passed since their stunning triumph at Oporto in Portugal, where they had completely out-manoeuvred *Maréchal* Soult's army, bottling it up within the city before forcing it to flee over narrow mountain tracks towards the safety of Spain; abandoning all of its artillery, baggage and treasure as it went. Soult would not be amongst the French generals to face Wellesley at Talavera, but his close proximity to the scene of the encounter was to have an unexpected influence upon the British commander's actions in the immediate aftermath of the battle.

During the early days of July, as the British advanced from Portugal into the Spanish region of Extremadura, Soult was busily re-equipping his demoralised host, the French II Corps, near the city of Zamora where, in compliance with a decree recently dispatched by Napoleon from Vienna, he would be joined by *Maréchal* Mortier's V Corps and *Maréchal* Ney's VI Corps, thus allowing him to assemble an army of some 50,000 men, of which he would be nominated commander in chief. Wellesley, although aware of Soult's whereabouts as he prepared for battle at Talavera, would remain completely ignorant of his recent reinforcements, considering him to be in command of just the 12,000 demoralised and ill-equipped troops he had chased out of Portugal. As such he expected no trouble from him.

At Talavera, *Maréchal* Victor and *Général de division* Sebastiani were eager for the fight, as was the intruder king of Spain, Joseph Bonaparte, who had come to the aid of both at the head of a scratch force of some 6,000 men which he brought from Madrid, a move he hoped would help ensure complete victory over the allied armies of Britain, Spain and Portugal in the high summer of 1809.

After advancing some 100 miles into Spain, it was in the vicinity of Almaraz, a small town lying just north of the Tagus, where Wellesley made his junction with Cuesta's Spanish army. By that time Britain's alliance with Spain had been active for some 14 months, and during that early period of the Anglo-Spanish alliance some joint military operations had already been carried out; notably the Royal Navy's rescue of the Marqués de la Romana's army from Napoleon's grasp in the Baltic during the summer of 1808, and Sir John Moore's abortive attempt to instigate an allied campaign against the French in northern Spain during the winter of that year. Moore's somewhat naïve and altruistic hopes for success in his mission would be ultimately dashed when he realised that, with the Spanish field armies in total disarray after their mismanaged attempts to halt Napoleon's renewed surge into Spain, the only hope he had of averting the total destruction of his own host was a precipitate retreat to La Coruña in the far north-west of the country, where the Royal Navy would come to the rescue once again. Neither of those commendable operations by Britain's soldiers and sailors had resulted in an actual joint Anglo-Spanish action against the French, but at Talavera such a longed-for clash was about to take place.

Wellesley and Cuesta were men of ego, neither of whom would be enthusiastic about the prospect of taking a subordinate stance in deference to his ally and nominal equal, but Wellesley arrived at Talavera with a string of outstanding military achievements behind him. Cuesta, on the other hand, had had a somewhat less than auspicious record since resurrecting his military career in the wake of the Spanish uprising of May 1808 and, if anything, his greatest failures during a lifetime of service to his country had occurred in the months leading up to Talavera, as we shall see. However, despite all of his earlier shortcomings against Napoleon's legions, it could be said that the Tagus campaign of 1809 was Cuesta's campaign. More willing to come to grips with the French invaders than many of his compatriot generals, it was his presence in Extremadura during the spring of 1809 which worried Victor to distraction, as he attempted to decide between a march upon Lisbon or Seville; and it was due to the ditherings of the Frenchman on the Portuguese frontier that Wellesley was able to disembark his force at Lisbon, adding to that of Cradock which, having formed part of the first British expeditionary force to Portugal in August 1808, had been isolated at the Portuguese capital since the evacuation of Moore's army. Assuming command of British forces, Wellesley made an unobstructed march upon Soult at Oporto. By then, despite having recently suffered a devastating defeat at the hands of Victor at Medellín, Cuesta was still lurking menacingly in the Spanish highlands south of the Guadiana, making the Frenchman reluctant to enter Portugal at the risk of being shut in by the Spaniard, whilst Wellesley was at large within her frontiers. Once Wellesley had defeated Soult, it was Cuesta's return to the south bank of the Tagus which caused Victor to shift his army eastward towards Madrid, thus creating the space and time for a unification of Anglo-Spanish forces in Extremadura, before marching on the heels of the Frenchman towards the capital.

The main aim of this story is not simply to re-fight the Battle of Talavera on paper, as there are many excellent descriptions of how this great clash of Napoleonic arms played out in the field already in print. Instead, the text will focus on the wider picture of events which took place in southern and central Spain between March and September 1809, the intricacies of which were further complicated by the individual personalities and the politicking of the three main protagonists on the allied side: Gregorio de la Cuesta, Francisco Venegas and Sir Arthur Wellesley. And if those three individuals were not enough to thicken the mix of any story, then the fault lines apparent in the Spanish command would be further deepened by the somewhat whimsical interpositions of the Spanish *Secretario de Guerra*, Antonio Cornel, who, from his political seat in Seville, was close enough to the theatre of operations to exert a further destabilising influence upon proceedings in the field.

British politics and intrigue would also have a debilitating effect on the fragile Anglo-Spanish alliance during the summer of 1809, as London agitated for the appointment of Wellesley as supreme allied commander on the Peninsula, an ambition encouraged by Cornel himself, as he schemed to retain a British presence in Spain as a means of ejecting the

French. However, when Britain and Austria became joint signatories to the Fifth Coalition, there arose a suspicion amongst the Spaniards that Wellesley's foray into Spanish territory was to be just one of three British diversionary operations agreed with the Austrians for their planned offensive against the French in central Europe, rather than a more permanent commitment to the Spanish cause. It was a suspicion which may well have enticed Cuesta to view Wellesley with a measure of wariness during their brief relationship, both before and after the Battle of Talavera.

The Spaniards harboured high hopes for the Tagus campaign of 1809, and though this may now seem somewhat fanciful, given the undoubted superiority of the French forces they would have to contend with, it should be recalled that, during the summer campaign of the previous year, they had defeated a substantial French army at Bailén in Andalucía, thus forcing their enemies back to the line of the Ebro and liberating Madrid in the wake of Joseph Bonaparte's installation upon the Spanish throne. But by the commencement of the winter of 1808/1809, Napoleon's counter-surge had returned control of Madrid and the north of Spain to the French. That the somewhat optimistic aspirations of the Spanish for the summer of 1809 were not ultimately realised was down to a number of factors, both military and political, and it is the hope of the author that each of them is about to be explored fully and impartially during the course of this story.

Though sometimes viewed in the context of a stand-alone action, the Battle of Talavera was actually the apogee of a long and complex military campaign, fought mainly in and around the valley of the Tagus during the spring and summer of 1809. Several commanders such as Wellesley, Beresford, Wilson, Cuesta and Venegas on the allied side, together with Victor, Sebastiani, Joseph Bonaparte, Soult, Ney and Jourdan on the French, would play a part, active or otherwise, in the large-scale manoeuvres and battles which took place as the Anglo-Spanish alliance attempted to gain control of Madrid and force the French to retire towards the river Ebro.

While Talavera was just one element of the Tagus campaign, there is no doubt that it was an important event which was to have a significant bearing on the way in which Wellesley would fight the war on the Iberian Peninsula during the succeeding five years. For the Spaniards, the campaign would mark the end of their attempts to fight the war against the French via a series of pitched battles on the rolling plains of the *meseta*, where the topography was particularly advantageous to the enemy due to their ever-present and overwhelming superiority in cavalry. That said, after Castaños' success at Bailén in the summer of 1808, the French were forced to retreat from central and southern Spain to the line of the river Ebro, but it was a feat the Spaniards would find impossible to repeat during the following year as they struggled to contain their enemy's counterstroke: an offensive which enabled the French to retake most of the territory they had surrendered. Dismayed by his elder brother's failings after Bailén, Napoleon had been forced to return from northern Europe in the autumn of the 1808 to take command of his newly and hugely reinforced armies south of the Pyrenees, and he was determined to resolve matters with his erstwhile ally. The impetus of the overwhelming offensive he unleashed in November 1808, soon pushed the Spanish armies towards the north-west and south-west hinterlands of the Iberian Peninsula. Caught up in it all, Sir John Moore's expeditionary force would be evacuated from the port of La Coruña by the Royal Navy in January 1809, after having been driven to its final, isolated position in Galicia by *Maréchaux* Soult and Ney.

Convinced that Spain was about to sue for peace, Napoleon decided to return to Paris once his pursuit of British and Spanish forces in the north had reached the cathedral town of Astorga, leaving what he thought was nothing more than a final mopping-up operation to Joseph and his coterie of jealous, ambitious and insubordinate marshals. With the British all but absent from the Iberian Peninsula, maintaining just a token force at Lisbon, attempts were being made by a somewhat detached trio of British officers, in the form of Colonel Sir Robert Wilson, Lieutenant Colonel William Mayne and Major John Grant, to reconstitute the Portuguese Army, which had been disbanded when the French occupied the country in November 1807. It was a continuing task which Wellesley would later delegate to William Carr Beresford at the outset of his Iberian campaign of 1809. Meanwhile Joseph, once more ensconced at the Palacio Real in Madrid, began the task of bringing the southern provinces of Spain under his control when the campaigning season of 1809 commenced. The Tagus, its valley and its none too numerous crossing points capable of accommodating the artillery and transport columns of a Napoleonic army, would become the primary focus for a renewed French drive into Andalucía.

It could be claimed that the first significant combat of the 1809 campaign on the Tagus was the Battle of Uclés, if only because of the fact that Francisco Venegas was in command of the Spanish Army of the Centre when it was defeated there on 13 January.[1] Setting that aside, we should consider the cavalry action which took place on 24 March at Los Yébenes, 30 miles south of Toledo, to represent the true beginning of the campaign. The engagement took place when some 4,000 Spanish cavalry belonging to the Army of La Mancha, then under the command of the Conde de Cartaojal, defeated the 600-strong regiment of Sebastiani's Polish lancers which formed the spearhead of his southward advance towards Andalucía. In wake of the action, Cartaojal decided to play safe and retreat towards the safety of the Sierra Morena, correctly judging that Konopka's lancers had represented just the tip of a significant French corps. Sebastiani's reaction was to send a force of some 7,500 infantry and cavalry in pursuit of the Spaniards, who crossed the Guadiana a little to the north of Ciudad Real before taking up a position which, inexplicably, offered little if any advantage for defence, located as it was in the midst of an extensive plain. Once the French had overcome the Spanish outposts at the bridge of Peralvillo, the outcome of the resulting battle at Ciudad Real on 27 March 1809 became a forgone conclusion. In the aftermath of the clash, the inevitable Spanish retreat towards the *sierra* to the south was conducted under incessant pressure from the French, and it was this demoralised Army of La Mancha which *Teniente General* Venegas was to inherit after Cartaojal's unavoidable dismissal; despite his own failure at Uclés.

Elsewhere, after the shattering defeat suffered by the Army of Castilla at Medina de Rioseco in July 1808, its commander in chief, Gregorio de la Cuesta, was to become embroiled in a bout of political infighting which would eventually result in his arrest, an act which almost put paid to his recently resurrected army career. In December, whilst on his way to face trial in Seville, he found himself under lock and key in the town of Mérida, where, in the face of the abject failure of various Spanish generals to stem the resurgent tide of French occupation, the people of the town began to agitate for Cuesta to be released and made *Capitán*

---

1   Uclés lies some 50 miles south-east of Madrid.

General of the region of Extremadura. Known for his willingness always to take the fight to his enemies, though not perhaps for his battlefield acumen, the *Merideños* could at least be assured that he would put up some resistance in the national cause.

Demoralised and mutinous after their recent defeats at Burgos and Madrid during November, the troops of *Mariscal de Campo* Benito de San Juan's Army of the Centre arrived at Talavera during the first days of January 1809, as they continued on their calamitous retreat. It was there where their crumbling discipline finally fell apart when they rioted in reaction to their plight; their commander in chief being shot down in cold blood on 7 January as he pleaded with his men for a return to order. In the meantime, and taking advantage of his new-found freedom, Cuesta had begun to detain and re-organise the Spanish soldiers he had discovered retreating through Mérida. These men he would use as a core around which to build a scratch force of about battalion strength, before marching to Badajoz at its head, and it was whilst he was there, in late December, that he was confirmed in post as chief of what came to be known as the Army of Extremadura.

With his much augmented and newly-christened force, Cuesta later tried but failed to prevent the French from crossing the Tagus, and once Victor had set foot upon its left bank there ensued a game of cat and mouse along the course of the river, which ended at Medellín. It was there, on 28 March, the day following Caraojal's defeat at Ciudad Real, that Cuesta suffered a similar but more bloody fate than his compatriot. To the casual observer it might seem that two such defeats in the space of two days would mark the point at which the French would have been expecting to make an essentially unobstructed advance into Andalucía, but it was not to be. Cuesta, tenacious as ever, re-organised his forces and maintained a Spanish presence in the highlands to the south of the Guadiana. In the meantime, the scarcity of provisions available to Victor's army for its projected march to the south eventually forced him to return to the north bank of the Tagus to avoid starvation. Later, as the summer heat began to accumulate and the British army prepared to advance from Portugal towards his right flank, Victor decided to retreat upon Talavera, allowing Wellesley and Cuesta to join forces in the region of Almaraz. Deciding it was time to make a stand, the Frenchman took up a line on the east bank of the Alberche, a tributary of the Tagus.

Meanwhile, to the south of Madrid, *Teniente General* Venegas had by then been made chief of the Army of La Mancha. However, his command was not to be an independent one, the Manchegans eventually coming under the auspices of Cuesta, with Venegas subordinated to him. It was an arrangement which, with the added complication of some spasmodic interjections from Spanish *Secretario de Guerra*, Antonio Cornel, would make for an uncomfortable campaign for Venegas as he attempted to modify and interfere with the instructions he received from his military and political masters, a state of affairs he tended to exacerbate via his own intrigues.

The prize within the reach of the allies during the high summer of 1809 was the occupation of Madrid and the withdrawal of the French to the line of the Ebro for a second year in succession. Had it been grasped it would surely have tested Napoleon's patience with his brother Joseph, once again commander in chief of all French forces in Spain, to breaking point. But, almost inevitably, complications soon began to appear on the allied side. *Maréchal* Soult would come to represent a serious threat in the rear of the Anglo-Spanish position, and would eventually force a separation of the British from their Spanish allies as Wellesley moved to cover the Frenchman's approach. There were some fleeting hopes that *Marechal do Exército* Beresford's force on the Portuguese frontier would be able to act as a deterrent to Soult, but doubts would slowly arise about the capabilities of the former's newly-formed army of Portuguese regulars, with the result that they would not take part in the campaign.

So, the scene was set for a complex campaign of move and countermove in the valley of the Tagus during the summer months of 1809. The allied armies to the south and west of Madrid were certainly numerous, more so than the French if we discount Soult's army; but the bulk of the Spanish troops being fresh conscripts they were barely trained if trained at all, the majority having had little if any experience of battle. In addition to this disadvantage, the allies would have to make use of exterior lines of communications along the convex face of the arc forming the front between the contending armies, whilst the French enjoyed the benefits of the interior lines of its concave face, as well as the advantages emanating from their occupation of the nearby capital. It would all make for an interesting contest. But for all its early promise, hopes that the allied victory at Talavera would mark a turning point in the war soon faded after Wellesley lost faith in the Spanish commitment, causing Cuesta's suspicions of British intrigues against him to grow. Before the end of the year, Wellesley would be back behind the Portuguese frontier, and after their bloody defeats at such places as Medina de Rioseco, Uclés, Ciudad Real, Medellín, Almonacid and Ocaña during 1808 and 1809, the Spanish would eventually be forced to take to the mountainous regions which mark the periphery of their country, where they could begin to conduct a more asymmetric war of attrition against the invaders.

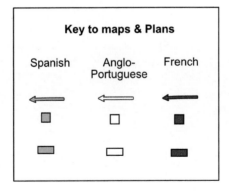

1

The Invasion of Portugal, and the Abdication of the Spanish Royal Family

In 1807, whilst Spain and France were still in alliance, their governments were conniving in a plan to mount an invasion of Portugal. It was in July of that year that Napoleon began to exert diplomatic pressure on the Portuguese, demanding that they close their ports to British shipping by 1 September and begin to comply with the strictures of his Continental System. The threats intensified during the month of August, when Portugal was invited to declare war on Britain and place its fleet at the disposal of the Franco-Spanish alliance, Napoleon having an undeclared aim of using it as part of a plan to gain control of South America. It was a move designed to generate some reluctance, if not outright defiance from the Portuguese, thus providing the alliance with a convenient *casus belli* by which a joint incursion into Portuguese territory could be justified. After some careful consideration, the Portuguese government proposed only a partial compliance with the demands placed upon it; a response which was gleefully received in Paris, as it still provided Napoleon with sufficient excuse to act. On 12 October 1807, a French army corps was launched towards Lisbon from its area of concentration near Hendaye on the Franco-Spanish frontier. By previous agreement, the expedition led by *Général de division* Jean-Andoche Junot, would be allowed to traverse the provinces of northern and western Spain in order to reach the Portuguese frontier, whence it would enter the country with orders to overthrow its government and establish a permanent occupation. Spain, in the person of its prime minister and head of the army, Manuel de Godoy, had an interest in obtaining any of the possible pickings from its neighbour's imminent dismemberment, having been promised a kingdom of his own in the Algarve as the *quid-pro-quo* for his agreement to provide three strong Spanish army corps to assist Junot in his mission. Looking on, King Carlos IV, the pusillanimous Spanish monarch of the time, was only too keen to display his eagerness to provide a ready-made breach in his country's defences against its powerful and expansionist neighbour, thinking it might put him in favour with Napoleon. But it was with uneasy feelings that the more cautious members of the Spanish government looked on as Junot's army began to trudge across the border and angle its march towards Madrid, and their apprehensions would soon be fully justified.

Soon, and without prior warning, a further three powerful French army corps would be launched into Spain from different points along the length of its Pyrenean frontier. In November 1807, Dupont led a column towards Madrid, before veering southwards in the direction of Andalucía. In January 1808, Moncey led his own corps into Biscay and Castilla la Vieja

(Old Castile) and a month later Duhesme led a strong force into Catalunya. As Spanish strong-holds south of the border were methodically emptied of their garrisons and re-manned with French troops, there was not a murmur of dissent from Madrid; but the mood of the Spanish people did begin to change. The Bourbon royals, frozen in fear of their futures if not their lives, failed to react until the anger of their subjects began to express itself on the streets of Spain's major towns and cities, the growing unrest amongst the Spanish populace eventually leading to a situation within the royal court whereby the heir apparent, Fernando, was elevated to the throne, replacing his father as king. But it was only when Napoleon's contempt for his southern neighbour led him to lure the Spanish royals to Bayonne as part of his plan to force an abdica-tion from Fernando in favour of his own brother, Joseph, that the Spanish people decided that enough was enough. In revolting against their erstwhile ally at Madrid on 2 May 1808, the hesi-tant state institutions of government and army were soon forced to intercede on behalf of the populace, thus sparking Spain's war of independence, *la Guerra de la Independencia*, against the French. Some days later, Fernando's continuing resistance to Napoleon's demands that he abdicate crumbled when he was threatened with execution. Taking advantage of the situation, the Emperor of France allowed royal protocol to be played out by insisting that Carlos re-ascend the throne, knowing full well that the elderly monarch would soon relinquish the crown once more. This, when it came to pass on 5 May, allowed Napoleon to force Carlos to cede to his brother, Joseph Bonaparte, and as the dreaded thread of news from Bayonne seeped into Spain, it was not long in reaching the Spanish capital, causing the populace in general to rise against the oppressors and put an end to the teetering Franco-Spanish alliance.

The Combat at Cabezón de Pisuerga, 12 June 1808

It would be impossible to analyse the 1809 campaign on the Tagus without focussing upon its main Spanish protagonist, *Capitán General* Gregorio de la Cuesta, his military abili-ties, his character and the enormous influence he exerted upon some of the major events marking the first 15 months or so of the war on the Iberian Peninsula. At an advanced age when the war commenced, and with a long military career behind him, we shall, after just a brief reference to his eighteenth-century campaigns, concentrate upon his role in the events which took place in Spain during 1808 and 1809. Sometimes the hero or villain of the piece, depending upon one's point of view, we shall attempt to give his case a fair presentation before leaving the reader to make up their own mind as to which of the two it was.

Amongst many Spanish historians with an interest in the Napoleonic era, Cuesta is remembered as a good soldier, having gained a measure of prestige on account of his victo-rious campaigns against the French Republic during the War of the Convention (also known as the War of the Pyrenees) of 1792 to 1795. In fact, at the time the Spanish Court was calling for a peaceful settlement of the conflict in 1795, Cuesta, displaying all the signs of stub-bornness and elan he became famous for, if not quite the recklessness he would later be accused of in 1808/1809, was leading a successful offensive against the French at Puigcerdá and Bellver, which was brought to an abrupt halt only when an emissary sent from Madrid ordered him to cease his operations, informing him that Spain had sued for peace and thereby lost the war. As the peace process got underway, Cuesta conducted an honourable and sincere political campaign against what he saw as a corrupt Spanish government led by

Manuel de Godoy. Tired of his continual protestations, Godoy ordered that he be exiled to the mountains of Santander province in 1801, where he would remain on half pay for some seven years until Fernando VII came to the throne in March 1808, during the period of Napoleon's early and stealthy incursions into Spain. It was Fernando, in one of his first acts as absolute monarch, who was to release Cuesta from his isolation and promote him to the position of *Capitán General* of the kingdoms of Castilla and León, and it was under that title that Cuesta would fight the combat at Cabezón some three months later.

As the Spanish uprising spread across the country in the wake of events at Madrid, groups of disorganised civilians would arm themselves with whatever weapons they could find, and after electing a local leader they would commonly determine to resist the French army if and when it appeared in the vicinity of their village, town or city. In some places, anyone with military experience could be called upon to act as a local commander and, depending upon the level of patriotic zeal displayed by their followers, they would sometimes be expected to take the fight to the enemy no matter how superior the invaders were, often with inevitable and tragic consequences.

It was a month before the Madrid uprising took place that Cuesta was promoted to *Capitán General* – the highest military rank attainable in Spain at the time. Then aged 67, he was probably thinking that his campaigning days were behind him after a lifetime of active military service, and it is said that when the Spanish revolt broke out, Cuesta was not exactly filled with enthusiasm for the national cause. This apparent lack of zeal may have come about due to an offer made to him by Napoleon on 25 May 1808, when he asked the old warrior to become Viceroy of New Spain (modern-day Mexico) in return for his support in the plan to make his brother king of Spain. Careful not to commit himself in haste, he studiously ignored Napoleon's enticement, but neither did he openly align himself with the cause of restoring the Bourbons to the Spanish throne. Once Joseph had been handed the crown, Napoleon wrote to Cuesta:

> The good opinion we have of you allows us to offer you the prospect of moving to Mexico in the capacity of Viceroy, so that the colony, which is so important to the motherland, may be secured. Your presence would allow us to avoid any unwelcome events which may arise as a result of popular discontent with the colonial government. We would also like you to designate three or four colonels, brigadiers or major generals to sail with you, whom you could appoint as local governors at strategic locations. We would be happy to write to the Lieutenant General and to the *Junta*, asking them to relieve you of your brevets and commissions in order that you may take passage on a frigate, or sail aboard a 64, one of the best ships of the line. In the meantime ... we can prepare other ships upon which you might like to sail should the ship of your choice be delayed or unavailable. Before sailing, I would like you to provide me with some proof of your enthusiasm [for my plan]. This important mission will allow you to acquire a new title in recognition of the esteem in which we hold you, and the good grace in which you are held by the king.[1]

---

1   Napoleon to Cuesta, 25 May 1808, H. Plon & J. Dumaine (eds), *Correspondance de Napoleon Ier* (Paris: Plon et Dumaine, 1865), no.13991, vol.XVII, pp.237–238.

By the beginning of June, Cuesta could no longer allow himself the luxury of maintaining his non-committal stance; by then fighting had broken out across Spain, and a French column under the command of *Général de brigade* Lasalle was approaching Valladolid, the seat of Cuesta's position as *Capitán General de Castilla y León*. As if to emphasise the fact that it was time for Cuesta to make a choice between his tacit acceptance of Napoleon's designs and his loyalty to the insurgent cause, crowds of *Vallisoletanos*, as the citizens of Valladolid are known, gathered outside his residence and began calling for him to help organise and lead the defence of the city as the French approached. It is said that, as Cuesta vacillated on the upper floor of his residence, a fanatical element of the mob, amongst whom there were many students from the University of Valladolid, began to erect a gallows in the street below with obvious intent. In the end he bowed to their wishes.[2]

After acceding to the demands of the crowd, there was hardly any time for Cuesta to settle into his new role before word arrived that the enemy was nearing Valladolid via the road leading to the bridge which crosses the Pisuerga at the small town of Cabezón, some 10 miles to the north of the city. At that he decided to lead a motley collection of students and citizens, together with a hotch-potch of small, regular army units, to Cabezón, all of them determined to stop Lasalle in his tracks.

There are two contrasting versions of what happened when Cuesta's scratch force took the field against the French at Cabezón de Pisuerga on 12 June 1808; both come to the same conclusion that the episode was a complete failure for the Spanish, but they differ in their apportionment of blame. One of them places the culpability for the disaster which followed squarely upon the shoulders of Cuesta, claiming that it was the *Capitán General* who insisted that almost the whole of his irregular troops, in effect some 5,000 raw civilians, including students, be placed in a line almost parallel to the Pisuerga, such that they straddled the road leading to the bridge which they were hoping to defend. The other blames the students and a number of fanatics amongst the crowd for the Spanish dispositions, claiming that they refused to heed the advice, or indeed orders, issued by Cuesta. Two of the four cannon available to the Spaniards that day were placed in the front-centre of the line before the bridge, with the remaining pair stationed on the opposite bank of the river, beyond the crossing, thus guarding the entrance to the village of Cabezón. Cuesta's 500 or so cavalry, the nearest thing he had to a regular army unit, were stationed on the left flank of the Spanish line in order to guard the fords which lay downstream towards Valladolid. The only force in place on the Cabezón side of the river, besides the two artillery pieces and their crews, were some small parties of infantry who were charged with the duty of repelling any attempt by the French to out-flank Cuesta's main position by fording the river. They were his only reserve.[3]

As already stated, there is little if any argument amongst historians regarding the actual Spanish deployment just described, only some contention about who was responsible for it. It was, shall we say, a somewhat unconventional arrangement of forces. In fact, it was the exact opposite to the standard military practice of the time, if not for all time. Most army commanders would shudder at the prospect of being caught in such a position – just a few hundred yards in front of a major river and directly in front of a bridge which defined

2   Charles Oman, *A History of the Peninsular War* (London: Greenhill Books, 1995), vol.I, pp.67–68.
3   Gomez de Arteche, *Guerra de la Independencia, Historia Militar de España* (Madrid: Imprenta y Litografía del Depósito de la Guerra, 1868–1903), vol.II, pp.25–35.

the only line of retreat – with no second line in place and no reserve to speak of on the far bank. Such a situation was bound to lead to deadly congestion at the bridge in the event of a panicked retreat.

When commenting on the combat at Cabezón, many Spanish sources tend to blame the ignorant ardour of the mob of students and civilians for the appalling dispositions taken up by Cuesta's force. They make the claim that the *Capitán General*, freshly pressed into service and in fear of his life should he refuse to lead, was in no position to stamp his authority on the rabble that had gathered round him, which was convinced that its patriotic passions would overcome the order, discipline and experience of the French troops they were about to face. The penalty for the merest expression of caution on his part would almost certainly have cost him his life; after all, he had already come close to feeling the noose around his neck when his initial hesitation in taking command was put to the test.

British historians tend to be less kind to Cuesta, their views of the Spaniard having perhaps been influenced, not to say prejudiced, by stories of the apparent obstinacy he displayed towards his British allies at Talavera in July 1809; such pronouncements on the part of Wellesley and others we shall give further scrutiny to as our story unfolds.

There is no need to dwell upon the detail of the fighting at Cabezón, as our aims are those of attempting to evaluate the personalities and competences of both Wellesley and Cuesta, as destiny drew them inexorably towards their meeting at Talavera. Suffice it to say that, when Lasalle assailed Cuesta's badly positioned line with the full force of his artillery, cavalry and infantry, the Spaniards were completely overwhelmed in short time and sent scattering for their lives, many taking to the waters of the Pisuerga for safety. After making his way back to Valladolid in the wake of the combat, along with his second-in-command, *Teniente General* Eguía, Cuesta mustered as many of the fugitives from the fighting as he could and made his way to Benavente, some 80 miles to the north-west. In the meantime, the French began to reap the spoils of their victory. However, Lasalle's column belonged to *Maréchal* Bessieres's II Corps, which had been charged with keeping open the communications between Spain and France as Napoleon's armies drove deeper into the kingdom. This meant that he was not permitted to linger at Valladolid, Bessieres insisting that he return to Burgos, a key point on the road system linking the two countries, to help ensure its defence.

Cuesta Assembles the Army of Castilla

After his retreat from Cabezón Cuesta, with the help of *Coronel* José de Zayas, began the task of recruiting and training what would come to be called the Army of Castilla. In such a thinly populated province, those found physically fit enough for service in the infantry of the new army would be scarce on the ground, though this was perhaps not the most pressing of Cuesta's problems. If he was ever going to challenge the French on the cereal-bearing plains of Castilla, then he was going to need a sizable and competent corps of cavalry; without such an arm his force would not be able to operate effectively, if at all, in open country, the French being particularly well served by a strong, skilled and experienced corps of mounted soldiers. He was thus forced to look to neighbouring provinces for help, but even before Madrid was in French hands, many of the individual regions of the country had begun to appoint local or provincial *juntas* as a means of maintaining a semblance of order, as well as resistance to the enemy. Many of those governing bodies ruled with as much autonomy as they could accrue to themselves, even to the extent of forming their own armed forces for the protection of their 'sovereignty' in the face of the ever-present threat of French incursions in search of treasure and provisions, or attempts at straightforward occupation. As such, the *Capitán General* would have to negotiate separately with the local centres of power.

Cuesta's appeals to the northern province of Asturias were largely ignored, the *junta* there had built up a force of some 15,000 men with which they intended to defend their mountainous frontiers, and its members were quick to point out to him that it was only in the mountains, where cavalry was of little use, that the Spanish could be successful against the enemy. In fact, some of the Asturians went so far as to suggest to the *Capitán General* that he join them in their mountain fastness, rather than attempt to fight the French on the plains of Castilla, but his obstinance soon came to the fore. Ignoring the sound advice of his northern neighbours, he was determined simply to come to blows with the enemy and liberate his territory from the invaders. Ultimately, in the face of his continual demands, the Asturians relented and granted him the use of the Regimiento de Covadonga, one of the best of several recently raised in the province.[4] The *Capitán General* then turned to the province of León where the *junta* was, if anything, more in need of resources than Cuesta himself, in order to place the region in a state of defence, as such its deputies would not contemplate the notion of directing any of its volunteers to the army being raised at Benavente. However, they did allow a small force of some 2,500 men to act as a detachment to Cuesta's army, on the condition that they would be used only as a covering force for the provincial capital.[5] At this point, there was just one more place to turn to for help: the province of Galicia in the north-west, which, due to a happy combination of circumstances and a recently appointed *junta* of some ability, had in place an army of some 30,000 men. Although somewhat uneven, the overall quality of the troops, together with their weaponry, was quite good. Some of the units then present in the province belonged to the regular regiments which had recently taken part in the Franco-Spanish invasion of Portugal before the two former allies went to war with each other. Besides these there were other regular battalions which had been stationed in Galicia whilst Spain was at war with Britain, their presence thought to be necessary as a deterrent against any attempts on the part of the British to capture or dismantle any of Spain's Atlantic seaports, such as El Ferrol and La Coruña. The regiments returning from Portugal were more or less at full strength, but those which had been on guard against British landings before the Anglo-Spanish alliance was formed would require some recruitment in order to fill their ranks. This was done by incorporating many of the recently signed-up volunteers. By 10 June 1808, those formations earmarked for service on or just beyond Galicia's frontiers, mainly the regular units just mentioned, had been concentrated at Lugo in readiness to commence their preparations for action against the French.

Training and instruction had no sooner begun at Lugo when news of the disaster at Cabezón arrived, soon to be followed by Cuesta's insistent calls for help and reinforcements. This threw the well-ordered preparation of the Galician army into complete panic

---

4   Arteche, *Guerra de la Independencia*, vol.II, pp.251–256.
5   Arteche, *Guerra de la Independencia*, vol.II, pp.256–257.

and confusion. A steady hand was required on the tiller, so the *Junta de Galicia* turned to *Teniente General* Joaquín Blake. Not yet 50 he was young for a Spanish general, and at one time had served as a subordinate to Cuesta himself. Blake wasted no time in reorganising the Army of Galicia into four divisions, with the addition of a strong vanguard commanded by *Brigadier* El Conde de Maceda. With a mind to prepare and equip his men for the coming rigours of a campaign against some of the best soldiers in Europe, Blake had decided to reinforce the garrisons guarding the passes of Manzanal, Sanabria and Foncebadón, all of them lying just beyond the Galician frontier with Castilla-León, thus securing control of access into the region of El Bierzo, which would thereby become a buffer zone to Galicia. With the latter thus sealed off from French incursions, his army could be hardened up for its coming trials. Had Blake been allowed the time he required to meld an effective fighting force, his efforts may well have paid handsome dividends, but Cuesta, impatient as ever, was demanding action. He wanted Blake to bring his army forward to Benavente, unite with him, and take the offensive to the French. Blake resisted at first, using his subordination to the *Junta de Galicia* as a shield against Cuesta's demands, but with typical insistence the *Capitán General* sent his deputy, *Coronel* Zayas, to Galicia to convince the *junta* of the need for taking the offensive. It was not long before Blake received instructions to march onto the plains of León and make a junction with Cuesta's Army of Castilla, and on 5 July 1808 his vanguard set off towards Benavente. Four days later the armies were in contact.

When the Galicians arrived at Benavente it became clear that their alliance with the Castilians would not be a harmonious one. The former regarded themselves as a race apart from the latter, their differences being emphasised by the Celtic origins of the Galicians, along with their local dialect of *Gallego*, a kind of Spanish-Portuguese patois. Geography wielded a further influence on identity; the Castilians inhabited the mainly arid expanses of Castilla where the dry crops of wheat, rye, barley and pulses thrived. This was in stark contrast to the rain-soaked mountains and valleys of Galicia, whose lush pastures supported meat and dairy farming industries, the produce of which was supplemented by rich fishing harvests collected from the cool waters of the Atlantic, which were the preserve of many a coastal community belonging to the remote province. These two citizen prototypes, each moulded in psyche and physique by their own climate, language, customs, diet and industries, did not make for comfortable bedfellows. Not surprisingly, no sooner had the leaders of this heterogeneous force come together at Cuesta's headquarters that quarrels began to break out, and it is here, once more, that we may gain an insight into some aspects of the *Capitán General*'s character.

Cuesta was firmly opposed to the concept of a joint and equal command structure for the two armies, and he began to insist that he be given overall control of the whole corps, making it clear that he could not imagine a situation where Blake could contest his leadership credentials. As to be expected, Blake was deeply wounded by Cuesta's attitude. He saw himself as the leader of the bigger and better part of the joint force and could not contemplate the idea that his army would, in effect, act as an auxiliary force to the Castilians. In fact, he was repelled at the thought of subordinating himself to someone he saw as a rude and arrogant compatriot who refused even to listen to his advice nor accept any of his plans, which is not to say that Blake was lacking in some peculiar traits of character himself.

There was another seemingly minor but extremely irksome incident which helped inflame Blake's feelings towards the chief of the Army of Castilla. It may have sprung from a lack of administrative insight on the part of Cuesta's staff; however, in the heated atmosphere which enveloped the two leaders, it appeared to Blake that he had been the victim of a deliberate and vile insult from his host. It all hinged around the lodgings to which Blake and his staff had been assigned in the village of Villalpando. In his magnificent history of the war, Arteche, in a somewhat understated manner, described the 'guest house' to which the Galicians were directed to as being, '*Incómodo á la vez que poco decoroso*' (uncomfortable, and at the same time somewhat lacking in decorum) which was about as close as he would go to describing it for what it was – a brothel! The whole affair rankled so deeply with Blake's staff that they continued to talk about it well into their later years. Ultimately, despite his protestations and rancour, Blake was forced to swallow his pride and submit to Cuesta's authority.

Once in charge, Cuesta's more commonly known failings were not long in coming to the surface. He was simply spoiling for a fight, and now that he had what on paper looked like a respectable force under his command, he would take no heed of any of the cooler heads around him; he was simply going to hurl his army at the French, smash them and sweep them from the territory he considered his own.[6] Without hesitation, on 12 July 1808, he marched at the head of the Army of Castilla on a pre-planned route towards Medina de Rioseco. It was one of two thrusts he would make upon the city of Valladolid, which lies some 25 miles south Medina de Rioseco. The second was the simultaneous advance of the Army of Galicia along a route leading more directly to the regional capital from its starting point at Villalpando, before continuing via Tordehumos, Castromonte, Villamayor, Monasterio de la Santa Espina and Villanubla.[7] Like this, thought Cuesta, he would be bound to encounter the French.[8]

The Battle of Medina de Rioseco, 14 July 1808

Cuesta's plan was to occupy Valladolid and hold it as a strongpoint of Spanish arms once in his possession. He thought that by doing so the French would be hampered in any movements they might wish to make from Burgos and Palencia towards León and Astorga, as to do so would expose their southern flank to an attack from the Castilians and Galicians in possession of the regional capital. A similar threat would apply to the French lines of communication linking Madrid with Burgos and the French frontier. Of course, the reader will recall that Cuesta had been previously forced to abandon Valladolid on 12 June, but that was due to Lasalle's triumph at Cabezón, since when the latter had been recalled to Palencia by Bessieres. Knowing that *Maréchal* Bessieres and Lasalle were now at Burgos and Palencia respectively, and that Valladolid was unoccupied, Cuesta calculated that the stronger of the two armies under his command, the Army of Galicia, should march on the regional capital from Villalpando via the route outlined above, whilst he led the Army of Castilla towards Medina de Rioseco. This would allow him to observe the route by which the French

---

6   Arteche, *Guerra de la Independencia*, vol.II, pp.272–274.
7   Archivo Histórico Nacional de Madrid (AHN): Diversas Colecciones 136, N.22: Anon. *Diario de Operaciones del Ejército de Galicia desde el día 14 de Julio [sic Junio] 1808*, entries for 12 and 13 July 1808.
8   Arteche, *Guerra de la Independencia*, vol.II, pp.258–269.

would approach from Palencia, once they had discovered that Blake was at or approaching Valladolid. Should the Galicians be secure in the city before the French appeared in front of Cuesta, then he would march from Rioseco to Valladolid and strengthen his grip on the place. If not, then he could either hold back the French from his position at Rioseco, or allow them to turn south towards Blake as he marched on Valladold, thus exposing their right flank to an attack from his Castilians. A fine plan – all things being equal; but there were great disparities between the two forces about to engage.

By the evening of 12 July, the Castilian vanguard was already at Rioseco. Blake was at that time still executing his march to Valladolid, having left his 2nd Division far in the rear to guard the pass of Foncebadón in the Maragatería, as well as that of Manzanal in El Bierzo. His 3rd Division was at Benavente, where it would remain as a reserve to fall back upon should he need to. Of the Galician formations committed to the advance his 1st Division was at Villabrágima and Tordehumos, his vanguard at Castromonte and his 4th Division, which was forming a flank guard on the right, was at Mota del Marqués. All of these formations passed the night at the places just mentioned, with the 4th Division ordered to be at Castromonte on the 13th, whilst the rest of his divisions remained where they were – with the exception of the vanguard, which was ordered to march to Villanubla that day so as to place it within touching distance of Valladolid. It was on the 13th, as his vanguard neared Valladolid, that Blake received news that the Castilians were about to find themselves in trouble at Rioseco; this left him with no choice other than to go to their aid.

It would seem that Bessieres had discovered the presence of Cuesta and Blake in his front, when the former reached Rioseco, and after gathering all of the reinforcements he could at Palencia, he decided to march towards his enemies once his advanced units had reported the positions of Cuesta's outposts, which were lying to the east of Rioseco. The scene was now set, and if things did not go exactly to the plan premeditated by the French *maréchal*, then the overall thrust of his tactics should still return him a handsome victory. Cuesta had underestimated his enemy, and both elements of his own force had now been caught fully exposed on the open, gently undulating plains of León, perfect cavalry country; as a result, his battlefield management skills were about to face a severe test on a scale far greater than that of the combat at Cabezón.[9]

When Blake arrived in person at Rioseco in response to Cuesta's call for help, he was some distance ahead of his army, which was hurriedly bending its march towards the little town after making a detour from its intended route to Valladolid. With no more ado he went to speak with the *Capitán General* at his headquarters. Both men then went together to the top of a nearby hillock to observe the flat lands before them and attempt to divine the probable approach route of the French. It goes almost without saying that they could not agree in their prognoses over how to react whenever and wherever the enemy might appear, so they decided to wait for signs of French activity before fixing upon a plan of attack or of taking up defensive positions. Of the two men, it would appear that Blake was the more uncomfortable with this unjustifiably relaxed approach. He was most anxious about his vanguard which, already in the outskirts of Valladolid when ordered to turn about, had the longest counter-march to make before arriving at Rioseco. Unable to sleep on the night of

9   Arteche, *Guerra de la Independencia*, vol.II, pp.275–276.

13/14 July, the commander of the Galicians rode through the encampments of those of his men who by then were situated on the southern edge of Rioseco, before continuing down the Valladolid road towards the troops who were still counter-marching towards the point of rendezvous. It was not long before he ran into them as they struggled along almost at the end of what would be a 30-mile march that day, having been forced to retrace their steps from Villanubla. Unable to console them with the prospect of a few hours rest, he ordered them into defensive positions before returning to Rioseco and turning out his 1st and 4th Divisions with the same instructions. Cuesta had not stirred during the whole of the night, rising to deploy his Castilians only as the Galicians were making the final adjustments to their positions in the field.[10]

The number of troops comprising the contending armies at Medina de Rioseco was quite considerable: the French were able to deploy some 15,400 infantry, 1,850 cavalry and 34 pieces of artillery, whilst the Spaniards fielded some 21,200 infantry, 710 cavalry and 20 pieces of artillery.[11] When dawn broke on 14 July 1808, it was clear that the Spaniards were about to face a tough trial during the course of the day. The ground, the lie of the land, did not suit them, though Blake seemed to have taken most if not all of the few advantages offered him by the topography. However, the landscape would not prove to be the major source of the problems experienced by the Spaniards once battle commenced; that, unfortunately, must be put down to human fallibility. When looking at battlefield maps for Rioseco, one does not need to be a military tactician of any great talent to realise the glaring shortcomings in the placement of the two Spanish armies. In brief they looked just like that; two separate armies occupying distinct areas of the battlefield, with a gaping space some 1,500 yards wide between them, neither formation having a strong flank. To confuse things further, by the time battle commenced, the armies of Blake and Cuesta had become somewhat intermixed in a rather haphazard manner due to the 4th Division of the Army of Galicia having been sent to reinforce Cuesta's army, where it took up a position some distance directly in front of the Castilians as though to form their front line. The remainder of Blake's army, the 1st Division and his vanguard, occupied part of the high ground comprising the Heights of Moclín, which are crowned by a twin peak, the one nearest the French position being lower than the other by just 70 feet. Inexplicably, Blake decided not to occupy the lower peak as a forward position, and when the French attacked they were able to haul a battery of artillery onto the plateau almost without opposition, giving them an advantage which they exploited to some effect (see Plate 1).

Amongst the Spanish archives there resides a document entitled, *Diario de Operaciones del Ejército de Galicia, desde el día 14 de Julio 1808*. When one comes to read its content, it soon becomes apparent that the composer of the title page meant to write '*14 de Junio*' rather than '*14 de Julio*' which, coincidently, was the actual date of the Battle of Rioseco. In fact, the time period covered by the diary runs from 14 June 1808 to 10 November 1808, and it contains quite a detailed account of the fighting at Rioseco. However, our main aim in this study is to examine how the battle was managed by the Spanish commanders in chief, rather than become deeply engrossed in the minutiae of combat, and there are just a few hints of that provided by the diarist; the one which catches the eye most is cited below.

---

10   Arteche, *Guerra de la Independencia*, vol.II, p.285.
11   Arteche, *Guerra de la Independencia*, vol.II, pp.654–667.

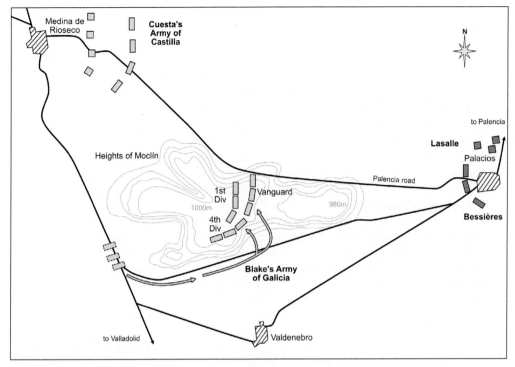

Plate 1. The Battle of Medina de Rioseco, early morning 14 July 1808.

By 4:00 a.m. on the day of the battle, with Cuesta and his Castilians still within the walls of Medina de Rioseco, Blake had already arranged his 1st and 4th Divisions on the battlefield in a position close to the Heights of Moclín. It was at about that time that his vanguard arrived on the scene after its counter-march from the outskirts of Valladolid, and it was as he was moving this unit into position that he received a message from Cuesta informing him that the French were forming up with the apparent intention of attacking along the Palencia road towards Rioseco. With reference to Plate 1, that is the road which passes to the north of the Heights of Moclín as it runs directly from Medina to Palacios before continuing on to Palencia, which is located away to the north-east, beyond the boundary of the map. At this point the diarist, whom we must assume to have been with Blake's Galicians judging by the title of his chronicle, takes up the story as follows:

At two in the afternoon [on 13 July] *General* Cuesta sent a courier to advise *General* Blake that the enemy was approaching by the Palencia Road, and that he should come and reinforce him. This disturbed all of his [Blake's] plans. *Ayudante* Ramón Calvet was sent to lead the 1st Division, *Ayudante* Joachín Zarate to lead the 4th and Barón de Alcalí the vanguard, all of them to be directed towards Rioseco such that the 1st and 4th Divisions arrived that evening along with the staff of headquarters. The moment they arrived, our commander in chief went with Señor Cuesta to reconnoitre the approaches …

It was impossible to provide the troops with any refreshment due to the confusion which reigned in Rioseco, where all of the troops belonging to the army of Señor Cuesta were located ... that night the generals convened a conference. At midnight, *General* Blake went to the places where his 1st and 4th Divisions were bivouacked, but the vanguard, which was still counter-marching the seven leagues from Villanubla, had not yet arrived. [After receiving their instructions] the 1st and 4th Divisions took up their arms and marched towards the approach [road] from Valdenebro: where they were formed by *General* Blake, placing part of the 1st in three closed columns ready to deploy en masse ... The 4th, in full order of battle, was placed on the left flank. The artillery had not been deployed by the time the vanguard arrived at three in the morning [of the 14th] and it was in this situation that *General* Cuesta sent a member of the Guardias de Corps to advise *General* Blake that the enemy was advancing by the Palencia Road and that he should bring his troops towards it. [In response] Blake sent all of his troops to the crest of the heights which covered our left and was at that time occupied by our light troops. When Blake arrived at the crest he could see nothing [of the enemy] so he ordered his troops to halt before dispatching some parties of scouts to search for them. Dawn was breaking by then and we were able to observe *General* Cuesta's troops moving out of Rioseco by the Palencia gate ... It was at that moment that *General* Blake decided to send his 4th Division to support the Castilians, so he formed them up in five columns ready to [march and] deploy [on the far side of the Palencia Road], leaving himself with [just] the vanguard and the 1st Division on the high plateau [of Moclín] which dominates Rioseco from its position between the roads to Valdenebro and Palencia ...[12]

We may now understand how and why Blake's 4th Division was sent to the aid of the Castilians, moving to Cuesta's side of the gap which lay between the two Spanish armies before the battle commenced: the movement was made entirely at the behest of Cuesta. It may be worth noting that, when the diarist talked of 'the high ground on our [Blake's] left', it may be safely assumed that he meant the heights of Moclín as, whilst the Galicians were marching out of Rioseco down the Valladolid road to take up position, the heights would have been on their left.

As we know, history has not always been kind to Cuesta, but was it entirely fair to make a scapegoat of him for the disaster which was about to unfold at Rioseco? When looking at Plate 1 it is easy to see just how mistaken the Spanish deployments were, and perhaps it was Cuesta's late start on the morning of 14 July which led to the somewhat eccentric geometry of the Spanish line. Had he begun to position his units at the same time as Blake, at about two in the morning, then a degree of coordination might well have been achieved. But the first question to ask is, why Blake did not inform Cuesta of his intentions to move his men into their battle positions during the early hours of the morning? If he had been warned, and given enough time, perhaps he would have moved his Castilians further down the left shoulder of the Palencia road, thus coming more into

---

12   AHN: Diversas Colecciones 136, N.22: Anon. *Diario de Operaciones*, entries for 13 and 14 July 1808.

line with Blake's divisions on the heights before the French attacked. Here, perhaps, lies the reason for the disjointed deployment of the Spaniards on the battlefield. Blake was an unwilling subordinate to Cuesta, but he should have at least consulted with his superior before deploying his men. However, such were the relations between the two commanders when the time came to face the enemy, that they were hardly willing to speak to each other, Blake, it seems, simply acted on his own initiative when deciding where he should position his men and when he would do it.

By 4:00 a.m. Blake's Galicians were in position on the Heights of Moclín, which lie to the right of the Palencia road as it runs from Rioseco to Palacios. The Castilians were to the left of the road some distance in the rear of the Galicians, and it would have been at about this time that Cuesta asked Blake to shuffle his forces to the left, thus moving them closer to the road as well as to Castilians. To comply fully would have meant abandoning the high ground he was occupying only to descend to an inferior position, thus leaving the heights undefended and open to French occupation; once in possession of them their artillery would have been in a perfect position to enfilade the Spanish line or at least rake it with oblique fire. That considered, there seems to have been little sense in Cuesta's order, as his army was already in position on the left of Palencia road, albeit in a somewhat withdrawn situation; all of which leaves one to suppose that he was still irked by Blake's earlier obstinacy and was attempting to impose his superiority of rank at the outset of the battle. That Blake, in partial compliance with the orders of his commander in chief, moved only his 4th Division to the left, seems simply to demonstrate the level of rancour which persisted between the two men.

Caught by surprise at Rioseco, there were no real anchor points on either flank of Cuesta's disjointed line; nothing to prevent the French from surrounding the Spaniards had they the need or wish to do so, but on seeing how dangerously exposed and disorganised his enemies were, Bessieres probably knew well that such a necessity would not arise.

Not knowing where the French were as he headed towards Rioseco, the thinking behind the route selected by Cuesta for the march of Blake was that his own Castilians would be on hand in the town to provide cover for the Galicians until they had reached Valladolid. With Blake on his right flank it would seem that Cuesta was guessing, correctly, as it turned out, that the French would appear from the direction of Palencia. But in the absence of intelligence on the location and strength of Bessiers and Lasalle as the two Spanish columns set off from the environs of Benavente and Villalpando, there seems to have been a kind of cautious approach adopted by the Army of Galicia, as illustrated by its diarist who noted that, as Blake's 4th Division made its march to go to the assistance of Cuesta: 'At a glance, it was easy to see that the information provided to our general about the foe's strength and the direction of his advance had been false. He had been told he would be facing 3 or 4 thousand men, but the enemy were at least 19,000 strong'.[13] In fact, neither of the Spanish commanders got to know exactly where the enemy was until they were within five miles of him, nor were they aware of his combined strength, a point borne out by the diarist.

---

13   AHN: Diversas Colecciones 136, N.22: Anon. *Diario de Operaciones*, entry for 14 July 1808.

The Fighting

The entry in the diary of the Army of Galicia for 14 July 1808, tells us that the fighting at Rioseco began at about 7:00 a.m. on that day, and that things began to go seriously wrong for the Galicians on the Heights of Moclín by mid-morning. Blake's diarist continued:

> At that point in time, and before his very eyes, our general found himself confronting the dilemma of observing the enemy making preparations for an assault, whilst being unable to take the advantage of attacking him before those preparations were complete, because of our lack of cavalry … At about seven in the morning we opened fire, but due to the open ground on our left, the men on that flank were completely without cover, allowing the enemy to occupy a small hill from which they kept up a lively fire, eventually putting them to flight …[14]

As both the Castilians and the Galician 4th Division were kept pinned to their ground at some distance in Blake's left and rear, Bessieres was able to push the Galician 1st Division and vanguard from the Heights of Moclín, scattering them in disorder and herding them away from Cuesta's army. When the French then turned their attentions to the Castilians, they were incapable of offering any effective resistance. By midday it was all over, the Spaniards streaming through Medina before taking the road to Benavente, leaving its inhabitants to the tender mercies of the victors.[15]

Cuesta's Account of the Defeat at Medina de Rioseco

In 1811, Gregorio de la Cuesta published what he somewhat grandly called his, *Manifiesto que presenta á la Europa el Capitán General de los reales Ejércitos, Don Gregorio García de la Cuesta, sobre sus operaciones militares y politicas …*[16] In other words, a report on his military and political activities from June 1808 to 12 August 1809 when, as his long-winded title goes on to say, he renounced his command of the Army of Extremadura. It is a document which some might see as an apology for his failures during the period stated, and we have only to read its sickeningly obsequious introduction by José Alexandro Fernández Blanco, to begin to obtain a flavour of what is to come as one reads on. Be that as it may, we may now examine what Cuesta had to say about Cabezón de Pisuerga and Medina de Rioseco. Firstly, with regard to Cabezón, he began by informing the reader about the success of his various efforts to bring a measure of calm and order to the civil and political situation at Valladolid, despite a widening occupation of Spanish territory by the advancing French; before going on to say of the action on the Pisuerga:

---

14   AHN: Diversas Colecciones 136, N.22: Anon. *Diario de Operaciones*, entry for 14 July 1808.
15   AHN: Diversas Colecciones 136, N.22: Anon. *Diario de Operaciones*, entry for 14 July 1808.
16   Gregorio de la Cuesta, *Manifiesto que presenta á la Europa el Capitán General de los reales Ejércitos, Don Gregorio García de la Cuesta, sobre sus operaciones militares y políticas, desde el mes de Junio 1808 hasta el día 12 de Agosto 1809, en que dejó el mando del ejército de Extremadura* (Valencia: José Ferrer de Orga y Compañía, 1811).

Général Bessieres, who took notice of [my] preparations, immediately dispatched a division of troops from Burgos under the command of *Général* Lasalle ...

Aware of these movements I ordered *General* Eguía, who happened to be present, to leave [Valladolid] at the head of a detachment of Guardias de Corps, which by chance had just returned from their sojourn at Bayonne,[17] and take with him others who, finding themselves at El Escorial, had fled in search of me in order to defend our good cause, [these were] the Carabineros Reales and two squadrons of the cavalry regiment, Reyna, along with some 400 civilians who had recently taken up arms. All of these were to cover the bridge at Cabezón in order to halt the progress of the enemy. Two days later I left [Valladolid for Cabezón] with another 200 civilians ...

With my people in position at the bridge of Cabezón, Lasalle arrived on the morning of 12 June 1808 with 6,000 infantry, 800 cavalry and six pieces of artillery, and [once his units were deployed, they] opened fire from several directions. My advanced positions and my artillery vigorously resisted [his assault] for about three hours, at the end of which, and with casualties mounting, we were forced to retire towards Rioseco and Benavente.[18]

It is noticeable that Cuesta talked of his 'advanced positions' as though he had deployed his forces in depth at Cabezón which, as is broadly accepted by historians, was not the case. There is no explicit mention that his 'advanced positions and ... artillery,' were actually located in front of the bridge at Cabezón in complete isolation, apart from two of his guns which he had placed on the far side of the bridge; an inexplicable deployment according to many commentators.

Having dealt with his defeat at Cabezón, Cuesta continued in his *Manifiesto* to provide the reader with his own version of events at Rioseco. What he said is worth some examination, as it provides the historian with something to hold in balance against the almost universal criticism and condemnation he has received from many contemporaries and others down the years, not solely for the defeat at Rioseco, but also for his actions before and after the battle. Here is what he had to say for himself:

We were given news that *Márechál* Bessieres was approaching [Rioseco] with respectable forces in search of us ... Seeing that there were two different approaches [by which the French could advance towards us] we [Blake and myself] determined to await news from our advanced posts about which of the two roads the French were using, before taking up our positions. We then agreed to meet at my quarters on the following morning; but after a long wait there along with my staff of headquarters, *General* Blake failed to arrive. Eventually I was told that he had left with all of his troops and had taken up a position on the summit of [the Heights of Moclín]. Once I saw what had happened, I left [Rioseco] with my own people and placed them on the [Palencia road] at some distance to the left of the

---

17 These were part of the personal guard that had accompanied King Fernando VII on his journey to Bayonne after he was summoned by Napoleon. It would seem that the French must have allowed them to return to Spain once the king had reached his destination.

18 Cuesta, *Manifiesto*, pp.4–5.

heights [on which Blake was posted]. It was along this road that the enemy was approaching.

I had just deployed my artillery and formed the infantry into two lines, placing the cavalry to the left of the front line, when my forward units advised me that the enemy cavalry were approaching. These were repulsed by [my own cavalry units, the] Guardias de Corps and the Carabineros Reales which, along with two battalions of the Asturians, had advanced to meet them.[19]

At this time one could hear a lot of musket fire coming from the heights … and I later discovered that Blake's vanguard, commanded by the Conde de Maceda, who was killed during the action, had put up a stubborn defence, despite the absolute lack of support from the Granaderos Provinciales de Galicia, who we soon observed descending the heights in disorder and fleeing as fast as they could towards Rioseco, their bad example causing the rest [of Blake's men] to follow.

On the left [Cuesta's left flank] the action against the enemy cavalry was energetically sustained and, although frequently repulsed, they continued to repeat their attacks against our horsemen, who were supported by my artillery and the two battalions of Asturians.

It must be said that, at the moment the attack began, *General* Blake sent one of his adjutants to me, who informed me that the enemy had appeared on the right of the heights [which Blake was defending] and were heading for Rioseco, adding that his commander in chief was in need of some cavalry in order to contain them; as such I ordered two squadrons of the cavalry regiment, Reyna, to march immediately to that point. All of this was in vain, as they failed to find any of the enemy. However, the movement was prejudicial [to me] as it weakened my cavalry force at the point where it was most needed, and during all of the time those two squadrons stood inactive, I was left with only the Guardias de Corps and the Carabineros Reales, who displayed great bravery in sustaining the battle.

When I observed that the Granaderos Provinciales de Galicia, the unit which had been holding the left of Blake's line, had abandoned the heights [of Moclín] in disorder, I immediately made a movement towards that place with my staff of headquarters and the two battalions of civilians who were closest to me, but as I arrived at the crest of the heights I was attacked by a corps of enemy infantry and cavalry. I was thus forced to retire and order the artillery, cavalry and infantry comprising the left flank of my army to do the same, as it was useless to resist the enemy, who was by then ensconced upon the heights.

When I arrived at Rioseco I met with Blake, and I could see that the whole of his troops were continuing to retire in disorder towards Benavente, leaving no hope that we could defend the town. As such, I continued my own retirement along with my staff of headquarters, my artillery, cavalry and a small number of the infantry, all heading towards Benavente, which I entered on the same day as *General* Blake …

---

19   These belonged to the Regimiento de Covadonga, lent to Cuesta by the *Junta de Asturias*.

> During the following two or three days the majority of our troops trickled in, but *General* Blake then decided to continue his retreat to Galicia without consulting with me, leaving me alone in Benavente with just a few men ...[20]

One may make of this whatever one wishes, but it has all the appearance of a clear and deliberate attempt by Cuesta to shift all of the blame for the defeat at Rioseco onto Blake's shoulders. One can easily discern that the *Capitán General* talked only of the weakness of the Galicians in face of the enemy, at the same time praising his own units, as well as the Asturian detachment fighting alongside them, and accusing Blake of calling upon him for cavalry reinforcements in order to protect his right flank when there was apparently no enemy threat visible from that direction. In fact, as we have already seen, it was Cuesta who had called for support from Blake even before the battle had begun, and it was his intention that all three divisions of the Army of Galicia make a flank march to join him. However, instead of completely abandoning the only good position in Spanish hands, thanks to Blake's early morning deployment, the commander of the Galicians sent only his 4th Division to help the Castilians. Had it been allowed to remain under Blake's command he might have been able to repel the subsequent French assaults on the Heights of Moclín, and as such disrupt Bessieres' plans.

In addition to his somewhat partial representations of the facts, Cuesta, throughout his *Manifiesto*, made continuous accusations of insubordination on the part of Blake. In contrast, the diarist of the Army of Galicia provided a much more objective description of the battle. Nowhere did he support Cuesta's assertion that he had sent a significant part of his cavalry to cover Blake's right, but he gave praise where it was due to Cuesta's cavalry units as well as Blake's vanguard, and eschewed any apportionment of blame for the failure to the Castilians. In a seemingly authentic passage, he went on to describe how and why Blake's 1st Division was displaced from its position on the Heights of Moclín, and how its subsequent disordered and disconcerting flight spread panic amongst other units. In comparison with Cuesta's description of the battle, that of Blake's diarist has much more of a genuine ring of truth about it.

The rout at Rioseco came about as a result of the incompetence, petty jealousies, and rancour at the heart of the Spanish high command. Perhaps the greater measure of the first came from Cuesta, as most Spanish, not to say British writers, tend to agree. In his five-volume history of the Peninsular War, *Historia del Levantamiento, Guerra y Revolución de España*, José María Queipo de Llano, Conde de Toreno, one-time Spanish Ambassador to Great Britain and member of the group of Asturian parliamentary deputies who fled to England at the beginning of the war, made the following astonishing accusation against Cuesta for the failure at Rioseco:

> [Bessieres] had judged that [the Spaniards] had formed themselves in two separate lines, and that the ignorance and lack of ability of the two [Spanish] generals had resulted in the placement of the soldiers at two distinct and distant locations... We believe that Cuesta had determined to operate only for his own glory, and to

---

20   Cuesta, *Manifiesto*, pp.6–8.

fight for victory only when his rival was on the verge of defeat, or at least greatly compromised; his offended pride making it impossible for him to comprehend the risks involved in such a reckless enterprise. On his part, Blake should have operated with greater care, and knowing how stubbornly inflexible Cuesta could be, he should have avoided offering battle with only a fraction of his army.

Lamentable day, owing to the obstinate blindness and ignorance of Cuesta, the lack of agreement between him and Blake and the weak and culpable condescension of the *Junta de Galicia*.[21]

So ended the story of Medina de Rioseco. In its aftermath, Blake managed without too much difficulty to retreat to Benavente and collect the 5,000 men of his 3rd Division, before marching into El Bierzo en–route to Galicia. Cuesta followed along in company with Blake as far as Benavente whence, after a brief and bitter exchange with his subordinate, the former made his way to León.

After suffering two crushing defeats in the space of little more than a month, Cuesta must have been expecting to face some kind of enquiry into his qualities of leadership. But within five days of their defeat at Rioseco there came news of one of the most extraordinary successes of Spanish arms during the course of the war. As the French invasion of Spain spread its tentacles from the Pyrenees towards the remotest corners of Spanish territory, *Général de division* Dupont led the French II Corps across the Sierra Morena towards the small Andalucían town of Bailén. It was there where Castaños brought him to battle on 20 July 1808 and inflicted total defeat upon him; the 15,000 survivors of his army afterwards being led to Cádiz, where they were placed aboard a number of rotting, old prison hulks dotted around the harbour.

The debacle at Bailén was to have significant ramifications, but the French may well have overreacted to the news of Dupont's defeat, when they decided to withdraw from Madrid and the central and southern Spanish provinces they had recently overrun; the intruder, King Joseph, making a precipitate retreat from the capital towards the defensive barrier of the river Ebro, together with his court, and calling in his far-flung armies as a precaution against another humiliating defeat at the hands of the Spanish.

Seemingly as surprised as their enemies were with the new situation, the Spaniards were slow in following up the French retreat, and amidst the confusion and euphoria of the occasion, any thoughts about a reckoning with Cuesta seem to have been dispelled. Then, as if to add to the heady scent of an anticipated, decisive and final victory hanging in the air, it was just three weeks after Bailén that news of Wellesley's arrival in Portugal, at the head of an army of some 15,000 men, was gleefully received by the populace of a newly liberated Madrid.[22] But as sole architect of the Spanish plan which led to Rioseco, Cuesta must take the main responsibility for its failings. Had the Galicians and Castilians succeeded in taking Valladolid before being confronted by the French, which was their original aim, then they may have been able to put it into a strong state of defence. A subsequent French siege, had it

---

21   Conde de Toreno, *Historia del Levantamiento, Guerra y Revolución de España* (Madrid: Imprenta de Tomás Jordán, 1835), vol.I, pp.379–380.
22   This was Britain's first expedition to Portugal during the course of the Peninsular War and it resulted in Wellesley's early victories at Roliça and Vimeiro before he was replaced as commander of the army.

been successfully withstood, might then have proved as disastrous for them as did the first siege of Zaragoza, then still at its height some 270 miles to the east. But as recent animosities amongst the Spaniards cooled, Cuesta would be allowed to live to fight another day, and in the following chapters we will examine just how well he rose to the challenge.

2

August to December 1808

Once Blake had set off for the safety of Galicia in the wake of the abject failure at Rioseco, Cuesta became aware of Bessieres' somewhat leisurely advance towards him at Benavente, thus forcing him to head north towards the city of León. But the French would soon be on his tail, and in the short breathing space afforded him whilst in the provincial capital, he decided to send the bulk of his infantry into the hills of Asturias, where they would find refuge from the French cavalry, no doubt recalling the advice earlier extended to him by the *junta* of that region. With just his own cavalry and artillery to worry about, by no means a numerous force, the *Capitán General* then took what many would have thought to be the foolhardy decision to retreat southwards down the León-Valladolid road, which runs parallel to the Benavente-León road up which Bessieres was marching, the two carriage-ways at that latitude being separated by a distance of just 15 miles or so. In fact, during their withdrawal, the Spaniards actually skirted the western edge of Medina de Rioseco, where the French rearguard was still waiting for its marching orders before following in the wake of the rest of Bessieres' army. Luck was with Cuesta in that he was eventually able to angle his march towards the southwest and head for Toro on the Duero without being discovered. But with the French withdrawal to the Ebro imminent, the heat would soon be off him – in the short term at least.[1]

Politics were never far from the front of Cuesta's mind, and despite the urgency of the military situation in northern Spain, he was about to become embroiled in a political struggle which could easily have ended his career. Just before leaving León he had met with Antonio Valdés, former *Capitán General* of the Armada, the navy's most senior rank, who had been present in León acting as president of the local *junta* when Cuesta arrived at the capital of his fiefdom. Aware that the French were pursuing him, he advised Valdés to decide between abandoning the city or remaining *in situ* to receive them in peace. After some reflection, the erstwhile naval officer finally decided to move to Ponferrada, together with two of his nephews and some of his political deputies, whence he would make for Lugo in Galicia. It was whilst he was there that he determined to unite the offices of the *Junta de León* with those of the *Junta de La Coruña*, and subsequently assume full command of the province of Castilla in his role as a member of the new joint body, thus placing the *Capitán General* of the region, Cuesta, under his orders. Insult was added to injury when Cuesta was ordered

---

1   Cuesta, *Manifiesto*, p.9.

by the new combined *junta*, and later by the commander of the Army of Galicia, Blake, to place the whole of his cavalry at their disposition. In doing so Cuesta would, in effect, relinquish his command of the Army of Castilla, as the few guns of his artillery would be the only formation belonging to it still under his direct command whilst his infantry was in Asturias.

The old soldier reacted by officially annulling what he termed the '*Junta de León en Galicia*' and, after forbidding all forms of local government in Castilla to submit to it, he began his march towards Toro. He then continued on to a location somewhere between Ciudad Rodrigo and Salamanca, where he commenced the work of re-building his army. By this time the effects of Castaños's victory at Bailén were beginning to show, one of which was the re-occupation of Madrid after it had been abandoned by the French during their retreat to the Ebro. Cuesta claimed it was at this point that a person he referred to as the *Diácono* (Deacon) *del Supremo Consejo de Castilla* invited him to move upon Madrid to maintain order in the capital in the absence of its recent occupiers. It should be noted that, as a result of his retreat from León, Cuesta had moved into the province of Salamanca, thus absenting himself from his area of jurisdiction; as such, *Teniente General* Eguía, his second in command, was sent to the capital with a small, combined force of cavalry, infantry and artillery, but, claimed Cuesta, he had given his deputy strict instructions not to enter the city if any of the armies of Valencia, Andalucía or Extremadura had arrived before him and were already stationed within the capital. This is exactly what happened, and Eguía returned to base leaving Madrid in the hands of Castaños.

The victor of Bailén soon called for a council of the commanders in chief of all the Spanish armies, at which it would be decided how best to react to the general withdrawal of the French from many parts of Spain. Cuesta was one of those summoned to Madrid, as was Blake, who, diplomatically perhaps, sent word that he could not attend, as he was advancing with the Army of Galicia along the southern foothills of the Cantabrian mountains as part of the ongoing Spanish pursuit of the French in northern Spain. He was thus substituted at the conference by the Duque del Infantado. It took several days for the council to come to its decision on how to handle the new situation in the country at large, a somewhat leisurely contemplation, it would seem, under the prevailing circumstances. One of the conference themes was the consideration of a proposal to elect a Spanish supremo to assume command over all of the somewhat disparate collection of regional forces which had come into being, but after failing to agree in favour of any of the candidates, things were left to continue as they were. Once business had been concluded, *Generales* Llamas, Castaños, Galluzo, Cuesta and Blake were ordered to advance to selected destinations; that of the Army of Castilla was the small town of Burgo de Osma which lay about 100 miles behind the new front line on the Ebro. It was at this point that Cuesta's political machinations commenced.

With the conference of military leaders at Madrid closed, Cuesta was informed that, as head of what he now referred to as the *Junta de Lugo* – the body claiming governance of Castilla *in absentia* – Valdés had been nominated by his two nephews for the new post of 'deputy representing the provinces of Castilla', in what was about to become the national government of Spain, the new *Junta Suprema Central*. Those provinces, Cuesta pointed out, were the very ones which Valdés had not long ago abandoned in the face of the enemy. So, when Cuesta discovered that he was travelling south to Madrid to take up his new post, he ordered Eguía to arrest him and incarcerate him at the Alcázar de Segovia, together with the Vizconde de Quintanilla, who was accompanying him as the nominated deputy for León, the nominating body again being the *Junta de Lugo*, which Cuesta claimed had no legal authority.[2] With both Valdés and Quintanilla under arrest, the *Capitán General* then ordered the authorities in Valladolid, now also free from French occupation, to nominate two replacements for them, but when the two substitutes selected arrived to take their places in the new *Junta Suprema* about to be inaugurated at Aranjuez, they were refused entry to the parliamentary buildings.

News of Cuesta's actions soon reached the ear of the venerable Conde de Floridablanca, then fulfilling the role of nominated president for the proposed new government, who responded by writing to the *Capitán General* on 16 September 1808, asking him to justify his actions with respect to Valdés. In a long-winded reply written on 17 September 1808, Cuesta recounted the whole story of his activities and adventures since being elected *Capitán General* of Valladolid, before emphasising the wider powers more recently invested in him as *Capitán General* of Castilla and León by the king, finally adding that he would refuse to give in to any of Floridablanca's demands. *Capitán General* Castaños then entered the fray, writing to Cuesta in a similar vein to that of the president elect and asking for Valdés's release, but Cuesta would have none of it. Instead, he ordered that the Conde de Cartaojal place Valdés on trial for attempting to force the regions of Castilla to accept the governance of the *Junta de Galicia*, then seated in La Coruña, claiming that Valdés's insurrection, as he called it, could easily have resulted in anarchy throughout Castilla. Fortunately, the immediate situation was defused when Cuesta was ordered to march for Burgo de Osma, as the Spanish armies continued their leisurely pursuit of the French towards the Ebro. By then he should have sensed that the Spanish establishment did not want or need any distractions, not to say petty distractions, from the business in hand: that of expelling the French from Spanish territory. But, being the man that he was, there was probably a widely held opinion forming amongst some of the Spanish political classes that Cuesta be finally put in his place before his troublesome character began to have a damaging effect on the national morale. Whilst the old warrior was absent from his fiefdom, Cartaojal, probably sensing where things were headed, decided to stay in Segovia rather than comply with Cuesta's orders to arrest Valdés.

At Aranjuez, it was decided that the new *Junta Suprema* would simply take on the role of a national government rather than elect one or, indeed, establish a temporary regency. It was a decision which would rankle with a number of senior army officers, including Cuesta, and would become the source of continual ramifications during the *Junta's* short tenure of power. Their first act was to order the release of Antonio Valdés from prison and drop all charges against him, before summoning Cartaojal and Cuesta to 'clarify any doubts' which may have remained with respect to Valdés's case.[3]

Cuesta arrived at the Royal City on 9 October 1808, and after a number of unproductive meetings with Floridablanca his case against Valdés was allowed simply to wither away, the president of the *Junta Suprema* quietly ignoring the general's continued demands for action. Ultimately, he received the news that Valdés, rather than being prosecuted, had been

2   Cuesta, *Manifiesto*, pp.10–12.
3   Cuesta, *Manifiesto*, pp.13–21.

formally declared a deputy for Castilla in the new governing body. In the aftermath of it all, Cuesta somewhat disingenuously claimed that the *Gazeta de Madrid* had been ordered to publish what he regarded to be a seriously defamatory article about him (see below) which, he claimed, became the cause of some reaction amongst the population of Madrid against the *Junta*. But for all his pains he was ordered to remain under what might best be described as a mutually agreed detention at Aranjuez for some time, all of which had the effect of turning the old soldier into an implacable enemy of the *Junta Suprema* and *vice-versa*, a situation which would contribute to the crisis which enveloped the Anglo-Spanish alliance during the Tagus campaign of 1809. The article in the *Gazeta* stated:

> The *Junta Suprema Guvernativa*, after considering the charges made against Don Antonio Valdés and the Vizconde de Quintanilla, both deputies nominated by the kingdom of León for the *Junta Reunida de Castilla y Galicia* … and their subsequent imprisonment by the *Capitán General de Castilla la Vieja*, Don Gregorio de la Cuesta; and having examined the powers bestowed upon them by that body, as well as the documents presented by the *Capitán General de Castilla la Vieja* concerning the imprisonment of said deputies: has decided that they will be admitted immediately to the sessions of the *Junta Suprema* as deputies for the kingdom of León, without prejudice and before being sworn-in, and ultimately that this agreement be published in the Gazeta for the satisfaction of all interested parties.[4]

Undoubtedly, the driving force behind this political manoeuvre was Floridablanca, but the elderly president would not survive to take up his own seat in the *Junta Suprema* after its relocation to Seville, passing away somewhat unexpectedly on the penultimate day of 1808. His resulting absence during the following months may well have had a bearing on Cuesta's rapid return to prominence within the army. But, in the meantime, there would be more pain for the old warrior whilst he remained in detention.

Upon answering his summons to Aranjuez, Cuesta had passed the command of the Army of Castilla to Eguía. By then it fielded just 4,000 or so men, and the *Junta* would soon displace Cuesta's deputy in favour of the Conde de Cartaojal, who would oversee the total dismemberment the force by sending some of its troops to make up for the recent losses suffered by the Army of Andalucía. Those remaining with Cuesta's army once the re-allocations were complete were then disbanded, thus extinguishing the existence of his host. Most people in his situation would have taken stock at this juncture: in summary, the *Junta Suprema* had shown itself deaf to his demands that Valdés be put on trial for sedition; instead it was Cuesta who found himself under arrest. In addition, his so-called Army of Castilla had not really come into the reckoning at the recently held conference of army commanders in Madrid. All of which should have been the clearest and final signal to him that, as far as the new order in Spain was concerned, he was yesterday's man; but it seems everything simply passed over his head, doing nothing to assuage his sense of injustice at the treatment meted out to him. Cuesta was a remarkably stubborn character, persistently putting the *Junta's*

---

4   *Gazeta de Madrid*, no.142, 8 November 1808, p.1446. Available at <http://www.cervantesvirtual.com/partes/282347/gazeta-de-madrid-1808/14>, accessed March 2021.

behaviour down to its opposition to his own insistence that Valdés be placed on trial for his 'desertion' from León to Galicia and his subsequent 'provocation' of the populace of Castilla in an attempt to provoke a so-called uprising. The thought that such a calumny might be the least of the *Junta's* concerns about him seemed never to have crossed his mind.[5]

Elsewhere in the Peninsula, the British army which disembarked under the command of Wellesley at Mondego Bay in Portugal from 1 August, had defeated Junot's army at Roliça and Vimeiro on 17 and 21 August 1808 respectively, but what had looked like a good start to a promising campaign soon became bogged down in issues relating to the leadership of the expeditionary force, Wellesley being succeeded in overall command as more senior officers arrived. There was also much, possibly too much, haggling in negotiations with the French over the terms of their ultimate surrender in Portugal, the discussions leading to the notorious Convention of Cintra under which Junot's defeated army, isolated in Lisbon with no help in sight, was transported to home territory aboard British ships. An enquiry into the terms of the convention would subsequently be held in England and would lead to some admonishment of those held responsible for the failure, Wellesley escaping the worst of the wrath which followed due to the apparently minor role he played in the Anglo-French talks, though there is some debate as to just how minor his role actually was. In fact, after defeating the French at Roliça and Vimeiro, Wellesley was superseded in command by Lieutenant General Sir Harry Burrard, who in turn was replaced by Sir Hew Dalrymple, and it was the latter who, in negotiations with the French, lobbied for a quick conclusion to the talks in order that the British army could expedite its march towards the Spanish frontier so as to relieve the pressure on the Spaniards. Eventually, Lieutenant General Sir John Moore took command of the troops in Portugal, and after Lieutenant General Sir David Baird had landed at La Coruña in northern Spain with a smaller auxiliary force, the British army was somewhat belatedly ready to make an attempt to catch up with the Spanish advance towards the Ebro after their success at Bailén, hoping to take part in what many in Spain were anticipating to be the final battles required to expel the French from the country.

By the beginning of October 1808, whilst Cuesta was at Aranjuez digesting the news of the imminent disbandment of his army, the Marqués de la Romana's host was being disembarked at Santander after being rescued by the Royal Navy from its perilous situation in the Baltic. With this addition of some 10,000 regular soldiers to the forces at Castaños's disposal, the outlook for the allied cause seemed bright, but things were about to undergo a dramatic transformation. Napoleon, looking on in despair from Paris as his armies in Spain remained motionless on the left bank of the Ebro, decided to act, and launched a much-reinforced French army into a new and devasting offensive across Spanish territory.

Cuesta is Presented with a Second Opportunity to Command

On 1 December 1808, whilst still in detention at Aranjuez, Cuesta heard news of a French breakthrough on the high mountain pass of Somosierra, some 50 miles north of Madrid. The man leading the French advance on the capital was Napoleon Bonaparte, who was

---

5   Cuesta, *Manifiesto*, pp.22–24.

hoping to bring the whole business south of the Pyrenees to a successful conclusion before winter could fully establish its paralysing grip.

The Emperor's march on Madrid meant that the *Junta Suprema*, still sitting at Aranjuez, was forced to flee to Seville in the far south of the country. Cuesta's somewhat informal confinement was not forgotten by the members of the *Junta* as they set off for Andalucía, and he was given orders to follow in their wake to Trujillo in Extremadura where he arrived on 6 December, remaining in the town for a short time after most of the members of the Spanish government had continued on their precipitate flight to the south. In his *Manifiesto* he claimed that, as the soldiers and civilians fleeing the French advance gathered in Trujillo, they were made aware of his presence in the town and began to clamour for his consent that they proclaim him *Capitán General* of Extremadura and commander in chief of the Spanish troops then gathered at Talavera after their recent rout from Burgos. Unsure about what to do, he eventually refused the pleadings of the crowd, but when he arrived at Mérida a few days later in company with some stragglers belonging to the government entourage, he claimed that:

> ... the people, along with two of the deputies of the local *junta*, were congregated in the town square in order to compliment me and ask me not to leave the place; claiming that the people of the town, as well as those of the province, wanted me to take command of the army. I responded that I could not do so without orders or approval from the [*Junta Suprema*] at which they decided to make an approach on my behalf, and I was fully convinced that the inhabitants of Mérida were resolved in their determination not to allow me to leave. When the solicitation was made, the members of the [*Junta Suprema* still present in the town] would not commit themselves to agree to the peoples' demands, using the pretext that they were not convinced that the citizens of [the whole of the province of] Badajoz shared the desires expressed ...

Cuesta went on to claim that, at that point, the people of Mérida decided to take matters into their own hands:

> The fact of the matter is that, when the [members of] the [*Junta Suprema*] left for Seville on the following morning, and the people of Mérida saw that a coach was being prepared for me in order that I follow them, there came a knock at the door of my lodgings and two good men were shown up to my room. [Once in my presence] they respectfully informed me that the people would not allow me to leave, nor would they be happy until I promised to comply with their wishes. At that the coach was ordered to leave ...[6]

Several months later, on 27 July 1809, the periodical, *Semanario Patriótico*, published a somewhat belated account of events regarding Cuesta's rehabilitation in the following terms:

---

6   Cuesta, *Manifiesto*, pp.26–27.

As the entourage of the *Junta Suprema* passed through Mérida, a deputation from the city's *junta* presented itself before the president asking, in the name of the people of the town and province, that the offices of Captain General and commander of their troops be assigned to Don Gregorio de la Cuesta, who at the time was present in the town waiting to continue with his retirement from Aranjuez. These demands had not been put to the vote by the *Junta Superior de Extremadura*, as they arose simply from the people's reaction to the miserable state of our military forces; the populous considering that the talent, spirit and opinion of *General* Cuesta were absolutely necessary for their reorganisation and recovery, in light of the recent disasters they had suffered. The president responded to the deputation that nothing could be done without the previous knowledge and cooperation of the *Junta de Badajoz*, which seemed determined to retain *Teniente General* Galluzo as commander in chief of the army on the Tagus. Nevertheless, after further solicitations that it recognise and assist in the election of the new general, the *Junta* [*Superior*] concluded that such a change might prove to be most advantageous under the prevailing circumstances. In consequence, Galluzo was deposed shortly after his arrival at Zalamea and sent to appear [before the *Junta Suprema*] in Seville. Cuesta then took command of the province and ordered that the relics of the army then stationed at Zalamea be transferred to Badajoz, where he established his general headquarters, and where, after a great number of stragglers had gathered in the city, he decided to unite all available forces in order to resist the enemy.[7]

It is interesting to note that the article referred to above was not published until the day on which the Battle of Talavera commenced. Printed in Seville at that time, there must surely have been some direct contact between the editorial staff of the *Semanario Patriotico* and the *Junta Suprema*, then sitting in the town, whose members may have had an influence on the piece's somewhat tardy appearance. Reading between the lines of the article, a cynic might become convinced that the *Junta* was shunning any idea that it was responsible for Cuesta's appointment as commander in chief of the Army of Extremadura. In considering the timing of its publication, and recalling what was then the general's history of failures at Medina de Rioseco and Medellín, as well as his known hostility to the *Junta Suprema*, were its members washing their hands of Cuesta should he be about to fail once more at Talavera? But enough of this for now.

Once freed from house arrest at Mérida, Cuesta began to busy himself, and between 10 and 27 December 1808 he collected together some of the remnants of the Spanish armies dispersed during the French onslaught across the north of Spain during the final months of the year. By the time he had finished, he had accumulated a force of some 900 men and 11 field pieces, at the head of which he marched for the city of Badajoz. It was whilst he was there that he received a royal order to take up formally the position of *Capitán General* of the region of Extremadura and its army, which, in reality, no longer existed.[8] Undaunted,

---

7   *Semanario Patriótico*, no.XXVII, 27 July 1809, pp.199–200. Available at <https://hemerotecadigital. bne.es/hd/es/viewer?id=37fcbae1-9bcb-4862-a29c-ee5f2f422ff6>, accessed May 2021.

8   AHN: Estado, 43, A: Junta Suprema Central de Sevilla to the Presidente de la Junta y Gobierno de Extremadura, 31 December 1808, pp.269–271 and Junta Suprema Central de Sevilla to Cuesta, 31

Cuesta immediately set about the task of re-establishing a viable military presence in the province, and the resulting, re-constituted Army of Extremadura would be the second scratch force put together by Cuesta since his return to active service. If nothing else, it highlighted the fact that he was at least willing to stand and fight the enemy whilst many other leaders in Spain – political and military – simply wanted to remove themselves from the path of the French advance by retreating into the deep south of the country.

December 1808, pp.272–273.

3

The Battle of Medellín

Commanded by *Mariscal de Campo* San Juan, the Spanish Army of the Centre had absorbed some isolated units from other Spanish armies as Napoleon's advance towards Madrid splintered all resistance in its path, and it was during the last days of November 1808 that San Juan found himself defending the final barrier to the capital, the pass of Somosierra in the Sierra de Guadarrama, which lies to the north of the capital. San Juan's position was by its very nature strong, and he should have been able to hold the French at bay for a considerable period of time; but a now famous charge made by Napoleon's Polish Lancers on 30 November 1808, managed to break Spanish resistance at the outset of the contest. Fleeing for their lives as the Poles disdained the hail of canister and cannon shot hurled at them as they charged up the pass, the Spanish defenders later vented their fury, if not their shame, upon San Juan, when he eventually attempted to rally them at Talavera some five weeks later, and it was in the midst of their rage that the unfortunate general was shot down as he spoke. It was whilst Cuesta was under detention that *Teniente General* Galluzo had been placed in charge of the remnants of the Spanish Army of the Centre after the murder of San Juan.

As he took up the reins of command, Galluzo decided to lead those of his men still willing to continue the fight to the south bank of the Tagus, where he began to draw up plans to hold the line of the river in an attempt to prevent the French from continuing their southerly advance into Extremadura and Andalucía; it was a policy which Cuesta would later adopt. Once the bulk of his force was on the south bank of the river, Galluzo's first act was a failed attempt to demolish the important bridge near Almaraz, its ancient stonework proving too sturdy for the manual efforts to dismantle it employed by the Spaniards.

The first skirmishes on the Tagus came about in late December 1808, when *Maréchal* Lefebvre launched a number of probing movements at various points along its north bank. At that time Galluzo was at the pass of Miravete with a force of about 5,000 men and a dozen pieces of artillery, the whole of which was assigned to block any attempts by the French to advance, should they cross the bridge. In command of a smaller force of some 800 infantry and 200 cavalry, *Mariscal de Campo* Trias was given responsibility for guarding the bridge at Arzobispo some 25 miles upstream, as well as that of El Conde (de Miranda) situated almost at the mid-point between the other two crossings. As Trias approached the bridge at Arzobispo, he ran into the party of Spanish engineers which had earlier been sent to demolish it; the men were retreating in haste due to the approach of *Général de division* Sebastiani. Caution taking the better part of valour, Trias too decided to retreat, leaving the somewhat narrow crossing to be occupied by the French on 25 December, and sending one of his cavalry officers to organise whatever defence he could at the bridge of El Conde, which also fell to the enemy. The failures at these two easterly bridges caused Galluzo to fall back on Jaraicejo with the bulk of his force, leaving just two battalions of infantry under Trias to defend the partly dismantled bridge near Almaraz; however, these were easily brushed aside when Lasalle's cavalry led the main French assault on the crossing, thus allowing their infantry to cross the Tagus without getting their feet wet.

On hearing the news that all three bridgeheads were in French hands, Galluzo decided to fall back on Trujillo as disorder once again began to reign amongst the Spanish troops, the result of which was an eventual wholesale retreat to Medellín where, after a further assessment of the situation, Galluzo decided to make for the distant sanctuary of Zalamea, which lies some 25 miles south of the Guadiana. Meanwhile, abandoned to his fate, Trias set out to collect the erstwhile defenders of the bridgeheads at El Cardenal, Almaraz, El Conde and Arzobispo, a task in which he excelled himself, eventually leading the 4,000 or so troops to safety via a long and circuitous route. It was these lamentable failures which were to lead to Galluzo's dismissal. Waiting in the wings at Badajoz, Cuesta would take up the reins of command as the new year dawned.[1]

The early weeks of 1809 were used by Cuesta to emphasise his return to power, actively engaging in communication with the *Junta Suprema* in Seville as he called for the money and resources necessary to meld his reconstituted Army of Extremadura into an efficient fighting force. Whilst the talks with Seville continued, orders were sent to the troops at Zalamea, instructing them to come and join their new commander in chief at Badajoz. As luck would have it, Cuesta had returned to prominence in a strategically vital region of Spain, and at a time when the French push towards Andalucía, temporarily stalled by the winter weather, was about to be revived as spring approached. But with the Spanish presence now growing in the region of Mérida and Badajoz, the French shied away from their temptation to march on Seville, and began to contemplate a limited withdrawal to the north bank of the Tagus.

At the Archivo Histórico Militar de Madrid, there is a collection of the correspondence which passed between the *Junta Suprema* and Cuesta, as his headquarters moved between Badajoz on the Guadiana and a number of towns dotted along the course of the Tagus, the latter taking a course lying some 70 miles to the north of the former as they both wend their ways across western Extremadura. Cuesta's wanderings were born more of necessity than whim, the old warrior being obliged to scour the banks of the Tagus in search of recruits, provisions and topographical intelligence, in preparation for the inevitable clashes with the forces of *Maréchal* Victor whenever they made their anticipated attempt to establish themselves south of the river. The series of archived letters covers the whole of 1809 and the early weeks of 1810, and on reading those relating to the first three months of 1809 it is easy to see just how worried the Spanish government was about the prospect of a French invasion of Andalucía. But before such an operation could be mounted, at least some of the bridges which spanned the Tagus as it wound its way through Extremadura would have to be taken by French forces and held. The task required of Cuesta therefore, was to deny the enemy

---

1   Arteche, *Guerra de la Independencia*, vol.V, pp.246–250.

possession of them; if that meant he had to destroy them then it should be done without hesitation, and this was continually stressed upon him via his correspondence with Seville. On 5 January 1809 the *Junta* wrote to its own *Secretario de Guerra*, Antonio Cornel, as follows, in order that he be aware of the task they were setting the elderly but by no means indolent soldier:

> The *Junta Suprema* ... has decided that today an officer will leave this place carrying documents for *General* Gregorio de la Cuesta, reminding him of all the previous orders it has communicated to him relative to his nomination. [Which were that he] is charged with defending all of those places and approaches which guard or provide access to the region [of Extremadura] and that he re-organise the army of the region, increasing its strength, its discipline ...[2] At the same time, he is informed that a force of just 150 French has been left at the bridge of Almaraz. This force he must dislodge at all costs in order to take possession of that important position, as well as all other such posts along the banks of the Tagus ...[3]

It was via this communication that the *de facto* campaign on the Tagus of 1809 was given formal status. But there was a second theme which ran through Cuesta's communications with the *Junta Suprema* during the first three months of 1809, and it was one which highlighted the state of Spanish arms at the commencement of the new year: that of a lack of regular troops. The immediate cause of the shortage was Napoleon's campaign in the north of the country during the previous autumn, which had more or less resulted in the destruction or dispersal of all those Spanish forces having the semblance of a regular army. The subsequent lack of trained soldiers, combined with a scarcity of uniforms, footwear, food and money, was always going to make it difficult for the Spanish to continue to resist Napoleon's well-tried, well-led and well-accoutred soldiers, but in Cuesta they at least had somebody who was willing to give it his all.

On 6 January 1809, whilst he was settling into his new post as *Capitán General* of Extremadura, Cuesta replied to the orders mentioned in the letter above, addressing his response to Martín de Garay, *Secretario General de la Junta Suprema* in Seville. After dealing with the usual formalities in the first part of his communication, he went on to describe the state of things in Extremadura, and a glance at Cuesta's words will provide the reader with an idea of the kind of force he would eventually bring to Talavera in July.

> I can assure you that I will omit nothing in carrying out the task you have asked me to undertake, despite the grave difficulties apparent.
> The army is completely disorganised, badly formed and dispersed, as well as being barely clothed and mostly without arms. The means to clothe it and provide it with footwear are very scarce or non-existent, and there is hardly enough money to cover the daily pay of the soldiers. This lack of means may well delay the remedy of so many faults, just as it has recently dashed our hopes of taking advantage of

---

2   Strictly speaking, the Tagus does not demarcate the northern limit of the region of Extremadura, whose northern-most province, Cáceres, actually straddles the river.
3   AHN: Estado, 43, A: Junta Suprema Central de Sevilla to Antonio Cornel, 5 January 1809, p.278.

the enemy's [recent] withdrawal from the banks of the Tagus, thus allowing them to return to their old positions and fortify them. Despite all of this, I have formed a vanguard of some 3,000 men from the least disorganised corps, with which [I intend] to occupy the bridges on [the Tagus] ...[4]

The importance of defending the line of the Tagus was stressed once more in a second letter from the *Junta Suprema* to Cornel:

The *Suprema Junta y Gobierno del Reyno* has resolved that you act with promptitude and advise *General* Gregorio de la Cuesta of the movement announced by the Duque del Infantado, in order that, with the greatest number of troops possible and encouraging the British [to give support] he may provide strong cover for the fords and bridges along the Tagus. Advise him that if he succeeds in this aim we could isolate the French now at Oropesa ...[5]

The reference to British army in the *Junta's* communication requires some discussion, as on 7 January 1809, the date on which the letter was written, Sir John Moore would have been leading his army along the final stages of its epic retreat to La Coruña, marching along a remote stretch of the royal highway which linked that place with the distant Madrid. In other words, the bulk of the British forces on the Peninsula were somewhere deep in the Galician highlands, way up in the north-west corner of Spain, far away from the Tagus and with the French in hot pursuit. If the *Junta Suprema* thought there were sufficient British forces in the region of the Tagus valley to help defend the line of the river, then it was sorely mistaken. As late as the beginning of April 1809, the British presence in Iberia consisted only of Lieutenant General John Cradock's force, some 13,950 men in all, some of whom had remained in Portugal after the evacuation of Moore's army from Spain by the Royal Navy.[6] It comprised some seven brigades of infantry, a brigade of cavalry and some artillery units; and its main and vital mission was that of safeguarding the port of Lisbon.

In 1809 there were just six major bridges spanning the Tagus between Talavera, which lies some 75 miles south-west of Madrid, and Alcántara on the Portuguese frontier; all of which, if in an undamaged state, were to some extent capable of carrying a Napoleonic army across the river. From west to east these were: the bridge at Alcántara, the Puente del Cardenal, the bridge at Almaraz, that of El Conde, and the bridges at Arzobispo and Talavera; the stretch of river they covered being about 125 miles in length. Taking each in turn, it could be said that the bridge at Alcántara, and perhaps the Puente del Cardenal some 50 miles upstream of it, lay too far to the west of the intended lines of operations of the French, and would therefore not be of much use to them in their planned drive to the south. It was also the case that the roads leading to and from both those bridges were not good, neither in their construction or state of repair. Of the two, that at Alcántara may have been sturdy enough, but the Puente del Cardenal, although closer to Talavera, may not have stood up to the kind of usage it would have to expect from the military. The bridge near Almaraz was well suited

4   AHN: Estado, 43, A: Cuesta to Garay, 6 January 1809, pp.280–282.
5   AHN: Estado, 43, A: Junta Suprema Central de Sevilla to Antonio Cornel, 7 January 1809, pp.284–285.
6   The National Archives, Kew (TNA): WO 17/2464: April 1809 Return.

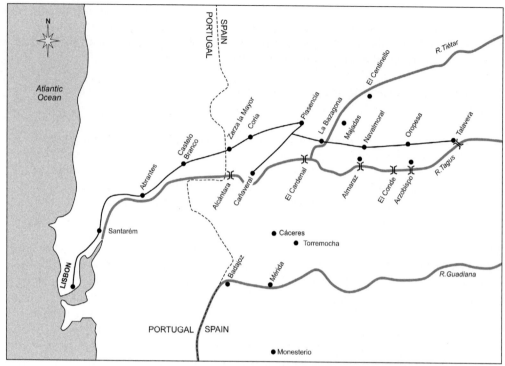

Plate 2. 1809. The six major bridges on the Tagus lying to the west of Madrid.

to military use and lay directly upon the main routes leading from central to southern Spain and to the south of Portugal. That of El Conde was poorly communicated and narrow; and the bridge at Arzobispo, though not on the main routes, was still close to them and sturdy, if perhaps a little too narrow for wheeled transport. The bridge at Talavera, though quite sturdy and close to Madrid, was poorly served by its approach roads. In summary, the bridges at Almaraz and Arzobispo were those which would have to be most closely guarded by Cuesta if he was to prevent a French incursion into Extremadura and Andalucía, a move which would give them control of the main routes to Portugal and Seville, by then the seat of the Spanish government.

Early Stirrings of the Tagus Campaign

Knowing that the French force from Talavera which had crossed the Tagus on 24/25 December was then concentrated at Trujillo, Cuesta was in motion as early as 11 January 1809, when he ordered his vanguard of some 5,000 men, under the command of *Teniente General* Henestrosa, to march from its base at Badajoz towards that place. Once in position, Henestrosa launched an attack on the town, forcing the French to fall back on Jaraicejo and Carrascal, but there would be no respite for them. A second assault by the Spaniards forced them back further to the pass of Miravete. On 23

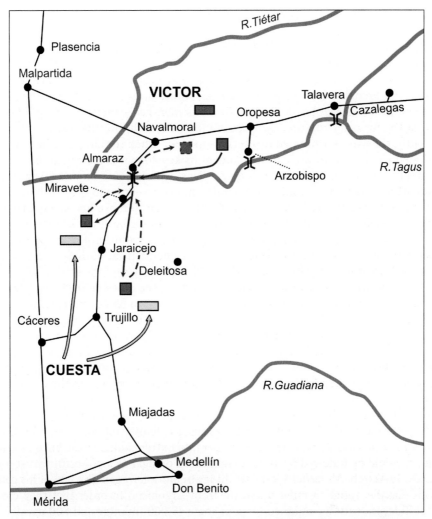

Plate 3. January 1809. Victor's attempt to establish a foothold on the south bank of the Tagus is frustrated by Cuesta's Army of Extremadura.

January, Cuesta led another force of some 4,000 newly-gathered recruits to Trujillo in support of his vanguard, arriving there on the 25th. With his forward units then reinforced he wasted no time in launching an attack on the pass at Miravete, forcing the French troops who were in occupation of it to withdraw, before pursuing them for some eight miles to the weakened but still stable bridge near Almaraz, where they re-crossed to the north bank of the Tagus whilst under fire from a unit of Spanish artillery which Cuesta had positioned on some nearby heights. As we have seen, the damage to the bridge near Almaraz had been caused earlier when Galluzo attempted to destroy it. His aim at the time was to demolish its main arches in what turned out to be a failed attempt to prevent the French from gaining a foothold on the south bank of the river, the very foothold which Cuesta had just succeeded in throwing back across the waterway.[7]

After the actions at Miravete and the Almaraz bridge, Cuesta left his vanguard on the south bank of the Tagus and withdrew his main force the short distance to Jaraicejo, where he established his headquarters. During mid-February he was receiving intelligence that the French were concentrating their forces once more between the bridge at Almaraz and that at Arzobispo. By this time his men had completed the job begun by Galluzo at the former structure, by dropping its main arch into the waters of the Tagus below. Sadly, the work terminated in a serious mishap, when the chief engineer and some 25 workmen went with the arch at the moment its keystone was dislodged, most of them being swept to their death. Be that as it may, at least Cuesta could now be fairly certain of the route which the French would have to take in order to cross to the south bank of the river in any significant force, but he took the precaution to move his headquarters from Jaraicejo to Deleitosa in order to keep a close watch upon both the bridges referred to above. Unfortunately his prudence went unrewarded as, by some unforgivable example of mismanagement, he was still unable to prevent the enemy from pushing two whole divisions, some 12,000 infantry together with 2,000 cavalry, across the bridge at Arzobispo on 20 February.[8] Trias, who was once again observing the crossing from Valdelacasa del Tajo with a force of some 3,000 men, was forced to retreat in face of the calamity. Luckily, the subsequent French advance towards Guadalupe was delayed at the pass of Hospital del Obispo by a force commanded by *Capitán* Balanzat. Nevertheless, the Spaniards were eventually outflanked and forced to resume their retreat after sustaining heavy losses, but their resistance had allowed Cuesta to send reinforcements towards the town, and the French were soon pushed back to Arzobispo where they re-crossed to the north bank of the river.[9]

With the French back on their starting line there would be only a brief respite for the Spanish. In the meantime, Victor was being promised extensive reinforcements by *Maréchal* Jourdan for the envisaged grand offensive deeper into Extremadura which, once successfully concluded, would be followed by an incursion into Portugal or a powerful thrust towards Seville. On 16 March, *Maréchal* Victor set things in motion by sending two of his generals, Leval and Lasalle, some 25 miles upstream from Arzobispo in order that they cross the bridge at Talavera with a combined force of some 13,000 infantry and 800 cavalry. Once on the left bank of the Tagus they turned west, sweeping the Spaniards along the course of the river to a point beyond the bridge at Arzobispo, thus allowing *Général de brigade* Villate to cross the river unopposed and join them. The French force was then divided into two columns, one being sent towards Mesas de Ibor to confront Cuesta's 1st Division under *Teniente General* Del Parque, the other towards Fresnedoso to attack his 2nd Division under Trias. Meanwhile, Cuesta's vanguard under Henestrosa was watching the bridge at Almaraz, whilst his 4th Division under *Mariscal de Campo* Portago, was in reserve. The overall intention of the French was to push Cuesta's raw recruits away from the south bank of the Tagus towards Mesas de Ibor and then further south towards Deleitosa. But by the time *Général*

---

7   Cuesta, *Manifiesto*, pp.32–33, and Arteche, *Guerra de la Independencia*, vol.V, p.253.
8   Cuesta, *Manifiesto*, p.33.
9   Arteche, *Guerra de la Independencia*, vol.V, pp.255–257.

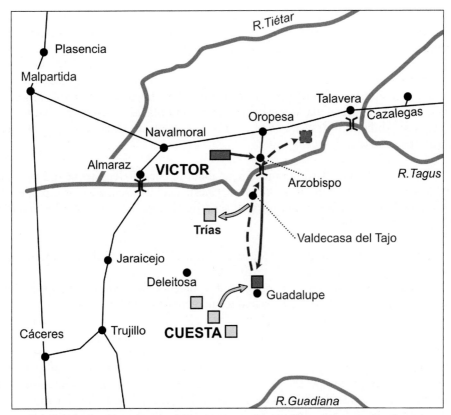

Plate 4. February. Victor's second attempt at crossing the Tagus is thwarted by Cuesta's counter attack at Guadalupe.

de division Leval's thrust eventually arrived at Mesas, Del Parque had begun to put up a stiff resistance along the banks of the Ibor river, slowing the French advance considerably; nonetheless, the Spaniards were eventually forced to fall back towards Deleitosa, where Del Parque was joined by Trias on 18 March. Once united the Spaniards were ordered to retire to the pass of Miravete, where Cuesta had established his headquarters during the previous day.

Finding himself confronted with strong enemy forces on his right flank, Cuesta finally realised his mistake, which was that, whilst observing Victor's preparations on the northern bank at Almaraz where, as well as massing his artillery, the Frenchman had openly displayed a collection of pontoons he was positioning close to the river, the Spaniard had been convinced that his opponent was about to make his main assault on the south bank of the Tagus somewhere in the vicinity of the broken bridge. In response, he had concentrated a large proportion of his own artillery and troops at the southern end of the bridge, ready to throw back the anticipated attack, leaving a strong reserve at the pass of Miravete. He explained the thinking behind these deployments in his *Manifiesto*:

On 17 March I transferred my headquarters to Miravete after having received notice that the greater part of the enemy army was marching towards Almaraz, bringing with them a large number of guns, many of them being of a heavy calibre. They were also transporting two flying bridges and 8 or 10 boats. My intention was not simply to support Henestrosa's vanguard from there but to make myself secure in the position, being convinced that the French would not be able to force their way [to Miravete] via Mesas de Ibor and Campilla, as I considered that route to be more difficult to traverse than to cross the Tagus at Almaraz via the means mentioned above ...[10]

However, with the French flanking movement about to cut off Henestrosa and the bulk of his artillery on the south bank near Almaraz, Cuesta decided to make a precipitate retreat towards Trujillo with Victor in hot pursuit, sending Henestrosa word that he should join him:[11]

At eleven on [the morning of] 19 March, I entered Trujillo with my column in the same formation as that when it left Miravete ...

The position at Trujillo ... is not suited to defence. Surrounded by a superior number of the enemy I would have had to surrender through a lack of food ... so I continued my retirement towards Santa Cruz del Puerto ... At six on the morning of the 21st I commenced my march towards the bridge at Medellín.[12]

Victor continued to push Cuesta south towards Mérida on the banks of the Guadiana, despite the Spaniard's attempts to slow the pace of his advance by whatever means he could. But on 23 March the commander in chief of the Army of Extremadura marched his men through Medellín, crossing the town's ancient bridge with the bulk of his force, having left a rear-guard under Henestrosa within the town itself. At this point the Spaniards had retreated a full 70 miles to the south, the distance which separates the Tagus from the Guadiana as those two great rivers approach the Portuguese frontier. Whilst at Medellín, Cuesta received the welcome news that the Duque de Alburquerque was coming to his aid at the head of the División de Andalucía.

In his *Manifiesto*, Cuesta claimed that, after having already spent the night of 23 March at Medellín, he decided that, rather than remain there and wait for Alburquerque to arrive, which, he said, would have resulted in a battle he was not yet ready for, he decided to feign a move towards the highway which ran between Mérida and Seville. This he would accomplish by marching via the villages of Villanueva de la Serena, Campanario, Quintana de la Serena and Higuera de la Serena. The tactic, he claimed, had the desired effect of causing Victor to divide his forces: one half of his army marching on Mérida, the other heading for Medellín. Whilst the French were in motion, Cuesta sent word to Alburquerque, ordering him to rendezvous with his army at Villanueva de la Serena, some 10 miles east of Medellín, where the proposed juncture took place on 27 March once Cuesta had completed his

10   Cuesta, *Manifiesto*, p.36.
11   Arteche, *Guerra de la Independencia*, vol.V, pp.266–270, and Cuesta, *Manifiesto*, p.35.
12   Cuesta, *Manifiesto*, pp.37–39.

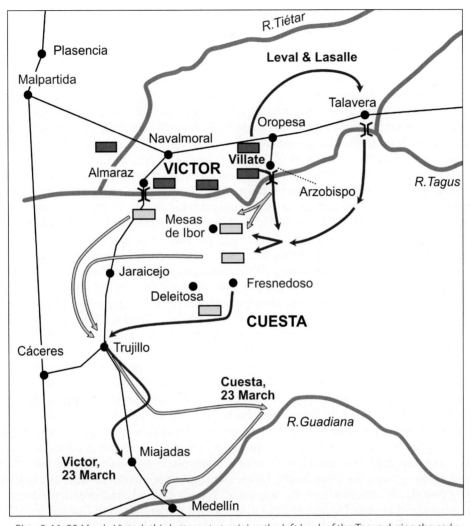

Plate 5. 16–23 March. Victor's third attempt at gaining the left bank of the Tagus during the early spring of 1809 is finally successful. Cuesta's resulting retreat to Medellín is also shown.

counter-march from Higuera de la Serena, the final leg of a round-trip of some 60 miles in four days. Unfortunately, his efforts to divide the French forces were not long lasting. The column which Victor sent to Mérida, some 25 miles west of Medellín, heard on its arrival that Cuesta was returning to the latter place and simply counter-marched to rejoin their commander in chief before the looming battle commenced. As a further blow to Cuesta's hopes for the day, Alburquerque arrived with just 4,000 men rather than the expected 10,000.[13]

---

13   Cuesta, *Manifiesto*, pp.30–41.

Early on the morning of 28 March, Cuesta led his men from their overnight camp at Villanueva to the town of Don Benito. In the meantime, the French began their preparations for battle in front of the formidable position at Medellín. As they left their headquarters and billets in and around the town, Victor's men were able to make use of the little bridge which crossed the Ortiga, in order to reach the battlefield and deploy. The Ortiga, lying immediately to the east of the town, is a tributary of the west-flowing Guadiana and runs roughly south to north into the great river, meeting it in such a way that it forms an obtuse angle to it with its left bank, and it is within that angle where Medellín sits. In analysis it would seem that the French must have been confident of success against their enemy because, should the opposite occur, the narrowness of the bridge on the Ortiga, which they would have to re-cross in the event of their having to retreat, would undoubtedly spell disaster for them.

Buoyed up by the stout rear-guard actions of his recent retreat, the Spanish commander appeared to have as much confidence in the prospects for victory as did Victor, so much so that, dispensing with the idea of a deployment in depth, he arranged his forces in a single, slightly disjointed though somewhat concentric line facing the enemy, his left, occupying some high ground close to the Ortiga, being somewhat separated from his right. It would be the right, with its right flank resting on the Guadiana, which would advance towards the French, who were arranged in battle order in front of Medellín. Whilst that manoeuvre was taking place, Cuesta's left would stand its ground, ready to advance with the intention of dislodging the enemy from the hill marking their right flank. The French left flank rested on the Guadiana. With hardly any hesitation once his men were in position Cuesta, typically himself once more, launched an all-out frontal assault upon the foe.

The Battle of Medellín may well be covered in detail in other works, should the reader wish to examine them, but in essence it is generally accepted that the Spanish troops gave good account of themselves during the course of several hours of intense fighting, especially so when one recalls that most of them were raw, recently enlisted recruits; essentially peasant civilians. There is broad agreement amongst witnesses that they courageously attacked the French positions as they marched head-on into a hail of artillery and musket fire, despite which they managed to penetrate their lines in some places and even capture some of the enemy artillery positions, albeit briefly, before running out of steam and ideas. But as Victor slowly exerted his influence over the battlefield, French methods and experience began to overcome the exhilarated spirits of patriotism carried in the breasts of Cuesta's men. Had defeat come to them sparingly from a magnanimous foe, nobody would have begrudged them any mercy granted, but instead, when it was clear that they were broken and in full retreat, the French pursued them with a merciless lust for blood. Firstly, as Victor's cavalry hunted down the fleeing Spanish infantry across flat, open country, they were slashed and sabred as the horsemen overtook them, eager to make an even more bountiful harvest from those further ahead. Many of the men who had not already expired from their wounds by the time the French infantry got to them were bayoneted to death, the rage of their foes showing no sign of abating. At the end of it all, of the 22,000 or so Spanish troops who set out from Villanueva on the fateful morning of Medellín, it is said that some 10,000 were killed, wounded or taken prisoner.[14] Once again, it would appear that Cuesta's do or die

---

14   Arteche, *Guerra de la Independencia*, vol.V, p.302.

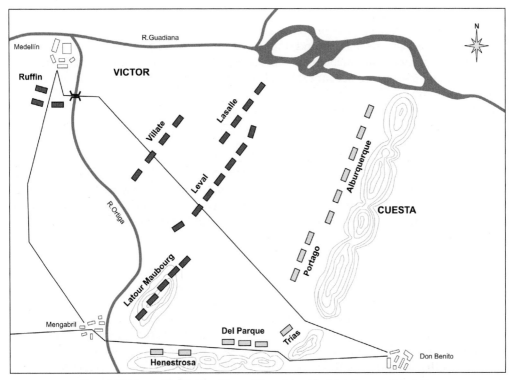

Plate 6. 28 March. Starting positions of French and Spanish forces at Medellín.

attitude had resulted in too much dying with not a lot of doing to show for it. He himself was wounded during the clash; knocked from his horse and trampled as he attempted to halt the retreat of some of his cavalry units at a crucial point in the course of the battle.

For what it is worth, Victor's account of Medellín was published in the *Gazeta de Madrid* on 3 April 1809 and reads as follows, but one should bear in mind that, at the time of the battle, Madrid was in French hands, with King Joseph Bonaparte seated at the head of what he regarded to be the legitimate government of Spain. Hence the flavour of Victor's article in the Madrid periodical:

His Catholic Majesty orders that it be made known that, on 28 March the 1st Corps of the army commanded by His Excellency, Marshal [Victor] Duke of Bellune ,won a new and decisive victory over the enemy army commanded by *General* Cuesta, at Medellín. 12,000 Spaniards have died by the sword and 4,000 have been taken prisoner; the rest, pursued by our light troops, managed to save themselves as best they could via whichever path or trail they could find. All of the enemy artillery, to the number of 25 pieces, as well as six flags, has fallen into our hands. Between 10,000 and 12,000 Spaniards have remained on the battlefield, and the majority of the senior officers and subalterns of Cuesta's army died on the day. The Spanish *Teniente General* [*sic*] Don Francisco de Trias, gravely wounded, was later found lying with the dead. Cuesta's army together with part of the Army of Andalucía was destroyed in the course of events. Field Marshal the Duke of Bellune has given praise to the generals, officers and troops who fought under his orders.

It seems almost incredible that our losses, when compared with those of the enemy and taking into account the scale of our success on that brilliant day, were less than 300 in dead and wounded; an advantage we owe to the impetuosity of our attacks and the vigour with which they were sustained.

This victory assures us of the conquest of Andalucía, which will soon be completely occupied by our troops.[15]

Cuesta's account of the battle is included in his *Manifiesto*. In it, he described how the early stages of the battle went well for the Spaniards; the infantry advancing with determination and pushing back the French to the point where the contest could have gone in his favour. It was at that critical point when things went wrong, and Cuesta placed the blame for what ensued squarely upon three of his cavalry regiments:

Our infantry did not hesitate as they continued their march at attack pace, even when the cavalry regiments of Almansa, Infante and two squadrons of Cazadores Imperiales de Toledo, which were flanking the advance, failed to attack the enemy infantry and cavalry. Instead they abandoned our soldiers and retired at the gallop, leaving the enemy at liberty to attack [our troops] from every direction. I was stationed on the right flank of the units forming our left line of attack when I noticed the retreat of the three corps just mentioned and dashed off in an attempt to detain them … [It was then when] I saw something which would capture the imagination of any general. Our corps of infantry grenadiers were marching with the greatest bravura, in closed ranks, and advancing to take one of the enemy's batteries, their commander, *Coronel* José de Zayas, at their head. All of this took place in sight of our cavalry as they retreated … With the enemy on top of me I called out to our horsemen, 'What is this? Halt! Cavalry! Return to those fellows, they are ours.' But all was useless, it was impossible to stop them, with the result that the enemy broke our infantry … The chiefs and officers I sent to attempt to contain the cavalry themselves became entangled amongst the fugitives … I was knocked from my horse and found myself amongst the enemy, whose charge took them over the ground on which I lay, injuring my leg …[16]

Cuesta went on to describe the courage displayed by his men as the battle slipped away from them, and used the latter part of his report to heap praise upon what must have been just about every officer who took part in the clash. But Medellín has been remembered by many as being perhaps the greatest military disaster to befall Spanish arms during the course of the Peninsular War. Sadly, two of the cavalry units which behaved so disgracefully on the day, those of Infante and Almansa, had been with the Marqués de la Romana's expedition

15   *Gazeta de Madrid*, no.93, 3 April 1809, p.459. Available at <https://www.cervantesvirtual.com/descargaPdf/num-93-3-de-abril-de-1809/>, accessed June 2022.

16   Cuesta, *Manifiesto*, pp.41–48.

to Denmark. Of the two, the troopers of Infante showed much spirit and determination in getting themselves from their remote cantonments on Jutland to the port of Nyborg on the isle of Funen, the initial point of embarkation agreed between British naval forces and La Romana's army in their joint rescue plan. As a result they were numbered amongst the 10,000 men of Romana's host returned to Spain by the Royal Navy in October 1808. The men of Almansa were based at Nyborg.

Behind the almost bland words of both Victor and Cuesta relating to the events of Medellín, lay the human tragedy of the numerous dead and maimed left on the field. There are but few personal accounts of the battle known to be in existence apart from Cuesta's, one of them appearing in the work of Albert Jean Michel de Rocca, who served as an officer with the French Hussars. The first edition of his book, *Memoires sur la Guerre des Francaise en Espagne*, was published in Paris in 1814, and an English version under the title, *In the Peninsula with a French Hussar: Memoirs of the War of the French in Spain*, was published in London by John Murray in 1815, the translation having been compiled by Maria Graham. An extract is provided below, giving an example of some of the things de Rocca had to say about the Battle of Medellín:

> General Lasalle's division of light cavalry was placed on the left; in the centre [stood] the division of German infantry and on the right General Latour Maubourg's dragoons.[17] Villate's and Ruffin's divisions were in reserve. The three divisions which formed our first line of battle had left numerous detachments in the rear to keep up our communications, so that we had scarcely 7,000 soldiers [on the battle-field]. The enemy before us presented an immense front more than 34,000 strong.
>
> The body of Germans began the attack; the 2nd and 4th Regiments of Dragoons having next charged the Spanish infantry were repulsed with loss and the Germans remained alone in the midst of the battle. They formed a square, and during the rest of the action vigorously resisted every effort of the enemy. With much difficulty, Marshal Victor renewed the fight by bringing up two regiments of Villate's division. The enemy's horse first tried in vain to break our right wing; a large body of it then fell at once upon our left which, for fear of being surrounded, was forced to make a retrograde movement upon the Guadiana [at the point] where it forms an elbow and straightens the plain towards Medellin. We retired for two hours, slowly and silently, stopping every fifty paces to face about and present our front to the enemy in order to dispute our ground with him, before abandoning it whenever he [was about] to drive us from it.
>
> In the midst of the whizzing of the bullets and the deeper sound of the bombs which, after cutting through the air, ploughed up the earth around us, the voices of the officers alone were heard; the closer the enemy pressed, the more coolly and collectedly did they give their orders.
>
> As we retired, the cries of the Spanish redoubled; their skirmishers were so numerous and so bold that they frequently forced ours back to their ranks. They

---

17   The division of German infantry mentioned was almost certainly Sebastiani's 3rd division of Germans under the command of Leval, which had been lent to Victor for his Medellín campaign.

shouted to us from afar, in their own tongue, that they would give no quarter and that the plains of Medellin should be the grave of the French. Had our squadron been broken and dispersed, the Spanish horse of the right would have burst through the opening upon the rear of our army and surrounded it; the plains of Medellín would then, indeed, have become, as our enemies hoped, the grave of the French.

General Lasalle rode proudly and calmly, backwards and forwards in front of his division. When the enemy's cavalry came within gunshot the skirmishers on each side retired, and in the space which separated us from the Spaniards nothing was seen but the horses of the dead, both friends and enemies, running wounded about the plain, some of them struggling to get rid of the cumbersome burden of their masters whom they were dragging with them.

The Spaniards had sent six chosen squadrons against our single one; they marched in close column [and] at their head were the lancers of Xeres [Jerez]. This whole body began at once to quicken their pace in order to charge us while we were retiring ...

Our hussars, who in the midst of the threats and abuse of the enemy had preserved the strictest silence, then drowned the sound of the trumpet as they moved onwards [with] a single and terrible shout of joy and fury. The Spanish lancers stopped; seized with terror they turned their horses at the distance of half pistol-shot and overthrew their own cavalry which was behind them ... Our hussars mingled with them indiscriminately and cut them down without resistance [as] we followed them to the rear of their own army. A little after our charge the whole of the Spanish cavalry, both right and left, entirely disappeared.

... Two regiments of Villate's division attacked the enemy's infantry on the right with success, [and] at the same moment those near the heights of Mingabril [sic for Mengabril].

In an instant the army that was before us disappeared like clouds driven by the wind. The Spaniards threw down their arms and fled; the cannonade ceased, and the whole of our cavalry went off in pursuit of the enemy.

Our soldiers, who had seen themselves threatened with certain death had they sunk under the number of their foes, and irritated by five hours' resistance, gave no quarter at first. The infantry followed the cavalry at a distance and dispatched the wounded with the bayonet. The fury of our soldiers was particularly directed against such Spaniards as were without military dress.

After taking part in the pursuit of the fleeing Spanish troops, a chase which it would seem lasted for some time, de Rocca made his way back to Medellín:

I returned to the town of Medellin a little before midnight. Silence and quiet had succeeded to the activity of battle and the shouts of victory. In the plain the only audible sounds were the groans of the wounded and the confused murmurs of the dying, as they raised their heads in prayer to God and the blessed Virgin. On every individual with whom the ground was strewed, death had stamped the expression of the passion which had animated him at the moment of his fall ...

Two regiments of Swiss and Walloon guards were stretched on the field in the very line they had occupied in battle.[18] Some broken ammunition waggons, [and] cannon with their teams of mules left to themselves, still marked the position which the Spanish army had occupied. Here and there lay wounded horses whose legs, being broken by the shot, could not stir from the spot on which they were soon to perish. Ignorant of death, and equally so of futurity, they lay grazing on the field as far as their necks could reach.

The French did not lose 4,000 men. The Spanish left on the field 12,000 dead and nineteen pieces of artillery; we made seven or 8,000 prisoners, but of these scarcely 2,000 reached Madrid. In their own country, the Spanish prisoners found it very easy to escape ...

The Spanish prisoners would say with a sigh as they pointed out a distant village to a grenadier who had to guard and lead them, 'Señor Soldado – Mr. Soldier – there is our native village; there are our wives and children. Must we pass so near them without ever seeing them again? Must we go so far off as France?'

The grenadier would answer ... 'If you attempt to escape I will shoot you, such are my orders, but I never see behind me.'

By this it would seem that a trace of humanity had soon returned to the French soldiers once the heat of battle was behind them.

De Rocca's final paragraph on the aftermath of the battle reads:

Thousands of enormous vultures had assembled from every part of Spain over the vast and silent field of death; placed on heights and seen from a distance against the horizon, they appeared as large as men. Our videts [sic] often marched towards them to reconnoitre, mistaking them for enemies. They never left their human prey on our approach till we were within a few paces of them, and then the flapping of their enormous wings echoed far and wide over our heads like a funeral knell.[19]

After the Battle

Four days after the Battle of Medellín the *Junta* wrote to Cuesta from Seville, and it would seem that news of the disaster in Extremadura was slowly seeping through to them. In their letter to the general, they did not give away much about what they might have known of the outcome of the confrontation, instead they asked Cuesta to instigate a regime of reporting to them twice daily by post:

---

18   It would appear that Rocca was mistaken when he says he saw, 'Two regiments of Swiss and Walloon guards were stretched on the field ...' Two battalions of Walloon Guards were present with Cuesta's army, but there were no Swiss Guards. See Oman, *History of the Peninsular War*, vol.II, pp.627–628.

19   Albert Jean Michel de Rocca, *In the Peninsula with a French Hussar* (London: Greenhill Books, 2013), pp.77–83. Some changes have been made to the original punctuation.

La Suprema Junta de Gobierno del Reyno, in considering how necessary it is that it receives news of the army under your command with all the frequency imaginable, in order that it may take such dispositions as demanded by the circumstances, has decided that you will establish a communication with it in relation to the army. This will take the form of two reports per day, with the expectation that, although they may be laconic in their content, each of them will provide His Majesty with news of anything that might [have] happen[ed], or state explicitly that nothing has happened, should that be the case. It is for your intelligence and compliance that I communicate this Royal Order to you.[20]

At first sight it might seem to the reader that the *Junta* had finally run out of patience as well as trust in Cuesta; but when examining the content of the Spanish archives it is clear that there was a flurry of activity at the *Real Alcázar de Sevilla* on 1 April 1809, and by reading some of the other items of correspondence sent out that day, one can see that, rather than there being an attempt underway at ousting Cuesta from his position as *Capitán General* of Extremadura, the *Junta Suprema* was actually falling over itself to heap praise and compassion upon him. Here is a sample of what they wrote:

Although the War Department has already expressed its satisfaction to Your Excellency for the heroic valour and commendable dispositions employed at the Battle of Medellín, His Majesty has now requested that I, in his royal name, give you due thanks for the consistent faith you continue to display in the salvation of our cause, despite the reverse suffered by our arms. Neither will the *Junta* lose faith so long as the state conserves in its bosom heroes who, like Your Excellency, know how to inspire the intrepidity and bravery of our armies, such as you did in the memorable action mentioned …[21]

In view of de Rocca's account of the battle, as well as the words put to paper by Cuesta, it might be fair to say that the Spanish soldiers who fought at Medellín gave more than a good account of themselves, and if Cuesta had managed to contain his usual impetuosity, and planned his battle tactics more carefully, who knows what his troops might have achieved. But the sorry truth appears to be that Cuesta's battle plan was singularly one-dimensional. His battlefield deployment consisted of a one-line formation; there was no reserve line, no mobile reserve, no defined line of retreat, in fact there would seem to have been no planning for a retreat at all; it was simply another all-or-nothing gamble with the lives of his courageous soldiers, who attempted to make it all work out by holding the field against their formidable enemy for up to nine hours. And it almost paid off; had the Spanish cavalry continued to provide close support for the infantry during the crucial phase of the fighting, then the whole might, just might, have pulled off an improbable victory. But in the final analysis the Army of Extremadura was, in the main, an army of untrained and untried soldiers, bravehearted no doubt, just like their commander in chief who, if not by any means

20   AHN: Estado, 43, A: Junta Suprema Central de Sevilla to Cuesta, 1 April 1809, pp.319–320.
21   AHN: Estado, 43, A: Junta Suprema Central de Sevilla to Cuesta, 1 April 1809, pp.321–322.

one of the best exponents of Napoleonic battlefield management, was a courageous man of arms always willing to take to the offensive against an enemy feared throughout the continent of Europe. If only he had had the sophistication to match his spirit.

Over the next few days, the chorus of praise for Cuesta and his army just kept on coming from Seville, and in its wake there followed a number of letters to various eminences and government departments, exhorting them to gather reinforcements, replacement equipment and fresh supplies; all to be sent to Cuesta. Here, for example, are the details of a letter and royal order sent by the *Junta Suprema* to its minister of war: 'I pass to you the Royal Order concerning the need to reinforce at all costs the Army Extremadura in order that, upon examining it without loss of time, you may consent to its execution.'[22]

The royal order referred to contained a long list of requirements including the likes of bread, meat, wine, salted cod, cheese, tobacco, uniforms, shoes, shirts, and so on. Then came letters the likes of that sent by the *Junta* to Cornel, requesting him to send some cavalry units from the area around Seville in order to reinforce Cuesta's army. Such was the flavour of the *Junta's* various communications with Cuesta until late April, when there appeared a clearly discernible alteration in emphasis and tone, all sparked, it would appear, by Wellesley's return to Portugal on 22 April; the British commander disembarking at Lisbon to take command of his recently arrived force of some 8,000 men to add to the 15,500 or so already there under Cradock, a number which included Major General Rowland Hill's 4,000 men lately arrived from Ireland, as well as Lieutenant General John Sherbrooke's 5,500 from England, who had disembarked on 12 March after an abortive sojourn at Cádiz. With an offensive British presence re-established on the Peninsula, the two allied commanders in chief would soon be drawn inexorably towards the field of Talavera.

Before moving on, we should perhaps attempt to understand the somewhat patriarchal if not wholly benevolent tone of the *Junta's* correspondence with Cuesta in the aftermath of Medellín, especially when one considers the treatment it had meted out to him after his failure at Rioseco and his clash of authority with Valdés and Floridablanca. When looking at the state of things in Spain during the early spring of 1809, one can see that the French offensive of the winter just passed had had a devasting effect on the various Spanish armies, most of which had been heavily defeated and scattered to the extremities of the country. So bad were things that the *Junta Suprema* itself decided to relocate from Aranjuez to Seville in the far south. One of the few glimmers of hope for the survival of the *Junta*, and indeed the country at large, had been Cuesta's spirited defence of the line of the Tagus during the early months of 1809. Sadly, all of that seemed to have been brought to an end at Medellín, but there were many in the *Junta* who, though carrying a healthy dislike for him, knew him well enough to be sure that he would not have considered the idea of outright capitulation for one second. That appreciation, combined with the knowledge that he and his army were the only things standing between themselves and the French, would seem to have concentrated minds in Seville. Their only option for at least slowing the expected French advance into Andalucía was to bury the hatchet with the old warrior and begin to support him, hence the flurry of supportive messages earlier mentioned. If one were to look for just a hint of cynicism in the *Junta's* apparent change of heart, then it may be found in the probability that its

---

22   AHN: Estado, 43, A: Junta Suprema Central de Sevilla to Cornel, 1 April 1809, p.323.

members were aware of Wellesley's impending return to Portugal. Should it be possible to keep Cuesta in the field somewhere between the Tagus and the Guadiana – or even south of the Guadiana – for a few weeks more, then Victor might find himself sandwiched between the elderly Spanish general in his front and Wellesley in his rear and right flank, should the British break out from Portugal in the region of the Tagus valley. By regrouping around Monesterio and Llerena in the wake of his defeat at Medellín, it could be justifiably argued that it was Cuesta alone who kept Spain in the fight during the temporary absence of a British offensive capability on the Iberian Peninsula.

The Situation of Maréchal Victor after the Battle of Medellín

After such an ultimately crushing victory at Medellín, it must have seemed to Victor that the road to Seville was open, and had things been as straightforward as perhaps some of the French high command thought they were, then such a move would have uprooted the seat of Spanish government once again, and sent it in search of an ever more difficult to find safe haven elsewhere; alternatively, it could have caused the Spaniards to sue for peace in acceptance of the hopelessness of their situation. But as the French historian, Thiers, remarked, 'It is certain that, in all the other countries, two battles such as those at Medellín and Ciudad Real would have decided a campaign and perhaps a war. But the Spaniards were not discouraged by their defeats.'[23] However, there were some extraneous factors which contributed to Victor's hesitation in advancing deep into Andalucía, preferring instead to station his army along the course of the Guadiana between Medellín and Mérida until he felt secure in his ability to proceed. Firstly, he had to secure his communications with Madrid, which meant he would have to sustain a significant detachment to watch over his pontoon bridge near Almaraz on the Tagus, knowing that the strong and active bands of *partidas de guerrilla* (Spanish irregulars) would destroy it if given an opportunity. A second crossing point on the Tagus, the bridge at Alcántara, would also have to be protected, and for that task the *Maréchal* had earmarked Lapisse's division. Absent from the recent battle at Medellín, *Général de division* Lapisse had been sent to reconnoitre the region of the Portuguese-Spanish frontier as far north as Ciudad Rodrigo. Finding the Spanish town in a good state of defence, Colonel Sir Robert Wilson's Loyal Lusitanian Legion having recently arrived there, he returned to Victor, who wasted little time in assigning him a new mission.

There were also two important nodes in the French commander's network of communications on the Guadiana, these were the bridges at Medellín and Mérida, and they would have to be safeguarded by garrisoning and fortifying each of those towns. South, beyond the Guadiana, lay Cuesta. If Victor was harbouring any hopes that the old warrior would be removed from command after his recent failure, then he would have been disappointed to hear that, in recognition of his efforts at Medellín, he was to be promoted to *Capitán General* of the Army of Extremadura, via a royal decree issued by the *Junta Suprema* on 1 April: 'The *Junta Suprema Guvernativa del Reyno*, in the name of our king, D. Fernando

---

23   M. A. Thiers, *Histoire du Consulat et de L'Empire* (Paris: Plon Brothers, 1851) vol.XI, p.56. The Battle of Ciudad Real took place on 26/27 March 1809, the eve of Medellín, and resulted in a heavy defeat of the Spanish under Cartaojal.

VII, and desiring to give to the troops of the Army of Extremadura a demonstration of the appreciation of their... bravery during the Battle of Medellín ... has decided that ... D. Gregorio de la Cuesta ... be promoted to Captain General ...' It was perhaps a well-deserved salute to the old warrior's energy and spirit, but one which, no doubt, would have stuck in the craw of his many enemies at Seville. In the meantime, Victor was loathe to cross the Guadiana; to have one great river in his rear was worry enough, but to put both the Tagus and the Guadiana between himself and safety might be to leave too much to chance. As the hiatus in Extremadura continued, Cuesta, via his regular communication with the *Junta*, began to receive news of some disturbing rumours which were swirling around in not too far away Seville. The essence of what was being picked up was that some form of clandestine negotiations had been instigated between a number of his officers and some of the members of Victor's staff:

> *La Junta Suprema Guvernativa* has, from various sources, come to understand that several officers belonging to the army under your command have held interviews and conferences with the French. As a result, His Majesty would like you to re-double your vigilance and zeal in the business at hand, which is most important to everybody. Take care not to allow the least indulgence to come before it, and do your best to discover what, in fact, may have occurred ...[24]

Cuesta's reply was soon winging its way to Seville:

> This being the first and only notice I have had of there having taken place interviews and conferences between the officers of this army and the French, I have found it impossible to discover even the most remote knowledge of such a thing. I would hope that Your Excellency might indicate to me any of the cases [which have occurred, in order that I may] investigate, remedy and punish ...[25]

It is impossible to know what, if any, contacts had been made with the French on the part of Cuesta's officers, but there does seem to have been something in the air regarding a secret approach to Victor on the part of the Spanish. On 4 May the *Junta* wrote to Cuesta as follows:

> Everything conspires to persuade us that the position of *Maréchal* Victor is not very advantageous, despite the favour he owes to fortune for his victory at the Battle of Medellín. The prompt organisation of the Portuguese troops under the direction of General Beresford; the [recent] disembarkation of General Wellesley and the British troops; the rapid march of those troops upon *Maréchal* Soult, who alone is too weak to resist them; the favourable results obtained by the Marqués de la Romana in León; the large reinforcements sent to the Army of Extremadura, together with their prompt organisation thanks to the untiring zeal and [illegible] capacity of Your Excellency, were all unanticipated by *Maréchal* Victor ... Under

---

24 AHN: Estado, 43, A: Junta Suprema Central de Sevilla to Cuesta, 18 April 1809, pp.367–368.
25 AHN: Estado, 43, A: Cuesta to Garay, 19 April 1809, pp.371–373.

these conditions, it would seem that an opportune moment has arrived to begin [the kind of] secret negotiations with the general about which Your Excellency and the *Junta* have spoken in the past. The *Junta Suprema* therefore authorises Your Excellency to offer him one million pesos, or property of an equal value in whichever part of Spain or America he may choose, should he surrender the army under his command, or contrive that it be completely defeated by Spanish troops …[26]

Cuesta's response, if he ever bothered to reply to this suggestion, was not to be found amongst those items of his correspondence examined by the author. But before leaving the subject of Medellín we should perhaps examine a rather melancholy exchange relating to it, which passed between the *Junta* and the old warrior. On 7 June 1809, some two and a half months after the battle, the general received the following letter from Seville:

La Junta Suprema Guvernativa del Reyno has received news that there remains on the battlefield of Medellín a number of unburied corpses, whose putrid miasmas are infecting the atmosphere and could become the cause of many ills, both in the country and amongst the army (which by the mercy of God remains free from disease). More such problems may arise in the current season as temperatures begin to rise. His Majesty, afflicted by these considerations and anxious to ensure that his fears will not be realised, has agreed that Your Excellency should take the most prompt and active measures to avoid any contagion which might necessarily occur, should the said corpses continue to remain in their present state, and advises Your Excellency that the most convenient measure to be adopted may be that of burning them, as it will be the easiest and quickest way of disposing of them; and at the same time the smoke and flames will purify the air.[27]

Cuesta replied as follows: 'Sir, … I do not think you can give credit to such dubious news without doing me an injustice. All of the corpses on the battlefield of Medellín have been buried, due to the measures I have taken since the French withdrew from the area and my advanced units arrived on the scene …'[28]

---

26   AHN: Estado, 43, A: Junta Suprema Central de Sevilla to Cuesta, 4 May 1809, pp.390–392.
27   AHN: Estado, 43, A: Junta Suprema Central de Sevilla to Cuesta, 7 June 1809, pp.411–412.
28   AHN: Estado, 43, A: Cuesta to Garay, 8 June 1809, pp.413–414.

4

Wellesley in Portugal, the Battle of Oporto and his Move into Extremadura

The evacuation of the bulk of Sir John Moore's army from Spain in January 1809, resulted in the concentration at Lisbon of all those elements of the original 1808 expeditionary force left behind when the ships bearing Moore's men set sail from La Coruña. Ironically, it was during that same month that Lieutenant General Sherbrooke had sailed from England in command of reinforcements destined for Cádiz, with the intention that they would advance into Spain to join Moore. But when his convoy arrived at its destination during the first week of March, the Spanish authorities would not allow the troops to disembark. The confusion arose due to a combination of London's failure clearly to communicate their recent change of plans to the Spanish government, and the suspicion amongst many in Seville that the British were simply keen to secure the facilities of a strategic military and commercial seaport. It was not the first time the British had been refused disembarkation at Cádiz; three regiments under Major General Mackenzie had been sent packing by their sceptical allies when they tried to land there a few weeks earlier, having been dispatched from Lisbon by Cradock, at that time the most senior British officer at the Portuguese capital. Rather than keep his troops cooped up aboard ship whilst the politicians argued, Sherbrooke, following Mackenzie's example, sailed with his 5,500 men back to Lisbon, arriving on 12 March and establishing a total British presence in Portugal of some 15,500 men.

Seemingly undaunted by the failure of Moore's expedition, the British government was determined to establish a strong presence on the Iberian Peninsula, even if it be confined to Portugal; a line of thought which may have arisen in London due to the fact that the resurgent French armies had occupied Madrid and most of the northern half of Spain before the spring of 1809. As plans matured, it was on 2 April 1809 that Castlereagh wrote to Wellesley providing him with a set of instructions for the campaign he had been chosen to lead:

> The defence of Portugal you will consider as the first and immediate object of your intention; but as the security of Portugal can only be effectually provided for in connection with the defence of the Peninsula in the larger sense, His Majesty on this account, as well as from the unabated interest he takes in the cause of Spain, leaves it to your judgement to decide when your army shall be advanced on the frontier of Portugal, [and] how your efforts can best be combined with the Spanish as well as the Portuguese troops in support of the common cause …

In any movements you may undertake you will however keep in mind that, until you receive further orders, your operations must necessarily be conducted with a special reference to the protection of that country [Portugal] ...[1]

Wellesley would have been pleased with the degree of licence afforded him by his political masters, thinking that his cause would be well served by partaking in combined operations with the Spanish against the common enemy, but his satisfaction would have been tempered when a second letter from Castlereagh arrived on the following day, written, no doubt, after he had heard the news of Sherbrooke's recent treatment at the hands of the *Junta Suprema*. From its content it was clear that, by their stubbornness in refusing Sherbrooke permission to disembark at Cádiz, the Spaniards could easily have killed off their best chance for obtaining British cooperation in their endeavours to rid themselves of the French invaders. So hurt was the Secretary of State for War by their actions that he withdrew the degree of licence he had afforded Wellesley for cooperating with the Spanish in his correspondence of the previous day, remarking in his latest letter that:

Upon the fall of Madrid and the retreat of the Spanish armies into the south of Spain, His Majesty was pleased to signify, through his minister to the Central Government of Spain, that [he] was to send an auxiliary army to sustain the Spanish efforts in that quarter, provided the British troops were assured of the port and fortress of Cádiz as a secure point of retreat in case of disaster in the field.

The government of Spain not having thought fit to accede to these preliminary and indispensable conditions, and having actually declined to permit the British troops under Major-Generals Sherbrooke & Mackenzie [to disembark at Cádiz] ... His Majesty does not feel he can, in justice to the safety of his own troops, again employ an auxiliary army in Spain ...

You will therefore understand that it is not His Majesty's intention in authorising you to cooperate with the Spanish armies in the defence of Portugal and of the adjacent Spanish provinces, that you should enter upon a campaign in Spain without the express authority of your government ... and that the service of your army (under the orders you have received) cannot be employed in general operations in Spain ... without a previous arrangement being settled to that effect between the two governments.[2]

Within a few days Wellesley would sail for Lisbon to join Cradock. It was the latter's force which Soult was hoping to crush during the course of his hoped-for re-conquest of Portugal in the name of France, although his operation had stalled at Oporto during the early spring of 1809. There are a number of theories about the reasons as to why Soult dallied so long at Oporto, the most credible of which makes the claim that, with the *Maréchal* happily ensconced in the pleasant environment of Portugal's second city, where he was constantly flattered by a treacherous and obsequious faction of its governors, he began to dream of

1   University of Southampton, Special Collections, Hartley Library (UoS): WP1/252/12: Castlereagh to Wellesley, 2 April 1809.
2   UoS: WP1/252/16: Castlereagh to Wellesley, 3 April 1809.

himself as the nation's next monarch. With that in mind, it would have been interesting to witness what became of the apparent state of bliss at Soult's headquarters when news arrived of the disembarkation of Wellesley at Lisbon on 21 April, bringing with him significant reinforcements for the units already in Portugal and creating what was about to become a new British expeditionary force on the Iberian Peninsula.

Within two days of arriving in Portugal, Wellesley had fixed on his plan of campaign. He would leave a small force in and around the Tagus valley to stall any attempt by *Maréchal* Victor to enter Portugal, and march north with the bulk of his forces to confront Soult. By this time, 24 April 1809, Cradock had already led a significant force to Leiria, some 90 miles north of Lisbon. It was whilst he was there that he received notice from Wellesley that he had been superseded in command and was to sail to Gibraltar to take up the governorship of the fortress. Meanwhile, *Maréchal* Soult had been stationary at Oporto for some weeks. At that time the city was served by the Ponte das Barcas (bridge of boats) on the Douro which was in a state of disrepair, having partially collapsed under the weight of traffic as Portuguese civilians had attempted to flee the city when the French arrived in late March. Feeling himself safe from attack from the south, Soult ordered repairs to be carried out, knowing that he could easily dismantle the temporary pontoons used to make the bridge serviceable, should the need arise. All of which suggests that he would have been surprised when Wellesley arrived on the south bank of the Douro on 11 May, causing him to remove the pontoons sooner than expected, and to have all of the river craft confined to moorings located on the north bank of the waterway. That done, he would no doubt have been feeling somewhat relaxed about the prospect of keeping the British at bay, whilst he decided how best to react to their unexpected appearance. As Wellesley contemplated the situation before him, he was brought news that the aptly named Lieutenant Colonel John Waters had managed to cross to the north bank of the river with the help of a Portuguese citizen. Once ashore, Waters was able to convince the owners of four river barges to navigate their vessels to the south bank and begin to ferry groups of British soldiers across the Douro via an improvised shuttle service. It was a stroke of luck which was to spell the end of the second French occupation of Portuguese territory. As the shuttle service continued to run without interference from the French, who were concentrated in the centre of the city some two miles downstream and out of sight of the operation, Wellesley succeeded in ferrying enough men across the Douro to make Soult's continued occupation of Oporto impossible. The *Maréchal* was then swiftly routed from his comfortable abode and subsequently forced to abandon his army's baggage, transport and treasure in order to avoid the total loss of his host. In fact, it was only by wit and luck that he succeeded in saving the bulk of his troops, marching them over a number of narrow mountain trails used mainly by local livestock drovers, before eventually stumbling across the border into Spain from a point close to the Portuguese town of Montalegre, whence he continued his march to Orense, arriving there on 19 May with his half-starved army after a forced march of some five days.

Meanwhile, by the end of April Cuesta, who was still at Monesterio some 60 miles south of the Guadiana, had almost completed the task of re-recruiting his Army of Extremadura by absorbing of a number of stragglers from the Army of La Mancha, recently defeated by the French at Ciudad Real. Whilst the Spaniard was rebuilding, Victor had to some extent concentrated his forces near the village of Torremocha, which sits between the Tagus and Guadiana at a location just south of Cáceres, thus allowing Cuesta to advance towards

Almendralejo, which lies some 30 miles south of Mérida and the Guadiana, where he would remain until the middle of June.[3]

Once Wellesley had completed the expulsion of Soult from Portugal, he began to move his forces south by way of Coimbra and Thomar, to Abrantes, where he arrived on 8 June. One of the reasons why he decided to move towards the Tagus may be found in his letter of 14 April 1809 to the Duke of Richmond, which he wrote whilst still in England having been delayed from sailing for Portugal due to contrary winds: 'The plan of operations for the French will be to move Victor's corps from Badajoz to Abrantes; then cross the Tagus; and as soon as that corps is ready to move on towards Lisbon, to bring on the other two weaker corps from Oporto and Salamanca; and the whole to join in the neighbourhood of Santarem'.[4]

From this one may discern that, even before he sailed for Lisbon, and despite Castlereagh's revised instructions of 3 April, Wellesley had already taken the decision to disrupt what he imagined were Victor's intentions. He would do it by striking at the isolated Soult at Oporto, after which he would march on Salamanca, or the south of Portugal, whence he would direct his next offensive upon Victor's army. Some of his musings were revealed in his letter to Frere of 29 April:

> I hope that the Spaniards will adhere to their determination of acting on the defensive, till I shall return to the eastward. They should reinforce Cuesta as much as possible. He has only 19,000 infantry and 1,500 cavalry, as he tells me in his letter of 23d ...
>
> I recommend that Cuesta should observe Victor's movements in the Alentejo, and follow them, if their object should be to invade Portugal ...[5]

Of course, actions against Victor in the Tagus valley would provide an opportunity for combined operations with the Spanish; as such, feelers were put out to Seville and to the commander in chief of the Army of Extremadura.[6]

The first hint of Cuesta's likely attitude towards the arrival of Wellesley may perhaps be perceived on page 51 of his *Manifiesto*. At that time, during early or mid-May 1809, he was at Fuente del Maestre in the midst of a minor campaign of move and counter move against Victor's forward units to the south of the Guadiana. It was then, he claimed, that without any prior consultation, he received instructions from the *Junta Suprema* to the effect that he should, '... do nothing, at the request of the commander in chief of the British Army of Portugal, and not attempt to commence any important operation until the union of his [Wellesley's] army with the Spanish army had been accomplished, a union he was hoping to

---

3   Cuesta, *Manifiesto*, p.51.
4   Wellesley to The Duke of Richmond, 14 April 1809, in J. Gurwood (ed.), *The Dispatches of Field Marshal the Duke of Wellington During his Various Campaigns in India, Denmark, Portugal, Spain, the Low Countries and France from 1799 to 1818* (London: Parker, Furnival and Parker, 1844), vol.III, pp.185–186.
5   Wellesley to Frere, 29 April 1809, Gurwood (ed.), *Wellington's Dispatches*, vol.III, p.197.
6   Wellesley to Cuesta 29 April 1809 and Wellesley to Garay, 29 April 1809, Gurwood (ed.), *Wellington's Dispatches*, vol.III, pp.197–199.

achieve after evicting Soult from Oporto.'[7] By which we may deduce that Frere had passed on the content of Wellesley's letter above to the *Junta* in Seville. Because of this, said Cuesta, he was forced to remain idle during the last 10 days of May.

Victor Withdraws to the Right Bank of the Tagus

Despite his severe beating at Medellín, Cuesta seemed still to be full of fight, encouraging his units to take the offensive to Victor whenever an opportunity arose, and by the end of May the Frenchman had withdrawn from the banks of the Guadiana to take up a position near Torremocha, as mentioned above, with the intention of dispersing a group of Cuesta's forces then gathering in the mountains near Guadalupe, which lies almost equidistant between the Tagus and Guadiana.[8]

Taking advantage of Victor's retirement, Cuesta sent his vanguard under the now *Brigadier* Zayas to probe the forward positions of the French, and it was during one of those raids that the Spaniards managed to round up some 14,000 head of livestock from the extensive grazing lands around Alange. In another of his forays into enemy territory, Zayas actually entered the town of Mérida during late May and early June, placing its Fort Conventual under siege. Unable swiftly to break the resistance of the French garrison within its walls, Cuesta realised that, even if he succeeded in taking the town, he would not be able to hold it should the French return in force; however, before he had time to issue Zayas with orders to disengage, a demoralised Victor sent a brigade of cavalry to rescue Conventual's garrison and carry it off to safety.[9] By now, it would seem that the French high command was becoming somewhat frustrated by Victor's hesitancy to move south, and when he was later ordered to return to the Guadiana by Joseph, he replied saying that it was too late. By then Cuesta had already pulled his troops back from Mérida and retired on Monesterio, 'taking with him the civil population of the region and destroying the mills, bakeries and crops as he went.'[10] As if to emphasise the difficulties facing the *Maréchal*, Zayas then struck again a few days later, defeating a sizable unit of French cavalry at Aljucén. It was at about this time that *Brigadier* Rivas, commander of the 2o Húsares de Extremadura, achieved a similar success in defeating a unit of Latour Maubourg's dragoons close to Medellín. With the growing activity of the Spanish, Victor had become well aware that his position in an isolated and devastated region of Extremadura was becoming untenable. As early as 24 May 1809 he wrote to his superior in Madrid, *Maréchal* Jourdan, complaining that his troops were already starving, but nothing came of it.

By the end of May 1809, Wellesley had made arrangements for an emissary from his staff to be placed on detachment with Cuesta's headquarters, the man he selected for the role was Lieutenant Colonel Richard Bourke, an Irish Whig in whom he saw great potential. When Bourke left to take up his post, he knew that his first task would be to glean from Cuesta his

---

7   Cuesta, *Manifiesto*, p.51.
8   Jean-Baptiste Jourdan, *Memoires Militaires du Maréchal Jourdan* (Paris: Ernest Flammarion, 1899), pp.190–191.
9   Cuesta, *Manifiesto*, p.51.
10   Jourdan, *Memoires Militaires*, p.191.

thoughts on how the coming allied campaign might be conducted. He was guided in his work by a memorandum written by Wellesley which contained a list of questions to be put to the Spanish general. The list was prefixed with a paragraph which read as follows: 'If the two armies under *General* Cuesta and [Sir Arthur Wellesley] are to cooperate in an attack on Marshal Victor, the cooperation must be on the principle of a junction; or of a cooperation with communication; or of a cooperation on separate lines, previously combined and arranged.'[11] In essence, Wellesley was spelling out the parameters within which he was willing to cooperate with Cuesta during a campaign against Victor.

The Bridge at Alcántara

The Loyal Lusitanian Legion came into existence when Chevalier Domingos António de Sousa Coutinho, a Portuguese minister involved in foreign affairs, approached Lord Castlereagh about the question of funding the reconstruction of the Portuguese army, which had been more or less disbanded during the French occupation of November 1807 to September 1808. The Secretary of State for War agreed to help, and at the beginning of August 1808 he appointed Colonel Sir Robert Wilson to raise a Portuguese army corps under the command of a collection British army officers which included Lieutenant Colonel William Mayne and Major John Grant, amongst others. The party set sail for Portugal shortly after Wellesley's first expedition to that country, which arrived in August 1808, but its members were not officially recognised as being part of the British army. Once disembarked, Mayne and his colleagues launched a recruitment campaign, aiming to enlist as many as 3,000 men, and whilst that was in progress, Wilson busied himself in the task of procuring the weapons, accoutrements and uniforms his troops would require. In spite of his strenuous efforts, he found that he could equip only some 2,000 of his volunteers.[12]

At the turn of the year Wilson, an inspiring leader, led a corps consisting of about 700 of his men across some very difficult country, in appalling weather, as they advanced from Lisbon to the fortified town of Almeida. Once there he was given news that the two British regiments comprising the garrison of the place were soon to be withdrawn, so he nominated Mayne as governor and, despite clear orders to the contrary, he then crossed into Spain at the head of a small detachment and made for the town of Ciudad Rodrigo. In effect, he was the swashbuckling leader of his own private army. On his arrival at the walled town he was surprised to find it without a garrison, especially so as word had begun to spread that the French were approaching; but this situation presented him with just the kind of challenge he seemed to relish. Soon the local governors had placed some 2,000 of their militia at his disposal, and with these men he was able to deny *Général de division* Lapisse any firm control of the region, employing the hit-and-run tactics of guerrilla warfare to attack small groups of the enemy wherever he found them.

---

11   Wellesley to Cuesta, 30 May 1809 (includes Wellesley's memorandum to Bourke), Gurwood (ed.), *Wellington's Dispatches*, vol.III, pp.260–261.
12   William Mayne, *A Narrative of the Campaigns of the Loyal Lusitanian Legion* (London: C. Roworth, 1812), pp.33–34.

When Beresford arrived in Portugal in February 1809 to take command of the Portuguese army, he also took control of the Loyal Lusitanian Legion, and relieved Wilson of his command. At that time the bulk of the force was occupying the puerto de Baños, a mountain pass which lies between the Sierra de Francia and the Sierra de Gredos, providing communication between the Spanish towns of Salamanca and Plasencia.[13] Shortly afterwards, Mayne was appointed as the legion's new chief, but Wilson was eventually returned to favour when Beresford reinstated him as commander of the force as it prepared to unite with Wellesley's army in time for its advance into Spain. By then it comprised two Portuguese battalions which were incorporated into the vanguard of the British force.[14] But it was during the time of Wilson's absence that the legion carried out one of its best-known exploits.

On 25 April 1809, Colonel D'Urban, at that time Quartermaster General of the Portuguese army, wrote to Lieutenant Colonel Mayne in his new and temporary role as commander of the Legion, which was then stationed at Castelo Branco:[15]

> I am commanded by Marshal Beresford to direct you to proceed immediately with the Loyal Lusitanian Legion under your command, to Alcantara …
>
> You will, of course, take with you the guns and howitzers attached to the legion; and on your arrival at Alcantara you will make such a disposition of your force as shall appear to you best for the defence of the passage of the Tagus at that place …[16]

On 8 May (four days before Wellesley's victory at Oporto) Cuesta wrote to Mayne as follows:

> The news I have received that 2,000 troops under your command have arrived at Alcántara, has given me the greatest satisfaction; the more particularly so, as I understand these to be the advance of a large army of British troops under His Excellency General Wellesley, [which is] bound for Spain.
>
> I should think Marshal Victor … will make a disposition to enter Portugal from Estremadura in order to relieve General Soult; and it will give me much pleasure to concert any plans for the impediment of the enemy's movement in the vicinity of Badajoz and Elvas … It is also probable they may try to pass the Tagus at Alcántara, and to move on to Castelo Branco in Portugal …[17]

Once on the banks of the Tagus, Mayne wasted no time in establishing a plan for the defence and, if necessary, the destruction of the bridge at Alcántara. In doing so he had brought his force of some 1,800 men of the Lusitanian Legion across the border from Portugal into Spain, together with 1,200 men of the Portuguese militia unit of Idanha,

---

13   The term 'puerto de Baños' occurs throughout this work. In English terms it is the equivalent of the 'pass of Baños' or 'Baños pass', as in the 'mountain pass of Baños'.

14   Richard Tennant, 'The Loyal Lusitanian Legion', *The Napoleon Series*, <https://www.napoleon-series. org/military-info/organization/portugal/LoyalLusitanianLegion/LoyalLusitanianLegion.pdf>, accessed May 2021.

15   Beresford was later to reinstate Wilson as commander in chief of the LLL.

16   D'Urban to Mayne, 25 April 1809, Mayne, *A Narrative of the Campaigns*, pp.220–221.

17   Cuesta to Mayne 8 May 1809, in Mayne, *A Narrative of the Campaigns*, pp.224–225.

and had taken possession of the crossing. Victor, knowing how valuable the bridge was to French plans to invade Portugal and, indeed, to those of supressing Spanish resistance in Extremadura, decided to take personal command of Lapisse's division, recently returned from the region of Ciudad Rodrigo, plus a further brigade of dragoons, and set off to capture it, arriving at Alcántara on 14 May 1809. With such a strong force at his disposal, he must have been surprised by the stout resistance put up by Mayne's troops, who had been well deployed and were able to use their artillery to good effect during the subsequent action. The legionnaires held their ground for some nine hours, but as French numbers and weight of artillery fire eventually began to tell, they were forced to retreat before taking up a second defensive position at the Portuguese end of one of the bridges which spanned the border-defining river Erjas, the Ponte de Seguro. Mayne had mined the bridge at Alcántara for just such a scenario, but when he fired his charges they did not quite bring down the arch upon which they were planted, leaving it viable for infantry if not much else.[18] In fact, Victor was able immediately to send a strong detachment across the partly disman-tled bridge in pursuit of Mayne's force as it retreated into Portugal, and by the end of the fighting the Lusitanian Legion had suffered 263 casualties: 103 killed, 143 wounded and 17 missing; Mayne claiming that the French had suffered appreciably more. It may be worth noting that the Idanha militia suffered less severely than the legion, having quit the field part way through the action.[19] With the bridge of Alcántara in his hands, Victor could have brought up the rest of his army and made a determined move upon Lisbon, but he was seemingly wracked with doubt. Lacking intelligence about the whereabouts and strength of British and Portuguese forces, but aware of Cuesta in his rear, he knew that it would be difficult to subsist in large tracts of Spanish Extremadura should he have to retreat under pressure, so he decided to withdraw, and simply marched back into Extremadura, no doubt contemplating his reduced options for the remainder of the campaigning season, and wondering how he would survive in such an impoverished region. In his memoires, Joseph's right-hand man at Madrid, *Maréchal* Jourdan, made reference to Victor's plight during the spring of 1809:

> When the king learned that the Duke of Dalmatia [Soult] was at Oporto with a British army to his front, he ordered the Duke of Bellune [Victor] to move to Alcántara and to station one of his divisions at Castelo Branco. However, the marshal responded that it was impossible for him to carry out the order due to the fact that his army would not be able to subsist in that region. In the meantime, he continued, the enemy had blown up the bridge at Alcántara making any move to the right bank [of the Tagus at that location] impossible.
>
> The king then ordered the Duke of Bellune to attack Cuesta's army, which had moved towards the Guadiana, but the marshal replied some days later that Cuesta had already retired upon Llema [*sic* for Llerena, a small town some 100 miles south of the Guadiana] taking with him the inhabitants [of the country] together with their livestock, and destroying the mills as he went, thus creating a desert between

---

18   Cuesta to Mayne, 8 May 1809, Mayne, *A Narrative of the Campaigns*, pp.224–225. The damaged arch did eventually collapse, but nobody has yet been able to place a date on when it happened.

19   Cuesta to Mayne, 8 May 1809, Mayne, *A Narrative of the Campaigns*, pp.241–245.

his army and that of the emperor, which caused the duke to claim that he could not subsist on the Tagus and that I Corps was in danger of complete dissolution within five days should he not receive orders either to enter Andalucía or return to the right bank of the Tagus.[20]

Wellesley and Cuesta Plan a Campaign on the Tagus

If anything, Victor's appearance at Alcántara, so close to the Portuguese frontier, had the effect of making up Wellesley's mind about what he should do after Oporto. In the aftermath of his victory he was attempting to decide between a number of options which presented themselves to him: a move against Ney in Galicia, a move towards Asturias, or a move south to unite with Cuesta. But when he began to receive news that Victor may well have been contemplating a thrust towards Lisbon after having chased Mayne away from Alcántara, there was really only one choice to make; he had to move south.[21] In fact, he had been expecting Victor to threaten Portugal, something which is clear from the content of his letter of 2 May to John Villiers, Britain's envoy to the Court of Portugal, and of that to Lieutenant General Paget of 4 May, in which he informed his cavalry chief that he was planning to attack Soult, but that he had left a detachment of British and Portuguese troops on the Tagus to observe Victor's movements.[22] As if to dispel what may have been a fog of doubt about his intentions in the minds of his overseers in London, Wellesley laid bare his forward thinking in a letter to Castlereagh dated 7 May 1809, just five days before his defeat of Soult at Oporto:

> I think I shall settle this part [the north] of the country in some way or other, and I shall then turn my attention entirely to Victor.
>
> I think it probable that Cuesta and I will be more than a match for the French army on the Guadiana; and that we shall force them to retreat. The tenor of my instructions will then become important and unless they are altered I shall be obliged to halt at the moment I shall have removed from the Portuguese frontier the danger by which it is threatened; possibly at that time at which the continuance of my advance might be the most important to the cause of the Spaniards.
>
> I wish the King's ministers to consider this point and to give me a latitude to continue my operations in Spain if I should consider them important to the Spanish cause and consistent with the safety of Portugal ...[23]

---

20   Jourdan, *Memoires Militaires*, pp.237–238. Note that Jourdan's reference to Cuesta's scorched earth tactic was employed after his defeat by Victor at Medellín.

21   Amongst the Wellington Papers, WP1/259 and WP1/260, held at the University of Southampton, there are a number of letters from Lieutenant General Mackenzie (WP1/259/50, WP1/260/17, 28, 39 ...) and John Charles Villiers, minister plenipotentiary to Portugal WP1/260/37, 43 ...) all warning Wellesley that Victor was about march upon Lisbon after his capture of the bridge at Alcántara.

22   UoS: WP1/262/5: Wellesley to Villiers, 2 May 1809; WP1/262/12: Wellesley to Paget, 4 May 1809.

23   UoS: WP1/262/27: Wellesley to Castlereagh, 7 May 1809.

In a similar spirit, the British commander wrote to John Hookham Frere, at that time acting as British plenipotentiary to the *Junta Suprema* in Seville, informing him that he was thinking of turning his attention to Victor once he had settled matters in Oporto and the north of Portugal, and perhaps attacked Ney in Galicia, after which he felt it would be safe to leave the east of Portugal on the defensive; before continuing:

> I conceive that I should act in the best manner for Portugal and for the whole of the Peninsula, by cooperating in a plan to oblige Victor to retreat, or if possible in his defeat.
>
> I fear that the letter which I have already written to *General* Cuesta and to Don Martín de Garay will have prevented you from making use of my name and induce the *Junta* Militias to adopt the plan of offensive operations in La Mancha in the same [illegible] as my promise to return to cooperate with Cuesta after I should have obliged Soult to withdraw from northern Portugal ...[24]

Having decided what his next move would be after his removal of the threat from Soult, Wellesley duly brought his army south from the northern fringes of Portugal towards Abrantes, which lies on the Tagus some 35 miles west of the Spanish frontier. By reading some of his dispatches from early June 1809, it is clear that Bourke had, as instructed, discussed his superior's proposals for the coming campaign with Cuesta, and had sent details of the Spaniard's response back to British headquarters. Wellesley's reply to him of 9 June may well have made for some uncomfortable reading for the envoy, as it would seem that Cuesta had proposed a number of schemes for joint allied operations, not all of which were to the British general's liking. Before listing them, we should remember that, at the time this correspondence was taking place, Victor was south of the Tagus at Torremocha in the region of Cáceres and Mérida, Wellesley was at Abrantes in Portugal and Cuesta was at Monesterio south of the Guadiana. However, by reading between the lines of Wellesley's reply to Bourke, it would appear that Cuesta must have been proposing the following alternatives: (1) A number of wide-ranging flanking movements using detachments from the allied armies, which would attempt to box Victor in and deny him an escape route via the crossing points on the Tagus. (2) That the British should come out of Portugal and cross the Tagus via the bridge at Alcántara, thus allowing them to operate on its south bank (assuming that both Victor and Cuesta were to remain in their current positions). Once in place, coordinated attacks by British and Spanish forces would be made against the French, hemming them in between the Guadiana and the Tagus. (3) That the British army should enter Spain and march on Plasencia.

After dismissing the first two of Cuesta's suggestions, Wellesley did see some advantage coming from the third, opining that, 'By this movement, should it be concealed from the enemy for a sufficient length of time, we must cut off his retreat by the bridge of Almaraz, and possibly [those of] Arzobispo and Talavera. If it should not be concealed, at all events the enemy cannot pretend to defend the Tagus.'[25] Whilst Wellesley was penning his dispatch

---

24   UoS: WP1/262/37: Wellesley to Frere, 9 May 1809.
25   Wellesley to Bourke, 9 June 1809, Gurwood (ed.), *Wellington's Dispatches*, vol.III, pp.281–283.

to Bourke, these incipient attempts to formulate an allied plan were already being overtaken by events.

Sitting at his headquarters in Torremocha, and aware that the allies had already attempted to destroy the Almaraz and Alcántara bridges, Victor became convinced that it was time to withdraw from his position between the Tagus and the Guadiana. It was in desperation that he wrote to Joseph Bonaparte on 8 June explaining the situation, but the King felt unable to assent to a retreat; no doubt fearing the wrath of his brother should he do so.

In order to understand just how difficult a time Victor was having, we need only to read the contents of a letter he wrote to Joseph on the day after he sent that mentioned above. Amongst the Wellington Papers at Southampton University there is a Spanish translation of a copy of this second letter, which was taken from a French courier by the name of Dubois when he was captured by a band of Spanish partisans somewhere between Talavera and Madrid. It is a truly harrowing *cri du couer* from a commander obviously at his wits' end:

> Sire,
> It is difficult for me to describe the state we are in. My situation is horrendous; I am literally watching the dissolution of the 1st Corps of the army. The troops are on the verge of starvation, I have nothing, absolutely nothing, to give them and they are desperate. The effects of this penury make me shudder, and they will be disastrous for our cause and for Your Majesty. I can foresee no remedy other than that which I had the honour to propose in my letter of yesterday [withdrawal to the north bank of the Tagus] and even if I am allowed to adopt it, it may be too late. The circumstances must oblige me to retreat towards Talavera de la Reyna, where I will find more resources than are available here. What will become of us in the midst of this calamity? We are in urgent need of help but where can we find it, and who, if anyone, can provide it?
>
> If Your Majesty abandons me in the wretched state I find myself in then my honour, my conviction and everything else will be lost.
>
> I will not be the cause of the disaster which threatens my troops but I will suffer the shame. Tomorrow I will be at Talavera de la Reyna, where I shall await the orders of Your Majesty, of whom I have the honour to be, with the greatest respect, his humble servant.
> Marshal Victor.
> P.S. I have discovered that the enemy are in possession of a pontoon bridge. If they intend to cross the Tagus they have the means to do it. The climate here makes it impossible for the 1st Corps to remain where they are. Never has there been a situation so despairing as theirs.[26]

Despite Victor's pleadings, he did not move to Talavera quite so soon as he was threatening to, and things were left to lie as they were until *Maréchal* Jourdan, who was accompanying Joseph in Spain, intervened on 26 June by sending notice to Napoleon's minister of war in Paris, Clarke, informing him that Joseph had finally relented and given permission for

---

26   UoS: WP1/267/26: Victor to Joseph, circa 9 June 1809.

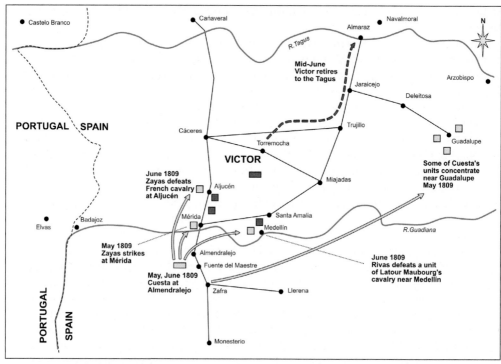

Plate 7. May–June. Cuesta maintains the pressure on Victor by pushing his forces across the Guadiana; at the same time threatening the Frenchman's left flank towards Guadalupe.

Victor to retreat to the right bank of the Tagus. In fact by then the much-relieved *Maréchal* had blown up Fort Conventual at Mérida and marched eastwards along the south bank of the river, eventually crossing it via the pontoon bridge near Almaraz, as well as by that at Arzobispo some 40 miles further upstream, returning the former to its previously inoperable state as he went by hauling to the north bank the collection of temporary pontoons which were in place, before burning them. Ultimately, the allies had been too slow to act in concert against Victor whilst he was isolated, and by 19 June the whole of his army was on the north bank of the Tagus. Safe in the knowledge that he would not now be trapped between it and the Guadiana, he extended his line eastwards from Almaraz and Arzobispo to Talavera. Zayas, active as ever, had followed the French as they made for safety, but Victor, being the soldier that he was, ensured that the Spaniards would not be allowed to interfere with his withdrawal, establishing strongpoints along the line of his retreat, whose garrisons would keep the Spaniards at bay until the bulk of his army had crossed the Tagus.[27] As the French retreated, Cuesta followed at a respectful distance, eventually placing himself within striking distance of Talavera but keeping to the south bank of the great river.

27   Arteche, *Guerra de la Independencia*, vol.VI, pp.231–232.

After their initial exchanges, the correspondence between Wellesley and Cuesta continued for the next few days in total ignorance of Victor's withdrawal, as such there is little of interest in its content. However, as both commanders continued to disagree about each other's proposals for an allied plan, it is clear that Wellesley was becoming more and more frustrated by the Spaniard's apparent obstinance. In a letter to Castlereagh his opening remarks include: 'My correspondence with *General* Cuesta has been a very curious one, and proves him to be as obstinate as any gentleman at the head of any army need be.'[28] Ultimately, it was resolved that the British should march from Abrantes to the Spanish town of Plasencia, which would place them on Victor's right flank so long as he attempted to maintain his current position, which at that time was between Bazagona on the Tiétar and Arzobispo on the Tagus. But the Frenchman did not fail to react as the British and Spanish forces approached, withdrawing his forces during the night of 23/24 June to concentrate them between Oropesa and Talavera by 26 June. In doing just that, and nothing else, he could see that the distress suffered by his troops through their chronic lack of provisions had hardly abated, despite the fact that they had consumed almost all that was available in the neighbourhood of the positions they had just vacated. Once at Talavera, Victor began to establish what would become a forward position on the east bank of the Alberche, and with the French clear of Almaraz, Cuesta brought his pontoons to a spot close to the broken bridge and established a replacement for the floating construction recently burned by the French.[29]

Wellesley was about to begin his first campaign on Spanish soil, and it would prove to be what we today might call a learning experience for him, and he would soon be complaining bitterly about the lack of transport and provisions made available to his force. We shall examine some of the things he said in this respect later on, but before we do so it might be fair to state that Wellesley's troubles in relation to transport and provisions had actually begun to appear in Portugal. In fact, some two weeks after his victory at Oporto, Brigadier General Edward Howorth, commander of the artillery, presented Wellesley with a return of the artillery's horses and mules, which showed that only 31 of the 105 horses and 14 of the 39 mules were fit for duty.[30]

Wellesley had concentrated his army at Abrantes before beginning his march from Portugal into Spain, a task which presented him with many difficulties, as most of his battalions had just taken part in the Oporto campaign. As a result, they were already in a state of significant fatigue when they were ordered to turn about and begin a series of long marches taking them south, but there were other problems besetting the British commander. If the soldiers were tired then so too were the large numbers of pack and draught animals used by the army, as witnessed by the examples above, and after some 10 weeks of incessant marching many of his troops were left with worn out footwear or none at all; the same was true of their clothing. Aware of what their needs would be and, it would seem, already doubtful that they would be furnished by the Portuguese, Wellesley had written to Castlereagh on 31 May requesting 30,000 pairs of shoes, 1,500,000 lbs of biscuit, 3,000,000 lbs of hay and 3,000,000

28   Wellesley to Castlereagh, 17 June 1809, Gurwood (ed.), Wellington's Dispatches, vol.III, pp.300–301.
29   Oman, History of the Peninsular War, vol.II, p.459 and Cuesta, Manifiesto pp.53–54.
30   UoS: WP1/261/11: Howorth to Wellesley, 25 May 1809.

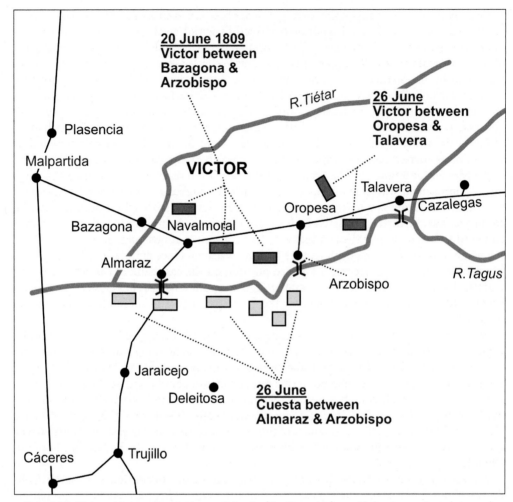

20 June 1809
Victor between
Bazagona &
Arzobispo

R.Tiétar

26 June
Victor between
Oropesa &
Talavera

Plasencia

Malpartida

VICTOR

Talavera

Bazagona   Navalmoral

Oropesa   Cazalegas

Almaraz

Arzobispo

R.Tagus

Jaraicejo

Deleitosa

26 June
Cuesta between
Almaraz & Arzobispo

Cáceres   Trujillo

Plate 8. 20–26 June. Victor retires to the north bank of the Tagus before withdrawing eastwards towards Talavera. Cuesta tracks the French movements from the south bank of the river.

lbs of oats, all of it to be sent from England to Lisbon.[31] Shortages of draught animals and provisions having been flagged up, it was at Abrantes where Commissary General John Murray wrote to the British commander on 1 July warning him of a shortage of transport: 'The scarcity of carts in this part of the country is now so great that unless those forwarded to Castello Branco are returned I feel the service here will be delayed.'[32]

Abrantes lies almost 100 miles inland from Lisbon, which was Wellesley's main supply base at the time, and all of the army's needs had to be brought up from the port by river

31   UoS: WP1/263/57: Wellesley to Castlereagh, 31 May 1809.
32   UoS: WP1/267/Folder 2/2: Murray to Wellesley, 1 July 1809.

craft to Santarem, the highest point on the river to which large ships could navigate, before being picked up by transport columns still learning their trade and carried overland to Abrantes. Wellesley described the difficulties thus: 'The transport of the army was not yet fully organised, its officers were lacking in experience, if not zeal, and orders were slowly executed. Many corps had, in the end, to start for Spain without receiving the much-needed stores, which were still trailing up from Santarem to Abrantes when [I] gave the signal to advance.'[33]

Worn out kit, tired soldiers and a transport system attempting to find its feet in a new environment were all factors in Wellesley's over-long stay at Abrantes, but the root cause of his paralysis throughout most of June 1809 was simply that of a lack of money. Writing to Frere on 11 June he said. 'I should now be ready to move into Spain in 2 or 3 days if I had any money: but the distress in which we are from want of that necessary article will, I fear, render it impossible …'[34] On the same day he wrote to Castlereagh describing the extent of the trouble he was in:

> I think it proper to draw your lordship's attention to the want of money in this army. The troops are nearly two months in arrears, and the army is in debt in Portugal a sum amounting to not less than £200,000. I know of no resource to answer these demands, excepting a sum amounting to no less than £100,000 expected from Cádiz in dollars, in exchange for Spanish gold, sent to Cádiz about six weeks ago, it not being current in Portugal.
>
> I conceive that the expenses in this country, including those of the ordnance, the advances to the Portuguese government, the pay of the army, and the extraordinaries, will not fall short of £200,000 per mensem [month]. The whole of this sum ought, for some months at least, to be sent in specie from Great Britain, otherwise the operations of the army will be cramped for want of money.[35]

Later on the same day, after having received a dispatch from Castlereagh dated 25 May (no doubt in response to Wellesley's letter of 7 May) in which he was given official permission to extend his operations in Spain beyond the provinces immediately adjacent to the Portuguese frontier, Wellesley replied that he was happy about his latest instructions but added, 'I fear I must delay making any movements whatever till the army shall receive a supply of money.'[36] In the same vein he wrote to Frere on 14 June telling him he could not move until he had received the money he was waiting for:

> One of the great difficulties I have in moving is the want of money; however, I have reason to expect that will be removed at an early period, either by the arrival of the *Surveillante*, from Cádiz, with £100,000 or by that of a vessel from England with a similar sum. The arrival of either would enable me to march forthwith.[37]

---

33   Oman, *History of the Peninsular War*, vol.II, p.451.
34   UoS: WP1/265/39: Wellesley to Frere, 11 June 1809.
35   UoS: WP1/265/42: Wellesley to Castlereagh, 11 June 1809.
36   UoS: WP1/265/44: Wellesley to Castlereagh, 11 June 1809.
37   UoS: WP1/265/58: Wellesley to Frere, 14 June 1809.

It was not until 16 June that Wellesley wrote to Murray informing him that the frigate, HMS *Surveillante*, coincidently the ship which had brought him to Portugal in April, had docked at Lisbon with the cargo of specie he was so desperate for, but it would be another 11 days before his army was ready to march for Spain, meaning he would not arrive at Castelo Branco until the final day of June; significantly, the same day upon which *Teniente General* Venegas's first advance from the Sierra Morena in the south came to an end, as we shall now see.

5

The Launch of Venegas's Campaign

Whilst Wellesley was bogged down awaiting funds at Abrantes, on the Spanish side Cuesta's host was about to be enlarged by the formal absorption of the Army of La Mancha, making it almost an auxiliary to the Army of Extremadura. This was the army which had been more or less destroyed at Ciudad Real in March whilst under the command of the Conde de Cartaojal. With tireless effort Venegas began to rebuild his newly acquired host, bringing it up to a strength of some 15,000 men by the middle of June, a growth in numbers fed mainly through the absorption of fresh recruits from Andalucía.[1] Venegas would be brought into play during the coming campaign, but being somewhat remote from his commander in chief and the immediate theatre of Talavera itself, meant that both control of, and communication with, his new force would prove to be a tiresome task for Cuesta. In the meantime Venegas's growing presence to the south of Madrid towards Andalucía was being increasingly felt by Sebastiani who, before being sent towards Toledo to counter any Spanish activity south of Madrid some five months earlier, had left his 3rd Division and its commander, Leval, with Victor, along with Merlin's corps of 1,200 cavalry. Now, after having descended from Toledo, he felt so threatened by the presence of Venegas that he had withdrawn his headquarters from the far south of La Mancha to the town of Madridejos, which lies to the north of the Guadiana and some 50 miles due south of Madrid, thus allowing his Spanish opponent to advance tentatively from the Sierra Morena and annoy his outposts.

Observing this from Madrid, Joseph would have been acutely aware of the delicacy of Sebastiani's position. With Victor now north of the Tagus, the former's right flank and rear were wide open to an attack from Cuesta, who had been gifted the run of the south bank of the great river, and from Venegas, who stood in his front. Such concerns caused Joseph to bring Sebastiani some reinforcements from the capital in order to deal with what was, in reality, a somewhat exaggerated threat posed by the Army of La Mancha. When the king arrived at the head of his personal guard and a brigade from Dessolles' division during the latter days of June, some 6,000 men in total, it was the signal for Venegas to retire to the safety of the Sierra Morena, his soldiers conducting some honourable rear-guard actions on the way as they were harried by the French. One such was led by the commander of the Spanish vanguard, *Brigadier* Lacy, at Torralba de Calatrava on 28 June, whilst *Teniente* Morán at Valdepeñas and *Capitán* Rosales at Alcubillas led some creditable rear-guard cavalry actions

---

1   Arteche, *Guerra de la Independencia*, vol.VI, p.233.

as the French took up the pursuit.[2] After examining this first phase of Venegas's campaign in detail below, we shall look at its second phase in a later chapter. Suffice it to say for now that, whilst this initial game of cat and mouse was taking place on the Guadiana, the British were still within the Portuguese frontier; and with Victor on the right bank of the Tagus Cuesta, by the third week in June, had occupied a line of posts south of the river between Almaraz and Arzobispo. All of which would suggest that Venegas may well have moved too early, and in doing so had stirred up the French to his disadvantage.

Venegas's First Advance from the Sierra Morena, 14–30 June 1809

It is now time to begin a close examination of the role which Francisco Venegas's Army of La Mancha played during the allies' 1809 campaign on the Tagus, and there are two significant primary source documents which we may draw upon in order to map out a detailed picture of his involvement. The first is a clear and comprehensive campaign diary kept by an as yet anonymous member of his staff at headquarters, who entitled it, *Diario de las operaciones del Ejército reunido del Centro y Andalucía* [aka *el Ejército de La Mancha*] *al mando del Exmo. Sr. D. Francisco Xavier Venegas, que principió en el 14 de Junio 1809;*[3] henceforth referred to as 'Venegas's Diary'. The second is a substantial document which Venegas published some two years after the Tagus campaign as a riposte to Cuesta's *Manifiesto* published in Palma de Mallorca in 1811, a document to which we have already made substantial reference. In fact, the ink must have been barely dry on Cuesta's missive when Venegas's work appeared during November of the same year, under the grandiloquent title of, *Vindicación de los agravios infundados, injustos y groseros con que el Capitán General D. Gregorio de la Cuesta ha intentado manchar la reputación del Teniente General y Virei de Nueva España, D. Francisco Xavier Venegas, en su Manifiesto impreso en Palma de Mallorca en 1811,*[4] which translates to, 'Vindication of the unfounded, unjust and vulgar insults with which *Capitán General* D. Gregorio de la Cuesta has attempted to cast a stain upon the reputation of *Teniente General* and Viceroy of New Spain, D. Francisco Xavier Venegas, in his Manifesto published in Palma, Mallorca in 1811,' henceforth referred to as 'Venegas's *Vindicación.*'

So much for the Spanish documentation relating to the Tagus campaign, but what about Venegas himself? A veteran of Spanish campaigns in the Mediterranean, North Africa, Gibraltar and the Pyrenees during the eighteenth century, he retired from the army in 1795, before returning to serve his country at the outbreak of the *Guerra de la Independencia*

---

2 Arteche, *Guerra de la Independencia*, vol.VI, pp.234–236. See also Oman, *History of the Peninsular War*, vol.II, p.457.

3 AHN: Diversas Colecciones, 125, N.5: Diario de las operaciones del Ejército reunido del Centro y Andalucía, al mando del Exmo. Sr. D. Francisco Xavier Venegas, que principia en el 14 de Junio 1809. Despite the title of the army used by the diarist for Venegas's army (*el Ejército reunido del Centro y Andalucía*) we shall henceforth refer to it by its informal title of el Ejército de La Mancha.

4 Francisco Venegas, *Vindicación de los agravios infundados, injustos y groseros con que el Capitán General D. Gregorio de la Cuesta ha intentado manchar la reputación del Teniente General y Virei de Nueva España, D. Francisco Xavier Venegas, en su Manifiesto impreso en Palma de Mallorca en 1811* (Cádiz: Imprenta del Estado-Mayor-General, 1811).

in May 1808. Present at the Battle of Bailén in July of that year, he was made second in command of the 1a División del Ejército de Andalucía by Castaños, before taking command of the 1a División del Ejército del Centro in the following November, as the second French advance into Spain arrived at the gates of Madrid. Wounded at the Battle of Uclés in January 1809 when in command of two divisions, he was forced into a short period of convalescence. However, his services would again be called upon some three months later as Spain continued to grapple with the French invaders.

It was whilst Venegas was recovering from his wounds that the French continued to consolidate their position in and around Madrid, and we may say that one of the first significant combats of the 1809 campaign on the Tagus was the cavalry action which took place on 24 March at Los Yébenes, some 30 miles south of Toledo. In this preliminary action to the Battle of Ciudad Real, a force of about 4,000 Spanish cavalry belonging to the Army of La Mancha, then under the command of the Conde de Cartaojal, defeated the 600-strong regiment of Sebastiani's Polish lancers which formed the spearhead of his southward advance towards Andalucía. The victorious Spanish unit comprised the vanguard of Cartaojal's army, which was advancing on Madrid from the south when *Brigadier* Bernuy and the Conde de Zolina became aware of the enemy presence in their front. Sensing that Konopka's lancers had represented just the tip of a significant French force in his front, Cartaojal decided to retreat towards the Sierra Morena after the action had been fought. Sebastiani's reaction was to send a force of some 7,500 infantry and cavalry in pursuit of the Spaniards, who crossed the Guadiana a little to the north of Ciudad Real before taking up a position which, inexplicably, offered little if any advantage for defence, located as it was in the midst of an extensive plain. Once the French had overcome the Spanish outposts at the bridge of Peralvillo, the outcome of the resulting battle at Ciudad Real on 27 March 1809 became a forgone conclusion. In the aftermath of the clash the inevitable Spanish retreat towards the mountains was conducted under incessant pressure from the French, and by the time the chase had petered out, Cartaojal had lost some 4,000 men killed, wounded or taken prisoner. It was this demoralised Army of La Mancha that *Teniente General* Venegas was to inherit after Cartaojal's unavoidable dismissal, and he would prove to be a somewhat controversial appointment.

In his *Vindicación*, Venegas provides the reader with a long and somewhat tortuous rebuttal of all the accusations and intimations of insubordination and incompetence levelled at him by his superior, Cuesta, in relation to his performance during the Talavera campaign; the latter having publicised his criticisms of the former in his *Manifiesto*. Despite his verbosity, Venegas did make a strong defence of his leadership during the summer of 1809, and in turn made many criticisms of Cuesta's own shortcomings as commander in chief of the Spanish forces fighting alongside their British allies. We shall now begin to examine the main thrust of Venegas's exculpatory publication.

He began his defence with a statement defining the crux of the problems he had to grapple with during his few tumultuous months in command of the Army of La Mancha, which was the almost universal lack of military experience amongst the majority of his troops, most of whom were the harvest of a *levee en masse* amongst the peasant population of south-central Spain conducted during the latter months of 1808. Many of these men had experienced their first taste of warfare under the command of the Conde de Cartaojal at the Battle of Ciudad Real on 27 March when, as we have seen, Sebastiani gained an easy victory over his opponent, the Spanish army suffering some 2,000 casualties before being routed by combined French and Polish forces, and another 2,000 during its retreat towards the mountains. Once free of the pursuing enemy as they trudged into the foothills of the Sierra Morena, those men still with their colours were greeted by three days of heavy rainstorms, with hardly any cover to shelter them as they attempted to regroup at the pass of Despeñaperros, one of the main gateways leading from the Sierra Morena into Andalucía. Such conditions only added to the dispersion which had taken place in the immediate aftermath of the battle, as sickness, demoralisation and exhaustion began to take their toll. Such was the state of things when Venegas took over command from Cartaojal on 6 April 1809. By 14 June, after some nine weeks of training and further recruitment whilst in the safety of the mountains, his new host had shaken off at least some of the depression resulting from its earlier experiences, and Venegas was able to march into La Mancha with a force of some 18,000 infantry, 3,000 cavalry, five companies of sappers, 20 guns and six obuses (a kind of light, naval artillery with short, large calibre barrels designed to fire explosive shells). By then a full one third of his men had been recruited since he took command; of the rest most were revitalised soldiers released from various hospitals after their recent campaign under Cartaojal. This meant that the majority of his host comprised men of little if any regular military experience, notwithstanding the trials recently undergone by many at Ciudad Real.[5]

Although he took up command of the Army of La Mancha in early April, the first entry in Venegas's campaign diary is for 14 June 1809, in which he stated that a message had arrived at his headquarters from his *general en jefe* (general in chief) Gregorio de la Cuesta, informing him that the French who had been at Valdepeñas had recently retreated northwards towards the Guadiana. It was this news which enabled Venegas to make a first venture forth from his stronghold in the Sierra Morena during early June and begin to explore the flatter lands to the south of the nascent river, whose source lies close to the town of Daimiel. By 17 June his divisions were strung out along a roughly north-south line connecting Almagro, Daimiel, Valdepeñas, Manzanares and Santa Cruz de Mudela, and it was as the Manchegans repossessed these and other towns of the region after the French withdrawal that they began to uncover evidence of a fate which would become all too typical for many such civilian settlements over the next four years, as the war on the Peninsula dragged on. Here is what Venegas's diarist wrote:

> Even the hardest hearts were softened as we entered the unfortunate province of La Mancha. The towns of el Virillo and Santa Cruz [de Mudela], which we saw for ourselves, provided an example of the melancholy scenes to be found in many more. Their distraught inhabitants, the majority of whom had yet to return to their homes, would find nothing but desolation on their arrival, and those who we came across were simply wondering about the streets bearing expressions which gave witness either to their reaction to the calamity recently suffered under the barbaric invasion, or to their satisfaction at finding themselves surrounded by their own troops.[6]

---

5   Venegas, *Vindicación*, pp.3–4.
6   AHN: Diversas Colecciones, 125, N.5: el Ejército de La Mancha, entry for 17 June 1809.

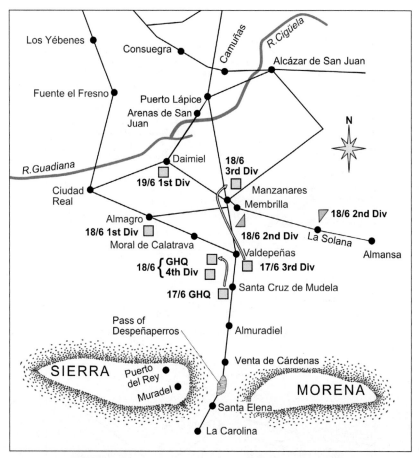

Plate 9. 17-19 June. The initial advance by Venegas's Ejército de La Mancha from the Sierra Morena to the south bank of the Guadiana.

It was on this day that Venegas received news that the French were in great strength at Daimiel and Villarrubia on the banks of the Guadiana, causing him to issue orders for his 1st and 2nd Divisions to suspend their forward movements whilst the 3rd Division continued to Manzanares; and for the 4th Division, together with army headquarters, to halt at Valdepeñas. It may be noted that at this point in time Wellesley was still at Abrantes in Portugal, and it would be another week or so before he commenced his march towards Talavera, as the money he was pleading for had failed to materialise. In the east of Extremadura, Cuesta was just beginning to occupy the south bank of the Tagus between Almaraz and Arzobispo, feeling his way upstream after Victor had completed his crossing to the north bank of the river. So, why, one may ask, was Venegas making his forward move-ment before Wellesley and Cuesta were in position to exert any appreciable pressure upon Victor? The answer, it would seem, probably lay in the state of the communications which existed between the allied armies, a problem which was to dog their performance during the weeks immediately before and after the Battle of Talavera.

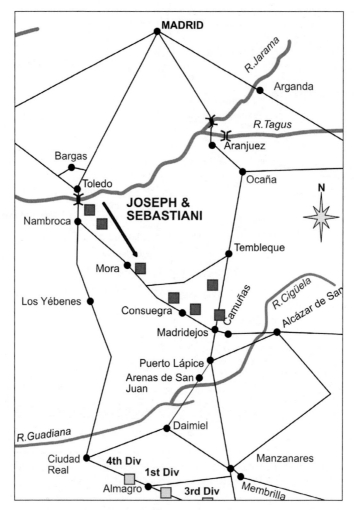

Plate 10. 19-20 June. Venegas's divisions are straddling both the Guadiana and the Cigüela. To the north, King Joseph and Sebastiani have united with the intention to push the Army of La Mancha back towards the Sierra Morena.

Little daunted by the reported situation at Daimiel, Venegas continued to shuffle his four divisions towards the Guadiana in search of the French until 19 June, when he received news from *Secretario de Guerra*, Antonio Cornel, that in the course of his retreat from western Extremadura, Victor had sent a force of some 4,000 men east towards Oropesa and that it might represent a reinforcement destined for Sebastiani. The movement of these men almost certainly represented the return to Sebastiani of his 3rd Division, together with Merlin's cavalry corps, both having been left with Victor for his Medellín campaign when Sebastiani first moved south. Just half an hour before receiving this information, Venegas had heard from *Brigadier* Girón at Almagro that a further 6,000 French had moved down from Madrid to reinforce Sebastiani, this news was later confirmed as the arrival on the scene of Joseph's force from Madrid. As mentioned earlier, the intruder king had instigated his move south in an attempt to guard what he saw as Sebastiani's wide-open right flank to the south of the Tagus. Venegas's reaction was to send orders to his 2nd and 3rd Divisions that they suspend their marches, but by 7:00 p.m. a further message arrived at Venegas's headquarters, this time from Cuesta, informing him that Victor had retreated eastwards upon Trujillo and Almaraz, and that he was following up closely, exerting pressure on the French and causing them to make long and fatiguing forced marches. That, said Cuesta, suggested that his own advance, combined with Wellesley's anticipated march to Plasencia, meant that it would be convenient for the allied cause if Venegas could keep up the pressure on Sebastiani, if possible drawing him a little to the east and away from Victor. With that in mind the commander of the Manchegans issued orders for his 2nd and 3rd Divisions to re-commence their marches to Villarta and Arenas de San Juan respectively, both these villages lying on the banks of the river Cigüela (sometimes written, Cigüela).[7] At this point, one must ask oneself why Cuesta was urging Venegas on when, if the Army of Extremadura was still to the west of Trujillo, the distance between the two Spanish armies was in excess of 200 miles. The British were even further away from Venegas, still in the act of concentrating at Abrantes in Portugal!

King Joseph Descends from Madrid to Reinforce Sebastiani

By 21 June, Venegas was continuing in his efforts to reinforce the Army of La Mancha, issuing orders for the distant *Brigadier* Zerain to re-unite with him by marching via Ciudad Real. He also sent a message to the *Junta de Granada* asking it to dispatch all of the cavalry, infantry and engineers it could spare, as he continued with his advance towards the Guadiana behind a screen of his various *partidas de guerrilla*.[8] As he moved further away from the safety of the Sierra Morena, it is clear that the commander of the Manchegans became somewhat uneasy about the slowness of his communications with Cuesta. Realising that he would require both a more rapid and more frequent notification of enemy movements the more exposed he became, he asked the army's Administrator of Post to establish a faster courier link between himself and his superior. Suspecting that Sebastiani was about to be reinforced by more detachments from Victor's army, he also asked that Cuesta keep up the pressure on the former's rear-guard in order to deprive him of any opportunity he may otherwise have of releasing some of his troops, at the same time stressing his need for prompt intelligence about any enemy movements.[9] By 24 June, Venegas was beginning to receive local intelligence strongly suggestive of the French making preparations to move against him. On the following day the information was more detailed, including mention of Sebastiani's strong reinforcements, recently arrived from Madrid under the command of 'José Napoleón', together with some units from Victor's army, as we have already seen. As a result, he began to prepare and position his four divisions for an early retreat. On the

7   AHN: Diversas Colecciones, 125, N.5: el Ejército de La Mancha, entry for 19 June 1809.
8   AHN: Diversas Colecciones, 125, N.5: el Ejército de La Mancha, entry for 21 June 1809.
9   AHN: Diversas Colecciones, 125, N.5: el Ejército de La Mancha, entry for 22 June 1809.

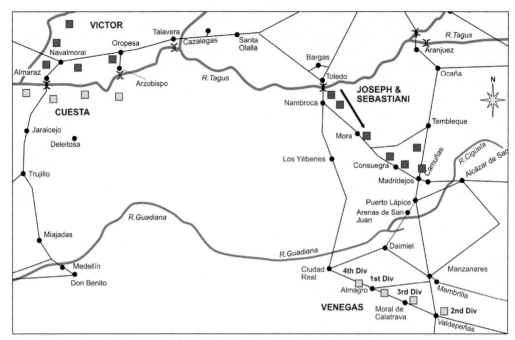

Plate 11. Fourth week of June. A wider picture of the campaign. To the west of Madrid Cuesta is preparing to cross the Tagus and force Victor towards Talavera. At the same time, King Joseph and Sebastiani are advancing on Venegas in the south, as the Spaniard concentrates his divisions for a retreat to the Sierra Morena.

25th a message from Cuesta arrived, instructing his subordinate to avoid a general action at all costs until the Army of Extremadura was able to cross to the north bank of the Tagus, a move which would allow both him and Venegas to operate in combination.[10] Three days later, orders written on 23 June arrived from the *Junta Suprema* which expressly forbade Venegas from sending any of his divisions forward, thus adding emphasis to Cuesta's recent message. On the 27th, the divisions of the Army of La Mancha were at the following locations: The 1st Division was at Moral de Calatrava on its way to Valdepeñas, the 3rd Division was also at Moral and the 4th, together with army headquarters, were at Almagro on their way to Santa Cruz de Mudela. There is no mention of his 2nd Division in the diary entry for 27 June; so one can only assume it to have been at its last-mentioned location, Consolación. In other words, Venegas was moving his army in a south-easterly direction towards the highway which would provide him with a good and direct line of retreat towards the mountains of the Sierra Morena, should he need it.[11]

---

10   AHN: Diversas Colecciones, 125, N.5: el Ejército de La Mancha, entry for 25 June 1809.
11   AHN: Diversas Colecciones, 125, N.5: el Ejército de La Mancha, entry for 27 June 1809.

Venegas Retreats to the Sierra Morena

In reality, and despite the promptings from Cuesta and the *Junta*, Venegas's first advance towards the Guadiana was almost at an end. Over the succeeding 24 hours, news of the recent French movements, together with estimates of their strength, left him no alternative but to continue to retire towards the sanctuary offered by the mountains in the south. After completing a well-ordered retirement to the safety of the *sierra*, his 1st Division took up positions at the puerto del Rey and Maradal, the 2nd at Villamanrique, the 3rd at El Viro, the 4th at Despeñaperros and army headquarters at Santa Elena. Compared with the performance of all too many Spanish commanders when faced with a strong advance by the French, in this instance that of Venegas was entirely creditable. Operating under the command of Gregorio de la Cuesta as he was, things could easily have gone wrong, as the mass casualties of Medina de Rioseco and Medellín might attest. During the course of his retreat from the Guadiana there had been one or two attempts by Cuesta to encourage his subordinate to take up a more belligerent attitude, but Venegas, well aware of the limitations of his raw and inexperienced troops, ignored them. In fact, he had shown a measure of subtlety in blunting or dampening his superior's impetuous urgings, giving the impression that he had little confidence in Cuesta (or, in fact, an innate dislike of him) an impression reinforced by the fact that he felt the need to remind his commander in chief that the safety of the Army of La Mancha was, in many ways, dependent upon prompt, regular and clear communication between the two. In this respect he had the presence of mind, not to say the cunning, to copy several tranches of the correspondence between himself and his chief to *Secretario de Guerra*, Antonio Cornel, in order that he be kept fully informed of what was passing at army command level, and on which dates. Indeed, in his diary entry for 19 June, Venegas noted that Cuesta had omitted to send him notice of an earlier movement made by Victor, an omission which could have had serious repercussions for him; that is, the return to Sebastiani of Merlin's cavalry corps and Leval's 3rd Division.

In summary, it would appear that Venegas could feel quite pleased with the outcome of his first operational activities in command of the Army of La Mancha. Knowing, by default or otherwise, that the Anglo-Spanish force had not yet concentrated in the region of Talavera, he would have understood that the time had not yet come for him to do anything more than feel for the enemy in his front. However, although in the unenviable situation of being subject to orders from Cuesta, who was some 175 miles away at Talavera, or to advice from Cornel situated some 170 miles distant at Seville, he had successfully attracted the attention of strong French forces from both Victor in the west and those under Joseph in Madrid, as well as from Sebastiani's corps; drawing them all south towards the Sierra Morena before retreating to safety.

The French reaction to Venegas's first sally from the mountains represented their intention to safeguard Sebastiani and to block the apparent advance on the capital by the Manchegans. Unfortunately, neither Wellesley nor Cuesta were ready to take advantage of this early diversionary move; such was the lack of coordination and preparedness amongst the allied armies. As for his own field tactics, the commander in chief of the Manchegans had managed to protect himself from the possibility of marching into trouble, by employing local irregular forces to act as scouting parties ahead of his planned movements, and whilst Joseph Bonaparte's attention was fixed upon Venegas, Cuesta would be safe from attack by Victor whilst awaiting Wellesley's arrival at Plasencia. To all of this it should be added that, in words once used by Wellesley himself, the commander of the Manchegans knew when to retreat and dared to do it – and without loss in this instance. Charles Oman goes even further in his *History of the Peninsular War*, despite an unfortunate qualification, when he said of Joseph's move into La Mancha:

> His excursion to Almagro had been almost as reckless and wrongheaded as Venegas's advance to Madridejos, for he had separated himself from Victor by a gap of 200 miles at the moment when the British army was just appearing on the Marshal's flank, while Cuesta was in his front. If the allied generals had concentrated their forces ten days earlier – a thing that might well have happened but for the vexatious delays at Abrantes caused by Cuesta's impracticability – the 1st corps [Victor's force] might have been attacked at the moment when Joseph lay at the foot of the Sierra Morena in a position too remote from Talavera to allow him to come up in time to succour Victor.[12]

In truth, Wellesley's 'vexatious delays at Abrantes' were not the fault of Cuesta, rather a failure at the heart of the British government to supply the British army with the specie it so desperately needed before commencing its march into Spain.

There are two ways in which to look at Venegas's first sally forth from the Sierra Morena during the second half of June. Seeing things in a positive light, one could claim that his actions had discouraged or prevented Victor from launching an attack on Cuesta before the arrival of Wellesley on the Alberche. As such he may well have already contributed to the later success at Talavera to a greater degree than is generally recognised, by attracting the attention of both Joseph and Sebastiani, thus causing them to march to the far south of La Mancha to keep him at bay. But this was not quite the intended role for the Army of La Mancha during the Tagus campaign. Far from simply causing a delay to the French concentration on the Alberche, Venegas was expected to prevent such a concentration from taking place at all. Having not yet fulfilled that ultimate mission, his early move towards Madrid could be deemed to have set the French hare running far too early, and as a consequence placed the allied plans in jeopardy. There is, however, another perspective from which Venegas's first advance should be judged, and it is this: rather than claiming that the Spaniard's movement had been too early, one could just as easily claim that Wellesley's march from Abrantes had begun too late for the allied master plan to succeed. It was during the second half of June, whilst Venegas's operation was forcing Joseph and Sebastiani to march south, that Wellesley was left twiddling his thumbs in Portugal whilst awaiting a delivery of specie. Had the British government acted with the requisite alacrity, he could have joined Cuesta on the Alberche whilst Joseph and Sebastiani were almost 175 miles away in the foothills of the Sierra Morena. Had that happened, the French would have been in some disarray and may well have lost possession of Madrid with worse to follow; but all of that is pure conjecture and it does not address the question of how the presence of Soult in the allied rear might have played out in such a scenario. Nevertheless, the question remains. Had the allies' best chance of victory on the Tagus already been lost by the end of June 1809?

---

12   Oman, *History of the Peninsular War*, vol.II, p.458. The distance between Talavera and Madridejos is closer to 150 miles than the 200 quoted by Oman.

6

Venegas's Hesitant Advance Towards the Tagus, 8 July to 11 August 1809

On 27 June, Wellesley commenced his march from Abrantes to the Portuguese frontier, arriving at Castelo Branco on the 30th. It was whilst he was there that he made his first requests for assistance from the Spanish, asking that some of their officers be sent to him on detachment, together with some local Spanish guides. On 3 July he crossed the border into Spain for the first time, marching via Zarza Mayor and Coria towards Plasencia, where he arrived on 8 July. At that point, with the Tiétar river to the east, the Tagus to the south and Cuesta awaiting him at his headquarters on the left bank of the great river, he must have felt that his long-anticipated allied offensive was about to take place.

The eagerly-awaited meeting between the two allied commanders took place on 10 July at Cuesta's headquarters in the village of Casas de Miravete, which lies about seven miles south-west of Almaraz, and we may glean something of how their conference progressed from a letter Wellesley wrote three days later to Frere:

> I received your letter of the 8th, at Gen. Cuesta's headquarters, to which I went on the 10th, in order to settle the plan for our future operations. I stated to the general my opinion that the principal attack on the enemy's posts on the Alberche ought to be made by the united forces of the British army and the Spanish army under his command; that it would be desirable to detach a corps consisting of 10,000 men, on our left, towards Ávila, to turn the enemy's right; and that Venegas, after having driven Sebastiani's corps across the Tagus, by which alone he is understood now to be opposed, should turn to his right, across the Tagus, either at Aranjuez or at Fuentidueña, and threaten Madrid by the enemy's left.[1]

The paragraph above exposes one of the main failings of the Tagus campaign: the lack of a regular, swift and reliable form of communications between the three nodes of command: Wellesley and Cuesta to the west of Madrid, Venegas to the south of the capital and Cornel in Seville, each separated from one another by distances ranging between 85 and 175 miles as the campaign progressed. In fact, with those distances in mind the use of the word 'swift'

---

1   Wellesley to Frere, 13 July 1809, Gurwood (ed.), *Wellington's Dispatches*, vol.III, pp.353–354.

might be meaningful only in a relative sense. For example, an express return journey of 100 miles by horse might have required at least three or four days to complete. So, despite Wellesley's reassuring words to Frere, by 10 July, Venegas had been nowhere near the Tagus, all of which should have served to illustrate that the allied armies would have to operate in much closer concert if they were to have any hope of recapturing Madrid, their primary objective. In his letter, Wellesley went on to say that Cuesta had objected to his wishes that the proposed 10,000-man detachment on the left should come from the Spanish army, the Spaniard preferring that the British should provide it. Apart from that one seemingly insignificant disagreement, Cuesta seems to have been happy with the rest of Wellesley's plan which, said the British commander in his letter, '... we shall begin to carry into execution on the 18th inst.'[2]

There are a few things to say about the planned flank movement on the allied left as proposed by Wellesley. Firstly, the idea of sending some 10,000 raw Spanish troops, and most of them would have been very raw indeed, on a 75-mile trek across open country populated, if not entirely dominated, by French troops, including cavalry, seems to suggest that he was not yet fully apprised of Spanish capabilities. Secondly, the hopes he was apparently entertaining that Venegas's army would be more than a match for Sebastiani's corps seem to have been equally misplaced. All of which suggests that the British commander had a few things to learn about the quality, morale and state of readiness of the majority of Spanish troops available for operations in central Spain, not to mention the abilities of some of their senior commanders.

Observers at the meeting between the two chiefs, such as Cuesta's Chief of Staff, *Teniente General* O'Donojú and Wellesley's Adjutant General, Charles Stewart, felt it was an awkward and not very cordial affair, but in his next letter to Frere, also dated 13 July, Wellesley remarked that, 'The General received me well, and was very attentive to me; but I had no conversation with him, as he declined to speak French, and I cannot talk Spanish.'[3]

We may now turn to Cuesta's *Manifiesto* for an idea of what was in the Spanish general's mind during the weeks leading up to his meeting with Wellesley:

> Victor crossed the Tagus with little loss and established himself on the opposite [right] bank [to that on which my forces stood]. On 20 June the Spanish army set up camp on the left bank, with its headquarters at Casas del Puerto.[4] The result of the French retreat was the same as that I had hoped to achieve via my combined operations with the allied general [Wellesley] that is to say, to push the enemy to the other side of the Tagus and away from the southern provinces of Portugal, something which General Wellesley would wish for in defence of that kingdom, which was his principal responsibility and occupation; this advantage also provided me with the opportunity to think about more important objectives.
>
> At this time Colonel Bourke was attached to my headquarters, commissioned by the English general to liaise with me about matters of mutual cooperation, and after

2   Wellesley to Frere, 13 July 1809, Gurwood (ed.), *Wellington's Dispatches*, vol.III, pp.353–354.
3   Wellesley to Frere, 13 July 1809, Gurwood (ed.), *Wellington's Dispatches*, vol.III, pp.353–354.
4   Here Cuesta uses the old name for the village, which became known as Casas de Miravete at the commencement of the nineteenth Century.

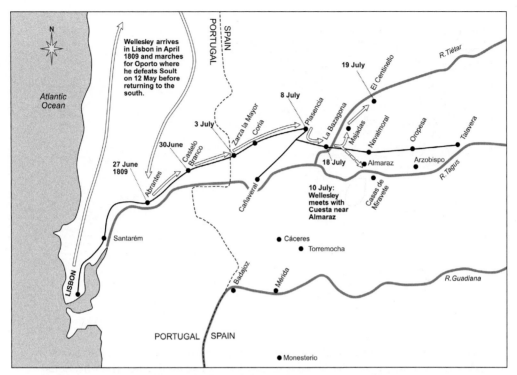

Plate 12. 27 June to 19 July. Wellesley's march from Lisbon to Oporto and his return to Abrantes before marching into Spain. The dashed white line represents Wellesley's visit to Cuesta's headquarters at Casas de Miravete.

various discussions it was clear that he was entertaining the possibility of pushing the French away, not only from Extremadura, but from both of the Castiles [Old and New] and of eventually forcing them across the Ebro via a combination of British forces from Portugal and Spanish forces from Extremadura and La Mancha, the whole of which would be almost twice as strong as those the enemy could field. Bourke communicated this new project to General Wellesley, thinking it to be founded on such solid principles that he would have the confidence to adhere to all of its tenets.

[Due to the heavy rains] it was not possible for Wellesley to continue his march [from Abrantes] to the Spanish frontier until 25 or 26 June, whence he went by Zarza la Mayor towards Plasencia with the idea of threatening the right flank of the enemy, had they remained in the position they had taken up on the right bank of the Tagus between the bridge at Arzobispo and the ferry at Bazagona on the river Tiétar [see Plate 12]. But by the night of the 23/24 June, *Maréchal* Victor had retired upon Oropesa and Talavera.

With that news I ordered the construction of our pontoon bridge next to the old stone bridge [near Almaraz] which had been broken in February, the use of which I had anticipated when ordering its transportation from Badajoz. I then pushed

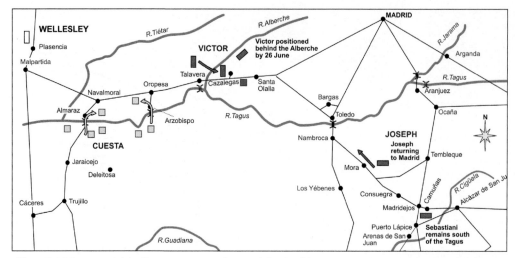

Plate 13. 23 June to 10 July. Cuesta moves to the north bank of the Tagus as Victor retires towards Talavera and the left bank of the Alberche. Wellesley's arrival at Plasencia on 10 July is represented, as is the commencement of Joseph's return to Madrid before joining Victor at Talavera. Sebastiani is north of the Guadiana, Venegas (not shown) lies to the south of the Guadiana.

the vanguard and some cavalry across the river and had them take up position in Almaraz … until 10 July, by which time the British had established their headquarters at Plasencia, thus allowing General Wellesley to visit me in order to concert the future combined operations of both armies.[5]

The Allied Advance to the Alberche

On the next two pages of his *Manifiesto*, Cuesta laid out the proposed future movements of all three allied armies over the coming weeks, defining in fine detail the routes to be taken by each, their halting points and the dates on which each significant milestone was to be reached, as they attempted to push the French back beyond Madrid. The scope of the envisaged operation was grand to say the least, encompassing a huge area of territory and taking for granted the idea that the distant elements comprising the allied forces would be able to work to his strict day-to-day timetable when executing their movements, all of which would result in their synchronised arrival at pre-determined locations, as they shepherded the enemy along in front of them. In fact, by the end of Cuesta's two-page description of the various battlefield dynamics he hoped to set in train, he concluded by stating that, '… [by] 23 July, our three armies will be occupying a continuous line some 25 leagues in length [about 75 miles] thus allowing us to paralyse the enemy, he being inferior in numbers, and

---

5   Cuesta, *Manifiesto*, pp.52–54.

prevent him from concentrating at any single point.'[6] All of which sounded very ambitious to say the least; the French, it seems, would have been willing to comply without objection. Thankfully, things went awry before any allied soldier had taken a pace towards the enemy, and it was Wellesley's first brush with the reality of the situation in Spain which threw the whole plan into disarray. Cuesta described what happened as follows:

On 16 [July] the English general sent the following letter to *General* O'Donojú,[7] explaining that the transport resources he was expecting from Ciudad Rodrigo had failed to materialise. I then passed it on to Cornel, *Secretario de Guerra*, in order that the [Spanish] government could attend to the problem:

Wellesley to *General* O'Donojú,
Plasencia, 16 July 1809.

My headquarters will be at Majadas on the 18th, on the 19th at Centenillo and on the 20th at Oropesa.

I feel I have to say that we march without many of the articles we need, due to the lack of a means of transport which means that, in this province, either it does not exist or they do not wish to provide us with it.

… I feel that it is only fair to my army and to His Majesty that I do not set out on any new operation until I have been provided with the means of transport that my army requires, and I think it only fair to give advance warning to *General* Cuesta that this is my determination.[8]

Here we see the first mention by Wellesley, not so much of his lack of transport, but of his somewhat naïve expectation, not to say sense of entitlement, that the Spaniards were somehow duty bound provide him with what would have been some considerable resources of wheeled transport and draught animals. Cuesta continued in his *Manifiesto*:

When the agreed day arrived for the troops under the commands of [Sir Robert] Wilson, Wellesley and myself to march, all set off on their respective agreed route without any changes to the proposed order, until the British army arrived at Oropesa and the units under my command at La Calzada. It was then when we were told that there was no source of water available along the royal highway to Talavera; that being the case the troops were unable to make their overnight stay at Peravenegas. [In light of this new information] it was subsequently agreed that I would march my men from La Calzada to the town of Velada, and that on the following morning the British army would continue its march from Oropesa to the Alberche in conformity with the pact agreed.[9]

---

6   Cuesta, *Manifiesto*, pp.54–56.
7   Cuesta's Chief of Staff.
8   Cuesta, *Manifiesto*, pp.56–57.
9   Cuesta, *Manifiesto*, p.57.

Three days later, seemingly having had some time to reflect on the joint plan of action agreed at Casas de Miravete, Wellesley wrote a second letter to O'Donojú from El Centenillo (Cáceres province):

> When the enemy shall retire over the bridge of the Alberche, near Talavera, it is probable that he will destroy it … [but] the British troops, for instance, may [at such a time] be engaged with the whole of the enemy force on the left bank of the Alberche, [whilst at the same time] the Spanish army may be *hors de combat* on the right bank by being unable to ford the river, or to repair the bridge … I still think that the two armies ought to cooperate with each other, as near as possible …
>
> When we shall cross the Alberche the engagement will have begun, the enemy will have assembled his force, and the distance of three leagues [10 miles] between the Spanish and British armies will be too much, and will expose both to some risk.[10]

After a further four days had passed, and as the British were preparing to cross the Alberche, Wellesley wrote to Cuesta from Talavera on 23 July: 'I have the honor to inform your excellency that 2 divisions of British infantry, and one brigade of British cavalry, will cross the Alberche tomorrow morning at 4 o'clock, and will proceed to the attack of the right of the enemy's position on the heights near Cazalegas.'[11] He then went on to state what he expected from the Spanish, as had been pre-arranged, and advised Cuesta that it might serve his attack on the bridge spanning the Alberche if he were to employ a battalion of light artillery. The two British infantry divisions allocated to cross the Alberche eventually materialised in the form of just one, Sherbrooke's 1st Division, though Mackenzie's 3rd Division did move up to the right bank of the river in support. The promised brigade of cavalry was that of Anson. There appears to be no record of a reply by Cuesta to Wellesley's letter, and on the following day there were more signs of his frustration with the Spanish general in a dispatch he wrote to Frere: 'I find Gen. Cuesta more and more impracticable every day. It is impossible to do business with him, and very uncertain if any operation will succeed in which he has any concern.'[12] Cuesta had the following to say about the period 21 to 23 of July:

> That night [21 July] the Spanish army bivouacked on the plains in the neighbourhood of Velada. Zayas's vanguard was situated at Gamonal, after having obliged the enemy to evacuate that post, thus allowing him to push his advanced guard on to El Casar, which the French also abandoned early in the morning … [We then waited] until the junction of the British army with ours was complete, before marching in column of battalions from Velada to Talavera. The enemy then retired towards the latter place at 11:00, closely followed by our troops and suffering significant

---

10   Wellesley to O'Donojú, 19 July 1809, Gurwood (ed.), *Wellington's Dispatches*, vol.III, pp.363–364.
11   Wellesley to Cuesta, 23 July 1809, Gurwood (ed.), *Wellington's Dispatches*, vol.III, p.364–365.
12   Wellesley to Frere, 24 July 1809, Gurwood (ed.), *Wellington's Dispatches*, vol.III, pp.367–368. It would seem that Wellesley had sent a note to Cuesta on 18 July, in which he set out his plans/hopes for attacking the French on 22 July. See also Wellesley to O'Donojú, 19 July 1809, Gurwood (ed.), *Wellington's Dispatches*, vol.III, pp.363–364.

loss before falling back to the area around the bridge which crossed the Alberche, whence their batteries played upon the British and Spanish cavalry causing the loss of some horses.

On the night of the 22nd, the allied armies ... bivouacked close to the Alberche in front of Victor's army ...

Just after dawn on the 23rd [I went with Wellesley] to the area close to the wooden bridge which spanned the Alberche, it was there where we observed the firing points, as well as the [French] forces in position to defend the crossing. Later, the English general carried out a reconnaissance of the section of the river opposite the British part of our line, as well as the ford some three miles upstream from the bridge, where he would be able to cross ... I proposed to him that we should attack the enemy immediately, but he opined that we wait until the following morning.[13]

However, Cuesta went on to confirm that on the evening of the 23rd, Wellesley, together with his headquarters staff and *General* O'Donojú, made a further, comprehensive reconnaissance of the enemy's position and strength, and that later in the night: '*Generales* Eguía and the Duque de Alburquerque came to visit me and told me that they had received intelligence that the Alberche was not fordable; a circumstance which placed in doubt the chances that our attack on the bridge [would be successful] ...'[14] This and other reasons, said Cuesta, compelled him to order Eguía and Alburquerque to take their respective divisions of infantry and cavalry upstream some two hours before dawn, until they came to the ford at which the British had determined to cross. The intention was that the two Spanish divisions would cross the Alberche with them and attack the centre of the enemy's line in order to protect the rest of the Spanish army as it crossed the wooden bridge some distance downstream. He then said that he sent O'Donojú and colonel of engineers, José Prieto, to inform the British generals of his new plan so that they could direct their divisions to the points of attack as indicated to them.

Returning to the question of the fordability of the Alberche, the source of the somewhat dubious intelligence about it being unfordable was identified in a footnote Cuesta added in his *Manifiesto* at this point:

The quartermaster of the army had told me that, as a consequence of the British having commandeered the 19 ovens in Talavera, the Spanish troops were in need of bread that day. At the same time, various persons belonging to the municipality of Talavera had assured me that the Alberche was not fordable, and that the [wooden] bridge was unsuitable for the transit of artillery ...[15]

Upon reading Cuesta's *Manifiesto*, it is clear that he had grave concerns about launching his raw recruits at the wooden bridge which, he said on a number of occasions, was heavily defended by troops and artillery on the French bank. Perhaps he was trying, rightly to be fair, to do all that he could to find an alternative means of crossing the Alberche than that of

---

13   Cuesta, *Manifiesto*, pp.58–59.
14   Cuesta, *Manifiesto*, p.59.
15   Cuesta, *Manifiesto*, footnote (1), p.59.

storming the bridge with his inexperienced troops, or at least affording them some support whilst in the act of doing so. Eventually the Spanish would be spared the stiff test they were about to be put to; the French withdrawing from the left bank of the river during the night of 23/24 July, leaving the allies to cross it at their leisure.

Victor Withdraws from the Alberche, Cuesta Pursues

Seemingly well pleased with the successful crossing of the Alberche, Cuesta wrote to Cornel on the morning of 24 July from El Bravo, informing him that the commanders of the allied army were surprised that they were able to cross the Alberche unopposed, due to the fact that the enemy had decamped during the night and withdrawn. He then added that it had been just about impossible for the troops of his vanguard to make contact with the French rearguard after they set off in pursuit. Writing a little later at 1:00 p.m. on the same day, he confirmed that he was still at El Bravo with his reserve and a division of cavalry, whilst the rest of his divisions and his vanguard were at Cebolla. The British army, he said, was at Cazalegas and San Román, with its vanguard at Santa Olalla together with his own advanced posts.[16]

Wellesley's letter to Castlereagh of 24 July largely supported all that Cuesta stated in his letter to Cornel, and by that time, he noted, Sir Robert Wilson with his 2,000 or so men of the Loyal Lusitanian Legion, plus two more Spanish battalions lent him by Cuesta, had joined him on the Alberche. As well as this he claimed that, on 18 July, the distant *Teniente General* Venegas had been directed to march upon Madridejos, some 75 miles directly south of Madrid, before making for Fuentidueña, where he could cross the Tagus before advancing to Arganda which is situated some 13 miles south-east of the capital. If the commander of the Manchegans had actually accomplished what had been asked of him, it would have meant that he would be some 95 miles north-east of Cuesta on his arrival at Arganda; granted, a much shorter distance than the 175 miles which separated the two whilst Venegas had been in the northern foothills of the Sierra Morena, but still enough to mean that communication between the Spanish commanders would have been slow. However, Wellesley's impression that the Manchegans were close to Madridejos was a little off the mark. Sadly, the Army of La Mancha was still some 35 miles south of Madridejos, with its commander in chief unwilling to advance on Sebastiani.

After describing the recent activities of the allied armies to Castlereagh, Wellesley once again complained forcefully about the lack of transport and provisions available to him:

> I have not been able to follow the enemy as I could wish, on account of the great deficiency in the means of transport within this army, owing to my having found it impossible to procure even one mule or a cart in Spain ... and I have since informed Gen. Cuesta, that I should consider the removal of the enemy from his position on the Alberche as a complete performance on my part of the engagement into which I had entered with him in his camp on the 11th inst., as that operation, if advantage

---

16   Cuesta, *Manifiesto*, p.60.

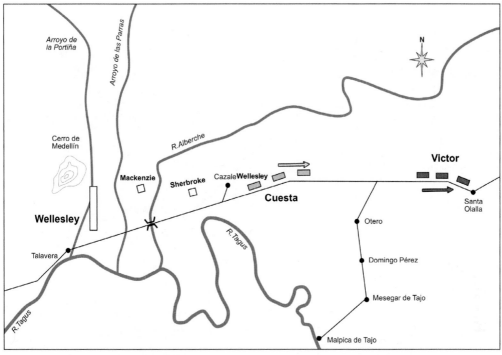

Plate 14. 24 July. Cuesta sets off in pursuit of Victor as he seeks the safety of a juncture with Sebastiani and King Joseph near Torrijos. Wellesley retains his outposts on the banks of the Alberche.

was duly taken of it, would give him possession of the course of the Tagus, and would open up his communication with La Mancha and with Venegas.

Within these 2 days I have had still more reason for adhering to my determination to enter into no new operation, but rather to halt, and even to return to Portugal, if I should not be supplied as I ought, as, not withstanding His Majesty's troops have been engaged in very active operations ... they have been in actual want of provisions for 2 days ... It is certain that at the present moment the people of this part of Spain are either unable or unwilling to supply them; and in either case, and till I am supplied, I do not think it proper, and indeed I cannot, continue my operations in Spain.[17]

By this letter we may note that Wellesley made his first complaint about a lack of provisions for his troops on 24 July, some six days after leaving Plasencia, where he had rested his army for a full 10 days before marching for Talavera. In fact, from his letter it is clear that he was claiming that his troops were running out of provisions by 22 July. However, according to the burghers of Plasencia, by the time he left the city on 18 July, en-route for his destination, his troops had been provisioned by the authorities of the town for several

---

17   Wellesley to Castlereagh, 24 July 1809, Gurwood (ed.), *Wellington's Dispatches*, vol.III, pp.368–369.

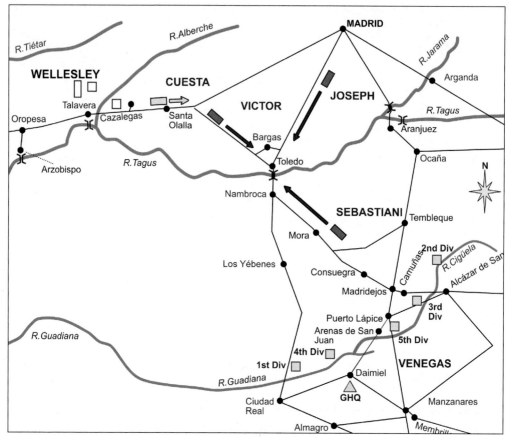

Plate 15. 24 July. The initiation of moves made by the French to concentrate maximum force before deciding which of the two allied forces to attack. The approximate positions occupied by Venegas's divisions on 24 July are also shown; in essence he was still on the banks of the Guadiana.

days in advance. Nevertheless, in a letter to O'Donojú on 25 July, the British commander re-emphasised his needs, but added some encouraging words to the Spaniard which seemed designed to give him the impression that the British commander was doing his best with regard to obtaining provisions for his army, in order to enable him to keep it in the fight: '…I am doing everything in my power to procure for the army [some] means of transport and provisions. I hope I have got some of the former … and in the meantime I might get something to eat. We are still in great distress for provisions, which I don't see any very early prospect for relieving.'[18]

---

18   Wellesley to O'Donojú, 25 July 1809, Gurwood (ed.), *Wellington's Dispatches*, vol.III, p.369.

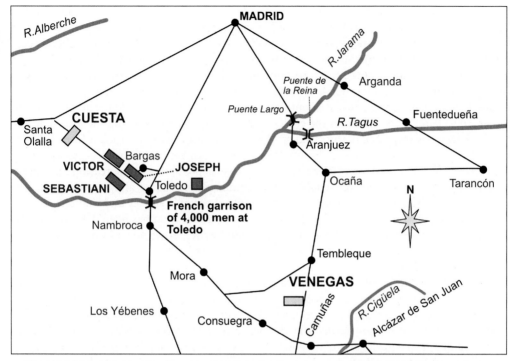

Plate 16. 25 July. The combined armies of the French advance towards Talavera from Bargas, as Cuesta makes preparations for a dash to safety towards Wellesley. In the south Venegas has crossed the Guadiana and is making a slow and careful advance towards Toledo and Aranjuez.

Venegas's Advance Towards the Tagus Commences

In the previous two sections of this chapter, we brought the timeline describing the movements of Wellesley and Cuesta to the west of Madrid, up to 24 July. But as we now switch our focus to Venegas's operations in the south, we shall revert to 4 July before re-running the timeline towards the fourth week of the month.

The content of the remaining sub-headings of this chapter represent an attempt to explain how the self-contained and wholly Spanish interactions between Seville, in the shape of Cornel, and the military command, in the shape of Cuesta and Venegas, defined the dynamics of allied operations to the south of Madrid during July and August 1809. By their nature those interactions were complex and controversial, and require a detailed examination of the correspondence between the three protagonists mentioned above, if we are to understand the political and personal undercurrents running through the Spanish efforts to maintain a southern front. And although hopes were high for Venegas's thrust, it was seen by many as being simply a distraction to French intentions to defeat the Anglo-Spanish army to the west of Madrid. As such, the author will indulge the reader's patience in presenting a somewhat extensive and intricate end to the current chapter.

After its first sally from the Sierra Morena, the Army of La Mancha had been pushed back to its initial start line just a week before Wellesley's appearance at Plasencia, and it was clear that the commander of the Manchegans would be expected by Cuesta and his British counterpart to venture forth once more during the coming operations in the Tagus valley, this time with more vigour. The long-awaited combined offensive was now fully in the offing, and Venegas's mission was to advance as far north as Toledo and Aranjuez, both places lying upon the banks of the Tagus and each some 40 miles south of Madrid, whence, from one or the other, he would be urged to launch an assault on the capital with the intention of keeping the French forces divided, thus sowing panic in the mind of Victor for the security of his retreat from Talavera should he be forced to withdraw. Of the two places, Aranjuez would be Venegas's primary objective as he attempted to pull Sebastiani as far east as possible, thus increasing his separation from Victor at Talavera; but would the Frenchman play his game, and, more importantly, would Venegas be able to coordinate his actions with those of Wellesley and Cuesta?

By necessity, there will be an element of overlap between what has been discussed in the pages immediately above and those immediately following, as we now examine the actions taken by Venegas during the period of the joint advance by Wellesley and Cuesta towards the Alberche and beyond.

After just five days spent in the mountains since his recent withdrawal from the banks of the Guadiana, Venegas began to receive intelligence informing him that the French in front of him were retiring towards Madrid, having recently evacuated Valdepeñas, Manzanares and Almagro. On 4 July, *Brigadier* Vigodet was ordered to advance with his 2nd Division from Villamanrique to Cozar and to send his cavalry to Membrilla; at the same time pushing his accompanying guerrillas on to La Solana, Manzanares, Santa Cruz and Valdepeñas, all of those towns lying south of the Guadiana.[19] Fortuitous or intentional, Venegas's forward move coincided neatly with Wellesley's arrival at Plasencia on 8 July, meaning that, finally, the French would have to be on the alert on two fronts as required by the allied plan. On 7 July, as his divisions were beginning to feel their way forward to the south bank of the Guadiana, Venegas received intelligence from Cuesta that Joseph Bonaparte, having withdrawn from the north bank of the river, had continued with his retirement and entered Toledo on the 5th with a force of some 10,000 men. Whilst there he was joined by a substantial number of infantry, plus nine pieces of artillery, all of which suggested that he was intending to carry out one of three alternative operations: defend the line of the Tagus; return to Madrid; or make a move along the valley of the river towards Talavera, some 55 miles to the west, in support of Victor. Further Spanish intelligence revealed the presence of a substantial force of French cavalry at Villarrubia de los Ojos and Arenas de San Juan, these supported by units of infantry at Consuegra, Madridejos, Villafranca de los Caballeros and Alcázar de San Juan, all of which lie a little to the north of the rivers Cigüela and Guadiana, thus indicating that the French had established a holding line, or a line of forward observation, well to the south of the Tagus, a move seemingly designed to keep the Manchegans away from Madrid whilst the French martialled their forces near Toledo for a march on Talavera.[20] On 8 July, knowing that it would now be safe for him to manoeuvre

---

19   AHN: Diversas Colecciones, 125, N.5: el Ejército de La Mancha, entry for 4 July 1809.
20   AHN: Diversas Colecciones, 125, N.5: el Ejército de La Mancha, entry for 7 July 1809.

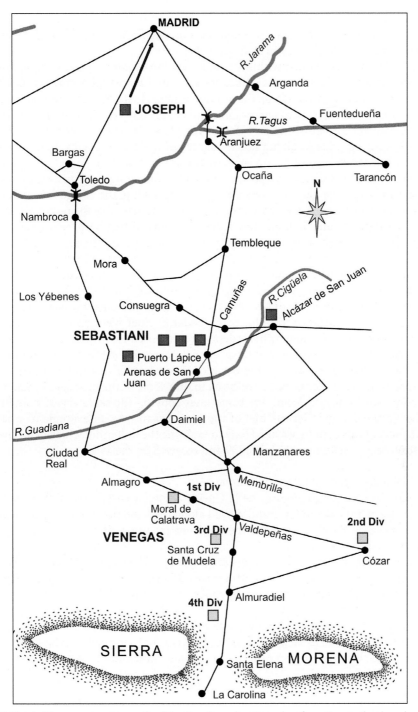

Plate 17. 12 July. Venegas remains south of the Guadiana despite orders from Cuesta that he advance via Tembleque to Ocaña and Tarancón by 18 July, before moving on to Fuentidueña by 21/22 July.

his army along the south bank of the Guadiana, Venegas ordered his 1st Division to El Viro and Moral de Calatrava, his 2nd to Alcobillas and Membrilla, the 3rd to El Virillo and Valdepeñas and the 4th to Santa Cruz de Mudela.

Lacy's 1st Division contained within its ranks a *campo volante*, a free-ranging unit used to carry out active forward reconnaissance missions and report all enemy activity to army headquarters. Should the situation on the ground be judged safe enough, they had permission to engage with any small, isolated enemy forces they came into contact with. Lacy had led this *campo volante* with some distinction before being placed in overall command of Venegas's 1st Division, scoring some small but notable successes against the enemy. But it would seem that, even when at the head of his division, he had not lost his taste for adventure, as it was he who, on leading his forward troops into Moral on 8 July, sought permission to push on to Villarrubia and expel the party of French known to be holding the village. Venegas, prudent as ever, ordered him to remain where he was and await the arrival of the rest of his division.[21]

With Sebastiani's available force now reduced to what it had been before the arrival of King Joseph, who was seemingly on his way back to Madrid in preparation to join Victor at Talavera, Venegas was still estimating that Sebastiani had some 12,000 men on the north bank of the Guadiana, with substantial forces in the rear. However, beyond Sebastiani's line the way was open all the way to Madrid, Joseph having left Toledo for the capital on the 11 July taking with him the whole of his force recently concentrated at the latter place.

Operating at some distance from his commander in chief, Venegas had commenced his campaign under a system whereby his orders were supposed to come directly from Cuesta's army headquarters. However, it would seem that *Secretario de Guerra*, Antonio Cornel, was not shy of sometimes sending the occasional royal order directly to Venegas via the daily dispatch from Seville, as well as relaying to him some of the messages he had received from Cuesta who, it would seem, was sometimes copying the secretary of state in on his dispatches to the commander in chief of the Manchegans. As an example of what could happen by way of this system, we need only to examine the first order which came by it from Cornel to Venegas, written on 12 July 1809 and received on the 14th:

> (Cornel to Venegas, 12 July 1809, *Número* 1):
> *Capitán General* Don Gregorio de la Cuesta advises that the enemy has crossed the bridge at Talavera in force and moved along the left bank of the Tagus towards Aldeanueva de Barbarroya, with the apparent intention of taking the bridge at Arzobispo in the rear …
>
> In view of this dispatch, and others related to it … H.M. expects Your Excellency to take all possible measures to attract the attention of the enemy, but without compromising the safety of the forces under your command.[22]

Here we may see that, although Venegas was a direct subordinate of Cuesta, and his Army of La Mancha considered as an appendage to the Army of Extremadura, the *Junta Suprema* felt it could issue him with direct orders as it saw fit. Knowing this to be the case, Venegas

---

21   AHN: Diversas Colecciones, 125, N.5: el Ejército de La Mancha, entry for 8 July 1809.
22   Cornel to Venegas, 12 July 1809, Venegas, *Vindicación*, sub-section Documentos, p.3, Número 1.

could, whenever it suited him, suppose it to be a higher authority than Cuesta and thus use its offices in an attempt to override some of Cuesta's orders during the course of the campaign, and it may have been via this device that the outcome of the campaign on the Tagus was eventually determined to the detriment of the allied cause. Venegas's supposition was strengthened by Cornel's regular use of the term 'S.M.' (*Su Majestad* – His Majesty) in his written correspondence, apparently to signify that the powers of the king, the highest in the land, were invested in him.

On the same day as he received Cornel's order above (14 July), Venegas was the recipient of a direct order from Cuesta to the effect that, so long as the number of French troops in La Mancha did not exceed 10,000, he should march on Madridejos whence, once all of his Divisions were concentrated at that place, he should advance on 17 or 18 July via Tembleque to Ocaña and Tarancón, such that he could push his vanguard on to Fuentidueña on the Tagus by 21 or 22 July, so long as the enemy's movements on the opposing bank of the river would allow it:

> (Cuesta to Venegas, 12 July 1809, *Número* 3):
> After receiving Your Excellency's letter of the 7th inst. I am aware that, as a consequence of the Intruder's movement from Madridejos towards Toledo and Talavera, together with the greater part of his force, you now have your cavalry at el Viso, Visillo and Santa Cruz, with your *campo volante* towards the Guadiana ...
>
> Should [the enemy] have less than 10,000 men, or so, in La Mancha, then it would be favourable to our cause if Your Excellency would advance with the whole of your force upon Madridejos, in the hope that it could concentrate there by the 17th or 18th inst., whence you should move on succeeding days via Tembleque to Ocaña and Tarancón, such that on the 21st or 22nd your vanguard or *campo volante* may advance to Fuentidueña on the Tagus, or even further to Arganda, in accordance with the information Your Excellency acquires of the enemy's movements along both banks of the said river. Should the British army and the army under my command commence their march towards Talavera on the 18th or 19th, then in the likelihood that the enemy simultaneously becomes aware of both our movement and Your Excellency's movement on Madrid from Madridejos, it would, at the very least, make him very uncomfortable in his position between the Tagus and the Alberche.[23]

No doubt, it was this order from Cuesta which caused Wellesley to suggest to Castlereagh on 24 July that Venegas would soon be at Madridejos.[24] However, Cuesta's stricture that his subordinate should avoid enemy formations of '10,000 men or so', would be put to use by Venegas as a convenient excuse never to take to the offensive, even when the need to do so clearly overrode this early note of caution from his chief. Besides his somewhat conspiratorial habit of copying his correspondence with Cuesta to Cornel, this was another ploy of

---

23   Cuesta to Venegas, 12 July 1809, Venegas, *Vindicación*, sub-section Documentos, p.4, Número 3.
24   Wellesley to Castlereagh, 24 July 1809, Gurwood (ed.), *Wellington's Dispatches*, vol.III, pp.368–369.

Venegas's which was to have an immediate and detrimental bearing on the allied campaign of 1809.

As suggested by Cuesta above, the overarching aim of the allies was that, with both himself and Wellesley commencing their joint advance on Talavera, a simultaneous move by Venegas towards Madrid from the south would prevent those enemy forces gathering between Santa Olalla and Toledo from concentrating against one or other of the allied armies. But in his *Vindicación* Venegas claimed that, even as Cuesta was writing his order of 12 July, as reproduced above, Sebastiani was on the Manchegans' immediate front with some 9,500 infantry, 2,500 cavalry and 18 guns, with a further 3,000 infantry at Consuegra and a strong garrison at Toledo; that is, a force considerably greater than 10,000 men, and therefore one to be avoided according to the stricture in Cuesta's order, notwithstanding the fact that the 'strong garrison at Toledo' actually comprised Joseph's retiring force, which was about to leave for Madrid, if it hadn't already done so. In fact, he initiated his return to the capital on 11 July, the day before Cuesta wrote his orders for Venegas's advance. Venegas's reaction to his superior's instructions was as follows:

> I cannot believe that [Cuesta] could judge it to be so easy and so certain that I could defeat Sebastiani; nor would it seem that there was any generosity of opinion or design in his asking me to attempt it, especially when one considers all of the precautions he himself was taking to avoid the enemy army he had in front of him …[25]

In his *Vindicación*, the commander in chief of the Manchegans then went on to invite the reader to ask themselves how he would have been judged had he complied with his orders and as a consequence suffered a severe beating, after having been warned by Cuesta himself not to attempt such an enterprise with the enemy present in strength before him, and having been ordered by the *Junta Suprema* only to 'call the enemy's attention towards himself,' whilst at the same time taking care not to place his army in danger.[26] Faced with this apparent dilemma, Venegas sought advice, or perhaps solace, from Cornel, writing to him on 15 July from his headquarters at Santa Cruz de Mudela in the northern foothills of the Sierra Morena. After making his own proposals for a more circumspect and limited forward movement than that demanded by Cuesta, using just two of his five divisions, he then posed a somewhat loaded question to the minister of war when he explained what his immediate superior was asking of him:

> (Venegas to Cornel, 15 July 1809, *Número* 4):
> But to advance on Madridejos, as indicated by *General* Cuesta, would result in a general action, and to advance to Tarancón and Fuentidueña before the combined Anglo-Spanish army had attacked Victor would expose me to the threat of being cut off by a combination of Victor's and Sebastiani's troops, making my retreat via Torrejoncillo, as proposed by *General* Cuesta, impossible … All of which would be

25   Venegas, *Vindicación*, pp.6–7.
26   Venegas, *Vindicación*, p.7.

in contradiction of His Majesty's orders that I should not put my army in danger. I place these considerations before Your Excellency so that you may issue me with definitive orders …[27]

This was an act of brazen insubordination, as well as a somewhat disingenuous assessment of Venegas's actual situation. Even if we take his figures as stated above to be accurate, Sebastiani's force immediately in front of the Army of La Mancha was no more than 12,000 strong, which was still of the order of the fairly arbitrary number set by Cuesta for preventing him from advancing. In such a situation, and with so much at stake, any commander worth his salt would have advanced. Venegas's refusal to do so, and instead play politics with Cornel, probably exposed a sinister trait in his character as well as a strong dislike of Cuesta. We should also note Venegas's use of the term 'His Majesty' when reminding Cornel of the orders he had earlier sent to him, hinting that he too could keep up the pretence that Fernando still held real and ultimate authority over the Spanish armed forces and that Cornel was simply his proxy. Somewhat rhetorically, Venegas went on to ask if Cuesta's idea of a combined allied offensive had been reduced to the proposition that the Manchegans should offer battle to Sebastiani. If so, he said, and they were victorious, then Cuesta would claim credit for the triumph, but if they were defeated he would waste no time in discrediting their commander in chief for his temerity in attacking a force much stronger than the 10,000-man limit he had imposed for such a move. Venegas then attempted to justify this allusion to malfeasance on the part of his superior, pointing to Cuesta's behaviour in the days immediately following the Battle of Talavera, which we shall examine later, and claiming it as proof that his commander in chief was determined to expose the Manchegans to danger with no intention of offering them the assistance demanded in the context of a truly combined military operation – remember that Venegas's *Vindicación* was written in retrospect of the Tagus campaign.

All of this chimed remarkably well with similar accusations made against Cuesta by Blake after the Battle of Rioseco, and one must wonder if Venegas knew of Blake's claims against the erstwhile *Capitán General* of Castilla-León at the time he wrote his *Vindicación*. In any case, the kind of adolescent reasoning employed in his argument, as expressed above, might tell us all we need to know of Venegas, and that he carried in his heart nothing but contempt for his commander in chief.

In essence he was committing an act of insubordination to his superior by challenging his order of 12 July that he advance on Sebastiani's forces, and inviting Cornel to support him in his actions. His refusal to obey his superior, and instead play politics with Cornel, probably exposed the arrogance of an overblown ego as well as a strong loathing of Cuesta. Returning to his *Vindicación*, one may see that the commander of the Manchegans went on to claim that, whilst awaiting a response from Cornel to his query about whether or not he should comply with Cuesta's orders to march on Fuentidueña or Arganda, he consulted with three of his divisional commanders: Lacy (1st), Vigodet (2nd) and Girón (3rd) about the possibility of them making a partial attack against the right or left flank of the enemy line which, he thought, would assist the allies' main attack at Talavera. All of them, he said,

---

27   Venegas to Cornel, 15 July 1809, Venegas, *Vindicación*, sub-section Documentos, p.5, Número 4.

demurred, claiming that it would result in a general action against superior enemy forces.[28] But surely the whole point of military hierarchies is that orders are passed down from above, not to be discussed and disputed, but to be obeyed.

Eventually, Venegas's worries about being asked to mount what he considered to be a premature move against Sebastiani were assuaged by Cornel's response to his letter of 15 July (see *Número* 4 above) in which the minister supported all of the reservations expressed by him about Cuesta's instruction that he advance on Fuentidueña and Arganda. All of which tended to confirm that the rift which had occurred between Cuesta and the *Junta* after the Valdés affair was far from healed, and that the *Junta*, still contemptuous of the old warrior, was willing to intervene in what were purely military matters by countermanding Cuesta's orders when they saw fit:

> (Cornel to Venegas, 17 July 1809, *Número* 8):
> The *Junta Suprema* ... having been made aware of the order communicated to you by ... Gregorio de la Cuesta, and of the reflections about it expressed in your reserved correspondence of the 15th inst. regarding the risks which your army will run by advancing towards Ocaña and Tarancón ... has resolved that ... Your excellency should advance to Madridejos, but that before continuing your advance you will require positive notice that *General* Cuesta's advance [towards Talavera and Madrid] continues and that the enemy's strength has not increased to a size which would expose you to the need of having to make a dangerous withdrawal ...[29]

Venegas replied to Cornel two days later as follows:

> (Venegas to Cornel, 19 July 1809, *Número* 9):
> I have received your royal order of the 17th inst. by which you commanded me to advance to Madridejos, but not to go any further until I have received notice that the general in chief, with who I am to remain in contact at the greatest possible frequency, is advancing; and that I must first be certain that the enemy has received no reinforcement to such an extent that I will be exposed to making a dangerous retreat before being able to take up a position favourable for defence. In my advance to Mardidejos, and in any subsequent movement, I must be guided by circumstances in all of my operations.[30]

Cornel's outrageous interference did not stop here. In a second letter written by Venegas to Cornel on 17 July, he informed the minister of the conference he had held with his divisional commanders, at which they agreed amongst themselves what they thought would be a better strategy than that decided upon by their commander in chief:

---

28   Venegas to Cornel, 17 July 1809, Venegas, *Vindicación*, sub-section Documentos, pp.6–7, Número 6.
29   Cornel to Venegas, 17 July 1809, Venegas, *Vindicación*, sub-section Documentos, p.8, Número 8.
30   Venegas to Cornel, 19 July 1809, Venegas, *Vindicación*, sub-section Documentos, pp.8–9, Número 9.

(Venegas to Cornel, 17 July 1809, *Número* 6):
I have made the journey to Manzanares, which I announced to you last night, and having deliberated with my commanders … about my project to attack the enemy's right flank at Villarubia using my 1st and 3rd Divisions with the 2nd and 4th in support … all of them have opined that, in view of the news that the enemy has received of our recent movements and positions, it is indispensable that the attack be general in its nature, which goes *en contra* to the plan currently under consideration.[31]

To which Cornel replied, praising Venegas for his military acumen and telling him, more or less, to do as he pleased as commander in chief of the Army of La Mancha. It was a travesty of military command protocol:

(Cornel to Venegas, 19 July 1809, *Número* 7):
The *Junta Suprema* … having been made aware of Your Excellency's correspondence of the 17 inst. informing it that, after corroborating with your senior officers that it would be advantageous for the allies to attack in a general action … and His Majesty, considering that Your Excellency will [by now] have received advice from *General* Cuesta confirming that on the morning of 20 July the whole of the combined army will be moving on Talavera, now believes that your thoughts could prove very useful and should govern your operations.[32]

There is one more detail over which to mull with respect to what amounted to a case of insubordination on the part of a senior Spanish officer, an act endorsed by Cornel, no less, and in doing so the reader may discern more than just a hint of Venegas's basic disingenuousness. It is that, after reading Cuesta's orders of the 12 July that he advance (they arrived on 14 July) he rushed his letter of complaint off to Cornel on the 15th (see *Número* 4 above). However, his superior had instructed him to concentrate his forces on 17 or 18 July. Had he begun his movement towards the point of concentration on the 15th, then by the time he was approaching Madridejos, both Wellesley and Cuesta would have been stirring on Victor's front – according to what Cuesta had told him in his orders (in fact, by 20 July, the two allied commanders to the west of Madrid had only got as far as uniting their forces at Oropesa). Had he been genuinely committed to Cuesta's plans, Venegas could have engineered an element of slip in his operational timetable in order to achieve the simultaneity of movement desired – had he known, day-to-day, the situation with his chief. That being the case he could have voiced his concerns to Cuesta and insisted upon a resynchronisation of movement between the allied forces. Of course, the existence of a swift and reliable system of communications would have to be a prerequisite to have afforded all three allied commanders the degree of coordination required for such intricate timing. Sadly, Cuesta's whole plan fell way outside the bounds of feasibility for such a system to have come into operation; the distance between himself at or around Oropesa, and Venegas at Santa Cruz

---

31   Venegas to Cornel, 17 July 1809, Venegas, *Vindicación*, sub-section Documentos, pp.6–7, Número 6.
32   Cornel to Venegas, 19 July 1809, Venegas, *Vindicación*, sub-section Documentos, pp.7–8, Número 7.

de Mudela, being some 175 miles. In terms of time, it would take at least three days for an efficient courier system to cover such a distance – some five or six for the return journey; a recipe for disaster.

On 14 and 15 July, Venegas moved his divisions forward as follows: the 1st to Manzanares – before being ordered to make a diversion towards Daimiel in response to a message received from Cornel dated 12 July (see *Número* 1 above), the minister having been informed by Cuesta of a recent movement made by *Maréchal* Victor towards the bridge at Arzobispo in combination with another towards Oropesa, both of which seeming to indicate that he was about to attack *Teniente General* Eguía near Mesas de Ibor. As such, the minister suggested to Venegas that a move by the Manchegans towards Daimiel might be a way of diverting French attention towards that quarter and away from the Army of Extremadura. In response, Venegas's 2nd Division was ordered to move to La Solana in support of the 1st with that idea in mind. The 3rd Division was ordered to Manzanares and the 4th to remain where it was at Santa Cruz.[33]

By 17 July, Cornel had informed Venegas that Cuesta's recent concerns about a possible attack on Eguía had diminished, Victor's apparent movement to the south bank of the Tagus having turned out to be only that of a cattle-raiding expedition, which ended in the disappearance of the French back to the north bank of the river along with their booty of captured livestock. As he dallied south of the Guadiana, intelligence about the enemy's strength and location kept coming into Venegas's headquarters from the *partidas de guerrilla* attached to the various divisions of his army. Ordinary citizens of ability and nerve were also willing to help, and on 17 July one Francisco Sepúlveda returned from a self-initiated spying mission encompassing 13, 14 and 15 July, to provide the general with a detailed breakdown of the size and location of Sebastiani's forces on his immediate front, which can be seen in Table 1.

Table 1. Estimate of French strength and location as submitted by Francisco Sepúlveda on 17 July 1809. The figures in the 'Carts' column are those as presented by Sepúlveda.[34]

Location	Infantry	Cavalry	Artillery	Carts
Alcázar de San Juan		680	2	2
Herencia		200		
Madrilejos	3,000	50	8	16
Consuegra	2,000	30	Unknown	
Camuñas	700	85		
Puerto Lapice		300		
Villafranca	3,000	25	8	
Villarrubia	700	1,200		
	9,400	2,570	18	26

---

33   Cornel to Venegas, 12 July 1809, Venegas, *Vindicación*, sub-section Documentos, p.3, *Número* 1. See also, AHN: Diversas Colecciones, 125, N.5: el Ejército de La Mancha, entry for 14 July 1809.
34   In his table, Sepúlveda writes 'Madrilejos' instead of Madridejos. He has also added up the figures in the final column incorrectly.

All of the places mentioned in Sepúlveda's report lie north of the Guadiana-Cigüela system. Conveniently for Venegas, the sum total of his obviously rounded figures for infantry and cavalry came to 11,970; just enough for him to justify his refusal to attack them, despite the urgency of his superior's pleading that he do so.

A Narrow Escape for Venegas and his Divsional Commanders

After receiving further local intelligence which suggested that Sepúlveda's estimate of French strength was a little on the high side, and that their forces at Villafranca, Herencia, Alcázar, Villarrubia and Consuegra (in essence the same units mentioned by Sepúlveda) were in fact no stronger than 8,000 infantry and 2,000 cavalry, Venegas decided that it was time to call his senior officers together to discuss the situation – this was to be the conference at Manzanares already mentioned above. On 17 July, whilst chairing the meeting with his 1st, 2nd and 3rd divisional commanders, together with his chiefs of the artillery and engineers, a party of some 200 French cavalry approached the nearby settlement of Daimiel, entirely ignorant of what was taking place just 10 miles away. Venegas, thorough as usual, had moved some of his units into positions around Manzanares before the conference commenced. But the French were also careful in their habits, sending forward a party of about 12 men to ensure that it was safe for their comrades to follow, and when they caught sight of the Spanish pickets they fled. They were soon caught up with, and in the running fight which ensued one French trooper was killed, one wounded and a third taken prisoner along with two horses. When questioned, the two survivors said they belonged to a unit of the Westphalian cavalry based at Villarrubia.

The Spanish conference seemingly ran to its natural conclusion despite the near-interruption and, as we know, the recommendation of the meeting at Manzanares was that it was not possible for the Army of La Mancha to mount an attack upon either of Sebastiani's flanks without it being part of a general engagement; a decision later endorsed by the *Junta Suprema*. As such, Venegas requested that the *Junta* furnish him with clear and unequivocal instructions under which to continue his campaign. Significantly, both Venegas and Seville seemed to have forgotten the latest intelligence they had received, which suggested there were no more than 10,000 French in front of the Manchegans, exactly the no advance limit suggested by Cuesta in his letter of 12 July (see *Número* 3 above) which meant that Venegas could have used his discretion in deciding whether or not to advance.

It was on the evening of 17 July that Venegas wrote to Cornel informing him of the outcome of his conference (see *Número* 6 above) which was that he and his generals had decided that it would be:

> ... absolutely impossible to attack either the left or the right of the enemy without exposing [the Army of La Mancha] to a general action, and as this was something prohibited by the government, we asked the general in chief for final instructions ... In response, Cuesta expressed his confidence in the prospects for success, due to the disposition of the divisional commanders and their troops, but added that, as it was always very difficult to make a successful retirement in the wake of suffering some misfortune, he had decided to defer to His Majesty for his sovereign

determination, suggesting to him that, to assure [the success of any] retreat to the [pre-designated points in the] Sierra Morena, should it be necessary to make one, the troops belonging to the Army of Reserve could be brought forward to augment the weak garrisons [at the said points] ...[35]

Of course, for the Spaniards, 'His Majesty' was Fernando VII, who was at that time languishing in confinement in France by order of Napoleon, which meant that the authority of 'His Majesty' temporarily resided with the president of the *Junta Suprema*. The person occupying that position at this time was the Marqués de Astorga.

On 19 July, after having remained idle for some 10 days in close proximity to the safety afforded by the nearby mountains to the south, Venegas sent out several *partidas de guerrilla* towards the towns and villages on the north bank of the Guadiana known to be held by the French. As their reports came in to headquarters later in the day, it was apparent that Sebastiani's units were still concentrated at or near Madridejos, some 20 miles north of the Guadiana, with all the appearance that they were about to retire to the Tagus and beyond. That evening, despite what had been said about the possibilities of a resulting retreat, the commander of the Manchegans received a royal order from Seville instructing him to move forward to Madridejos, where he should halt until the *Junta* had received news of Cuesta's activities on the Tagus. Perhaps Cuesta's approach to 'His Majesty', as mentioned by Venegas above, was about to produce the desired effect. As usual, the latter imposed his own safety-first regime on the manner in which he carried out the order, instructing *Brigadier* Castejón to advance with his 4th Division from Santa Cruz to Membrilla whilst he awaited the latest intelligence about the situation in Madridejos, all the time keeping Cornel advised of his actions. At this point in proceedings some alarming news arrived from Valdepeñas, telling of a dangerous contagion which was sweeping through the town's population. In the absence of any civil assistance, Venegas ordered that his *Jefe de Medicina* (Chief of Medicine) Juan Manuel de Arepila, remain in the town until he had put in place a regime of treatment and containment for the disease, after which he returned to the army, leaving a doctor and pharmacist on hand to continue with the restorative programme prescribed.[36]

Sebastiani Withdraws but Venegas Refuses to Follow

Now, if ever, was the time for Venegas to spring into action and advance determinedly to the Tagus if the allies' plan was to succeed. He had already wasted 10 hugely important days since recommencing his advance, by hiding from difficulties which in reality did not exist. At midnight on 19 July, he finally set in motion his own proposed but limited advance on Madridejos, occupying a line connecting Membrilla, La Solana, Manzanares and Daimiel, still all places on the south bank of the Guadiana. His 5th Division (Zerain) was at Ciudad Real and his *partidas de guerrilla* were occupying various advanced posts.

---

35   AHN: Diversas Colecciones, 125, N.5: el Ejército de La Mancha, entry for 17 July 1809.
36   AHN: Diversas Colecciones, 125, N.5: el Ejército de La Mancha, entry for 19 July 1809.

According to the commander of the Manchegans, it was at about this time that Sebastiani made a tactical retreat towards Madridejos from Villarrubia and Alcázar de San Juan, with two objectives in mind. The first being that of shortening the distance between Victor's left flank and his own right flank which, if accomplished as hoped for, would allow the French much more freedom to decide which of the allied armies to bring to battle. That done, the selected army would be attacked and defeated whilst the other was held in place until the full force of the French could be brought to bear upon it and defeat it in turn. The second thought in Sebastiani's mind, as imagined by Venegas, was that of enticing the Army of La Mancha to cross the Guadiana and the Tagus in pursuit. Should he (Venegas) take the bait then the Frenchman would launch a counter attack to pin the Spaniards against either of those rivers and destroy them. At this point in his Vindicación Venegas reminds his readers that, both the orders of the *Junta Suprema* not to engage with the enemy, and Cuesta's instructions not to take on any enemy force composed of more than 10,000 men, still obliged him to remain on his present ground to the south of the Guadiana; Sebastiani's combined force, he claimed, amounting to some 22,000 men according to a dispatch he had received from *Brigadier* Vigodet.

Divisions	Men
Général de Brigade Rei	5,000
Alemana	7,000
Polaca	6,000
Caballería	4,000
Total	22,000[37]

The dispatch also made reference to some intelligence he in turn had received from a Don Miguel Rosales, commander of a local guerrilla force.[38] At that, yet another golden opportunity to disrupt the French was about to be allowed to slip away.

By the time Venegas saw these figures, *circa* 19 July, Joseph had already left Toledo for Madrid some eight days earlier, which meant that the numbers of French between him and the capital actually amounted to Liger-Belair's 1st Division of about 8,000, Valence's 2nd Division comprising 1,600 Polish cavalry, Leval's 3rd Division of some 4,500 Germans and Merlin's 1,200-strong cavalry brigade: in other words the whole 15,500 men of Sebastiani's IV Corps, rather than the 22,000 claimed by Rosales. Happy to seize upon the guerrilla leader's dubious numbers, Venegas claimed that, 'It would have been stupid to have attacked an army of 22,000, whose cavalry and artillery alone outnumbered the sum total of my own force,' before adding that the French force at Talavera, thus weakened by this significant detachment apparently facing him, just as was hoped for in the allied plan, fully justified his assertions that Wellesley and Cuesta could now attack Victor's 40,000 men with numerical

---

37   Venegas, *Vindicación*, p.11. *Général de Brigade* Rei: Most probably Jean Pierre Antoine Rey's brigade of infantry, part of Sebastiani's 1st Division commanded by *Général de brigade* Liger-Belair. Alemana: Most likely Leval's German division. Polaca: Apparently Valence's Polish cavalry division. If so, its strength should have been listed at about 1,600. Caballería: Probably Merlin's cavalry brigade.

38   Venegas, *Vindicación*, p.9.

advantage, and under far less risk of suffering a reverse than that which would be run by the Manchegans should they continue to advance.[39]

Flushed with the *Junta's* endorsement of his refusal to attack Sebastiani's units lying between the Guadiana and Tagus, Venegas could not resist taking another sarcastic swipe at Cuesta:

> Fully demonstrated the solid foundations and reasons for my refusal to chance my luck in a battle, it is worthwhile repeating the difficulties of the advance, some might say the dash to Arganda, as proposed by *General* Cuesta, only to be followed by the retirement via some form of magic or flight required to return me to the *sierra* from Torrejoncillo and San Clemente, all of which would be aided by the rugged terrain of the mountains which, in truth and as far as I know, do not exist; and always by roads which crossed nothing but flat, open plains, [as though it were] no mean disadvantage when pursued by 4,000 French cavalry.[40]
>
> And who could imagine that, in the inconceivable case that the enemy would have opened the way for me and allowed me to advance to Fuentidueña or Arganda, he would not then have concentrated there a considerable army composed of Sebastiani's troops and a large detachment from Victor's forces? Having done so, would I have been allowed the luxury to retire via Torrejoncillo to the strongholds in the *sierra*; that is, to march without being attacked for some 30 or 40 leagues across some of the flattest lands on the peninsula?
>
> ... *General* Cuesta, hallucinated by his ideal plan, took no regard of French intentions to give themselves the option of allowing Victor to reinforce Sebastiani or vice-versa, according to circumstances. And in his blindness to the difficulties and dangers of the movements and operations he advised me to execute, he was attempting to turn me into another Don Quijote who launched himself, without plan or purpose, at the windmills of the province in which he was forced to operate. Any circumspection on my part deserving only of the epithets of ignorance, ineptitude, malice and envy.[41]

Such was the attitude of Cuesta's immediate subordinate.

The Junta Suprema Finally Orders Venegas to Advance

From what has gone before it would seem that, as far as Venegas was concerned, he was fully complying with the orders he had received from the *Junta Suprema* by simply calling the attention of the enemy's advanced posts towards the Army of La Mancha along the whole

---

39   Venegas, *Vindicación*, p.11.
40   One can only surmise that Cuesta must have been suggesting that Venegas, if forced to retire, should head in an easterly direction, via Torrejoncillo del Rey, towards the mountains of Cuenca, or in a south-easterly direction via San Clemente in the province of Cuenca. Both routes may have offered him more protection from the French cavalry, but would have taken him far away from Wellesley and Cuesta.
41   Venegas, *Vindicación*, p.12.

length of its line, just south of the Guadiana, his guerrillas being in continuous contact with the French. This is the way things remained on Venegas's front until 24 July, by which time Wellesley and Cuesta had been in contact with Victor on the Alberche for a day or two, meaning that the commander of the Manchegans had thrown away the chance of the allies applying two simultaneous if distant pressure points upon French resources.

On 20 July, Venegas received intelligence of fresh French movements on the Tagus directly south of Madrid, as well as others on the north bank of the Guadiana, all to the effect that the enemy garrison at Toledo had been reinforced by the arrival of some 3,000 infantry, and that a further five regiments of French infantry, along with some cavalry and eight cannon, had arrived at Mora, just 20 miles north-west of Madridejos, which was still the intended destination for the Army of La Mancha's long delayed advance, the almost inevitable reaction to which being Venegas's decision to suspend his march upon that place.[42] Once again, it would seem that Venegas's prudence, not to say devilry, had been rewarded.[43] But then Lacy, at Daimiel with the 1st Division whilst his guerrillas were operating on the north bank of the Guadiana, sent news that the French force recently arrived at Villarrubia, just a few miles up the road from him, had since retired northwards; and on questioning the town's mayor, the commander of the *partida* was told that the French detail consisted only of some 600 cavalry; there was no mention of infantry or artillery, all of which suggested that this particular group of horsemen was part of a foraging or scouting party. At this point, one can sense from the hesitancy of his movements that Venegas was still shadow boxing, apparently waiting for a safe opportunity before advancing towards the Tagus, but the question is, was he being over-cautious or duplicitous in his intentions, thus putting the whole of the allied campaign at risk of failure?

It was on 21 July 1809 that Venegas received Cornel's message of the 19th informing him implicitly that the *Junta Suprema* had decided it was finally time for him to launch an attack upon the enemy; confirming that Cuesta and Wellesley would launch an attack on Victor on 20 July, unless prevailing circumstances at the time provided good enough reason to suspended it (see *Número 7* above). This implies that Cornel's orders were written prior to 20 July. It was, in effect, a royal order – and taken as such by Venegas. In other words, with Wellesley and Cuesta in motion, Venegas could now partake in the general offensive he had been agitating for, by advancing beyond the Guadiana, but would he comply?

A note of the arrival of Cornel's order at Venegas's headquarters was made in his campaign diary entry for 21 July, the diarist going on to add, somewhat ironically, that Venegas then replied to the *Junta* demanding that the general action be suspended.

In his [royal] order of the 19th, the minister of war informed [*Teniente General* Venegas] of the approbation by the *Junta Suprema* of the plan to attack the enemy via a general action, and confirmed to him that the combined army would commence

---

42   Oman, *History of the Peninsular War*, vol.II, p.499. In fact, a 3,000-strong brigade of Dessolles' division was added to the 1,000 or so Spanish troops enlisted with the French who made up the town garrison at the time. See also, AHN: Diversas Colecciones, 125, N.5: el Ejército de La Mancha, entry for 20 July 1809.

43   AHN: Diversas Colecciones, 125, N.5: el Ejército de La Mancha, entry for 21 July 1809.

its movement on the 20th, unless an unforeseen change of circumstances called for the suspension of its execution.

A reply to the royal order was sent, informing [the *Junta*] that, as circumstances had changed [since Venegas's dispatch of the 17th to Cornel] the movement [required of him] should be suspended, as the task of calling the attention of the enemy [towards the Army of La Mancha] had now succeeded, as evidenced by [the arrival] in Mora of five infantry regiments, together with some cavalry from Toledo.[44]

Incredibly, Venegas was now openly questioning Cornel's direct orders, and in doing so further compromising the chances of an allied victory on the Tagus in the summer of 1809.

It would seem that the French units mentioned by Venegas above were those noted by the diarist on the 20th, when he recorded that the commander of the Manchegans had reacted to their appearance in Mora by ordering the suspension of his own movement on Villarubia, a place he judged to be too close to the French presence in Mora, thus risking the chance that his 1st and 3rd Divisions might run into the enemy. The diarist went on to note that Venegas, rather than advancing, was in the act of concentrating his divisions in readiness to receive the French, and that he had sent notice of their movement to Cuesta as proof that Victor's forces in front of both him and Wellesley had been diminished, the relevant dispatch being that of 21 July which Venegas wrote whilst at his headquarters at Membrilla:

> (Venegas to Cuesta, 21 July 1809, Número 10):
> Sebastiani's army in my front … is composed of 12 to 13,000 men of all arms, and has just been reinforced by five regiments of infantry, some cavalry, 8 pieces of artillery and 25 carts of munitions from Toledo, all having entered Mora at one in the morning on the 19th. This news has determined me to maintain my line connecting Daimiel, Membrilla and La Solana, along which, with my divisions well concentrated, I am sure that I may repulse the enemy if I am attacked, leaving him with the disadvantage of having the rivers Guadiana and Cigüela in his rear, with all the difficulty of having to cross them should we be victorious.
>
> In executing this plan I shall be fulfilling my principal objective of attracting the attention of the enemy which, as a result, will diminish the size of his army in your front; and if, as an effect of the movements being executed by the combined Anglo-Spanish army, the enemy alters his [movements] with respect to the forces in my front, thus offering me the opportunity of advancing against him, I will take advantage of it, bearing in mind the details of your own operations as described to me.[45]

On the same day, and in a similar vein, Venegas wrote to Cornel repeating the details of the first paragraph of his dispatch to Cuesta above, before going on to say:

> (Venegas to Cornel, 21 July 1809, Número 14):

---

44   AHN: Diversas Colecciones, 125, N.5: el Ejército de La Mancha, entry for 21 July 1809.
45   Venegas to Cuesta, 21 July 1809, Venegas, *Vindicación*, sub-section Documentos, p.9, Número 10.

Due to the arrival of his reinforcements, the enemy has re-occupied his old positions at Herencia and Alcázar de San Juan [both on the north bank of the Guadiana]
and although I have prepared orders for an advance to Villarta, Arenas [de San
Juan] and Villarubia [all on the banks of the Cigüela] I have decided not to issue
them, as I am now resolved to remain in [in my current positions of Daimiel, La
Solana, Manzanares and Membrilla]. This will mean that, should the French decide
to attack me, they will suffer the disadvantage of having the rivers [Guadiana and
Cigüela] in their rear. Zerain is in the act of bringing his division to reinforce Lacy
at Daimiel.[46]

Here we have solid proof not just of Venegas's tendency for procrastination, but of his dere-
liction of duty in refusing to obey a direct order as issued by the *Junta Suprema* on 19 July
(see *Número* 7 above) just as he had done on receiving Cuesta's order of 12 July (see *Número*
3 above).

His uneasiness about what he was being asked to do was clear in both his dispatches to
Cuesta and Cornel of 21 July (see *Números* 10 and 14 above) and in his diary entry for the
same date, when, in effect, he suggested to Cornel that he had already completed the basic
task required of him during the campaign: that of keeping the French forces divided, and
as a result the intended movement of his corps in unison with that of Wellesley and Cuesta
should be suspended. In fact, he went on, his divisions had been united precisely to receive
an attack from enemy forces, whose presence on the Guadiana bore witness to a diminution
in the strength of Victor's army, all of which, he claimed, had been directly communicated
to Cuesta. In truth, the French units referred to by Venegas in his dispatch to Cuesta of 21
July were almost certainly those belonging to Sebastiani's 3rd Division and Merlin's corps
of cavalry earlier mentioned, Venegas seemingly quite happy to give the impression that
Victor had reduced the strength of his own forces in order to reinforce Sebastiani, rather
than having simply returned to Sebastiani what was Sebastiani's.

When reading his campaign diary at this point, it is easy to discern that Venegas thought
he could see the hand of Cuesta at work when reading between the lines of Cornel's dispatch
of 19 July (see *Número* 7 above) which implied that it was now finally the time for the
Manchegans to advance on the Tagus. Having ignored his chief's direct orders that he make
an immediate frontal attack on Sebastiani,[47] Venegas was convinced that Cuesta had then
approached the *Junta Suprema* and pressed for its members to re-issue his orders of the
12th (see *Número* 3 above). If true, it would explain Cornel's intervention of the 19th (see
Número 7 above) by which he asked, more forcefully than Cuesta, that Venegas advance on
Sebastiani in concert with the combined army's movements,[48] but on receiving Cornel's
instructions, the commander of the Manchegans decided to let his feelings be known in no
uncertain fashion when he noted: '… the project has no solid basis, due to the difficulties
involved in its realisation and the extravagance and fatuity displayed by its author'.[49]

---

46 Venegas to Cornel, 21 July 1809, Venegas, *Vindicación*, sub-section Documentos, pp.12–13, Número 14.
47 See his reasoning for his insubordination to Cuesta in his dispatch to Cornel (Venegas to Cornel, 15
    July, *Número* 4) and see Cuesta's order, (Cuesta to Venegas 12 July, *Número* 3), both above.
48 Cornel to Venegas, 19 July 1809, Venegas, *Vindicación*, sub-section Documentos, pp.7–8, Número 7.
49 AHN: Diversas Colecciones, 125, N.5: el Ejército de La Mancha, entry for 21 July 1809.

On 22 July, as if to confirm Venegas's assertions that his presence on the Guadiana had forced Victor to send reinforcements to Sebastiani, Lacy sent details of intelligence extracted from a French deserter who had been stationed at Mora, some 10 miles south of Toledo, which stated that there were no fewer than nine infantry regiments camped at the town, as well as some Polish cavalry; the latter having just received orders to march for Toledo.[50] The deserter's story would seem to have been supported by a Spanish escapee from the castle at Consuegra, some 12 miles south of Mora, who claimed that there were some 7,000 French infantry in the town together with an accompaniment of cavalry. The two stories almost certainly bore witness to the concentration at both Mora and Consuegra, not of fresh reinforcements sent by Victor, as asserted by Venegas, but of the bulk of Sebastiani's IV Corps which, it would seem, was making its way to Toledo before departing for Talavera. On the same day, 22 July, more such intelligence came from Grimarest, commander of Venegas's 3rd Division, when he reported that some 7 or 8,000 of the enemy were in the vicinity of Villafranca, Madridejos, Consuegra and Puerto Lápice, all of it providing Venegas with some justification for his reticence to comply with his orders to make an immediate attack upon the enemy as part of the purported general action by the allied armies, despite the fact that Lacy's French deserter had added that by 22 July the French force had commenced its march towards Toledo, making it clear that they were marching away from Venegas and towards Cuesta, rather than the opposite as claimed by Venegas.

As things were coming to a head, news continued to flow into Venegas's headquarters, including notice that his 5th Division, absent for so long under the command of Zerain, had finally re-joined the army at Daimiel on the 22nd.

It was at this point, whilst Venegas continued to stall, that the allied plan for concerted action against the French on the Tagus began to fall apart. By all means Venegas was right to be cautious in the face of the French and not attempt a suicidal advance against a far superior enemy, but the intelligence he was receiving between 20 and 22 July strongly suggested that Sebastiani had already commenced his move towards Victor at Talavera, and that the troop movements reported to him, rather than depicting a strengthening of Sebastiani's IV Corps in his front, actually represented the first preparatory movements by the Frenchman for his relocation to Talavera. If there had been a perfect moment for the allied plan to begin to bear fruit then surely this was it. Had Venegas begun his advance towards Toledo and Aranjuez on or about 22 July, Sebastiani would have been caught in two minds about whether to reinforce Victor at Talavera or remain in place to the south of Madrid. Whether through fear or malice, Venegas failed to comply with his orders from Cuesta until it was too late, leaving both his superior and Wellesley to face a foe which was some 15,000 stronger than it otherwise would have been had he done his duty. Instead, he had been hanging around in the territory south of the Guadiana between 9 and 24 July, latterly claiming that it was too dangerous to attack what was in truth only an observational force left on the north bank of the Guadiana by Sebastiani after he had led the bulk of IV Corps to Victor's aid.

50   AHN: Diversas Colecciones, 125, N.5: el Ejército de La Mancha, entry for 22 July 1809.

Venegas Finally Decides to Cross the Guadiana

On 23 July there was more news from Lacy at Daimiel, whose scouts were then well advanced at Puerto Lápice which lies just north of both the Guadiana and the Cigüela and a short distance to the south of Consuegra. In his dispatch he reported that no enemy forces were to be seen in that direction; however, he included the disturbing news that the corpses of three enemy soldiers had been discovered in an olive grove near Villarrubia. Apparently the victims of some members of the local populace, they had been beaten and stoned to death. Ironically, just before this gruesome discovery, Lacy's patrol had taken charge of a dozen or so German deserters from the French army, all of whom had been happy to put their signatures to a propaganda leaflet encouraging their comrades to come over to the allied side. As this kind of thing was a tactic in common use at the time, it reinforced the feeling amongst the Spanish high command that something had to be done to prevent such atrocities as had just been reported, otherwise their enticements to the enemy would prove fruitless. Lacy therefore sent out strict orders to the authorities at Fuente del Fresno and Malagón, both lying within the neighbourhood of Villarrubia, threatening severe punishment on the local justices if they did nothing to halt 'such excesses so contrary to the public cause.'[51]

Meanwhile, despite all the concerns expressed by Venegas with respect to Cuesta's promptings that he launch an attack on Sebastiani, on the morning of 24 July the commander of the Manchegans finally issued a general order that his army be put in motion at dawn on the following day. The 1st Division was to move to Villarrubia with orders to move on to Las Labores should there be no sign of the enemy at Consuegra or Madridejos; the 2nd Division was to advance to Herencia; the 3rd to Villarta, the 4th to La Casa de Magara and the 5th to Arenas de San Juan, all places lying on the banks of the Cigüela, a tributary which in that region flows from north-east to south-west towards its confluence with the Guadiana. Army headquarters remained at Daimiel on the south bank of the Guadiana. By this time, the French high command would have been fully aware of the imminence of a general action at or near Talavera, not least because of Cuesta's advance to Santa Olalla and beyond on the 24th. As such, it would seem that they had decided to shorten their line in front of Madrid by drawing Sebastiani's right flank in towards Victor's left flank, at that time close to Bargas and the capital (see Plate 19) so that the former could consolidate the small holding force he was about to station along the north bank of the Tagus, thus allowing him to take the bulk of his army to Talavera.[52] In fact, the French general ultimately decided to leave behind just 4,000 men at Toledo, taking with him some 15,000 to reinforce Victor, a force which in itself was not too far short in numerical terms than that commanded by Wellesley. Despite the fact that the French were now nowhere to be seen as his divisions advanced from the Guadiana at a somewhat leisurely pace, Venegas still refused to countenance a determined move against Sebastiani's skeleton force now in front of Madrid, as such he had clearly failed in his main mission by allowing Sebastiani to slip away and make his presence felt at Talavera.

---

51   AHN: Diversas Colecciones, 125, N.5: el Ejército de La Mancha, entry for 23 July 1809.
52   AHN: Diversas Colecciones, 125, N.5: el Ejército de La Mancha, entry for 24 July 1809.

If there had been any excuse for the slowness of Venegas's advance to the Guadiana from the area in and around Santa Cruz de Mudela and Valdepeñas, it would likely rest on the fact that his cavalry was much inferior to that of the French. Knowing this, Sebastiani maintained a screen of his horsemen across the Spaniard's line of advance, through which their Spanish counterparts dared not venture, thus leaving their chief almost completely blind to the Frenchman's movements as he led the bulk of his force towards Toledo, before uniting with *Maréchal* Victor. In the words of *Brigadier* Girón, commander of Venegas's 3rd Division:

> I remained in Manzanares until the evening of the 24th [July] when I marched for Villarta [de San Juan] preceded by the cavalry.
> The enemy was not present in great force in La Mancha and had little intention of launching any operations there, but they retired slowly, manoeuvring in such a way as to slow our advance as much as possible. By this time, threatened by the Spanish and English armies from the direction of Extremadura, they could not mount a formal resistance in La Mancha. As such, it could be said that Venegas did not advance with enough determination to assist the operations of Wellesley and Cuesta as agreed.[53]

Something of an understatement, perhaps.

Venegas Complains of a Lack of Communication from Cuesta

It was during the middle fortnight of July that Venegas had complained bitterly of Cuesta's lack of communication and direction at such an important juncture of the campaign, saying that he had heard nothing from him since 12 July. By the 25th he was claiming that he was in complete ignorance of his chief's movements and thus unable to coordinate his own manoeuvres with those of the combined Anglo-Spanish army, leaving him unsure whether to direct his advance towards Toledo or Madrid. In desperation whilst at his headquarters in Herencia on 26 July, he sent *Coronel* Cebrián to Cuesta's headquarters with the following dispatch containing a summary of the intelligence he had just received, and a request for instructions on how he should proceed:

> (Venegas to Cuesta, 26 July 1809, *Número* 11):
> At five in the morning on the 23rd, the enemy began to move from their positions at Consuegra, Camuñas, Villafranca, Alcázar [de San Juan], Herencia and Villarrubia, some of them marching for Mora, others for Tembleque, all of the former places being completely evacuated by the evening of the 24th. His [original] force, when added to that which came down from Toledo, some 15 or 16,000 men of all arms, I would judge to be about 22,000. Of these, so my *confidents* assure me,

---

53   Juan Sañudo and Leopoldo Stampa, *La Crisis de una Alianza* (Madrid: Ministerio de Defensa, 1996), p.196.

some 14,000 infantry and 3,000 cavalry have gone to Toledo, the remaining 4,000 infantry and 1,000 cavalry having taken the road to Tembleque.[54]

It would appear from this that, as late as the eve of Talavera, Venegas was still attempting to convince his superior that Victor had sent some considerable resources to reinforce Sebastiani in his front, disingenuously failing to concede that these units represented a return to Sebastiani of his 3rd Division and Merlin's cavalry brigade. As we have seen, with these two units, plus his 1st and 2nd Divisions, Sebastiani actually took some 15,500 of his own men to Talavera, almost the whole of his force, leaving just a covering detachment at Toledo, and it was at about this time that King Joseph began his march from Madrid to Talavera, via Toledo, with the force he had earlier used to reinforce Sebastiani. At this point, Venegas sent word to Cuesta of his own movements in response to those of the enemy, explaining that he felt his divisions were now well placed to allow him to make a move either to his right, towards Aranjuez, or to his left towards Toledo, as he explained to Cuesta in his dispatch of 26 July: …

(Venegas to Cuesta, 26 July 1809, *Número* 11):
As soon as I became aware of this news [Sebastiani's withdrawal from the Guadiana] I ordered the five divisions of my army … to advance towards the Cigüela and afterwards to the following locations: 1st Division or vanguard to Turleque, the 2nd to Camuñas, the 3rd to Consuegra, the 4th, 5th and headquarters to Madridejos. This will allow me to continue my movement to the right, or head for Toledo, depending upon the news I receive of the movements and advantages gained by Your Excellency's army. All of this I communicate to Your Excellency for your intelligence; and with the aim that, with Your Excellency fully aware of my own situation, [you] may provide me with your orders and instructions so that I may cooperate with Your Excellency's plans …[55]

To sum up and attempt to clarify all of the reported movements made by Sebastiani's army north of the Guadiana between 5 and 25 July, it would be fair to say that the French commander was organising his forces such that the bulk of his artillery and infantry could commence their march towards Torrijos, where they would unite with the armies of Victor and Joseph, before marching towards Talavera. That there were a number of confusing intelligence reports regarding the strength and whereabouts of Sebastiani's units during that period of transition was almost inevitable, especially so when taking into account the movements of his cavalry as it formed a protective screen between the bulk of his forces and the Spaniards.

We have just seen how Venegas had complained about a lack of communication from Cuesta, stating that he was in complete ignorance of his chief's recent movements up to 25 July. Relieved he must have been then, when a dispatch from Cuesta dated the 25th arrived, detailing how things had come to such a pass. In his message he explained that, after

---

54   Venegas to Cuesta, 26 July 1809, Venegas, *Vindicación*, sub-section Documentos, pp.9–10, Número 11.
55   Venegas to Cuesta, 26 July 1809, Venegas, *Vindicación*, sub-section Documentos, pp.9–10, Número 11.

replying to Venegas's letter of 7 July, he became concerned at not having received confirmation from his subordinate of its arrival, and had since discovered that the said reply had never reached the commander of the Manchegans. With that he brought him up to date as follows. As mentioned, Cuesta's letter is dated 25 July from Santa Olalla, having been on the tail of Victor as the Frenchman withdrew from the Alberche towards Toledo and his union with Joseph and Sebastiani:

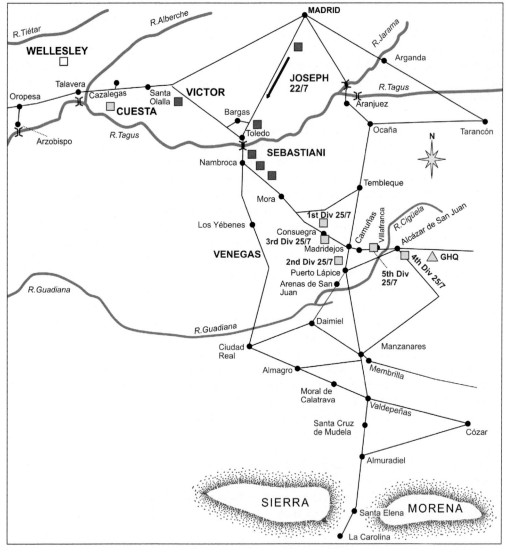

Plate 18. 25–26 July 1809. Sebastiani has withdrawn to Toledo, Joseph has left Madrid to join Victor at Bargas. In the south Venegas has finally crossed the Guadiana and moved his divisions up towards Madridejos and Consuegra.

(Cuesta to Venegas, 25 July 1809, *Número* 12):

All of the above [here Cuesta refers to Venegas's letter of the 7th which he appended to his dispatch of the 25th] compelled you to send to me to know if you should put your troops in motion against the enemy should his forces in La Mancha not exceed 14 or 15,000.

[I would say that] such an operation should produce some great advantages ... and, as has been said before, would prevent Sebastiani from uniting with the 23,000 men of Victor's army and the 10,000 which the Intruder is bringing from Madrid via Toledo ... to attack the British army and my own ... I will leave it to Your Excellency to decide whether you should make a movement towards Ocaña and Aranjuez, or on Toledo ...[56]

Once again, we see how Cuesta, seemingly afraid of using the imperative, failed to give clear and concise orders to Venegas, treating him as an equal rather than a subordinate. It was a lack of clarity which contributed significantly to the disaster which followed.

As Venegas's units arrived at their destinations on the 25th and began to probe further ahead, intelligence from both his *partidas* and the local population, indicated that the Sebastiani had begun his withdrawal towards the Tagus as early as the 23rd, giving signs that he was heading for Toledo and Tembleque, with the ultimate destination of Talavera in mind. Anticipating what was happening, all too tardily it must be said, Venegas issued fresh orders that night, the 25th, for his units to continue their advance: the 1st Division to Consuegra, the 2nd to Camuñas, the 3rd to Madridejos, the 4th and army headquarters to Herencia, and the 5th to Villafranca, all of these places lying some 40 miles south of Aranjuez (see Plate 18). By 26 July, the eve of Talavera, all had arrived at their destination – but to what purpose? Venegas claimed that he was now ready to move on Toledo and threaten Victor's rear, or on Madrid, bearing in mind, he said, that 'La Mancha was not abundant in provisions and other necessities, despite *General* Cuesta's arbitrary assumptions; the province having been devastated by the enemy it was in penury for many indispensable articles, thus making it impossible for me to make the rapid movements I wanted to ...'[57] The beginnings of an excuse for his failings it might seem.

It is now time to return to the Talavera front and begin to analyse the kind of relationship that developed between the British and Spanish allies just before, during and immediately after that defining action.

56   Cuesta to Venegas, 25 July 1809, Venegas, *Vindicación*, sub-section Documentos, pp.10–11, Número 12.
57   Venegas, *Vindicación*, p.15.

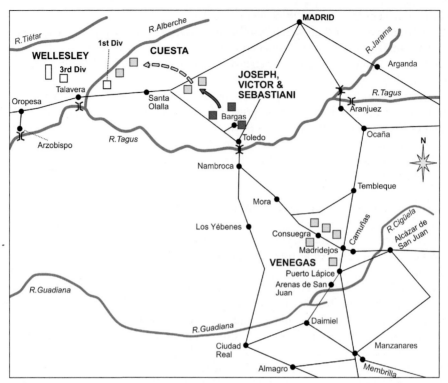

Plate 19. 26 July. With Victor, Joseph and Sebastiani concentrated at Bargas, Cuesta is forced to retreat to the Alberche. Venegas remains around Consuegra, some 45 miles south-east of Toledo and some 80 miles south of Madrid.

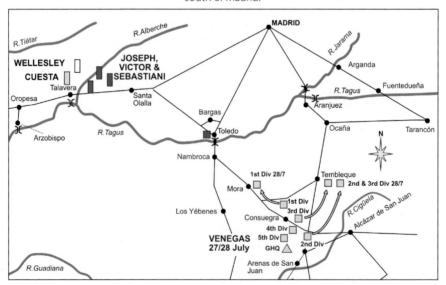

Plate 20. 27–28 July. Venegas's divisions are in motion towards Toledo and Aranjuez, both places lying on the banks of the Tagus. It was during those two days that the Battle of Talavera was fought.

7

The Battle of Talavera

Chapter 4 ended at the point where Wellesley and Cuesta were manoeuvring for position in front of *Maréchal* Victor's army on the Alberche, and we may now return our focus to Talavera by examining a letter from Wellesley to the Duke of Richmond dated 25 July, just two days before the serious fighting in that sector commenced:

> We formed a junction with the Spanish army under Gen. Cuesta on 20th at Oropesa, and on the 22d our advanced guards drove in the enemy outposts at this place [Talavera]. We were to have attacked him in his position on the Alberche yesterday morning; but Victor retired in the night, and has gone towards Toledo, I believe, to join himself with Sebastiani. Whether they will offer us battle again when joined, or will retire to the northward, I cannot tell. We have certainly closed upon Madrid on both sides, with Venegas' corps of 20,000 men at Arganda, and Sir R. Wilson's Portuguese and Spanish corps of 4,000 at Escalona; and I think the question whether they will offer us battle or not depends upon their means of defending Madrid without the assistance of their main army. I think, however, that, with or without a battle, we shall be at Madrid soon: and I think it best for the Spaniards that they should never fight any general action.[1]

Despite Wellesley's impression of Venegas's progress, by 25 July he was nowhere near Arganda, which lies just 20 miles south-east of Madrid. In fact, his five divisions were at that time concentrated in the vicinity of Consuegra, some 35 miles south of Toledo, which itself lies almost 50 miles south of Madrid. It was on this day, 25 July, that Cuesta wrote to Cornel from Santa Olalla as follows:

> After advising Your Excellency yesterday evening of my arrival at El Bravo, I continued with my march to Santa Olalla with the reserve and the cavalry divisions, where I found the 1st and 2nd infantry divisions together with the vanguard. The enemy was at Alcabón, a league from this place, and at Torrijos, which is two leagues away, but during the night they retired towards Toledo ... My troops

---

1 Wellesley to the Duke of Richmond, 25 July 1809, Gurwood (ed.), *Wellington's Dispatches*, vol.III, p.370.

marched seven leagues yesterday, after passing a day and night under arms, so I am obliged to remain here until nightfall, and I must also allow time for the English army, which is at Cazalegas and San Román with hardly any provisions and baggage, to reach me.

The enemy boasts that he is going to await us on the plains of Toledo; but I don't believe it and I don't expect it. I know nothing of Madrid nor *General* Venegas who, if he has followed my instructions, will be engaged in obstructing the enemy's retreat. I am assured there are hardly any troops in Toledo. Neither have I had news of Sebastiani who, I believe, will unite with Victor before they continue their retreat towards Aranjuez.[2]

From his comments to Cornel, it is clear that Cuesta thought he had Victor in full retreat along the Tagus valley towards Venegas who, he imagined, would have been in contact with Sebastiani's forces and exerting pressure on the Frenchman's line of retreat towards Aranjuez, as ordered. In fact, the commander of the Manchegans had by this point moved only as far north as Madridejos, allowing Sebastiani to slip away and unite with Victor near Toledo. The reader should refer to Plate 18 for a picture of the whereabouts of Cuesta, Wellesley, Venegas, Victor, Joseph and Sebastiani on 26 July, the day after Cuesta had written to Cornel once more:

This morning I advised you of my arrival at Santa Olalla with part of the troops under my command, and that I was proposing to allow them some rest … but since then I have learned that the armies of Victor and Sebastiani have united in the region of Toledo, and that Joseph Napoleon left Madrid three days ago with 10,000 men, heading for Cazalegas. I am also aware that, when Victor retreated, he decided to march from Navalcarnero towards Toledo and is now at Bargas, which lies some two leagues from that city …

General Wellesley, as I have informed you, remains on the banks of the Alberche, he tells me that the scarcity of bread and other baggage is preventing him from joining me as quickly as he had hoped, but is doing all that he can to ensure that he does … If my suspicions that [the French] intend to attack me are confirmed before the English arrive, then I think it would be better for me to retire and unite with them …[3]

Cuesta's Pursuit of Victor Comes to a Shuddering Halt

In his dispatch, Cuesta went on to tell Cornel that he was doing everything he could to get Wellesley to join him. In fact, Wellesley had simply ignored all of his ally's pleading in that direction and remained on the Alberche. The Spanish general's next dispatch to Cornel was written from the banks of the Alberche, indicating that the French had in fact attacked

---

2   Cuesta to Cornel, Santa Olalla, 25 July 1809, Cuesta, *Manifiesto*, p.61.
3   Cuesta to Cornel, 25 July 1809, Cuesta, *Manifiesto*, p.62.

him and forced him back from Torrijos and Santa Olalla towards the British position near Cazalegas.

Torrijos lies some 25 miles east of Cazalegas and some 40 miles east of Talavera; and Cuesta, with his usual eagerness to engage the enemy, had advanced much too far without the requisite support and had suffered the inevitable chastisement. When describing his forced withdrawal from Torrijos, he gave generous praise for the performance of Zayas and his vanguard, who were forced to take on the role of rear-guard during the retreat, and to Alburquerque and his cavalry who did their best to stem the French advance.

Numbered amongst the casualties suffered during the actions which followed, was the gallant colonel of the Dragones de Villaviciosa, Barón de Armendáriz, who had given good service to the Marqués de la Romana during the Royal Navy's evacuation of his expeditionary force from the Baltic during the summer of the previous year. Badly wounded on this occasion, the baron was taken prisoner by the French after his dragoons had been chased into a field, the perimeter of which, except at the single point of ingress and egress, was delineated by a deep, wide ditch. Unable to extricate themselves they were charged by the pursuing French cavalry and cut to pieces. Just one man amongst them managed to escape the fate of his comrades: a British officer, better horsed than the Spanish troopers, whose mount was the only one capable of clearing the ditch and carrying its rider to safety.[4] In fact, it was not the first time that the Villaviciosa dragoons had been caught in a tight spot; during the Denmark campaign some of them, along with their mounts, had been forced to swim the chilly Baltic waters separating the islands of Funen and Tassing in order to reach the Royal Navy's final embarkation point on Langeland, before being evacuated. Unfortunately, there was to be no escape for them on this occasion.[5]

All of the difficulties just described should have been foreseen by the Spaniards. In fact, in a letter to O'Donojú written on the very day of Cuesta's troubles at Santa Olalla, Wellesley had remarked, 'I should recommend to Gen. Cuesta to be very cautious in his movements, particularly of the main body of his army, and to direct his march rather to the right towards Toledo than to the left towards Madrid.'[6] It is not known if O'Donojú was presented with an opportunity to pass on Wellesley's words of advice before Cuesta was attacked.

Whilst his vanguard was struggling to slow the French advance, Cuesta led the rest of his force back to the Alberche. It was near there, close to the wooden bridge mentioned earlier, where he re-formed his divisions on its left (east) bank, and there has been some conjecture as to his reasons for not putting the river between himself and the French at the first opportunity, as we shall shortly discover.

Anticipating the kind of trouble Cuesta was heading for when he decided to advance, the British commander in chief had placed Sherbrooke's 1st Division on the east bank of the Alberche at a point some distance beyond the wooden bridge, whilst Major General John Randoll Mackenzie's 3rd Division, though remaining on the west bank of the river, was instructed to take up a position much closer to the bridge, thus acting as a reserve.[7] Once

4   The Earl of Munster, *An Account of the British Campaign in 1809 under Sir A. Wellesley in Portugal and Spain* (London: Henry Colburn and Richard Bently, 1831), p.70.
5   John Marsden, *Napoleon's Stolen Army* (Warwick: Helion, 2021) p.80.
6   Wellesley to O'Donojú, 25 July 1809, Gurwood (ed.), *Wellington's Dispatches*, vol.III, p.369.
7   Oman, *History of the Peninsular War*, vol.II, p.501.

the Spanish units had re-crossed to the west bank on the morning of the 26th, Sherbrooke marched his division back to Talavera, leaving Mackenzie to take up an outpost position near the Palacio de Salinas, at that time a collection of dilapidated buildings overlooking the Alberche from the west. With Cuesta feeling himself safe he remarked, 'I very much doubt the enemy will attack us here, and my doubts will be much increased if it is true that they have detached 15,000 men to Madrid, having regretted leaving it so undefended.'[8] With this remark, one may assume he was convinced that Venegas would have been at the gates of the capital, which was sadly not the case, as the map below indicates.

Having mentioned the Palacio de Salinas above, this might be an appropriate time to examine the story of Wellesley's apparent stroke of luck in evading capture there. On 25 July, the British commander was at Cazalegas, which lies some 15 miles east of Talavera, beyond the Alberche. It was there, whilst amongst the men of Sherbrooke's division as they awaited the retreating Spaniards, that he wrote the following to O'Donojú:

> I have just returned from Cebolla, where I heard that Gen. Cuesta was about to retire across the Alberche. I have ordered Gen. Sherbrooke to remain here with his corps till to-morrow morning …
>
> I think that, supposing the Spanish army should cross the Alberche, it would be desirable to occupy and fortify the sandhill on the left [east] bank of that river, near the bridge. But it would probably be best not to cross the river this evening, but to let the troops halt on this [the east] side, holding the heights with your advanced guard; and give us time until tomorrow morning to consider the position in which it would be most expedient to place the combined armies to receive the attack which it is to be hoped the enemy will make upon us.[9]

In his history of the war, Oman describes Cuesta's return to the Alberche as follows:

> He [Wellesley] rode out himself to meet the Spanish general, and begged him to carry his army beyond the Alberche, as it would be extremely dangerous to be caught with such an obstacle behind him, and no means of retreat save a long bridge and three fords. But Cuesta tempted providence by declaring that he should encamp on the further [east] bank, as his troops were too exhausted to risk the long defile across the bridge after dark. His sullen anger against Wellesley for refusing to follow him on the 24th was still smouldering in his breast, and the English were convinced that he remained on the wrong side of the river out of pure perversity, merely because his colleague pressed him to put himself in safety.[10]

Oman's description of what happened at the Alberche on 25/26 July contrasts sharply with that of Wellesley who, rather than accuse Cuesta of some stubborn refusal to take his troops across the Alberche as soon as they arrived at its east bank, actually claimed it was his own idea to have them wait for the morning light before crossing the river via the wooden bridge.

---

8   Cuesta, *Manifiesto*, p.63.

9   Wellesley to O'Donojú, 25 July 1809, Gurwood (ed.), *Wellington's Dispatches*, vol.III, p.370.

10   Oman, *History of the Peninsular War*, vol.II, p.501.

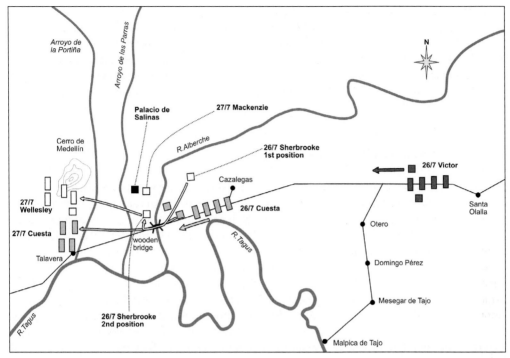

Plate 21. 26/27 July. Cuesta moves to the right bank of the Alberche via the wooden bridge. Mackenzie takes up a forward position at the Palacio de Salinas Sherbrooke retires to the main British position.

In light of this fact, it would seem that Oman's harsh words against Cuesta were hardly justified.

At 9:00 a.m. on 27 July, Wellesley sent a dispatch to Sherbrooke from Talavera, instructing him to vacate the sandhill on the east bank of the Alberche and cross the river: 'As soon as you shall receive this, you may withdraw across the river. Leave Mackenzie's division and the cavalry at their old position in the wood [on the west bank] and come yourself with the Germans to town.'[11]

The Palacio de Salinas, which Sir Charles Oman refers to as the Casa de Salinas, was, he said, a 'ruined house' at the time of the battle, if so then its current state of repair suggests that it has benefitted from a good deal of restoration in the course of the past two centuries or so. It is located on a hill on the right bank of the Alberche, quite close to the place where the 'wooden bridge' stood in 1809 (see Plate 21). At about the time Sherbrooke was making use of the bridge to march his division across the Alberche, a number of infantry units belonging to Lapisse's division were fording the river some distance to the north. Out of sight from the British, including the men of Mackenzie's division still stationed on their elevated position on the west bank of the river, the French soldiers weaved their way through the olive groves towards the Palacio de Salinas. There is some anecdotal evidence that, by

---

11   Wellesley to Sherbrook, 27 July 1809, Gurwood (ed.), *Wellington's Dispatches*, vol.III, p.371.

then, Wellesley had made his way to the old house and had decided to climb onto its roof to observe the progress of Sherbrooke's withdrawal. He had not long been there when, to his astonishment, he heard a sharp and growing exchange of musket fire to his left as the French ran into Donkin's brigade of Mackenzie's division. In very short time he was down from the roof and up in the saddle, riding for safety, leaving behind a combat which soon grew to respectable proportions before the situation was stabilised, with a cost to the British of some 440 men.[12]

First-hand Accounts of the Battle of Talavera

Rather than re-process some of the many secondary source descriptions of the fighting which took place at Talavera, it might be better to provide the reader with the accounts of the battle given by Wellesley and Cuesta themselves, with the addition of some personal notes made about the action by Lieutenant Andrew Leith Hay of the 29th (Worcestershire) Regiment of Foot, all three being presented below in as near a chronological order as possible.

According to Wellesley's dispatch to Castlereagh of 29 July, it was Major General Mackenzie's division, as we have just seen, which sustained the first shock of the French attack when Lapisse's infantry appeared on the right bank of the Alberche and advanced upon the isolated forward position of the British army. Stationed on the low height occupied by the Palacio de Salinas some distance in front of the British line, Mackenzie was quite exposed and therefore unable to withstand the French assault, which was launched at about 2:00 p.m. when their sharpshooters went forward with all of their usual *élan* and, despite some solid resistance from the 1/45th and 5/60th, he was forced back towards the main British position, allowing the bulk of Victor's army to begin to take up its initial battle positions on the heights overlooking the Portiña brook, a minor, south-running waterway on whose right bank the allied line was situated.

In his post-battle communique to Castlereagh, Wellesley related the salient points of the resulting action thus:

> The enemy immediately commenced his [main] attack, in the dusk of the evening, by a cannonade on the left of our position, and by an attempt with his cavalry to overthrow the Spanish infantry, posted, as I have before stated on the right [of our line]. This attempt entirely failed. Early in the night, he pushed a division along the valley on the left of the height occupied by Gen. Hill, of which he gained a momentary possession; but Major Gen. Hill attacked it instantly with the bayonet, and regained it. This attack was repeated in the night, but failed; and again, at daylight, on the morning of the 28th, by 2 divisions of infantry, and was repulsed by Major Gen. Hill.[13]

---

12   Oman, *History of the Peninsular War*, vol.II, pp.503–504.
13   Wellesley to Castlereagh, 29 July 1809, Gurwood (ed.), *Wellington's Dispatches*, vol.III, pp.370–375.

As reproduced in his *Manifiesto*, Cuesta's battle report to Cornel contained the following description of the commencement of the action at Talavera:

> Last night I wrote to Your Excellency from the left bank of the Alberche, informing you that I feared we were about to be attacked by the force which the enemy had gathered at Toledo, should I remain separated from the English.[14]
>
> This consideration led me to return to the river yesterday morning and take up the position agreed with General Wellesley, both armies forming a line in front of Talavera and taking advantage of the [walled] enclosures or whatever else the lay of the land offered.
>
> We had barely formed our line in this position when, at five o'clock in the evening, the enemy appeared in a strength we could only estimate to be about 40,000 men, of which 5,000 were cavalry. They immediately launched an attack on our line ... directing their principal force towards the left, which was occupied by the English, in an attempt to overrun that flank ... the outcome being that the enemy was repulsed on two occasions with heavy losses in dead and wounded, the action having continued until half past eight in the evening. The English have also suffered losses, especially in officers.[15]

The two quotations above provide the reader with an idea of the impressions gained by the two allied commanders during the early phase of the battle, as the fighting continued throughout the afternoon, evening and night of 27 July 1809. From what was said by the two men, one can begin to picture how the approximately two-mile long position held by the allies was formed. Essentially, it ran north-south from the height known as the Cerro de Medellín in the north (how evocative, considering Cuesta's recent disaster at the town from which the hill takes its name) to the southern outskirts of Talavera, at the point where the old road running along the right bank of the Tagus enters the town just a little to the west of the Arroyo de la Portiña.[16] It was at that spot where the allies had stationed a field battery, its guns ready to sweep the causeway clear of any enemy troops approaching from the east in an attempt to threaten their right flank (see Plate 21). The British manned the northern segment of the line down to about the centre point of the position marked by the Pajar de Vergara, beyond the east bank of the Portiña, where they had thrown up a second strong artillery position. It was there where the left of the Spanish line lay; their right being marked by the first-mentioned battery on the right bank of the Tagus.

Day One, 27 July 1809, Andrew Leith Hay's Account

Lieutenant Andrew Leith Hay sailed from England in June 1809 and disembarked at Lisbon on 2 July. From there he travelled in company with Captain John Tucker on his way to join the 29th Foot, and it was not until 23 July that the men arrived at their regiment's camp

---

14   Cuesta is referring the combined forces of Victor, Joseph Bonaparte and Sebastiani.
15   Cuesta, *Manifiesto*, pp.63–64.
16   Arroyo: Spanish for stream or brook.

near Talavera, thus ensuring they were present at the forthcoming battle where the 29th formed part of Stewart's brigade, a formation assigned to the 2nd Division commanded by Major General Rowland Hill. On 26 July, the eve of the battle, he was to witness the effects of Cuesta's retreat from the direction of Santa Olalla towards the Alberche. This is what he said about it:

> During the 25th [July] we heard nothing of the Spanish army, but on the following day the report of artillery announced its return – not unaccompanied. The cannonade was distant, but evidently becoming less so. Runaways and stragglers passed to the rear; the weather was very fine; from the vicinity of the Santa Olalla road we derived great amusement: it was covered by a succession of groups habited in various costumes.
>
> On the morning of the 27th we learned that part of *General* Cuesta's army had passed to the rear; while battalion after battalion formed a continuous line of march in the same direction. From amidst clouds of dust, disorderly chattering assemblages of half-clad, half armed men, became occasionally visible; again, regiments marching in perfect order, cavalry, staff officers, bands of musicians, flocks of sheep and bullocks; artillery, cars, carriages and waggons, varied the animated, confused, and singular scene on which we gazed.[17]

Leith Hay then went on to describe how, once the Spanish army had passed by, he and his comrades continued with their chores in the shelter of an olive grove until O'Donojú arrived, excitedly spreading the word that the French were across the Alberche and would be upon the allies very shortly. For which, in the words of Leith Hay, he was merely thanked and told that the 29th would get under arms once orders to that effect were communicated to them.

The 29th were destined to take up position on what would turn out to be the hottest spot in the allied line, the Cerro de Medellín which, during the time they were in the olive grove, had not yet been occupied. It would be a full hour before they received instructions to make their way up the allied line towards the height, passing on the way the ranks of Spanish and British infantry already stationed in position, and looking on as the men of Mackenzie's division retired through their files and across the line of the 29th's march whilst making their retreat from the advanced position they had been forced to give up just before darkness began to fall. It was not long after this that the 29th were ordered to advance at the double on the final leg of their dash towards the hill, and as they reached the summit they found that:

> A considerable body of French were in possession of the height. Their numbers rapidly increasing, the drums beat the *pas de charge*; while at intervals voices were heard, some calling out they were the German Legion, others not to fire. It was so dark that the blaze of musketry alone displayed the forms of the assailants.
>
> The leading company of the 29th poured in a volley when close to the bayonets of the enemy. The glorious cheer of British infantry [then] accompanied the charge

---

17   Andrew Leith Hay, *Narrative of the Peninsular War* (Driffield: Leonaur, 2013), pp.86–87.

which succeeded ... The enemy was pushed down the hill, abandoning the level ground at its top, thickly strewed with dead bodies or wounded men. No second attempt was for some time made to carry this important point. The 29th remained in possession of the ground, lying on their arms in the midst of fallen enemies. The furred *shakos* of a dead French soldier became my pillow for the night.[18]

We shall leave the final words relating to the action of 27 July to Cuesta, who summed up the day from a Spanish perspective with the following paragraph: '[Our losses] have not been considerable, and in general terms our troops have been brave and firm, apart from three or four corps who made some mistakes about which I will talk later.' The somewhat anodyne words he uses to describe the failings of some of the Spanish units on the night of the 27th belie the gravity, not only of the failings of a minority of his soldiers, but also of his own shortcomings in dealing properly with the matter after the battle had run its course, which we shall describe a little later.

Day Two, 28 July 1809 and the Days Immediately Following

In his dispatch to Castlereagh, Wellesley gave but a brief account of the events which took place on 28 July:

The general attack began by the march of several columns of infantry into the valley, with a view to attack the height occupied by Major Gen. Hill. These columns were immediately charged [by our cavalry] and although the 23d dragoons suffered considerable loss, the charge had the effect of preventing the execution of that part of the enemy's plan. At the same time, he directed an attack upon Brig. Gen. Alex. Campbell's position in the centre of the combined armies, and on the right of the British. This attack was successfully repulsed ...

An attack was also made at the same time upon Lieut. Gen. Sherbrooke's division, which was in the left and centre of the first line of the British army. This attack was most gallantly repulsed by a charge with bayonets by the whole division ...

Shortly after the repulse of this general attack, in which apparently all of the enemy troops were employed, he commenced his retreat across the Alberche ... leaving in our hands 20 pieces of cannon, ammunition, tumbrils and some prisoners.

Your Lordship will observe that the attacks of the enemy were principally, if not entirely, directed against the British troops. The Spanish commander in chief, his officers and troops manifested every disposition to render us assistance, and those of them who were engaged did their duty; but the ground they occupied was so important, and its front at the same time so difficult, that I did not think it proper

---

18   Leith Hay, *Narrative of the Peninsular War*, p.88.

to urge them to make any movement on the left of the enemy while he was engaged with us.[19]

Returning to Cuesta's battle report written for *Secretario de Guerra*, Antonio Cornel, we may examine what he said about the second day of the battle and its immediate aftermath:

> Very early this morning the enemy renewed his attack and has continued until 7 o'clock this evening, but he has been consistently repelled, and I expect that will continue to be the case. José Napoleón was present until this evening, but we know he has since retired with his guard to Santa Olalla, and that 98 carts loaded with wounded have crossed the Alberche with him.
>
> I do not have time to enter into details, having been under arms on the battlefield with my troops for three days. We have had absolutely no provisions in that time nor the means to access them, as the commissariat absented itself from this theatre and from both armies as soon as the first shots were fired.[20]

On the morning of the 28th, Andrew Leith Hay and the 29th were still holding the Cerro de Medellín, from whose summit they had expelled the French after they had been in brief occupation of it on the previous evening, and they were determined to keep it in their possession:

> Just before daybreak was an anxious moment, and when the first glimmering light appeared, the attention of all was naturally riveted upon the enemy's position to ascertain what troops were opposed, where his cannon were placed, and to what extent we were to be assailed. Twenty-two pieces of artillery had their mouths directed towards us ... to the right of the French cannon were perceived columns of infantry. A renewed battle for the hill became certain ...
>
> When it became perfectly light, a signal gun put the enemy's columns in motion, the whole of his artillery opening almost immediately after ... The 29th were ordered to lie down a short distance behind the brow of the hill ... By this judicious arrangement, the regiment suffered little from the cannonade ...
>
> When the French columns had mounted the ascent, and were so near as to become endangered by the fire of their own artillery, a scene of great animation was exhibited. The summit, which had appeared deserted, now supported a regular line of infantry. Near the colours of the 29th, stood Sir Arthur Wellesley, directing and animating the troops.
>
> General Ruffin had nearly surmounted all of the difficulties of the ground, when a fire burst forth that checked his advance ...
>
> After the repulse of the 1st Corps, great indecision seemed to prevail in the enemy's army.[21]

---

19   Wellesley to Castlereagh, 29 July 1809, Gurwood (ed.), *Wellington's Dispatches*, vol.III, pp.371–377.
20   Cuesta, *Manifiesto*, p.64. It would seem that the Spanish, like the British, were also short of rations after the battle.
21   Leith Hay, *Narrative of the Peninsular War*, pp.89–91.

Despite their lack of immediate success, the French did not desist at this early hour of the day, and there were more attacks to come, all of which were aimed at breaking that part of the British segment of the allied line which extended from the right of the height being defended by the 29th. It was only hard fighting and a tenacity in defence that held the enemy at bay and eventually forced him to withdraw. By that point in the proceedings the 29th's day was done and they became mere spectators of the rest of the day's action. 'The 29th regiment, reduced by the fall of one hundred and eighty-six officers and soldiers, bivouacked for the night on the same spot as on the preceding …'[22]

Cuesta's report for the succeeding days continued as follows:

Talavera 29 July:
I reported to you from the battlefield that at seven o'clock yesterday evening, both the enemy attacks and our defence against them continued obstinately.

Hostilities ceased at nightfall, but the enemy did not abandon their positions until just before dawn when they commenced their retreat, crossing the Alberche on their way to Cazalegas and Santa Olalla after having given up all their hopes of breaking us or forcing us out of our position.[23]

Talavera 30 July:
The enemy, in the shape of 10,000 infantry and cavalry, are still to be seen on the heights of the far bank of the Alberche … Both [British and Spanish] armies are occupied with seeing to the wounded, amongst whom there are many French, and burying the enemy dead of whom there are so many that I have had to order my troops to burn them.[24]

Talavera 31 July:
Upon pushing our advanced posts closer to the enemy, he responded by opening a desultory fire upon them. Some time later he brought up a sizeable corps of artillery … It would seem that … Victor's total force, with the exception of that part of the Imperial Guard which retired with José Napoleón to Madrid, is about two or three leagues from here. Their intention would seem to be that of awaiting the arrival of Soult in order to attack us in front and rear; at that point, if we were to detach part of our force to go in search of one of the marshals, then the rest would be too weak to resist the other, as such we must attack Victor, despite his increased strength, before the arrival of Soult, who we believe to be close to Plasencia. This question must be resolved tomorrow.[25]

22 Leith Hay, *Narrative of the Peninsular War*, p.95.
23 Cuesta, *Manifiesto*, p.64.
24 Cuesta, *Manifiesto*, pp.65–66.
25 Cuesta, *Manifiesto*, p.66.

Pour Encourager les Autres

A little earlier we made reference to the failings of some of the Spanish units during the night of 27 July, when they were overcome by panic and deserted their positions in the front line, causing havoc in the rear areas as they ran from the sound of the guns, some of them continuing in their flight all the way to Oropesa.[26] According to Arteche, the panic spread to the British units manning the earthwork thrown up at the Pajar de Vergara, who thought that the line had been broken.[27] Cuesta, enraged by what he saw, would not let it pass, and decided to make an example of the units involved. Commenting on this episode, the Conde de Toreno confirmed that, 'Cuesta intended nothing less than decimating them (*diezmarlos*) … [However] the English general interceded and managed to calm his passion, but only after he had already had 50 of them shot.'[28] John Spencer Cooper of the 7th Fusiliers witnessed at least some of what took place:

> Early in the morning of the 30th, twenty-five Spanish soldiers, dressed in white and attended by several popish priests, were marched up to the front of our regiment and shot. One, a young lad of 19 or 20 years of age, dropped before the party fired. But it was of no use, for after a volley at 10 paces distance had been given by about 50 men, the whole party ran forward, and firing through heads, necks, breasts, &c, completed their horrid work. The executioners having tools with them, the bodies were hidden in shallow graves in a few minutes. These unfortunates belonged to a regiment that had given way in the late battle.[29]

The Spaniards went some way towards redeeming themselves from the dishonour of the flight of the three battalions, when Alburquerque's cavalry stemmed the French advance before pushing them back beyond the allied line, the Spanish flank artillery raking them with fire as they went.

At the distance of some 200 plus years from such incidents as Cuesta's punitive actions described above, it would perhaps be wrong to cast judgement upon him in these pages.

With respect to their positive contributions to the victory at Talavera, one can examine the various actions which the Spaniards were involved in during 28 July. It was Leval's Germans, part of Sebastiani's 4th Corps, which opened the afternoon attack, when they advanced before their supporting corps were ready to move, and found themselves alone in front of the Pajar de Vergara. It was there where the British had just been reinforced by the arrival of two Spanish battalions, along with *Capitán* Uclés's battery of four heavy calibre guns to add to those of the British already within the earthwork. Blasted by the artillery and assailed by Campbell's infantry, the Germans managed to recover themselves before returning to the attack against Campbell's division. It was then that some Spanish infantry

26   The front line Spanish battalions involved were los Provinciales de Trujillo, los Provinciales de Badajoz and los Leales de Fernando VII. Arteche, *Guerra de la Independencia*, vol.VI, p.302.

27   Arteche, *Guerra de la Independencia*, vol.VI, p.302.

28   Conde de Toreno, *Historia del Levantamiento*, Vol. III, p.61.

29   John Spencer Cooper, *Rough Notes of Seven Campaigns, 1809-1815* (Staplehurst: Spellmount, 1996), pp.24–26.

and a section of two of their guns under *Teniente* Santiago Piñeiro took Leval's men in flank, preparing the way for what would be remembered by the Spaniards as one of their most brilliant cavalry charges, when the Regimiento del Rey rode in to scatter the enemy, capturing 10 of his guns, four of which were brought into the Spanish line.[30]

To the north of the battlefield, beyond the Cerro de Medellín, lie the foothills known as the Peñascales de la Sierra de Segurilla, the two features separated by a wide valley. It was to this depression where Alburquerque's cavalry was sent to reinforce the two brigades of British horsemen commanded by Anson and Fane. *Mariscal de Campo* Bassecourt's 5th Division was sent a little further north to form the extreme left of the allied line, taking up a position in the Peñascales. As a further detail, *Teniente* Entrena's section of two heavy guns (12–pounders) had been moved to the southern slope of the Cerro de Medellín. All was then set for the famous charge made by the 1st and 23rd Light Dragoons. According to the Spaniards, Alburquerque's cavalry also took part in the charge, and Arteche includes in his work the Duque's account of the action:

> After the commencement of the general attack, the division under my command followed all of the movements of the English cavalry, charging at the same time as it did. And although the great ditch between it and the enemy prevented it from getting amongst the French, the artillery of my division, under the command of Diego Entrena and Pedro Ladron de Guevara, advanced with the English and caused considerable damage to the enemy during the morning, flanking one of his batteries and silencing it in very short time.[31]

While by no means an exhaustive coverage of the Spanish contribution to the victory at Talavera, the short section above may well provide the reader with at least a notion of their involvement, something which has been generally overlooked by some British writers over the years.

To sum up in this matter, it would be fair to say that much has been made of Cuesta's obstinacy and brittleness when dealing with his British allies and, indeed, with some of his fellow Spaniards. In fact, Wellesley mentioned this trait in his character on at least two occasions, and it is something which British historians have often referred to, especially in the context of Talavera. However, after agreeing to the battlefield disposition of his troops as suggested by Wellesley, he then stood with them as they faced yet another stiff test under his command, and it is perhaps the case that both he and his infantry have never received from British observers the plaudits they deserved for their (mostly) stolid performance on the right flank of the allied line during the whole of the battle. The Spanish cavalry was also conspicuous at Talavera, especially during the second day of fighting, and it was whilst Wellesley observed the preparations being made by the divisions of Ruffin and Villate for an

---

30 Arteche quotes Eguía's assertion that the Spanish infantry battalions involved were los Provinciales de Badajoz, los Provinciales de Trujillo, los Imperiales de Toledo, los Provinciales de Guadix, el Regimiento de Osuna (two battalions) and los Voluntarios Extranjeros. Arteche, *Guerra de la Independencia*, vol.VI, p.314, f/n. 1. Note that the first two mentioned were involved in the panic which took place on the previous night.

31 Arteche, *Guerra de la Independencia*, vol.VI, p.321, f/n. 1.

attack on the British left flank on 28 July, that Cuesta was asked to provide any assistance he could spare. Again, he responded positively by sending Bassecourt's infantry division and Alburquerque's cavalry division beyond the Cerro de Medellín to help his ally, as described above, both of which played an important role in frustrating what the French had hoped would be a decisive move. Once again, perhaps it is time to ask if enough attention has yet been given by historians to the Spanish efforts in shoring up both the allied flanks at Talavera.

Private George Woolgar's Letter

Finally, we may take a look at an exquisite little cameo piece of contemporary documentation, in an attempt to catch the flavour of things during the height of Wellesley's activities before, during and after the Battle of Talavera. It is an item kept amongst the National Army Museum's collection of documents and comprises a letter from a Private George Woolgar of the 16th (Queen's) Light Dragoons, who were with Cotton's brigade of Lieutenant General Payne's cavalry division at Talavera. Posted home by Woolgar to his brother-in-law and sister on 23 November 1809, and dated 'Villavariaga,' Portugal, 26 October 1809, it provides a fascinating picture of his experiences between 2 July and 9 August of that year; and as such it deserves to be quoted in full. Woolgar's spelling might be said to be somewhat phonetic and his punctuation a little original, but this only enhances the letter's authenticity and charm:[32]

> To,
> Mr Wm Lewin,
> No. 20 Victualling Office Row,
> Grove Lane,
> Deptford,
> England.
>
> Dear Brother and Sister
> The last time I wrote to you was from Thomar we marcht from Thomar the 2^d July over a mountainous country we wear a 11 days on our march without halting, the Sun Exsesive hot & the roads very dusty.
>   We arrived at Placentia the 13th we halted here 4 days to rest & shoe the horses 16th inst we marcht the whole of the British army over the mountains a very bad road very hot & dusty and scarcely any water to be met with on the road; we where fortunate enough to camp 2 of the days by rivers – on the 20th we joind the Spanish army they had 10,000 midlin cavalry 20,000 midlin infantry very Iregulery dres^t. 21th – this afternoon the British were drawn up in line for the inspection of Sir Arthur Wellesley & the Spanish Genl Cuesta, the line of the British reach^t 4 miles – we

---

32   National Army Museum (NAM): 1999-09-54-1: Letter written by Private George Woolger, 16th Light Dragoons, to his brother-in-law, Mr William Lewin, 26 October 1809, <https://collection.nam.ac.uk/detail.php?acc=1999-09-54-1>, accessed, April 2021.

then campt near Alcanagon. 22^d 4 A.M. it was a beautifull sight to see the English & Spanish Armys march on the fine plains of Aratara – colours flying trump^{ts} sounding & men in high spirits. About ½ 8 A.M. we came up with the enemy at ½ past 9 the action began with a smart cannonade from which was soon returned from the enemy however the French did not stand long They retreated 3 miles beyond Tallavera & crost the Teagus & made another stand and fire^d with cannon till dark – Nothing Particler happened till the 26th when we herd cannonading at some distance which was a collum of the Spaniards engaged with the enemy. The Spaniards was obliged to retire as also Genl Sherbrook which had advanced the 24th. This day we was the whole of the British cavalrey were orderd to be out at 2 A.M. of the 27th July. we then advanced towards the Out Post when arived we found Genl Sherbrook retreating our cavalry then coverd his retreat Genl Sherbrook crost the Teagus 3 miles from Talavera with his 2 brigades to take possesion of the wood, the enemy crosst the river undiscovered by us 4 miles still higher and atacked our infantry with strong collums our infantry stud them sharply for some time till ordered to retire onto the plain The French wou^d not follow us onto the Plain – there sharpshooters fired smartly on us for some time & teazed us until there horse artillery had time to bring 2 brigades of guns to the edge of the wood with which they give us an uncommon smart cannonade which obliged our cavallrey to quit the plain & retire towards Talavera the French then crossd the Teagus & ocqpid the plain together with there sharpshooters follow^d us up close – by this time our infantry had formd the line, the British on the left Spanish on the right a little before sunsett the battle became very hot which contined till nearly 12 P.M. the remaing part of the night was employde in arranging cannon on 2 hills which took possetion of which if the french had gaind wou^d have turned our army.

As soon as light apeard on the 28th the battle was renewd with a most tremendious cannonade from the contending armys which continued for some hours without interruption, our infantry was sharply put to it. our Reg^t sufferd much we lost 8 men & 21 horses in about 15 minuts bessides what we lost the day before – about 2 PM the battle became dredfull. All this large plain was all in a smoake from cannon and musketerey and when the french give way ther dead and wounded lay in almost whole ranks – the french stormd the 2 hills 6 times and were as often drove back with great slaughter till both hills were coverd with killd and wounded – too much praise cant be given of the 29th, 31th and guards, 48th foot – in short everey Reg^t did ther duty they stud like stone walls. disdaining to flinch dispising there numbers, they were 3 to one & we had scarcely any bread or water these two trying days & excessive heat & and hard fighting, still I found none grumble Provision Verey scarce as the french have layn here 7 month and made such havock with everey thing they found this country & they knew everey nook of the country for miles round which was of great advantage to them in this battle, both sides fought hard – the french had near 100 guns and we had not more than 40 & short of amunition the battle continued till dark till neither side cou^d see where to fire a shot. the British remain on the field of battle all night the french retreated during the night and left 20 guns behind them – we remain on the field till 10 A.M. 29th July – but enemy [never] apeard to renew the action we were then ordered to our old

camp ground it was shocking to see the killd & wounded on both sides some with both legs of others both arms or one arm of in short wounded in all parts men and horses lay together mangld in a shocking manner – all the houses in Talavera are filld with English french and Spanish wounded, many die with loss of blood some with ther wounds – 3 Aug[t] we were ordered to march to Oropesa on the road back to Placentia as marshal Soult was coming in our rear – at 2 A.M. we were orderd to sadle we did so, at a 11 we were orderd to make for Ponte Arzo del bispo we had had no bread for the two last days here we had 1 biscuit & half served to each mess, which was 10 men. – 5th August we march at 4 AM over a mountainous country, water scarce & bad no bread – 6th Aug[t] march[t] at 4 AM still over mountains – we now begin to feel the hardships and calamitys of a retreating army – cars break down bullocks drop down dead with fatigue & hunger Artillery horses also – likewise troop horses and the infantry are obliged to yoak to the guns to draw themselves up these steep mountains – it was 3 o clock on 7th Aug before we halted as we were forced to cover the artillery we then rested till 6 AM to be at our horses at 10 we marcht again over the highest mountains I ever saw infantry still at the guns about halfway we came to more levell ground we march[t] 9 leagues: water scarce & bad no wine to be had for money This day a handfull of Rye flour was served out no bred we halt here one day 9th Augt, this day we had 5 small biscuits served out which was precious [little for] our famisht harts – we now think ourselves out of danger a little, we now begin to receive a little more bread – however we have made a good retreat to places with easy marches – here we can have any thing if we have money – in portugale water is plentifull & good we are preparing for the field again we expect to meet them again about the middle of next month or not a tall – I hope we shall be ordered home, when please god I see you again I can give you a better account than by letter – I hope to find you & all the family in a good state of health – as thank god I injoy mine at present give my love to W[m] – step[n] – geo[r] & Mary – I hope you will write to my mother & B[r] – W[m] – as I have not wrote to them & let them know I am in good health – I have wrote to my wife & recv[d] ananser she was well if you should go any ways near her you will call on her & see how she and the child are I therefore conclude for the present & Remain your loving Brother
    Geo[r] Woolgar.[33]

---

33   There are a couple of things to note about Woolgar's letter. Firstly, the postmark appears to read, 'VILLA VI, OZA, 4 O'CLOCK NO 23 1809 EV,' and it is possible to fill in the blanks by inspecting Wellesley's dispatches bearing the date, 23 November 1809, or thereabouts. On doing so we find a letter he addressed to Villiers, dated Elvas 25 Nov. 1809, the second paragraph of which begins, 'I have been at Villa Viçosa since Wednesday …'. Assuming 'EV' in the post mark to signify 'Elvas' it would indicate that the location from which Woolgar posted his letter was Villa Viçosa, about 15 miles south-west of Elvas. Secondly, when Woolgar talks of both the British and French crossing the 'Teagus' [Tagus] he is undoubtedly confusing it with the Alberche.

8

After the Battle

Once the fighting at Talavera was over, Victor withdrew the bulk of his forces in the direction of Madrid, leaving just a holding force on the east bank of the Alberche. The battle may have been won by the allies but the situation in central Spain was still far from clear, and this, together with other considerations, such as Wellesley's concerns about Spanish logistics and state of military preparedness, were going to have a bearing on his future plans. However, his first consideration was for the thousands of wounded men who would have to be removed from the battle area to those buildings in Talavera which could serve as hospitals; but he would not be allowed to linger in the vicinity of the city for much longer. Unbeknown to the British commander, Soult had recently received considerable reinforcements to his II Corps in the shape of Mortier's V Corps from the vicinity of Valladolid and Ney's VI Corps from Galicia, all of which had concentrated in the area just north of Salamanca, and were now marching to position themselves somewhere in the rear of Wellesley and Cuesta, with the intention of cutting off their retreat to Portugal; the combined strength of Soult's new command now amounting to some 50,000 men. The *Maréchal* would have to be either confronted or avoided before any move could be made upon Madrid or, indeed, before any retreat into Portugal could be considered by the British. On the French right (west) flank, Victor had his own dilemmas to contend with; his ultimate aim was to keep Cuesta and Wellesley on the Alberche whilst Soult approached, but he also had to keep a wary eye on Venegas, who was by then on the south bank of the Tagus and finally threatening to move on Madrid. Could the Army of La Mancha be dealt with on the Frenchman's left (east) flank by sending a strong detachment of his troops to destroy it? To do so might well expose those who remained on the Alberche to an allied attack, whilst they were still reeling from the clash at Talavera.

On 31 July, Cuesta received a letter from Venegas informing him that his vanguard had finally advanced to Aranjuez, which sits some 35 miles south of Madrid on the banks of the Tagus, and was in possession of the Puente de la Reyna, should he have to use it to enter the city from the east, or remain where he was and continue to attract the attention of Victor.[1] In his *Manifiesto* Cuesta claimed that, even at this late hour, Venegas's march on Madrid was of the greatest importance to the allied cause, adding that, although now reduced in

---

1   The Puente de la Reyna, or Puente de la Reina, spans the Tagus at a point about one mile to the east of Aranjuez city centre.

numbers after the recent battle, the army under Victor's command was still some 37,000 strong and determined to defend itself. His implication being that Venegas should still do everything he could to draw off some of the Frenchman's forces still to the west of Madrid, which supposed that the Manchegans should strike at the capital.[2] The question was, would Venegas now finally throw his full weight behind the allied plan, or was it all too late for that? In the immediate aftermath of Talavera, Cuesta wrote to Cornel on 29 July informing him that:

> According to what the French prisoners have told us, we know that, during the attack of yesterday morning, the whole of Joseph's Guard, in which he placed all his hopes, was repulsed and defeated, and as a result he has fled towards Santa Olalla.
>
> I have just discovered that his army, much chastened, has directed its march towards Toledo; it is without provisions and with no means of subsistence. Finally … I can only add that this has been the most glorious and important battle of the whole war, and that I expect it will open a path towards the Ebro as soon as we have all that we need to sustain the troops.[3]

At this point Cuesta's reports to Cornel began to illustrate the growing dilemma faced by the various actors in the drama unfolding across central Spain during the summer of 1809. Here are his *Manifiesto* entries for the beginning of August:

> Talavera, the morning of 1 August:
> At dawn this morning we were surprised to discover that the enemy had decamped and taken the road to Torrijos, according to those of our light detachments which followed him. We have also taken some prisoners and deserters recently, who declare that Sebastiani retired towards Toledo yesterday, probably because of *Brigadier* Lacy's threatening attack, and it is likely that, together with Victor, he will march to the defence of Madrid and halt the advance of Venegas, to whom I have sent news of this movement.
> Yesterday, troops belonging to *Maréchal* Soult entered Béjar …[4]

> Talavera, the evening of 1 August:
> This morning I informed Your Excellency that all of the enemy forces we had in front of us had disappeared and that our light troops had followed them to Santa Olalla, taking some 32 prisoners.
> On the insistence of Sir Arthur Wellesley, although in my concept to little advantage, tomorrow I will detach the 5th Division, along with 300 cavalry, in the direction of Plasencia and the pass of Baños, all under the orders of *General* Bassecourt. The hope is that they will arrive in time to impede the passage of *Maréchal* Soult,

---

2   Cuesta, *Manifiesto*, p.67.
3   Cuesta, *Manifiesto*, p.65. Note a further reference illustrating the fact that the Spanish were short of provisions in the immediate aftermath of the Battle of Talavera.
4   Béjar is situated on the road between Salamanca and Plasencia and lies some five miles to the north of the mountain pass at Baños.

who is heading towards Plasencia. However there are hopes that General Beresford, together with his 25,000 Portuguese, will pursue and intercept him or that, once he learns of our recent victory, he will alter his plans knowing that Victor is unable to assist him, and therefore keep his distance from our front.

In any case, Bassecourt should slow the advance of Soult and prevent him from destroying the bridge at Almaraz or intercepting that important and necessary communication.

Talavera, 2 August:

Nothing to report from the enemy in front, but it would seem that they are moving towards our flank.

Brigadier Marqués de la Reyna, commander of the troops [some time ago] detailed to defend the pass of Baños, has informed me that, being unable to resist the forces of *Maréchal* Soult, he has retired upon the Tiétar, and that the enemy entered Plasencia at two in the afternoon yesterday.[5] In consequence, I have spoken with General Wellesley about [the prospect of] marching on Soult and confronting him, before he comes any closer to Talavera in an attempt to join forces with Victor and launch a combined attack [upon us]. [As a result] Wellesley has determined that the British army will march on Soult at dawn tomorrow, leaving the Spanish army at Talavera with me in order that I present a front to Victor and cover [the British] operation; like this he will remain ignorant of the separation of our forces, to which effect it would help if Brigadier General Wilson remained with his troops in an advanced position at Escalona on our left.[6]

We may suppose that in three days time the French, Portuguese and British will meet and that the business will be quickly decided. In the meantime, should Victor and Sebastiani decide to attack me with superior forces, I will retreat and reunite with the British.

As of yesterday, Lacy was still in front of Toledo and *General* Venegas at Ocaña and Aranjuez.[7]

It is quite striking to see how, on 1 August, Cuesta thought there was 'little advantage' in sending troops to help De la Reyna defend the pass at Baños, and by the following day mention, almost in passing, that the Marqués had been overwhelmed by the French at that very place.

On the following day, just before Wellesley left for Oropesa in search of Soult, Cuesta received copies of some captured enemy correspondence, amongst which there was a letter from Jourdan to Soult, as well one from Joseph Bonaparte to *Colonel* Hugo, at that time French governor of Ávila. Both letters were post marked Bargas (just north of Toledo) and

5   The reader should note that De la Reyna's troops had been sent to guard the pass of Baños several days before Cuesta sent Bassecourt to that place.

6   Colonel Sir Robert Wilson, commander of the Loyal Lusitanian Legion. See Plate 25 for the movements of Wilson's Legion.

7   Cuesta, *Manifiesto*, pp.67–69. From what Cuesta says, it would seem that the Marqués de la Reyna had been detached to the puerto de Baños some days before 1 August.

are included in Appendix V of Cuesta's *Manifiesto*. Ávila lies some 40 miles north of Santa Olalla and has a direct communication with Plasencia via the pass of Béjar, so it would seem that Joseph and Jourdan were communicating with Soult by sending their couriers around the left flank of the allies. Here is what Joseph wrote to its French governor:

> It is of the greatest importance that I obtain news of the march of *Maréchal* Soult by return of post. The outcome of important events will depend upon my knowledge of the date of his arrival in Plasencia, more so the date of his arrival at Almaraz. I hope he does not have to await the arrival of Ney's army before putting himself in movement. From Plasencia he must march immediately to an encounter with the British army, which will be being pursued by I Corps (that is to say, the army of Victor).
>
> Please ensure that a copy of this letter finds its way to *Maréchal* Soult [and] send me a daily update on the progress of his march.
>
> All is going well, but will go better should *Maréchal* Soult be at Almaraz on the 31st [July].[8]

From Joseph's letter, it is clear that his main concern was that Soult take possession of the bridge near Almaraz on the Tagus. That achieved, the options for Wellesley's retreat to Portugal would be much reduced.

Jourdan's letter to Soult is a much longer affair, but its crux is contained the final paragraphs; these cover the events which took place during the hours immediately following Joseph's withdrawal from Talavera towards Santa Olalla:

> The king is aware that the army of Venegas is at Toledo and Aranjuez ... Our movement on Plasencia will force the English army to separate itself from that of Cuesta and return to Plasencia. In consequence, on the 29th I Corps [Victor] took up a fallback position on the Alberche, whilst His Majesty overnighted at Santa Olalla with IV Corps [Sebastiani] and the reserve in order to prevent the enemy making an attempt on Toledo, and to make Venegas sorry should he cross the Tagus at Aranjuez and march on Madrid.
>
> Now that you know, *Monsieur Maréchal*, of all that has occurred in the position occupied by the army, His Majesty has ordered me to inform you that, should your movement on Plasencia fail to force the English army to separate from the Spanish army, then it will be only with difficulty that the king will be able to confront the forces which have united in his front.[9]

Cuesta summed up the importance of the captured documents in his report to Cornel as follows:

---

8   Joseph Bonaparte to the French governor of Ávila 31 July 1809, Cuesta, *Manifiesto*, Appendix V, p.108. See also TNA: FO 72/74: Spanish letters to Canning, 6 July 1809 to 10 August 1809, p.298.
9   Jourdan to Soult, 30 July 1809, Cuesta, *Manifiesto*, Appendix V, pp.108–112. See also TNA: FO 72/74, Spanish letters to Canning, 6 July 1809 to 10 August 1809, pp.300–303.

Talavera 3 August.

... the letters, after giving notice of the battle of the 27th/28th, announce in the strongest terms possible the level of interest which would be generated for 'the cause' by [Soult's] arrival at Plasencia in as short a time as possible, and his continuation from that place in order to attack the British army which, he is assured, consists of 25,000 men. This clearly infers that Soult's strength must also be at or about 25,000, which makes the possibility of a British victory doubtful.[10] By another source, I have come to know that Victor is on the move from Maqueda to Santa Olalla, which indicates that he is awaiting Soult's arrival in order to attack us from front and flank.

The urgency of not leaving the British army to be exposed at Almaraz, or of leaving my army here in a position completely exposed on the left due to the departure of the British, has convinced me that I must march tonight to unite with General Wellesley, leaving here all the appearance of a vanguard so that the enemy will not perceive my movement and will continue to respect the position at Talavera, to which I propose to return once we have beaten Soult. In the case that Victor attacks Talavera with all of his strength, I will at least have avoided the chance that I may not have been able to defend it.

I have given notice of this movement to *General* Venegas, and to General Wellesley ...[11]

This marked something of a change in Cuesta's usual comportment. Judging by his previous actions at Cabezón de Pisuerga, Medina de Rioseco, Medellín and, in fact, his early behaviour at Talavera when he set off in pursuit of Victor, one might have expected him to stand his ground at the prospect of a clash with the French. Overall, his analysis of the situation in this case seems to have been extremely sound, but how would his move towards Wellesley and away from Madrid affect Venegas? More importantly, was he communicating effectively with Venegas and keeping him completely up to date with the changing situation on the Alberche? In an appendix to his *Manifiesto* there are copies of the correspondence between himself and Venegas regarding his intentions after Talavera, in the first two letters of which he insisted that Venegas advance on Madrid, whilst in the third, written on 3 August, he informed him that both he and Wellesley were marching to confront Soult in the region of Plasencia:

I have received reliable news that, having traversed the pass at Baños, *Maréchal* Soult is now at Plasencia, [as such] the English army decided to leave here early this morning to confront him somewhere between Almaraz and the river Tiétar. In the meantime the Spanish army remained at Talavera, maintaining its position. However, after the English departed, I received reliable information that Soult was bringing a much greater force than was previously thought, as such I have

---

10   By Cuesta's reckoning it would seem that the Spaniards were still unaware of Soult's recent reinforcement by Ney and Mortier. His strength was actually some 50,000 men.

11   Cuesta, *Manifiesto*, pp.69–70.

determined to leave [this place] tonight in order to reinforce the English and ensure the [success of] the action against Soult …[12]

Venegas Continues to Advance on Madrid

It is now time to return to the situation with regard to the Army of La Mancha, having switched our attention to Talavera on 25 July at the point where the bulk of Venegas's divisions were positioned between the Tagus and the Guadiana and billeted around the villages of Camuñas, Madridejos, Herencia and Villafranca, as they felt their way towards Aranjuez and Toledo. Venegas's diary records that, on 26 July, the eve of Talavera, his divisions would shuffle a little further to the north as follows: the 1st Division to Turleque, the 2nd to remain at Camuñas, the 3rd to Consuegra, the 4th, 5th and army headquarters to Madridejos, all of those places being some 50 miles south of Aranjuez on the Tagus (in referring to Plate 18 the reader will gain an idea of just how carefully Venegas was proceeding, even at this late hour).

As Lacy's 1st Division moved through the Spanish countryside, they received intelligence that between 24 and 25 July a column of some 10,000 French, almost certainly Sebastiani's IV Corps, was seen heading towards Toledo, where they were met by Joseph Bonaparte and the men of his Guard, plus a brigade belonging to Dessolles' division, about 6,000 men in total. Other reports put the number of Sebastiani's troops on the move at that time to be about 16,000, which tallies almost perfectly with Oman's number of 15,456 for the strength of the IV Corps at Talavera. In other words, all of the troop movements reported during the days leading up to Talavera would appear to be those made in preparation for the final leg of both Joseph's and Sebastiani's marches to join Victor. Later news indicated that the whole of IV Corps had marched directly from Toledo to Talavera without having rested the horses belonging to its cavalry, and that for most of the 25th and 26th *los paisanos* (the country folk) living near Toledo could hear the rumble of cannon fire from the direction of Cebolla which, if true, probably marked the French attack on Cuesta in and around Torrijos, Santa Olalla and Cazalegas, which took place on 26 July.[13]

As Sebastiani's men vacated the various towns to the south of Madrid, they took care to set fire to the local bridges spanning the Tagus, such as that at Barcas and the Puente de la Reyna on the eastern fringes of Aranjuez, in an attempt to destroy them. All of this was done in the knowledge that Venegas would almost certainly advance towards the capital in their absence. At 2:00 p.m. on the 26th, Venegas sent *Teniente Coronel* Cebrián to deliver a dispatch to Cuesta, informing him of the commencement of the enemy's retreat from the Guadiana on 23 July and the subsequent pursuit mounted by the Army of La Mancha; asking for instructions on how best to proceed with his operations.[14]

As issued on 27th, Venegas's marching orders for 28 July would take his 1st Division closer to Toledo, the 2nd to Ocaña, the 3rd to La Guardia and the 4th, 5th and army headquarters

12   Cuesta to Venegas, 3 August 1809, Cuesta, *Manifiesto*, pp.116–117.
13   Oman, *History of the Peninsular War*, vol.II, p.648. See also AHN: Diversas Colecciones, 125, N.5: el Ejército de La Mancha, entry for 26 July 1809.
14   AHN: Diversas Colecciones, 125, N.5: el Ejército de La Mancha, entry for 26 July 1809.

to Tembleque, all of those places being within 30 miles of Aranjuez (see Plate 20). In essence these movements would mean that Venegas would not begin to arrive on the south bank of the Tagus until 29 July. Lacy, in command of the 1st Division, was informed that his move upon Toledo was intended to draw most of the French units still south of Madrid to that place, and that he should try to take possession of it and hold the enemy force there in position, thus allowing the rest of Venegas's force to repair the Tagus bridges in the vicinity of Aranjuez, before crossing the river to take the enemy in the rear, cut their line of retreat and enter Madrid. All of this was communicated to Cuesta in Venegas's dispatch of the 27th, in which he also asked Cuesta what he should do next, adding that, in his own mind, the best thing he could do was to follow his own plan as outlined above.[15] In the meantime Don Felipe de la Corte had led an advanced party to Aranjuez to take possession of the fords and bridges there, and *Coronel* Riglos, commander of the *partida de guerrilla* operating with the 3rd Division, was at Ocaña (refer to Plates 18–20 for an idea of the geography and troop movements).

On 28 July Lacy, then at Nambroca just south of Toledo, received what was clearly some incorrect intelligence from within the city, to the effect that Joseph had left for Talavera that day with some 12,000 men. Whether or not this was a reference to the movement of Joseph's personal guard and Dessolles' brigade, or that of Sebastiani's corps, it was inaccurate both in the numbers of men stated (too big to be Joseph's force, too small to be Sebastiani's) and the date of the movement given, which was too late by several days. Nevertheless, it gave a strong indication that Toledo was now occupied by a reduced garrison of some 3,000 men, an indication confirmed by a later report from one, Ventura Jiménez, an agent operating inside the city, in which he claimed there were just 1,900 French troops within its walls and that the citizenry was 'disposed to fall upon them.'[16] But even that claim had to be treated with a degree of circumspection, as the garrison strength was actually closer to 4,000, notwithstanding the fact that about half of the troops were Spanish.

Venegas's 2nd Division was at Ocaña that day, just 10 miles from Aranjuez, the 3rd was approaching that place from La Guardia and the 4th following up along with army headquarters. The 5th Division was at Yepes some 10 miles due south of Aranjuez.[17] All of the movements made by Venegas during 27 and 28 July coincided with the Battle of Talavera, and it must be said that, apart from the 3,000 or so troops left to garrison Toledo by Sebastiani, the commander of the Army of La Mancha had been incapable of preventing a single French soldier from taking his place amongst the massed ranks which were to assail Wellesley and Cuesta at Talavera. It was an abject failure.

On 29 July Venegas's 1st Division was at Toledo, his 2nd and 3rd divisions had finally arrived at Aranjuez and the 4th and 5th were at Yepes and Ocaña, respectively. But with Sebastiani and Joseph still in the vicinity of Talavera, the gates of Madrid should now have offered an irresistible prospect for the Army of La Mancha. Had the allied plan of campaign been for the move upon Madrid from the west to be the diversionary attack and Venegas's push from the south the main assault on the capital, then it would have worked perfectly, Madrid now being at the mercy of the Venegas's army. Unfortunately, that scenario was

15   Venegas to Cuesta, 27 July 1809, Venegas, *Vindicación*, sub-section Documentos, pp.11–13, Número 13.
16   AHN: Diversas Colecciones, 125, N.5: el Ejército de La Mancha, entry for 28 July 1809.
17   AHN: Diversas Colecciones, 125, N.5: el Ejército de La Mancha, entry for 28 July 1809.

diametrically opposed to the one conceived, and the allies' scheme had come apart to such an extent that it was the French who had now been presented with an opportunity to defeat the Spanish and British forces in detail. This, in fact, was what they had originally set out to do, by concentrating all of their strength to deal with Wellesley and Cuesta whilst Venegas was held at bay on the south bank of the Guadiana during the middle weeks of July. That they had effectively failed to deal with the former two at Talavera in the first instance, did not mean that their plans had been ultimately foiled. Having drawn Venegas to the south bank of the Tagus, he was now within comfortable striking distance for Sebastiani as he withdrew from the recent battle area, as such he could seek him out and destroy him whilst the combined allied army was held at bay on the Alberche by Victor, in effect the reverse of their original plan but viable in the sense that Venegas ought now to be easy meat, and once dispensed with the weakened Wellesley and Cuesta could be overwhelmed by Victor and Soult, the latter drawing ever closer in the rear of the allies, hoping to cut off their escape route to Portugal.

The French had suffered significant losses at Talavera, but a second confrontation was now in the offing and Sebastiani would soon be detached to deal with the Army of La Mancha, leaving the combined army at the mercy of Soult and Victor. The allies' game was up. Cuesta may still have been entertaining the idea of a glorious march to the Ebro, but Wellesley had his eyes firmly set on the Portuguese frontier. The Manchegans, with hardly a Frenchman between them and the Tagus, had failed expeditiously to cross the Guadiana from the south during the days leading up to the battle at Talavera, and a French counter stroke was now in the offing.

In reality, Venegas's inexperienced army would probably have been annihilated had he attempted to force the pace to the south of Madrid, unless, that is, he could somehow have held Sebastiani on or near the Tagus, just below the capital, before bringing him to battle on the eve of Talavera, but that would have demanded some exquisite timing, as well as an unlikely level of compliance on the part of the French; things which were clearly not within Venegas's gift. The Manchegans, in the shape of Lacy's 1st Division, actually arrived on the south bank of the Tagus whilst the Battle at Talavera was raging, but even with the path to the capital almost denuded of French forces, Venegas still failed to push on. Two days later, with Victor and his reinforcements having failed to destroy the British and *Extremeños* at Talavera, the French were not about to give up the fight. If there was to be a second battle on the Tagus then at least Wellesley would be present in much reduced strength after his losses in the first confrontation; and having tested Cuesta's abilities to destruction at Medellín, Victor must have thought that a swift chastening of Venegas by Sebastiani would allow him to join forces with Soult and crush the combined army at the second time of asking, thus accomplishing his desire to defeat the allied armies in detail if not quite in the manner he had originally envisaged. All he had to do was to keep Wellesley and Cuesta where they were, whilst Sebastiani turned on the decidedly weaker and more vulnerable Manchegans. Once the plan was set in motion, he himself would remain in the vicinity of the Alberche, in order to prevent Wellesley and Cuesta from breaking into the capital by threatening one or other of their flanks, either of which moves would dissuade the combined army from going to the aid of Venegas; and all the time Soult would be drawing closer. The jaws of a potentially fatal trap were beginning to close upon the allies.

Venegas at Aranjuez

By 12:30 p.m. on 29 July, Venegas was at Aranjuez eager to hear from Lacy. Worried about a lack of communication from Cuesta, he sent a courier to Toledo to collect news from the commander of his 1st Division, and at the same time ask him for any recent information he may have received from the Spanish commander in chief, as he himself had heard nothing from that direction since the 25th.

Ignorant of any news from the west of Madrid, Lacy replied that when he arrived at Toledo he stationed his troops on the heights above the Puente de Alcántara, and that when he sent his first units to cross the bridge and lay siege to the city's Alcázar, they became involved in a long, bickering fight with the French garrison before withdrawing.[18] Whilst Lacy was making his show at Toledo, the rest of Venegas's divisions took control of the Puente de la Reyna at Aranjuez, together with a number of fords both up and downstream from the bridge itself. By this time, intelligence from Madrid suggested there were no more than 2,000 French troops in the capital, and that the populace, having heard of the approach of the Manchegans, were openly preparing to welcome them into the city with celebrations, the likes of which were to be mimicked by the members of the *Junta Suprema* in far away Seville, who had gone so far as to make detailed plans for the arrangements to be taken care of once the subsequent fall of capital had been announced. In fact, Cornel had issued a royal order on 27 July to the effect that, once the expected evacuation of the French from Madrid had taken place, Venegas was to provide a garrison for the capital from the Army of La Mancha, before taking up the role of *Capitán General de Castilla la Nueva*.[19]

By 11:00 a.m. on the following morning, 30 July, the picture began to change when news arrived from Lacy informing Venegas that numbers of French cavalry and infantry were approaching Toledo from the direction of Talavera, thus forcing the 1st Division to retreat to the Monasterio de Sisla some three miles to the south. It was quite clear to Lacy that these units were the vanguard of Sebastiani's troops retiring from the scene of the recent battle. At midday a message from Cuesta finally arrived at Venegas's headquarters. Written on the battlefield of Talavera at 9:00 a.m. on the 29th it was sent to inform him of the allied victory of the 27/28 July and the subsequent retreat of the French towards Toledo, the sender adding that he had proposed to Wellesley that, once their troops had been rested and fed, they should march together in pursuit of the enemy. The commander of the Army of La Mancha duly noted in his diary that, on dissemination of the news from Talavera, a *Te Deum* was sung in the church of one of the local parishes, and that each soldier belonging to his host was allowed *un quartillo de vino* (half a litre of wine) in celebration of the happy tidings. Venegas then replied to his commander in chief, reminding him that, in complying with his orders, he was not intending to go in search of the enemy until the whole of the allied armies were ready to mount a combined operation against them. Reading between the lines it is not difficult to imagine that Venegas was suggesting to his chief that, should he be in need of new orders, they ought to be dispatched as soon as possible and should relate to the

---

18   This is the Puente de Alcántara at Toledo, not to be confused with the Puente de Alcántara at Alcántara in the province of Cáceres, close to the Portuguese border. In fact the word, *alcántara*, derives from the Arabic word, *al-qanṭara*, meaning bridge.

19   AHN: Diversas Colecciones, 125, N.5: el Ejército de La Mancha, entry for 29 July 1809.

coordination of the proposed allied advance. Once again, Venegas copied the details of his communication to Cornel – should things eventually go awry, it would seem.[20]

Written at 9:00 p.m. on the previous night, a further message from Lacy arrived at Venegas's headquarters on the morning of 31 July. It informed the general of the disorderly arrival of some 7,000 French troops at Toledo. All the signs that they had been roughly handled at Talavera were, he said, plain to see. As such, he stated that he was not fearful that they might attempt to cross the Tagus and attack him; in any case, he said, he had the bridges in front of him well secured and guarded against just such an eventuality. Later news from Lacy noted that the French had taken possession of the bridge on the Tagus just south of Montalbán, which lies some 15 miles west of Toledo at the mid-point between that town and Talavera, a key point should the French be planning further operations. The commander of Venegas's 1st Division added that he had established a post of *partidas de guerrilla* at a point some 10 miles from the bridge in order to guard against any advance towards him, ending his dispatch with a note to the effect that most of the French troops earlier mentioned had moved out of Toledo on the day following their arrival, marching off along the north bank of the river in the direction of Mocejón to the north east. This and other news about enemy movements towards the Puente Largo, a crossing point on the Jarama river just north of Aranjuez, caused Venegas to follow the advice of Girón and send a force of five battalions, together with cavalry and artillery, to guard that bridge, before directing the remainder of his 2nd and 3rd Divisions to occupy the Puente de la Reyna on the Tagus, situated in the eastern suburbs of Aranjuez itself.[21]

By 1 August, Girón was sending messages to army headquarters to the effect that his scouts had advanced some 12 miles up the royal highway which runs from Aranjuez to Madrid, and that they were only some 20 miles from the capital.[22] Then, on the following day, Lacy sent notice to Venegas of a message he had received from Cuesta at Talavera to the effect that Victor's army, which had been stationed some eight miles in front of him, had 'disappeared towards Toledo and Torrijos' during the night of the 31 July (see earlier). At 7:00 a.m. on the morning of 2 August, the commander of the Manchegans received a message from Cuesta which chimed with that he had sent to Lacy.[23] In it, he informed his subordinate that Joseph had returned to Madrid with his much-reduced corps of Guards, and that on 31 July Victor had been on the left bank of the Alberche with some 27,000 men. He then went on to tell him that under such circumstances, and with the agreement of Wellesley, he, Venegas, should advance with the whole of his army towards Madrid 'without a moment's loss,' in the hope that the imposter king and his troops would be forced to 'enclose themselves in the Retiro or make a precipitate retreat,' adding that this suggested operation would 'alarm Victor to such an extent that he would be obliged to detach a considerable portion of his forces to the city,' thus reducing the numbers which he and Wellesley would have to face should they decide to attack the French marshal. Like this, continued Cuesta, the allies could make their longed-for combined movement against Victor, pushing him towards Madrid where he would have to offer battle or commence what might turn into

20   AHN: Diversas Colecciones, 125, N.5: el Ejército de La Mancha, entry for 30 July 1809.
21   AHN: Diversas Colecciones, 125, N.5: el Ejército de La Mancha, entry for 31 July 1809.
22   AHN: Diversas Colecciones, 125, N.5: el Ejército de La Mancha, entry for 1 August 1809.
23   Cuesta to Venegas, 31 July 1809, Venegas, *Vindicación*, sub-section Documentos, pp.20–21, Número 26.

a difficult retreat. On the other hand, should things not go to plan, Venegas could always retreat via Arganda, keeping his chief permanently informed of his intentions. It was almost as an afterthought that Cuesta ventured the news that '*Maréchal* Soult, with 12,000 men of all arms, is advancing in our rear, having arrived at Béjar [on 29 July].' In fact, as we have seen, Soult was at the head of an army of some 50,000 men.[24]

As a result of these instructions from his superior, Venegas sent orders to Zerain, recently returned to the Army of La Mancha along with his 5th Division, to march with his own and Lacy's 1st Division from Toledo to Aranjuez, leaving just a covering force behind so that, with the whole of his army concentrated at the latter place, he could launch the desired assault on Madrid.

As an additional entry in his diary for 2 August, Venegas recorded that at 5:00 p.m., 'I received another express from Cuesta repeating the news that Victor had disappeared from his front, but this time adding that, "... the day before yesterday, *Maréchal* Soult, with 12 to 14,000 men, entered Béjar and continued towards Baños, where he probably forced the pass with the intention of uniting with Victor. As such," continued Cuesta, "I am anxious to know the effect that your approach on Madrid will produce, because if the city has not yet been reinforced then I think its acquisition is very achievable".'[25] However, in response to Cuesta's obvious promptings that he make a determined move on Madrid, Venegas replied:

(Venegas to Cuesta, 2 August 1809, *Número* 28):
I conceive it would be difficult and daring for me to march on Madrid as you advise.

The enemy, combining his marches, must now be at Toledo ... in which case, should I march on Aranjuez tomorrow, where I expect my 1st and 5th Divisions to arrive, the French will be marching in my left rear or on a route parallel to that of my own; and if they have marched via Torrijos directly on Madrid they will overtake me and I will have them interposed between my army and the capital.

In either case, Your Excellency will observe the difficulty or impossibility that the combined armies [Wellesley and Cuesta] will arrive in time to assist my army in its uneven fight against the superior numbers of Victor and the various corps which may sally forth from Madrid to assist in the operations against us. Nevertheless, by tomorrow night my army will be concentrated at Aranjuez, and if the circumstances ... suggest that my march on Madrid will be successful I will carry it out; but at the moment I am inclined more to wait at Aranjuez for new orders from Your Excellency, and with your permission I would like you to take into consideration that I think it indispensable that our movements are combined, if so my army will embark on its own without a moment's loss.[26]

Once again, we have an example of Venegas's haughty insubordination towards Cuesta. On the following day, 3 August, he wrote to his superior once more, this time informing him

---

24   Cuesta to Venegas, 31 July 1809, AHN: Diversas Colecciones, 125, N.5: el Ejército de La Mancha, entry for 2 August 1809. See also Venegas, *Vindicación*, sub-section Documentos, pp.20–21, Número 26.
25   Cuesta to Venegas, 1 August 1809, AHN: Diversas Colecciones, 125, N.5: el Ejército de La Mancha, entry for 2 August 1809. See also Venegas, *Vindicación*, sub-section Documentos, pp.21–22, Número 27.
26   Venegas to Cuesta, 2 August 1809, Venegas, *Vindicación*, sub-section Documentos, p.22, Número 28.

of some new intelligence he had received suggesting that Joseph Bonaparte was at Illescas, some 10 miles north-west of Aranjuez, with some 30,000 men, and that the French were putting it about that they were going to attack him at the royal city; going on to say that:

(Venegas to Cuesta, 3 August 1809, *Número* 29):
Setting aside the truth of this for the moment, there is no doubt that yesterday they attacked our guerrillas at the Puente Largo, and that the enemy army is on my left flank … if it has not already advanced [to gain contact with us]. All of which gives proof to what I said yesterday, having calculated correctly the marches of the French.[27]

Towards the end of his diary entry for the previous day, 2 August 1809, Venegas had written:

Together with his orders of the 31st ult. the *Secretario de Guerra* included copies of the two reports of the battle at Talavera supplied to him by *General* Cuesta, and being of the opinion that I too had received the said reports, he supposed that my army would have advanced to cut off the enemy's retreat. In this the *Suprema Junta* had supposed well, but it is not what I have actually done, due to my previous orders from Sr. Cuesta that I do all that I can to avoid an encounter with Victor's army.
I have sent the *Secretario de Guerra* a copy of Sr. Cuesta's dispatch of the 31st ult. [see *Número* 26 below] together with my answer [to him] [see *Número* 28 below] and I have given him notice of the dispositions which, in consequence, I have taken.[28]

Once again, we see Venegas referring back to Cuesta's earlier orders, in which he unfortunately stipulated a maximum strength for French forces that the Army of La Mancha should be willing to confront during its march on Madrid. However, the whole landscape of the situation in and around the capital had changed drastically in the wake of the battle at Talavera; Venegas knew it but wanted to ignore it, hence his pedantic referral to the now surely obsolete orders previously issued by his commander in chief.

The relevant details from the two documents referred to by Venegas above; those he forwarded to Cornel were as follows:

(Cuesta to Venegas, 31 July 1809, *Número* 26):
According to the latest news we have acquired, Joseph is returning to Madrid accompanied by his much-reduced Guard. Victor remains almost in sight with some 26 to 28,000 men on the left bank of the Alberche … Soult with some 12,000 men … is advancing in our rear, having arrived at Béjar the day before yesterday.
Under these circumstances I have agreed with General Wellesley to write to Your Excellency … instructing you to march with all of your troops on Madrid without a moment's loss …[29]

---

27   Venegas to Cuesta, 3 August 1809, Venegas, *Vindicación*, sub-section Documentos, p.23, Número 29.
28   AHN: Diversas Colecciones, 125, N.5: el Ejército de La Mancha, entry for 2 August 1809.
29   Cuesta to Venegas, 31 July 1809, Venegas, *Vindicación*, sub-section Documentos, pp.20–21, Número 26.

Subsequent to this dispatch, Cuesta had sent a second on the morning of the following day, 1 August 1809, in which he informed Venegas that Victor's army had de-camped and marched towards Torrijos and Toledo.[30] It was in the light of what was said in both these dispatches that Venegas replied to Cuesta on 2 August as follows, sending a copy to Cornel:

> (Venegas to Cuesta, 2 Aug. 1809, *Número* 28):
> ... [Your] second dispatch, in which you informed me that Victor had de-camped in the direction of Torrijos and Toledo, makes me think that a march by me on Madrid would now be more difficult and risky, and that you should send me new instructions.[31]

Along with these two enclosures, Venegas wrote a note to Cornel pointing out that it would have been easy for him to enter Madrid earlier when he had the opportunity, rather than remain inactive due to the orders he had received from Cuesta telling him stay where he was – only to receive orders now, instructing him to march on the capital with all the difficulties it entailed. To put it mildly, this analysis would seem to be a travesty of the truth. As we have seen, Venegas was never keen on advancing to Madrid, no matter what Cuesta's orders were. But the big question is, why was he still so unwilling to obey his orders to advance beyond the Tagus during the first days of August 1809? In his diary entry for 3 August he recorded that:

> At 11:00 this morning, a message was sent to Cuesta informing him that we have been advised by *General* Girón that some 30,000 of the enemy were at Illescas and the surrounding area, which proves, no matter their exact number, what I told Cuesta yesterday, that depending on the time elapsed since they struck camp [at Talavera] they would be on our left flank if not further in advance [by now]. That being the case it should demonstrate to the *Capitán General* [Cuesta] that, in order to bring the French to battle with some advantage, the combined army [of Wellesley and Cuesta] will have to advance and form a line with mine.[32]

This last point had been put to Cuesta by Venegas in an earlier communication, making it clear that, despite his commander in chief's promptings, he was unwilling to pitch his army against the French without the direct support of the British and the Army of Extremadura. The final entry in Venegas's diary for 3 August records that he had sent his congratulations to Cuesta and Wellesley for their victory at Talavera. A somewhat tongue in cheek remark, it would seem.[33]

With the allied campaign now in serious danger of ending in disaster, Venegas seemed to think the time had come to lay all of the blame for the impending defeat at Cuesta's feet by using his uncomfortably chummy relationship with Cornel to prepare the ground for

30   Cuesta to Venegas, 1 August 1809, Venegas, *Vindicación*, sub-section Documentos, pp.21–22, Número 27.
31   Venegas to Cuesta, 2 August 1809, Venegas, *Vindicación*, sub-section Documentos, p.22, Número 28.
32   AHN: Diversas Colecciones, 125, N.5: el Ejército de La Mancha, entry for 3 August 1809.
33   AHN: Diversas Colecciones, 125, N.5: el Ejército de La Mancha, entry for 3 August 1809.

his own ascendency after, so he seemed to think, the inevitable demise of his superior; his conceit and ambition apparently knowing no bounds.

The French Concentrate for an Attack on Venegas

On 4 August, Venegas received an urgent message from Lacy informing him that he was on his way to headquarters to discuss the difficulties, or otherwise, of maintaining his position in front of Toledo, for fear of being attacked by superior forces. However, we have already seen that, by that time, Venegas had sent a dispatch to both Lacy and Zerain (2 August) assuming them to be at Toledo and ordering them to come to Aranjuez. It may have been the case that Lacy was already on his way there when he wrote his message, which Venegas received on the 4th, or that the message and the dispatch crossed in transit. In support of Lacy's concerns, Girón had that day already reported the presence of the French at Illescas, with another 4,000 at Yuncos, as well as other smaller detachments at Azaña, Cobeja and Alameda. Then, in a fast-moving scenario, an astounding piece of news arrived from Cuesta at 5:30 p.m.:

> (Cuesta to Venegas, 3 August 1809, *Número* 30):
> I have received reliable news that, having traversed the pass at Baños, *Maréchal* Soult is now at Plasencia, [as such] the English army decided to set off from here early this morning to confront him somewhere between Almaraz and the river Tiétar. In the meantime the Spanish army remains in its position at Talavera. However, after the English departed, I received reliable information that Soult was bringing a much greater force than was previously thought, as such I have determined to leave [this place] tonight in order to reinforce the English and ensure the [success of] the action against him. Once that has been accomplished we shall return to seek out *Maréchal* Victor, who for the present is unaware of my [intended] movement … I understand that the intruder king, together with the forces he did not lose [at Talavera], is marching on Illescas and has not sent any troops towards Toledo, where *Generales* Zerain and Lacy were located yesterday … I send this information to you persuaded that you should avoid any attempt by Joseph and Sebastiani to move against the Army of La Mancha, and under the premise that you should not take part in general actions against superior troops.[34]

Once again, we have an example of the mixed messaging passing from Cuesta to Venegas, the kind of which had sown the seeds of convenient confusion (for Venegas) about how the commander in chief of the Army of La Mancha should react to the presence of the enemy in his front. Sometimes he was ordered not to engage unless the French were below a certain strength, whilst on other occasions he was being encouraged to throw caution to the wind

---

34   Cuesta to Venegas, 3 August 1809, Venegas, *Vindicación*, sub-section Documentos, pp. 23-24, Número 30. In his *Manifiesto*, Cuesta said he was already at Oropesa with Wellesley on 4 August when he heard of Soult's actual strength. See also, AHN: Diversas Colecciones, 125, N.5: el Ejército de La Mancha, entry for 4 August 1809.

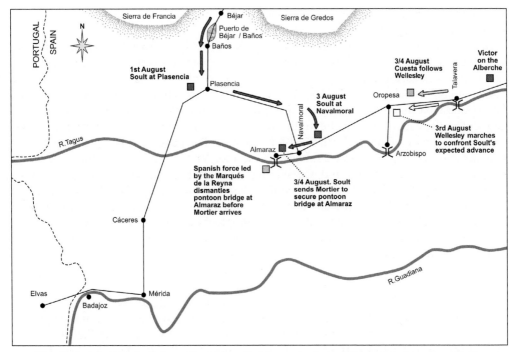

Plate 22. 1–4 August. Soult forces the puerto de Béjar and arrives at Plasencia before advancing to Navalmoral, sending Mortier to capture the pontoon bridge at Almaraz. Fortunately, Spanish forces commanded by the Marqués de la Reyna manage to dismantle the bridge before the French arrive. To the west, Wellesley marches to confront Soult and Cuesta follows.

and simply attack the enemy, all of which provided him with the opportunity to superimpose his own subjectivity onto any situation in order to suit his purpose. Cuesta should never have allowed him such a measure of leeway, something he could have achieved by giving him a well-defined and consistent set of parameters within which to operate, and if he had known of his subordinate's connivence with Cornel then he should have done all that he could to nip it in the bud, rather than tolerate his constant backsliding.

As was his wont, Venegas wasted no time in forwarding a copy of Cuesta's message to Cornel at Seville as part of his dispatch of 4 August (*Número* 38) reminding him of the plan which he himself had earlier suggested.[35] Cuesta too was to be a recipient of that plan – that Wellesley and the commander of the Army of Extremadura should both advance to unite with his Army of La Mancha, so that the whole of the allied army could then bring Joseph and Victor to battle. This, he re-iterated, was the best course of action to adopt, claiming that Soult's arrival at or close to the eventual site of the contest would hardly matter, as he was not strong enough to face the allies. However, he continued, the retrograde movement by Wellesley and Cuesta currently underway would effectively abandon the Army of La

---

35   Venegas to Cornel, 4 August 1809, Venegas, *Vindicación*, sub-section Documentos, p.28, Número 38.

Mancha to its fate. Such an outcome, he continued, would necessarily force him to retreat in the face of much superior forces.

In persisting with his opinion that an all-out general action against the French offered the best chance of victory, it would seem that Venegas had paid little attention to Cuesta's assertion that Soult was now much stronger than the allies originally thought him to be, the very assertion upon which Cuesta had based his latest resolve to march to Wellesley's aid.[36] To be fair to Cuesta, it should be said that he was probably thinking that, once Wellesley became aware of Soult's actual strength, he would almost certainly decide to avoid fighting an action against him and commence his longed-for retreat to Portugal. That being the case, both Cuesta's and Venegas's armies would be easy meat for Victor, Joseph, Sebastiani and Soult. In essence, and with that in mind, Cuesta may well have been genuinely doing his utmost to keep the British in the fight for Madrid when making his decision to follow Wellesley.

In view of what would turn out to be the ultimate fate of Venegas's army, it may be instructive to include the second and final paragraph of his dispatch to Cornel of 4 August, in which he foresaw with some accuracy the end result of his army being left entirely to its own devices in facing the full strength of the enemy:

> (Venegas to Cornel, 4 August 1809, *Número* 38):
> Your Excellency knows perfectly well that this army, inferior to the enemy in numbers, has been abandoned and forced to rely entirely upon its own resources, when even the *Capitán General* [Cuesta] himself recognises that the French are superior in the art of manoeuvre. [It would appear that] I am therefore left with no other recourse than to carry out a shameful and second retreat, which will be hated by the people of the towns we now occupy, and who we are about to leave behind. It will be a retreat that will leave our soldiers crestfallen and demoralised, and will dilute the national spirit, especially amongst the population of the region. [And it is] these palpable truths which have resolved me to stand and fight if I am attacked, preferring that the enemy smashes me to pieces rather than consider the idea of flight. Your Excellency will now see how much better my situation would have been if I had ignored the restraints placed on me by the *Capitán General*, and marched on Madrid in the belief that I would receive the help I was promised from the combined Anglo-Spanish army.[37]

The content of Venegas's final sentence above is difficult to comprehend. How, after weeks of hiding behind Cuesta's 'constraints' in order to refuse to advance, even at times when Cuesta had suggested that they may be ignored or loosened, and after he himself had sometimes exaggerated the enemy strength in his front in order to refuse an order to advance, could he now make such a statement? One can only say that it displays an element of low cunning in his attitude. In fact, Venegas's dispatch does not bear the hallmark of a clear prescience of mind; neither can it be regarded as a self-fulfilling prophecy from a disillusioned and demoralised general, nor the disingenuousness of a guilt complex. Instead, it has

36   AHN: Diversas Colecciones, 125, N.5: el Ejército de La Mancha, entry for 4 August 1809.
37   Venegas to Cornel, 4 August 1809, Venegas, *Vindicación*, sub-section Documentos, p.28, Número 38.

a desperate sound of faux martyrism about it, the commander in chief of the Manchegans seemingly ready to sacrifice his army after being apparently abandoned by his superior.

With the fighting at Talavera now over, it was clear that the allies were not about to reap the hoped-for harvest from their battlefield triumph; disharmony and mistrust reigning amongst their commanders. Wellesley, it would seem, had decided that his supply problems were never going to be resolved, and was, in effect, already marching back to Portugal. Cuesta sensed it, and even he was not willing to remain where he was as the darkening clouds of overwhelming French strength began to gather; instead, he would throw in his lot with the British and withdraw. The unfortunate, or should that be the contrary, Venegas was about to reap the whirlwind he had helped to sow, and he knew it. Where, one might ask, was this spirit when it was most needed? If there had been a moment at which it was acceptable to risk the annihilation of the Manchegans for the greater cause of an overall allied victory, then it was during the final week of July 1809, when a courageous and determined attempt on Madrid might have clinched the laurels of a famous victory. Had this stark realisation caused him to dwell upon the fact that his own failings of character may well have sealed the fate of the allies in the summer of 1809? Oman, in his *History of the Peninsular War*, remarked:

> What the allied generals never expected was that Venegas would let Sebastiani slip away from his front, without any attempt to hold him, and would then (instead of marching on Madrid) waste the critical days of the campaign (July 24-29) in miserable delays between Toledo and Aranjuez, when there was absolutely no French field-force between him and Madrid, nor any hostile troops whatever in his neighbourhood save a weak division of 3,000 men in garrison at Toledo. The failure of the Talavera campaign is due even more to this wretched indecision and disobedience to orders on the part of Venegas than to the eccentricities and errors of Cuesta. If the Army of La Mancha had kept Sebastiani in check, and refused to allow him to abscond, there would have been no battles on the Alberche on July 27-28, for the French would never have dared to face the Anglo-Spaniards of the main host without the assistance of the IV [Sebastiani's] Corps.[38].

Wellesley and Cuesta in the Aftermath of the Battle of Talavera

So far in this chapter, we have concentrated on the interplay between the main protagonists on the Spanish side of the Anglo-Spanish alliance during the first four days of August 1809. We may now examine the interaction which took place between the British and Spanish during that same period, beginning on 31 July.

In the immediate aftermath of the battle at Talavera, Wellesley's first thoughts were to encourage Cuesta to go after the French as they retreated towards the Alberche, whilst he

---

38   Oman, *History of the Peninsular War*, vol.II, pp.478–479.

rested and refreshed his British contingent where it was, with the intention of moving on Madrid when all was ready, 'if not interrupted by some accident on our flank.'[39]

By 31 July he was aware of Soult's approach on Plasencia, though it would appear that he was another of those still ignorant of the sizeable reinforcements the *Maréchal* had received since his expulsion from Portugal in May. Hoping to block his old adversary's march from Béjar to Plasencia, it was on this day that Wellesley wrote to O'Donojú from Talavera:

> Adverting to the intelligence which has been received of the movement of a French corps towards the Puerto de Baños, I cannot avoid requesting that you would press his Excellency Gen. Cuesta to detach towards that quarter, on this night, a division of infantry with its guns, and a Commanding officer upon whose exertions and abilities he could rely ... At all events this division will not be missed here, and it will be in a position to observe the enemy, if he should have crossed the mountains before the arrival of the division. But if the division should arrive in time, it will perform a most important service to the common cause ...
>
> P.S. I have to observe that His Excellency is equally interested with me in preventing this irruption into Plasencia, as the enemy's first step will certainly be to interrupt His Excellency's communication with Seville by the bridge of Almaraz.[40]

Later, on receipt of intelligence indicating that, far from retreating towards Madrid after the battle at Talavera, Victor's main force had actually halted on the left bank of the Alberche just a few miles from the battlefield, the British commander became alert to the fact that he still had a strong enemy force to his front whilst another was attempting to approach from the rear. With this in mind he wrote a further letter to O'Donojú:

> In addition to the official letter which I have written to you this morning, respecting the advance of the enemy through the Puerto de Baños, I cannot but observe to you that the situation of both [the Spanish and British] armies will become very critical in such an event. There is but one way to avoid it, besides stopping the enemy advance through the Puerto de Baños, and that is, to urge on the advance of Gen. Venegas towards Madrid ...
>
> I shall be obliged to you if you would explain these my sentiments to Gen. Cuesta.[41]

Wellesley's hopes, as expressed in his correspondence with O'Donojú, were that Soult could be prevented from breaking out of the mountains of the Sierra de Gredos, and that the hoped-for advance of Venegas to the south of Madrid would cause Victor to detach some of his forces to cope with it, thus allowing him to attack the *Maréchal* on the Alberche in combination with Cuesta. But despite the hard-earned success at Talavera, the dead hand of Spanish politics would soon begin to pluck at the strings of discord between the allies. It would seem that Martín de Garay, *Secretario General de la Junta Suprema*, had become

---

39   Wellesley to Beresford, 29 July 1809, Gurwood (ed.), *Wellington's Dispatches*, vol.III, pp.379–380.
40   Wellesley to O'Donojú, 31 July 1809, Gurwood (ed.), *Wellington's Dispatches*, vol.III, p.382.
41   Wellesley to O'Donojú, 31 July 1809, Gurwood (ed.), *Wellington's Dispatches*, vol.III, pp.382–383.

involved in the background politicking and was attempting to establish some kind of permanent and direct correspondence with Wellesley, who nipped his intentions in the bud by writing to Frere on 31 July, requesting him to inform Garay that he (Wellesley) had no authority to correspond directly with any Spanish ministers. Once the diplomatic niceties were dispensed with the British commander moved on to raise some urgent issues with the plenipotentiary:

> It is not a difficult matter for a gentleman in the situation of Don M. de Garay to sit down in his cabinet and write his ideas of the glory which would result from driving the French through the Pyrenees; and I believe there is no man in Spain who has risked so much, or has sacrificed so much, to effect that object than I have. But I wish that Don M. de Garay, or the gentlemen of the Junta, before they blame me for not doing more, or impute to me beforehand the probable consequence of the blunders, or the indiscretion of others, would either come or send here some-body to satisfy the wants of our half starved army, which although they have been engaged for 2 days, and have defeated twice their number, in the service of Spain, have not bread to eat. It is positively a fact that, during the last 7 days, the British army have not received one third of their provisions; that at this moment there are nearly 4,000 wounded soldiers dying in the hospital of this town [Talavera] from want of common assistance and necessaries, which any other country in the world would have given even to its enemies; and that I can get no assistance of any description from the country. I cannot prevail upon them even to bury the dead carcasses in the neighbourhood, the stench of which will destroy themselves as well as us.
>
> I cannot avoid feeling these circumstances; and the Junta must see that, unless they and the country make a great exertion to support and supply the armies, to which the inevitable attention and the exertion of every man and the labor of every beast in the country ought to be directed, the bravery of the soldiers, their losses and success, will only make matters worse and increase our embarrassment and distress. I positively will not move, nay, more, I will disperse my army, till I am supplied with provisions and means of transport as I ought to be.[42]

Wellesley's frustrations would continue to mount over the coming days, as we shall see; but, never one to waste a convenient crisis, he would come to learn some valuable lessons about what he could and could not expect from the Spaniards when campaigning on Spanish soil. These lessons would convince him that any future dependence he might place upon his allies, in terms of logistics and combined operations, at least, would probably prove to be unfounded, and that he would have to be, as near as possible, fully self-sufficient for transport, food, draught animals, guns and ammunition, wherever he went in Spain. All of which would mean that he would have to build and maintain a reliable supply train and, what might prove to be a more risk-strewn or difficult enterprise, have the means to estab-lish secure and reliable communications along his lines of operations when campaigning at

---

42   Wellesley to Frere, 31 July 1809, Gurwood (ed.), *Wellington's Dispatches*, vol.III, pp.383–384.

any distance from the Portuguese frontier. As he began to grapple with these ideas in the aftermath of Talavera, he would become more determined to form a basis upon which to construct his projected strategy for continuing the war on the Peninsula.

By 1 August the French had withdrawn from the left bank of the Alberche and retreated towards Santa Olalla, by this move Wellesley supposed that they would continue their withdrawal to the Guadarrama, a tributary of the Tagus which rises in the mountains to the north of Madrid and runs southwards, a little to the west of the capital, before flowing into the great river just west of Toledo, whence Victor *et-al* could bring their whole force to bear upon either Venegas or Wellesley and Cuesta, should any of them make a move against Madrid. Wellesley wrote to Castlereagh on this day, summing up his situation thus:

> My public letters will give you some idea of our situation. It is one of some embarrassment, but of which I think I shall get the better, I hope, without fighting another desperate battle, which would really cripple us so much as to render all our efforts useless. I certainly should get the better of everything, if I could manage Gen. Cuesta; but his temper and disposition are so bad, that it is impossible.
>
> Venegas' movement will probably relieve our front. I think it probable also that the French will not like to press through the Puerto de Baños, having Beresford's army on their rear, and a victorious army on their front; and, indeed, that point would be quite secure, if I could prevail upon Gen. Cuesta to reinforce his troops at Béjar, so as to secure that point as I understood it to be.
>
> We are miserably supplied with provisions, and I do not know how to remedy this evil. The Spanish armies are now so numerous that they eat up the whole country. They have no magazines, nor have we, nor can we collect any; and there is a scramble for every thing.[43]

Here, in three short paragraphs, we have Wellesley complaining about Cuesta's character, his apparent lack of military acumen and energy, and about the lack of provisions for his own army; themes he would return to in the coming weeks. He also went on to comment upon the lack of military capabilities displayed by Cuesta's army at Talavera, but he did not cast any aspersions upon the courage of the individual Spanish soldiers who, in the main, did their duty. However, he did note what he referred to as the 'want of officers properly qualified' and the 'miserable state of discipline' displayed by the Spanish troops.

On the following day, in a letter he wrote to Frere, he returned to the subject of his wounded, who continued to have a miserable time some five days after the battle at Talavera had ended, before going on to raise further concerns about the lack of food for his troops:

> The state in which our men in hospital are from want of sheets and shirts induces me to request of you to prevail upon the [Spanish] government to have 5,000 or 6,000 of each sent here from Seville without loss of time: 200 mules would carry the whole, and I would pay for them.

---

43   Wellesley to Castlereagh, 1 August 1809, Gurwood (ed.), *Wellington's Dispatches*, vol.III, pp.386–387.

I have seen a letter from the government to Gen. Cuesta, stating that they had determined to send us a large quantity of salt beef. If, instead of salt beef, they would form in this neighbourhood a magazine of 300,000 or 400,000 lbs. of biscuit, they would enable us to get on and to take advantage of our successes.[44]

To be fair to the Spanish citizens living in the immediate neighbourhood of Talavera, it would seem that they at least were striving to help with the supply of food for the troops, but their best efforts were going unnoticed and therefore unrecognised by the majority of Wellesley's men; the reason being that they were regularly waylaid and robbed as soon as they came into contact with the soldiers, as implied in a general order issued by Wellesley at Talavera on the 2nd:

2. The soldiers plunder the inhabitants bringing in provisions, not withstanding the repeated orders given upon the subject, and the knowledge which they all have, that this practice must tend to their own distress.
3. The Commander of the Forces desires that particular attention may be paid to former orders, requiring that no soldier should quit his lines, excepting on fatigue, in charge of an officer or non-commissioned officer, unless he is dressed according to the standing orders of his regiment with side-arms.
    The rolls must be called in camp every two hours, and commanding officers of brigades will give directions of what proportion of officers of each regiment are to be present. The Provost and his assistants must patrole the neighbourhood of the camp constantly, and the assistants must relieve each other.[45]

In the second of three dispatches he wrote to Castlereagh on 1 August, Wellesley informed the minister that Victor's rearguard had, '... left the Alberche last night at eleven o'clock, the whole army marched to Santa Olalla, I conclude, with an intention of taking up a position on the Guadarrama, with a view to be able to throw their whole force upon Venegas, or upon this army, if either should move towards Madrid.'[46] However, he still held out hope for the allies prospects for manoeuvring the French away from Madrid without another battle, thinking that Soult may not be strong enough to have a significant effect on proceedings. In the first of the three dispatches to Castlereagh, he said:

On the 30th [July] we received intelligence that provisions had been ordered for a French corps of about 10,000 or 12,000 men, on the road from Alba de Tormes towards Béjar, in the Puerto de Baños, which affords the best road through the range of mountains which separates Plasencia and Estremadura from Castille. I had hoped that this pass had been effectually secured by the Spanish troops, otherwise I should certainly not have moved from Plasencia ... and as I cannot prevail upon Gen. Cuesta to detach a sufficient force to secure that important point,

44   Wellesley to Frere, 2 August 1809, Gurwood (ed.), *Wellington's Dispatches*, vol.III, p.387.
45   Wellesley's general orders for 2 August 1809, Gurwood (ed.), *Wellington's Dispatches*, vol.III, p.386.
46   Wellesley to Castlereagh, 1 August 1809, Gurwood (ed.), *Wellington's Dispatches*, vol.III, p.388.

I am apprehensive that this French corps will pass through the mountains into Estremadura in our rear ...

Gen. Venegas's corps arrived upon the Tagus on the 28th and 29th; and he attacked Toledo with a detachment under Brig. Gen. Lacy, and moved himself to the bridge of Aranjuez.[47]

From this it is clear that, as late as 1 August, Wellesley was still convinced that Soult's approaching force comprised just 10 to 12,000 men, which probably accounted for the relaxed attitude displayed in his eventual decision to intercept and defeat it, whilst Cuesta held Victor at bay on the Alberche; and even at this late hour, it would seem that he continued to place some confidence in Venegas's hoped-for move on Madrid actually materialising. With regard to his constant prompting of the Spaniards to send a force to secure the puerto de Baños, we saw in the previous chapter that Cuesta, somewhat tardily, detached Bassecourt to fulfil Wellesley's hopes.

Wellesley Prepares to Turn on Soult

Realising that he would soon have to move away from Talavera, Wellesley wrote to O'Donojú on 2 August asking him to communicate with Colonel Henry Mackinnon, who had been instructed to place a watch over the British hospital at Talavera in an effort to supply the wants of the sick and wounded, and to apply to Cuesta for his assistance; in particular with a view to detailing some of his men to attend to the cleaning of the hospital buildings.[48] Besides this, Mackinnon was given a set of personal orders for the removal of men who were able to travel, should the Spanish have to withdraw from Talavera. Then, on the following day, the British chief received the news he had been fearing: Soult was in his rear at Plasencia. Despite his earlier pleadings for Cuesta to send a division of his troops to guard the puerto de Baños in order to keep the French maréchal at bay, the Spanish troops did not commence their march until 2 August, the day after Soult's appearance at Plasencia, which meant that they had completely failed in their mission. Cuesta made a rather matter-of-fact reference to this failure when writing the entries for 1st and 2nd August in his *Manifiesto* (see start of this chapter).

When the allied commanders met to discuss the now imminent threat from Soult, Cuesta proposed that half the allied army should march immediately in order to retrieve the situation. To this, Wellesley remarked to Frere, '[I told him that] if by half the army he meant half of the Spanish and English corps, I would not consent to the proposal, and that I would either stay or go with my whole corps. He then desired that I would choose, and I offered to go.'[49] With that the British commander wrote to Beresford: 'The movement of Soult through the puerto de Baños has deranged all our plans, and I am obliged to return to drive him out.'[50]

47   Wellesley to Castlereagh, 1 August 1809, Gurwood (ed.), *Wellington's Dispatches*, vol.III, p.386.
48   Wellesley to O'Donojú, 2 August 1809, Gurwood (ed.), *Wellington's Dispatches*, vol.III, p.388.
49   Wellesley to Frere, 3 August 1809, Gurwood (ed.), *Wellington's Dispatches*, vol.III, p.389.
50   Wellesley to Beresford, 3 August 1809, Gurwood (ed.), *Wellington's Dispatches*, vol.III, p.388.

Wasting not a moment's time, the British commander was at Oropesa by the following day, 3 August, whence he wrote to O'Donojú once again, recommending that Venegas be ordered to '...keep the enemy in a state of alarm for the safety of Madrid, by the road of Fuentidueña and Arganda, as the only one by which he can oblige the enemy to keep his forces divided.'[51]

Cuesta Decides to Follow Wellesley in Pursuit of Soult

Judging by the content of a second dispatch from Wellesley to O'Donojú on 3 August, it is clear that, in a letter from the Spaniard bearing the same date, O'Donojú had informed the British chief of Cuesta's decision to follow in his footsteps. In his reply Wellesley wrote, '... I acknowledge that I do not conceive the enemy are likely to attack you or to harass me, as they say they will, for some time, and I wish that Gen. Cuesta had remained a little longer'; before signing off with the comment, 'Depend upon it, you are mistaken in Soult's strength; and that Victor, without Sebastiani and the King, who cannot move while Venegas is where he is, can do us no harm. P.S. I conclude that you will take care to establish a strong post at Arzobispo, and destroy the bridge at Talavera.'[52] The British commander could hardly have been more wrong.

British headquarters at Oropesa was to be a busy place on 3 August, and with fresh intelligence about Soult's movements coming in throughout the day there was need for a continual correspondence with Cuesta. As a result, a further dispatch was penned to O'Donojú in which Wellesley informed him of Soult's arrival at Navalmoral, about 13 miles or so from Cuesta's pontoon bridge near Almaraz which the Spanish were still holding, having made preparations to destroy it on the approach of the enemy. At this juncture, apart from Venegas, who was at Aranjuez, and Sebastiani, who was near Toledo, the various contending armies were strung out along the road which shadows the north bank of the Tagus between Navalmoral, where Soult was, Oropesa where the British were, Talavera where Cuesta was and Santa Olalla where Victor stood, in other words, the combined army was trapped between Soult in its rear and Victor in its front. This meant that the only safe route to the south bank of the Tagus still open to Wellesley and Cuesta, was that which led from Oropesa to Arzobispo, some 10 miles to the south, where the town's narrow old bridge remained intact.[53] Later, some welcome news confirmed that the Marqués de la Reyna, commander of a small corps consisting of about four battalions detailed some weeks earlier by Cuesta to guard the puerto de Baños and the approaches to Almaraz, had fought a long-running and honourable rearguard action against Soult's vanguard as it advanced via the heights of Navalmoral towards the Tagus; all of which culminated in the Marqués's decision to dismantle the pontoon bridge left there by Cuesta some weeks earlier. De la Reyna should have been reinforced by Bassecourt's division in a plan to occupy the pass at Baños, but this was aborted on 2 August when Cuesta learned that Soult had already chased off the marqués before continuing his advance to Plasencia.

---

51   Wellesley to O'Donojú, 3 August 1809, Gurwood (ed.), *Wellington's Dispatches*, vol.III, p.390.
52   Wellesley to O'Donojú, 3 August 1809, Gurwood (ed.), *Wellington's Dispatches*, vol.III, pp.390–391.
53   Wellesley to O'Donojú, 3 August 1809, Gurwood (ed.), *Wellington's Dispatches*, vol.III, p.391.

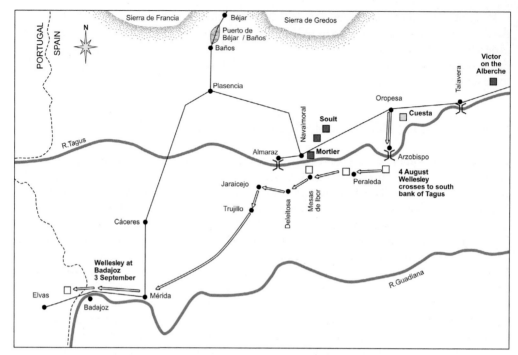

Plate 23. 4 August-3 September. Wellesley halts at Badajoz in the final stage of his retreat to Portugal.

As a result of de la Reyna's action, Soult's probing force, in the form of one of Mortier's divisions, would be prevented from gaining the south bank of the river in the rear of Wellesley and the Spanish commander in chief. Spanish sources claimed that de la Reyna's force suffered significant casualties during their creditable action against the French, that being the case, their intervention marked a significant contribution by the Spaniards to the Tagus campaign, by which both Wellesley and Cuesta were able to escape entrapment by the enemy. It is a detail which has been somewhat overlooked, or underplayed, by British writers (see Plate 22).

By this time Wellesley had been made aware of Soult's actual strength, and it was on 4 August that the British chief arrived at Arzobispo where he wasted no time in crossing to the left bank of the great river, seemingly having made up his mind to retreat to Portugal come what may. During the following two days he recorded that he was at Peraleda de Garvin and Mesas de Ibor, as he continued towards the Portuguese frontier along a route which would take him through Deleitosa, Jaraicejo, Trujillo, Mérida and Lobón, before halting at Badajoz on 3 September.

In his *Manifiesto*, Cuesta gave the following account of events affecting his army during 4 August and the days immediately following. The reader should bear in mind that he constructed a good part of his *Manifiesto* by inserting the series of reports/dispatches he sent to Cornel during the course of the campaign:

Arzobispo, 4 August:

Last night I wrote to Your Excellency from Talavera informing you that I was about to march with the intention of reinforcing the British army, which had left for Oropesa. I arrived at that place early this morning … I had a conference with General Wellesley, whose opinion it was that we should march to the bridge at Arzobispo in order to secure our flank, and to retreat if circumstances demanded it. The English general put this measure into immediate effect, and I have followed him this evening after awaiting the arrival of our 5th Division (Bassecourt) which I had detached towards the river Tiétar two days ago.

Sir Arthur Wellesley has crossed the bridge [at Arzobispo] and taken up a position on the left bank [of the Tagus]. My position is on the right bank in front of the town …

On my arrival at Oropesa I was surprised to find that the British army was still there, as I had expected them to have advanced towards Navalmoral to receive the 1st Division of the enemy army which, until then, we had estimated to be a force of some 12 to 15,000 men, but whilst at Oropesa we learned that its total strength was about 34,000. I spoke with the English general about both our armies going in search of *Maréchal* Soult … but Wellesley replied that he would not enter into any action without securing his retreat beforehand; as such he marched for the bridge at Arzobispo without delay, leaving me with mixed feelings. I felt we had a good chance of beating Soult before he could concentrate the whole of his forces, placing our own between his and the bridge in order to safeguard our retreat; but seeing the determination of the English general, I soon realised that I had to follow him, and that night I camped on the right bank of the Tagus, close to the bridge at Arzobispo which the British had already crossed on their way to Mesas de Ibor.[54] On the following day we saw some small parties of the enemy … so I decided to cross the bridge and establish myself on the left bank, leaving my vanguard on the right. In an attempt to speed up the operation, I sent the Duque de Alburquerque to confer with the people of the town in an effort to discover if the ford a little upstream of the bridge might be used by our cavalry. He soon returned after having been informed that the fording point was inaccessible, as such it was necessary for me to pass the whole of the army and its artillery across the bridge, which was very narrow.

By the 6th the enemy forces had increased considerably … [so] I ordered that the vanguard cross the bridge, leaving garrisons for its towers, as well as for the bridgehead, on the left bank; in the meantime the various divisions were stationed in a nearby wood so that they would be shielded from the blazing sun. I instructed the division of 3,000 cavalry under the command of the Duque de Alburquerque to take up a position at Azután, and to keep a watch on the fords as well as the road which runs along the left bank of the Tagus to the wooden bridge at Talavera. I then transferred my army headquarters to Las Casas de la Oliva.

On the 7th, with the army's supply of food and provisions exhausted, I was forced to march via La Peraleda to Las Mesas de Ibor, leaving the 5th Infantry Division

---

54   Cuesta's continuing thirst for battle caused Wellesley to remark in a letter to Frere, 'As usual, Gen. Cuesta wanted to fight general actions', Wellesley to Frere, 4 August 1809, Gurwood (ed.), *Wellington's Dispatches*, vol.III, p.392.

at the bridgehead, under the command of *Mariscal de Campo* D. Luis Bassecourt, and the 2nd Cavalry Division at Azután under the command of the Duque de Alburquerque ... with instructions to go to the aid of the infantry if necessary.

When the army arrived at Peraleda de San Román, and was readying itself to march by some very bad roads for Las Mesas de Ibor, I received a message from *General* Bassecourt informing me that the enemy cavalry had crossed the river [Tagus] by the ford nearest to the bridge [at Arzobispo] with the clear intention of taking his division in the rear, thus forcing him to abandon the bridgehead [on the south bank] and retreat into the nearby mountains ...

In view of this I ordered *General* Henestrosa to take his 1st Cavalry Division, together with Zayas's vanguard, and remain in post at Peraleda until the arrival of Bassecourt's division, so that they might halt the enemy vanguard.

The loss of the bridge at Arzobispo filled me with surprise. According to the forces I left there and the dispositions that I made, I was confident that the enemy would not so easily break through, but the loss of the bridge was occasioned by some carelessness, combined with a measure of reckless behaviour on the part of the cavalry division under the command of the Duque de Alburquerque at Azután. Not only had Alburquerque failed to send part of his force to cover the ford closest to the bridge, he had also allowed his men to keep their horses unsaddled and unbridled, so that when Bassecourt sent news that the enemy was crossing, they arrived late on the scene and in complete disorder in their intention to prevent it. But instead of attempting to re-unite and attack in good order the 800 French cavalry, who were fording the river in the face of some stiff resistance being offered by a party of 300 1st Extremadura Hussars of Bassecourt's division, they simply divided into various groups and retreated in the same disorder as they had arrived, some towards Guadalupe, some to Valdelacasa and the rest to wherever took their fancy.[55]

Continuing with his story, Cuesta went on to describe his difficulties when it came to subsistence in the territory to the south of the Tagus. Just as Victor had found it impossible to remain there after Medellín, he too was beginning to suffer in face of the scarcity of provisions:

In that critical situation, we were in such straits due to a lack of supplies that [even] army headquarters was without rations of any sort for four or five days. The odd muleteer would arrive selling bread, but they would charge five or eight *reales* per pound, all of which meant that the troops were 10 days on quarter rations. And whilst the divisional commissaries were able to collect a quantity of bread and meat from various villages, it was never enough to cover our needs.

The royal treasury, passive and careless in this urgent matter, before and since the Battle of Talavera, did more to obstruct the measures taken by the divisional commanders than to facilitate the supply of necessities. The answer given by the

---

55   Cuesta, *Manifiesto*, pp.70–73. Despite Cuesta's claim that he became aware of Soult's true strength on 4 August, he actually knew of it a day or two earlier.

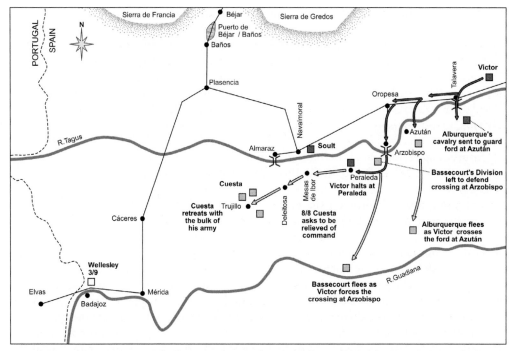

Plate 24. 6–12 August. Cuesta has taken his army onto the south bank of the Tagus, leaving his 5th Division to hold the bridge at Arzobispo. Alburquerque fails to hold the ford at Azután, allowing the French to gain the south bank of the Tagus.

quartermaster general to the continuous admonishments he received, was always that he had given all the orders and taken all the necessary steps that were required; in the end all to no avail. Nothing could be found with which to nourish the troops, and eventually various diseases began to run through their ranks – the daughters of their abject destitution. Of all this I gave continuous complaint and notice to the *Junta Central*, via the Ministry of War, but nothing was done.

This state of affairs contributed in no small way to the misfortune of a campaign which had begun so gloriously, as did the order which the *Junta Central* sent to Venegas on 17 July that he should not obey the instructions I had given him on the 12th that he draw the attention of General Sebastiani to the Army of La Mancha before the commencement of the Battle of Talavera. Had he done so it would have reduced Victor's available force by some 12,000 French troops, as the alternative would have been to allow Venegas to enter Madrid with impunity at the head of 27,000 men. Any military expert will know that such conduct [as that displayed by the *Junta* and Venegas] was akin to the malicious sacrifice of the fatherland at the time.[56]

---

56   Cuesta, *Manifiesto*, pp.73–74.

The Loyal Lusitanian Legion During the Tagus Campaign

Sir Robert Wilson's Lusitanian Legion, together with the 5th Portuguese Caçadores, was chosen to act as Wellesley's left or northern flank guard as he advanced from Plasencia to Talavera. Regarded as being too weak in numbers to take on the task alone, Cuesta agreed, during his talks with Wellesley at Miravete, to detach two of his units: the Tiradores de Mérida from Zayas's 1a División and the 3er Regimiento de Sevilla from Manglano's 4a División, to join Wilson's force.[57] Once united, the whole corps of some 4,000 men pushed ahead of the main allied force, acting more as its vanguard than a flanking unit as its leader's adventurous spirit took hold. Marching from Venta de Bazagona on the Tiétar on 15 July, he was at Arenas de San Pedro on the 19th and at Escalona on the Alberche by the 23rd (see Plate 25).[58]

Continuing their advance, on the eve of Talavera the legion entered the small town of Navalcarnero, lying some 60 miles northwest of the battlefield. Out on a limb, but apparently disdaining the possibility of being attacked in such an exposed situation, Wilson decided to continue his march towards Madrid, entering what today is one of its western suburbs, Móstoles, with the intention of pushing on to the capital. It was whilst he was in the small town that he got wind of the battle taking place at Talavera, and decided to reunite with the Wellesley's army. By 28 July, as the fighting raged across the Portiña brook, he almost stumbled into the French rear as he neared Cazalegas. Realising the danger he was in he turned around and made for Escalona.[59] It was there, as he awaited further instructions from Wellesley, that he received intelligence indicating that Soult's army was at the puerto de Baños, on its southerly march towards Plasencia, with the intention of placing itself across the allies' line of retreat.

On 3 August, six days after defeating Victor at Talavera, Wellesley marched to confront Soult, thinking his strength was no more than 15,000, but when details of the true size of the Frenchman's force reached him from Cuesta, he decided to take evasive action and crossed to the south bank of the Tagus at Arzobispo. On 5 August, feeling himself safe, he wrote to Wilson, instructing him to communicate with Cuesta and, whilst awaiting his reply, to continue his march via Calera y Chozas to Arzobispo, before joining him on the south bank of the Tagus, finally warning him that Soult was at Navalmoral de la Mata and informing him that the Marqués de la Reyna had dismantled the pontoon bridge at Almaraz.[60]

When Wilson arrived at Velada en–route to Arzobispo, he discovered that the French were in possession of the road between Oropesa and Talavera, thus barring his way to the crossing point on the Tagus. At that he marched for Las Ventas de San Julian and Centenillo on the Tiétar, having decided to cross the peaks of the Sierra de Gredos in the region of Bohoyo, before heading for Barco de Ávila on the Tormes and moving on to Tornavacas. From there he marched his corps over more rough country to Béjar and Baños, where he arrived on 11 August. It was when he was heading south from Baños towards Aldeanueva del Camino, on the last leg of his journey to rejoin Wellesley, that he observed a French column

57   Wellesley to O'Donojú, 13 July 1809, Gurwood (ed.), *Wellington's Dispatches*, vol.III, pp.351–352.
58   Wellesley to Castlereagh, 24 July 1809, Gurwood (ed.), *Wellington's Dispatches*, vol.III, p.368.
59   Oman, *History of the Peninsular War*, vol.II, p.570.
60   Wellesley to Wilson, 5 August 1809, Gurwood (ed.), *Wellington's Dispatches*, vol.III, p.394.

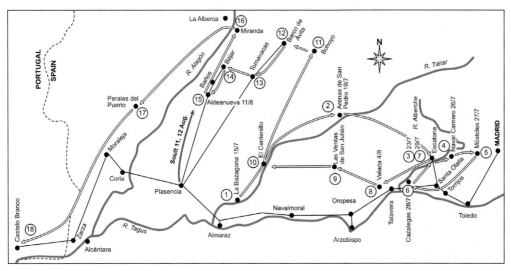

Plate 25. 15 July-20 August. Movements of Sir Robert Wilson's Loyal Lusitanian Legion during the Tagus campaign.

marching in the opposite direction towards him. This was the 12,000 or so men of Ney's corps making their way north to Salamanca, now that Wellesley had effectively escaped the trap being laid for him by Soult and Victor. Leaving just 200 of his Spanish infantry at Aldeanueva as a blocking force, he returned to Baños to organise more substantial defences there. Despite his efforts, the French were too strong for him, scattering his units from their defensive positions along the pass and forcing them up into the hills and beyond, inflicting some 400 casualties amongst them as they went.[61] Once regrouped, Wilson led his men west via Miranda del Castañar and Perales del Puerto, eventually crossing into Portugal and reuniting with Wellesley at Castelo Branco. It could be said that the Legion's actions had been more of a guerrilla campaign than a flank duty, and had Wilson marched into an unguarded Madrid from the west, whilst Venegas was on the north bank of the Tagus in the vicinity of Aranjuez, then the results of the 1809 campaign might well have been better than they turned out to be.

61   Wellesley to Marquess Wellesley, 15 August 1809, Gurwood (ed.), *Wellington's Dispatches*, vol.III, pp.423–424.

9

The Battle of Almonacid

At 4:30 a.m. on the morning of 5 August, Venegas rode to Aranjuez to inspect, organise and position his troops in expectation of an attack by the French. Having returned to his headquarters at Ocaña, he was having dinner when an urgent message arrived from Girón, commander of his forces in the royal city. The news he sent was not good; the French had advanced and crossed the Jarama river via the Puente Largo. As a result, Lacy, recently arrived from Toledo on the 3rd, had withdrawn and taken up position at a place close to the Puente de la Reyna, as earlier indicated by Venegas for just such a circumstance, leaving his vanguard at Doce Calles. As the day wore on, worrying tidings from Girón kept arriving at headquarters, such as the news that strong French columns had been observed heading for the ford at Añover on the Tagus, which lies some three miles to the west of Aranjuez.

According to Venegas's diary, it was at precisely 8:21 p.m. on the evening of the 5th that Girón's first report of fighting close to Aranjuez arrived at headquarters, in it the *Brigadier* reported that, 'Firing has [now] ceased along the whole of the line. The enemy, in considerable force, launched three major attacks upon us, as well as a number of smaller ones, all of which were repulsed. The fire has been terrible, but the coolness and bravery of our troops has been above all praise.'[1] Later reports from Girón indicated that the French had eventually retreated to the Cuesta de la Reyna. With all this in mind, one must wonder what Venegas would have thought had he known that, whilst his Army of La Mancha was holding the line of the Tagus at Aranjuez, Wellesley's army was streaming across the bridge at Arzobispo some 100 miles downstream, its commander having come to the conclusion that Madrid was not for the taking and that it was time to return to the safety of the Portuguese frontier. Cuesta too was at Arzobispo, waiting for his chance to follow in the footsteps of the British, the plight of the Army of La Mancha, it seems, counting for little in the mind of the retreating allied commanders.

With regard to the French attack at Aranjuez, Venegas's first thoughts were that it was merely a reconnaissance in force, but as the strength of the enemy's move on Añover became more apparent, he realised that the assault on the royal city was more of a diversionary attack, launched to distract him and pin him to his ground, and that the main thrust by the French was that which was taking place on his left, with the intention to take him in flank and rear. It was now time for him to retreat. The 2nd and 3rd Divisions were

---

1   AHN: Diversas Colecciones, 125, N.5: el Ejército de La Mancha, entry for 5 August 1809.

to commence their march at dawn by heading for La Guardia, the 1st Division to a position betwixt Dos Barrios and La Guardia and the 4th Division, together with army headquarters, to Tembleque. Girón was ordered to suspend his action at Aranjuez and Lacy to dismantle the Puente de la Reyna on the eastern edge of the town. By the end of the day the 1st Division was still at Aranjuez, the 2nd at Ocaña, the 3rd at La Guardia, the 4th and army headquarters at Tembleque, all places to be found on the road leading directly south towards Madridejos.[2]

As an indication of the state of communications between Cuesta, Venegas and Seville, prevalent at the time, it was not until the evening of 7 August that Venegas received the following dispatch from Cornel, giving his approval for the dispositions taken by the Army of La Mancha in uniting all five of its constituent divisions at Aranjuez in readiness to march upon Madrid:

> The *Suprema Junta de Gobierno del Reino* has received your dispatches of the 2nd and 3rd inst. which contain copies of the dispatches Your Excellency sent to the general in chief [Cuesta] about the movement of that army [Cuesta's & Wellesley's force] on Madrid, and His Majesty finds your reasoning to be so well founded that the chiefs of the combined Anglo-Spanish armies should do all that they can to adopt it. However, His Majesty does not know which resolution they have actually taken as, since receiving Don Gregorio de la Cuesta's dispatch dated the 1st inst., he has heard no more.
>
> At this moment in time your second dispatch of the 3rd has just arrived announcing the arrival of Lacy at Aranjuez on that night ...[3]

Clearly, this was the endorsement Venegas was seeking from Cornel for his insistence that Cuesta and Wellesley participate with the Army of La Mancha in a general advance on Madrid, and yet another example of the manipulative nature of the relationship between the former two. In fact, when reading between the lines of Cornel's reply immediately above, one begins to wonder if Venegas was not actually treating Cuesta as a subordinate via his secretive correspondence with Seville; the Minister of War acting as a proxy for Venegas by agreeing with his dispositions before urging Cuesta to act in line with them. To add strength to such thoughts, there were some rumours circulating of a pact already having been made between Venegas and Cornel whereby, once the Talavera campaign was over, the commander of the Manchegans would replace Cuesta as head of the combined armies of Extremadura and La Mancha. And there is some anecdotal evidence that Cuesta's friends in Seville had informed him of the plan. If so, it might further explain his circumspection towards his political masters and their British counterparts.

No sooner had the Minister's message arrived at Venegas's headquarters on the 7th than Cuesta's final order that he launch his long-delayed operation against the capital was delivered to him by courier. But by then Venegas's advance on the capital had already

---

2   AHN: Diversas Colecciones, 125, N.5: el Ejército de La Mancha, entry for 5 August 1809.
3   Cornel to Venegas, 5 August 1809, Venegas, *Vindicación*, sub-section Documentos, p.61, Número 50. The two dispatches from Venegas to Cuesta referred to by Cornel were almost certainly: (1) Venegas to Cuesta, 2 August 1809 and (2) Venegas to Cuesta, 3 August 1809. Both are referred to earlier.

been postponed due to a last-minute change in circumstances. In his diary Venegas wrote that, in yet another communication with his headquarters that day, Francisco Saavedra, then the *Junta Suprema's Secretario de Estado*, had sent details of 'certain precautions' to be taken with respect to the decision to enter Madrid.[4] So apparently sensitive were these precautions that Venegas did not define them in his diary, noting only that a summary of all the events which had taken place at his headquarters that day had been passed to Antonio Cornel. The one thing he did note, however, was that the proposed move on the capital 'did not take place due to a change in circumstances.'[5] Nevertheless, if we were to hazard a guess as to what Cornel's message contained, it may have been the news that, despite Cuesta's earlier declaration that both he and Wellesley would go to the aid of Venegas once they had dealt with the threat offered by Soult, both those commanders had since given up on that rosy prospect, if Wellesley had ever seriously entertained it at all, and were now retreating ever more deeply into Extremadura. As we have seen, Cuesta sent notice to Venegas on 3 August of Wellesley's departure for Oropesa, as well as his own intention to follow the British commander, all of which was logged in the entry for 7 August in Venegas's diary, suggesting that that was the date on which the news was received. In other words, by 7 August, Venegas was aware of Wellesley's and Cuesta's retrograde move to confront Soult, but not of their latest intention to continue their retreat towards Portugal. All of which makes it likely that it was via Saavedra's message that Venegas learned of his total abandonment. The upshot of it all being that the Manchegans were now completely isolated and at the mercy of the armies of Soult, Victor and Sebastiani.

During the night of 7 August and the morning of the 8th, *Brigadier* Lacy was communicating intelligence about the build-up of French forces in and around the ferry point and ford at Añover, and at Borox, respectively, the former being in his left rear, the latter in his left front, slightly west of the confluence between the Jarama and the Tagus, assuming the general was still at Aranjuez. By 11:00 a.m. on the 8th, the commander of the Venegas's advanced post observing the Puente de Alcántara in Toledo, was informing him that the French were also concentrating near that town. It was at this point that Venegas decided to send his 4th Division to Nambroca, via Almonacid, to reinforce Zerain's 5th Division, which suggests that Lacy had returned to Toledo from Aranjuez on 7/8 August.

French Forces Cross the Tagus

At 6:00 a.m. on 9 August the French made their move; crossing the Tagus at Toledo and threatening the divisions of Zerain (5th) and Castejón (4th) which were forced to retreat towards Almonacid. On hearing the news, Venegas ordered his remaining divisions to march immediately for that location, where he hoped to stop the French advance and push them back towards the Tagus. Somewhat ironically, an order from Cornel dated 6 August arrived at army headquarters on the evening of the 9th, advising Venegas to take care that

---

4   AHN: Diversas Colecciones, 125, N.5: el Ejército de La Mancha, entry for 7 August 1809.
5   AHN: Diversas Colecciones, 125, N.5: el Ejército de La Mancha, entry for 7 August 1809.

Victor did not fall upon him now that he did not have to concern himself about the presence of the Anglo-Spanish army on his front, as it had marched 'to receive Soult.'[6]

On the eve of the Battle of Almonacid, 10 August 1809, Venegas's diarist made the following entry in the journal of his chief:

> The writer of this diary remained in Tembleque when the general set off for Almonacid, leaving it in the custody of the secretary. It was he who was charged with the responsibility of transporting it to wherever circumstances dictated. Said circumstances forced him to make a precipitate retreat from Tembleque, which meant he was absent from the general's company until the afternoon of 19 August, when they met at La Carolina. At that place he was presented with some relevant papers from which he was able to make some retrospective entries in the diary. These were necessarily brief in their content due to the level of activity apparent during recent days, a circumstance which has made the writing of detailed documentation an impossibility, to such an extent that many orders were never put in writing …
>
> The government order of 7 August, which I should have received today, I cannot find and neither can I find the minutes of the document which was sent to the Court.[7]

The diarist, apparently Venegas's secretary according to the passage above, then went on to collate the documents pertaining to the dates 11–18 August which he was given on his arrival at La Carolina, a small town lying to the south of Valdepeñas beyond the pass of Despeñaperros on the road to Bailén. Hence the very brief/empty entries covering that period in Venegas's operational diary. From 18 August the diary entries return to their former level of detail and continue through to 29 September, recording the many comings and goings of the French in the territories to the south of Madrid, but there is nothing of any great note to remark upon. However, as the Battle of Almonacid could be regarded as the final significant clash of the Talavera campaign, we shall reproduce some of the very brief description of the battle written up by the diarist as part of his retrospective entries for 11–18 August, all of which will mean that our immediate interests have been admirably served by the punctilious person who was responsible for its keeping. Fortunately, under the direction of their commander in chief, a set of more comprehensive descriptions of what took place at Almonacid were submitted by his divisional commanders, and we will examine them shortly. Firstly, the diary entries for 11 and 12 August:

> At five in the morning [on 11 August] the army was attacked by the enemy in its position at Almonacid, and by seven o'clock the firing had intensified and extended along the whole of the line. The enemy attacked in considerable numbers … [and] our troops put up an honourable resistance for some nine hours. However, when the enemy took possession of a height which formed the left of our line, they gained

---

6   AHN: Diversas Colecciones, 125, N.5: el Ejército de La Mancha, entries for 7–9 August 1809.
7   AHN: Diversas Colecciones, 125, N.5: el Ejército de La Mancha, entry for 10 August 1809.

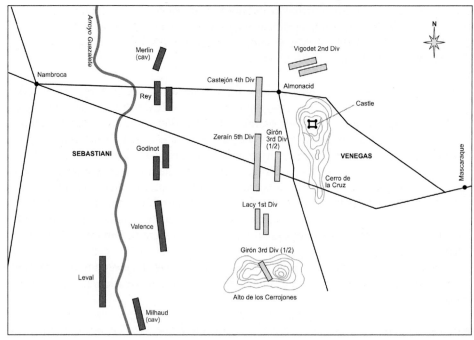

Plate 26. 11 August. the Battle of Almonacid. Venegas positions his troops for what was to be a last stand against Sebastiani.

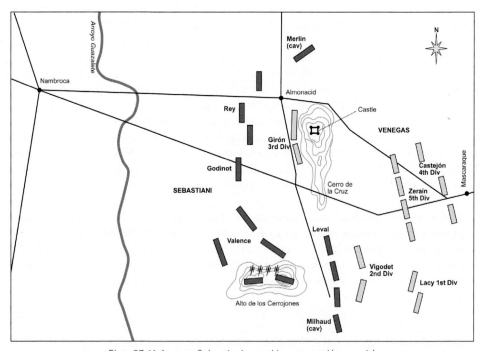

Plate 27. 11 August. Sebastiani routs Venegas at Almonacid.

an advantage of position by which they were on the point of rolling up all of our divisions, thus forcing our commander in chief to order a retreat ... On this day the honour of the nation was sustained and much blood was spilt on both sides ...

The general, realising the necessity of retiring to the safety of the positions in the *sierra*, gave orders for *General* Carvajal to advance and take post at La Carolina, where he was to re-unite the volunteers of the region with the stragglers who continued to arrive.

On 12 August the general in chief left for Herencia by way of Argamasilla de Alva, where he met with his commanders of division and issued them with verbal orders that they continue to occupy the [strong] points in the *sierra*.[8]

Notes on the Battle of Almonacid by Venegas's Subordinates

Brigadier *Lacy, Commander of the 1st Division*
As we have just seen, it was on the day following his defeat at Almonacid that Venegas requested his commanders of division to send him their personal account of events, all of whom complied within a few days, and their dispatches are included in the *Documentos* section of his *Vindicación*. Unfortunately, they all take the form of a broad-brush summary of the fighting, followed by a long list of the names of soldiers or units who were deemed by their respective commanders to have performed well on the day. Lacy, commander of the 1st Division, was sparing in his description of the fighting, noting only that the height marking the left flank of the Spanish position was attacked and taken by the French, causing the Spanish division defending it (Girón's 3rd Division) to retreat in disorder. This in turn, he claimed, left him with little alternative other than that of retreating to the *cerro del castillo*, (the hill on which the castle stood) where the Spanish troops put up a spirited defence before being forced to cede the position. Such was the panic amongst the men of Girón's and Lacy's divisions as they retreated from the *cerro* that they, together with the fleeing Spanish cavalry, crashed into Vigodet's 2nd Division which was by then attempting to hold a reserve position in the rear.[9]

Brigadier *Vigodet, Commander of the 2nd Division*
It would appear that Vigodet made a valiant attempt to fight his division in good order during the course of the battle. After taking up his initial position to the right of Almonacid, his battalions were forced to move when they became unsettled by some units of Spanish cavalry as they came charging through the town in panicked retreat. At this he sent one of his officers, Francisco Medrano, in pursuit of them to re-establish order, a task he succeeded in only to a limited degree. With either the 3rd or 4th Division posted on a height in his front, he could not say which, Vigodet claimed that he observed the French advancing from the town:

---

8   AHN: Diversas Colecciones, 125, N.5: el Ejército de La Mancha, entries for 11-12 August 1809.
9   Lacy to Venegas, 22 August 1809, Venegas, *Vindicación*, sub-section Documentos, pp.39–40, Número 41.

Two strong [enemy] columns of infantry marched from the town and attacked a height in my front which was occupied by our 3rd or 4th Division. I ordered my division to advance to support it; but seeing that the troops on the height were beginning to retire, I ordered [my men] to halt and deploy in order of battle facing the town ... once formed, with the artillery on our flanks and centre, I ordered all six pieces to open fire ... against the enemy columns, which were stopped and forced to retire ... It was whilst we were deployed in this position that I was ordered ... to move into an olive grove on my left ... so that I could offer some support to the retreating army ... I was later ordered to gather together what troops I could and retire towards Mora. Suddenly, I was attacked by a column of enemy infantry, so I instructed my troops to deploy in order of battle facing the enemy formation. As we did so our artillery gave us some protection with their fire of grapeshot and ball, which managed to contain the enemy ...[10]

Vigodet claimed that, as disorder spread amongst the retreating Army of La Mancha, he observed the French cavalry preparing to take him in flank or rear, at which he ordered his men to form in column and begin their retreat. As he continued to retire, he reached a collection of vineyards just as a number of ammunition carts parked nearby exploded, thus spooking the Spanish cavalry units which were protecting his infantry and allowing the advancing French cavalry to get amongst his rearguard and sabre some of the men. After making another desperate attempt to stem the French tide, Vigodet was forced to withdraw, eventually joining the general retreat towards Consuegra, Turleque, Madridejos and Villamanrique.

Brigadier *Girón, Commander of the 3rd Division*
Girón, commander of Venagas's 3rd Division, was given the task of defending one of the key points on the Spanish line; the Heights of Cerrojones marking its left flank. From what he said in the account of the fighting he submitted to Venegas, it would appear that he may have been ordered to occupy the height somewhat late in the day, as the French columns were by then already on the move:

Between 7 and 8 in the morning I was at my lodgings observing the skirmishes of our guerrillas. I then [noticed] several strong enemy columns appear, leaving me in no doubt that we were going to be attacked, so I mounted my horse and went ... to place myself at the head of my division. Your Excellency instructed me to position the batallón de Velez-Málaga as vanguard and to position the batallón de Alpujarras on the *cerro del castillo*, acting as a rear-guard beyond the town [of Almonacid]. Later you ordered me to join the reserve with the remaining three battalions of my division ...

---

10   Vigodet to Venegas, 19 August 1809, Venegas, *Vindicación*, sub-section Documentos, pp.40–44, Número 42.

Eventually, after receiving various orders and counter orders from Venegas, Girón was instructed to reinforce the height marking the left flank of the Spanish line, which he did 'with the utmost order and promptness' whilst under fire from the enemy:

> ... who made a determined attack against our left. As I arrived on the heights there, I saw one of our battalions engaged with the enemy on the plain below, who forced it to retreat. I decided to attack straight away, but [it was] as I commenced my march at the head of the 1a Reales Guardias Españolas ... [to go to their aid that] the corps [below] began a precipitate and disorderly retirement. At this ... I returned to occupy the heights I had just abandoned. When I was half way up the hill, the troops who were engaged with the enemy on our right ... began to retire in disorder. I was forced to go amongst them, making great efforts to have them reform and re-occupy the hill; unfortunately all of my efforts were in vain. The enemy, who were by then in possession of the height, opened fire upon us ... [and] we were at such a disadvantage that we ultimately had to abandon our position after suffering no small loss.
>
> The battalions of my division [eventually] managed to recover their exact formation once they had concentrated on the side of the hills surrounding the town, all this whilst they were under a rain of shot and shell ...
>
> After some time had passed, Your Excellency ordered me to descend with three battalions and take up position in a nearby olive grove ... but shortly after deploying, the heads of some enemy columns appeared at very close range ... I then ordered the retreat as a consequence of an instruction I had received from Your Excellency, which was that I take up a position in the rear to avoid being surrounded.
>
> Once I arrived at the prescribed position I received a new order from Your Excellency, this time that I retire towards Mora in order to cover the retreat of the whole of the army ...[11]

That evening, 11 August, Girón arrived at Madridejos and continued his retreat throughout the night, passing through the towns of Herencia, Membrilla, Valdepeñas, Santa Cruz, and El Visillo, as he led his division towards the Sierra Morena.

Brigadier *Castejón, Commander of the 4th Division*

Under the command of Castejón, Venegas's 4th Division took up position on the right flank of the Spanish line at the commencement of the action. Its commander in chief noted, '... soon an enemy column appeared on the left of our line, which was already under fire from the enemy artillery, thus indicating it to be the true point of the attack ...'

After sustaining appreciable losses from the enfilading fire coming from his left once the French occupied the height there, Castejón ordered a partial withdrawal of his troops to a hill in the rear. There, after momentarily forcing back the French, he was forced to retreat once more when the enemy artillery began to enfilade his new position, taking a

---

11   Girón to Venegas, 22 August 1809, Venegas, *Vindicación*, sub-section Documentos, pp.44–46, Número 43.

heavy toll of his troops. Accompanied by some Spanish cavalry for the first part of their retirement, the 4th Division was soon abandoned by the horsemen who, in their flight, said Castejón, rode over his infantry, breaking up their formation and leaving the artillery to their fate. Once the French cavalry who were the cause of the panic got amongst the Spanish foot soldiers, 'they were sabred with impunity' before order could be restored, after which Castejón retreated to the Sierra de Mora and on to Turleque, Madridejos and Herencia.[12]

Brigadier *Juan de Courten, Commander of the 5th Division*

Due to the absence of *Brigadier* Zerain, the last of Venegas's divisions, the 5th, was under the temporary command of Juan de Courten. As such, it fell to him to write the dispatch describing the experience of the 5th Division at Almonacid which, in the opinion of the author, is probably the most accurate and enlightening of the five submitted by Venegas's divisional commanders. As such it is well worth dwelling upon, as it is also a concise piece of writing and provides a vivid and untrammelled description of the action:

> At the same time as the [other] divisions came under arms, and realising that the enemy was about to launch an attack on our line, I gave orders that the men of the 5th Division, who were holding a position chosen to allow them to support the four-gun battery at the centre of the line, to do the same. I placed the 1er batallón del 1er Regimiento de la Infantería de Córdoba to the right of the guns ... with the 2o Regimiento de la Infantería de España on their left ... and formed a rear-guard comprising the 2o and 3er batallones del 1er Regimiento de la Infanteria de Córdoba. The Regimiento de Carmona formed a vanguard in front of the slope of the height [on which we were positioned] with the Regimiento de Sevilla stationed on the slope of the castle height itself.
>
> Our position was the first that the enemy attacked, initially by the fire from a strong battery of eight heavy guns, throughout which the troops maintained their position with the greatest firmness and calm despite the destruction they suffered from the cannon shot, which sometimes carried away six or eight men at a time. This is how it remained until the [French infantry approached] and opened a fire of musketry, which our men once more sustained until they came within half a musket shot, even though our artillery poured in its fire of shrapnel as they ascended the hill. We saw them retreat on two occasions to re-form, but [it was at about that time that] our left began to retire, allowing the French to gain the height on our flank, where they seized the opportunity to bring their artillery to bear upon us. In this situation, seeing that the enemy was attempting to surround us, I ordered a retreat to the castle heights which was carried out in the best possible order. It was there where I kept the troops in order of battle until our artillery retired, and it was during this interval that an adjutant [of army headquarters] arrived with orders that the Regimiento de Córdoba enter the castle, an order I decided was impossible to execute. By then the position on our left had been completely abandoned,

12   Castejón to Venegas, 17 August 1809, Venegas, *Vindicación*, sub-section Documentos, pp.46–49, Número 44.

allowing the enemy to gain full control of the height despite the lively musket fire directed upon them. Under these circumstances, and observing that the rest of the divisions on our right were doing the same, I continued my retirement ... ensuring that the march was carried out at a regular pace according to circumstance. Should the enemy cavalry have approached with the intention of charging us I would have marched the men at double pace ...[13]

In Venegas's campaign diary, the entry for 13 August records that a dispatch describing the events relating to the Battle of Almonacid was sent by him to each of Cornel and Cuesta, and it must have been one of the final dispatches the latter was to receive whilst still in command of the Army of Extremadura, as we shall see. That said, there is little more to dwell upon with respect to the Battle of Almonacid and its aftermath. Once back in safe territory, the various units of the Army of La Mancha went to ground in the Sierra Morena. As with Cuesta, Venegas's days as an army commander were also numbered, but he was to remain in post as commander in chief of the Army of La Mancha until 29 September 1809, when he was suddenly called away by the *Junta Suprema*. His diarist recorded that event, which took place during an overnight stop he made on his way to carry out a forward reconnaissance on the banks of the Guadiana, which indicates that the French must have withdrawn to a line closer to the banks of the Tagus, in the wake of Talavera and Almonacid:

The general in chief and his entourage halted at Villarrubia, whence he made his way back [to headquarters at Daimiel] in obeyance of a royal order issued on 27 September which was received this night, advising that Don Francisco Venegas was to take up the role of second in command to *General* Blak[e] in Catalunya, replacing the Marqués de Coupigny, who has been nominated as a *vocal* in the *Junta General Militar*, thus necessitating his move to Seville.[14]

If Venegas felt a little hard done by at being asked to play second fiddle to Blake, then his disappointment would not have been long lasting, as a later communique from the *Junta Suprema* informed him that, rather than make his way to Catalunya to join Blake, he was to make for Cádiz where he was to take up the role of governor, a post he continued to hold until August 1810, when he was nominated Viceroy of New Spain (modern day Mexico).[15]

Of all the seemingly contrary decisions taken by Venegas during the mid-summer months of 1809, perhaps that of resolving to stand and fight at Almonacid is the most difficult to understand. For the whole of June and July of that year he was being urged, sometimes frantically, by his commander in chief, Cuesta, to press the French forces to south of Madrid, but all to no avail. Embroiled in, and sometimes orchestrating intrigues against Cuesta, he seemed more determined to bring down the old warrior than do anything to help save the allied campaign on the Tagus. Looking back upon it, Cuesta's willingness to provide the commander of the Army of La Mancha with a generous measure of leeway for his operations

13   Juan de Courten to Venegas, 9 September 1809, Venegas, *Vindicación*, sub-section Documentos, pp.49–51, Número 45.
14   AHN: Diversas Colecciones, 125, N.5: el Ejército de La Mancha, entry for 29 September 1809.
15   AHN: Diversas Colecciones, 125, N.5: el Ejército de La Mancha, entry for 29 September 1809.

on the Guadiana and Tagus was sadly mistaken. The insertion of an early clause in Venegas's operational instructions, that he should not pitch his inexperienced army against Sebastiani should the Frenchman's available forces number more than 10,000 or so, was too restrictive, not to say naïve, given his penchant for mischief making. Operating at great distances from his superior, it was easy for Venegas to claim that he was faced by just such numbers whenever he received an order to advance, thus allowing himself the option of not doing so; an option he chose on every occasion when put to the test. But even on the occasions when Cuesta used the imperative in his instructions, ordering him to advance no matter the odds against him, Venegas was quick to recruit Cornel to his cause of inactivity, suggesting to the Secretary of State for War that he knew better how to fight the enemy than did Cuesta. So why, after showing such reluctance to enter into battle against Sebastiani when acting in concert with Wellesley and Cuesta, did he suddenly decide to throw caution to the wind after that pair had set their armies on a retreat towards the Portuguese frontier? His answer to that question seems to have been that he could not bring himself to abandon the people of La Mancha to another period of occupation by the French, preferring, as we have seen, to see his army smashed rather than retreat without offering any resistance. Surely, if there had ever been an opportunity for Venegas to strike a blow against French occupation, then it was presented to him on more than one occasion during the second half of July. If his men were ultimately to be sacrificed, it would have been better that their sacrifice had not been in vain, which may well have been the case had he discovered his fighting spirit as he approached the banks of both the Guadiana and Tagus in mid-July. As commander in chief of the Spanish armies during the Tagus campaign, it was Cuesta who shouldered the blame for ultimate failure. Had he dismissed Venegas from the command of the Army of La Mancha and appointed a more willing chief, Madrid may have fallen into allied hands during the summer of 1809. But he was never fully comfortable whilst under the auspices of his political enemies in the *Junta Suprema*, and would have surely realised that *El Favorito*, Venegas, was secure in his post.

10

Cuesta's Final Days in Command of the Army of Extremadura

On 8 August, as he continued his retreat along the south bank of the Tagus, Cuesta arrived at Mesas de Ibor where he took up a defensive position with the intention of offering battle to the pursuing French. However, by then Victor had given up the chase after arriving at La Peraleda, no doubt recalling just how much his army had suffered during its previous sojourn on the south bank of the Tagus. This meant that the Army of Extremadura would remain undisturbed where it was for the next four days, which was just as well, because it would seem that the rigours of the summer campaign were by this time beginning to tell on the health of the army's commander in chief, as he noted in his *Manifiesto*:

> … despite the severe scarcity of provisions suffered by the army, the Spanish troops displayed once more their powers of consistency and durability under the call of duty, a quality in which they were superior to all other European soldiers once a level of discipline had been established amongst them.
>
> However, the workload and fatigues which I was forced to endure, despite my poor and deteriorating health, inclined me to seek out the shade of an *encina* (holm oak) during those inclement days, unable even to mount my horse. In that state I decided to hand over to my second in command, *Teniente General* Don Francisco Eguía, before seeking permission from the *Junta Central* to visit the thermal spa of Alhama. In the meantime I travelled to Trujillo via Deleitosa under great difficulties.[1]

Whilst at Deleitosa Cuesta received the following reply from the *Junta*:

> The *Suprema Junta de Gobierno del Reyno* gives notice of the receipt of your letter of the 12th inst., informing it that you have passed the command of the army to *Teniente General* Don Francisco Eguía … due to a deterioration in your health which no longer allows you to tolerate the fatigues of war, a disability exacerbated by the worsening of the initial paralysis you suffered last year. In response His

---

1   Cuesta, *Manifiesto*, pp.75–76.

Majesty offers you his sincerest sympathies, noting that the army has been deprived of a general whose knowledge, talents and skills, both political and military, are deserving of the highest esteem from both the *Junta Suprema* and the nation as a whole.[2]

It is worth noting that Cornel made mention of Cuesta's 'paralysis' of the previous year, which would seem to indicate that he had suffered a stroke sometime during 1808; if so it might explain Charles Stewart's comments on seeing him during Wellesley's first face-to-face meeting with the Spanish general at his army headquarters in Casas de Miravete, having accompanied his chief on his visit to the Spanish camp.[3] He noted of that journey:

Unfortunately, in conducting us towards the bridge of boats upon the Tagus [at Almaraz] our guides lost their way and darkness had, in consequence, set in before we approached the camp. This was the more to be regretted, as Cuesta had drawn out his whole force, for Sir Arthur Wellesley's inspection. The troops had been under arms during four hours, in momentary expectation of our arrival: whilst the poor old man himself, whilst still lame from the effects of his bruises at Medellín, remained on horseback at their head, during the greater part of that time.

Our arrival at the camp was announced by a general discharge of artillery, upon which an immense number of torches were lighted, and we passed the Spanish line in review by their blaze. The effect was very singular. As the torches were held aloft, at moderate intervals from one another, they threw a red and wavering light over the whole scene, permitting, at the same time, its minuter parts to be here and there cast into shade; whilst the grim and swarth visages of the soldiers, their bright arms and dark uniforms, appeared peculiarly picturesque as often as the flashes fell upon them … Nor was old Cuesta himself an object to be passed by without notice, even at such a moment and under such circumstances. The old man preceded us – not so much sitting on his horse as held upon it by two pages – at the imminent hazard of being overthrown whenever a cannon was discharged, or a torch flared out with peculiar brightness. Indeed, his physical disability was so observable as clearly to mark his total unfitness for the situation which he held. As to his mental powers, he gave us little opportunity of judging; inasmuch that he scarcely uttered five words during the continuance of our visit.[4]

And so, after his stolid performance at Talavera and his wrangling with Venegas throughout the month of July 1809, the old warrior finally slipped from the scene, having packed a lot of fighting into the 15-month period between May 1808 and August 1809, both in military and political terms. Rumbustious and cantankerous at times, he did not make friends easily; but he was a fighter, and perhaps the only fighter Spain had when she needed them most. Of course, fighting a battle is one thing, winning it another, but despite the fact that his French

2   Cornel to Cuesta, 15 August 1808, Cuesta, *Manifiesto*, pp.76–77.
3   Charles Stewart (later Charles Vane or Charles Vane-Stewart) was the 3rd Marquess of Londonderry. He was also the half-brother of Robert Stewart, Lord Castlereagh.
4   Charles William Vane, *Story of the Peninsular War* (London: Henry Colburn, 1848) pp.175–176.

adversaries in Castilla and Extremadura were probably convinced that they could always defeat him, they knew that any confrontation with his scratch armies may not always be won cheaply. Ultimately, it was by dint of his obstinance, as well as a streak of pedantry, that he was usually remembered by military friends and foes alike, be they Spanish, British, or French, and by historians; traits which have tended to cast him in the role of disruptor of the fragile harmony which characterised the British and Spanish alliance during 1808 and 1809. But did he have good reason to be sometimes less than gracious to the *Junta Suprema* and to his ally, Wellesley, during that period? Perhaps he did, and it is a theme we shall investigate in the final chapters of this story.

11

Wellesley's Thoughts on the Tagus Campaign of 1809

Despite several promptings to write his own history of the Peninsular War, Wellington always refused to do so for a number of reasons, the main one being that he would be most reluctant to have to name some of his officers in connection with controversial or unpleasant circumstances, thus tarring their reputation for ever more. As a result, the only comprehensive compilation of his thoughts about the war are to be found amongst the pages of his copious correspondence with many of the major figures associated with the conflict, a correspondence which he carried on throughout the entire period of its duration. It is to that superb historic record we now turn, in an attempt to fathom his feelings during his first foray into Spain.

The Supply of Transport and Provisions to Wellesley's Army

The British army crossed the border separating Portugal and Spain on 3 July 1809, halting at Zarza Mayor on the right bank of the Alagón at a point some 10 miles north of its confluence with the Tagus. Until then it had been operating exclusively within the Portuguese frontier since Wellesley's arrival at Lisbon on 21 April.

After its halt, the army continued its march via Coria to Plasencia, where it arrived on 8 July. Two days later, Wellesley visited Cuesta's headquarters at Casas de Miravete for their first ever face-to-face meeting, during which they discussed plans for their anticipated attack upon *Maréchal* Victor. Apart from some manageably innocuous comments from Wellesley regarding Cuesta's personality and idiosyncrasies, it would seem that the two men handled their relationship in an acceptable if not exemplary fashion during the days leading up to the Battle of Talavera, which is not to say that the British commander was entirely without complaint concerning arrangements relating to the supply of provisions and transport for his army during its sojourn in Spain. In the context of his time in that country, his first remarks on this subject appeared in a letter dated 16 July, which he wrote to Cuesta's close subordinate, O'Donojú, a figure who would play an active role as his superior's chief liaison officer with the British:

I am sorry to say that we shall march but ill provided with many articles which we require, owing to the deficiency in the means of transport in our possession; and this country is either unable or unwilling to supply them. I have sent a Commissary to Gata and Ciudad Rodrigo, but he has not been able to procure one mule; and I fear that he will not be more successful at Béjar, as there appears to be a general disinclination to give that assistance to the army which every army requires, more particularly in a country unprovided with magazines or strong places.

Nothing shall prevent me from carrying into execution the arrangements which I settled with Gen. Cuesta when I had the pleasure of seeing him, although to do so will be attended with the greatest inconvenience, on account of the deficiency of the means of transport, which I then hoped this country and Ciudad Rodrigo would have afforded; but I think it but justice to the army under my command, and to His Majesty, to determine that I shall undertake no new operations till I shall have been supplied with the means of transport which the army requires ...

I shall be obliged to you if you will lay this letter before Gen. Cuesta for his information, and tell him that I shall send a copy of it to Mr. Frere for the information of the government. I beg you at the same time to inform Gen. Cuesta that I am convinced that Señor L. de Torres and Col. O'Lawlor have done everything in their power to procure for the army the means of transport which we have required.[1]

We should note that Wellesley wrote the above as he marched his men out of Plasencia after a 10-day halt at the town, during which it would seem they had been well provided with rations, a claim implicitly supported by the absence of any complaint about a lack of provisions in Wellesley's letter. His main bone of contention at this stage seems to have been that of a lack of transport, though mutterings about an absence of provisions would soon arise. These issues were to feature as a common theme throughout his correspondence during late July and early August 1809. However, it was not the case that the British commander in chief had been entirely free of difficulties relating to transport during the spring of that year, as he fought to expel Soult from Portugal. On his arrival at Plasencia on 8 July, for instance, he wrote to his deputy paymaster general, Boys, after receiving a letter from him via the quartermaster general, claiming that he had been unable to bring up the military chest from Abrantes in Portugal because he had found it impossible to procure conveyance:

The QMG has communicated to me your letter of the 5th, which has astonished and disappointed me not a little. I cannot understand why you did not move at an earlier day, after I had quitted Abrantes, nor for what reason you did not make it known to me, at an earlier period, the difficulties in procuring conveyance for the military chest, if these difficulties prevented its removal ...[2]

1   Wellesley to O'Donojú, 16 July 1809, Gurwood (ed.), *Wellington's Dispatches*, vol.III, p.360.
2   Wellesley to Boys, 8 July 1809, Gurwood (ed.), *Wellington's Dispatches*, vol.III, p.345.

The British commander brought this topic up with his commissary general in a subsequent letter of the same date, explaining that the resultant lack of cash had caused him much embarrassment and that,

> All these evils would have been avoided if Mr. Boys had been supplied with 30 carts … It is impossible that any man can pretend that Portugal, or even the neighbourhood of Abrantes, could not supply 30 carts for this service. I cannot and nobody can believe, that, if proper methods had been adopted, a sufficient number of carts could not have been procured to remove the treasure at an early period.[3]

Wellesley made a more general complaint to Villiers, bringing it up almost as a footnote to a letter he wrote to him, again on 8 July, and from his words it is easy to form the impression that transport, or the lack of it, had been as problematic for the army in Portugal as it would prove to be in Spain:

> I shall be very much obliged to you if you will mention to the government the great inconvenience that the army has felt, ever since its arrival in Portugal, for the want of the assistance of the Civil government to procure the supplies it has required, particularly of carriages and mules. For the latter I have written to you, I believe, not less than 10 letters; but they have not yet assisted the British army with one, and the magistrates of the country have rather prevented than aided us in procuring carts.
>
> I hope that now we have left the country more attention will be paid to our demands, and that I shall not want that which alone I shall require from Portugal, the means of moving the money and ordnance stores which I shall want from Lisbon …[4]

All that said, it would seem that, at this early stage in his role of commander in chief of British forces on the Peninsula, it was not only a lack of wheeled transport that was causing Wellesley so much trouble in his attempts to keep his army supplied with its needs. In fact, his own Commissariat appears to have been more than capable of contributing to his difficulties, as implied in a letter he received from Deputy Commissary General Dalrymple about a complaint made to him by a commissary, ostensibly about having been subjected to a measure of abuse by General Sherbrooke. In turn, Wellesley wrote to Sherbrooke as follows:

> I enclose a letter which has been forwarded to me by Dep. Commissary Gen. Dalrymple from Mr. Commissary, ––– containing an account of transactions at Castello Branco, which does not differ materially from that which you gave me of the same transactions.

3   Wellesley to the Commissary General, 8 July 1809, Gurwood (ed.), *Wellington's Dispatches*, vol.III, pp.345–346.
4   Wellesley to Villiers, 8 July 1809, Gurwood (ed.), *Wellington's Dispatches*, vol.III, pp.348–349.

I am not astonished that you and the General officers should feel indignant at the neglect and incapacity of some of the officers of the Commissariat, by which we have suffered and are still suffering so much; but what I have to observe, and wish to impress upon you, is, that they are gentlemen, appointed to their office by the King's authority, although not holding his commission; and that it would be infinitely better, and more proper, if all neglects and faults of theirs were reported to me, by whom they can be dismissed, rather than that they should be abused by the General officers of the army. Indeed it cannot be expected that they will bear the kind of abuse they have received, however well deserved we may deem it to be; and they will either resign their situations, and put the army to still greater inconvenience, or complain to higher authorities, and thereby draw those who abuse them into discussions, which will take up, hereafter, much of their time and attention.

I don't enter into the grounds you had with being displeased with Mr. –––, which I dare say were very sufficient; but I only desire that, in all these cases, punishment may be left to me, who alone can have the power of inflicting it.[5]

So long as such problems existed with his transport, they would remain the root cause of a number of serious and consequential difficulties which Wellesley would have to contend with. If they could be dealt with on fairly amicable terms whenever they arose in Portugal, due to the nature of the Anglo-Portuguese alliance, the same could not be said about Spain. Once across the border and finding himself without the provisions which could have been brought forward into Spain by a properly equipped and organised supply train, his army would soon resort to the kind of plundering of the local populace which he abhorred. However, if he were to ask the Spanish army to offer some assistance by providing food for his men, under the promise that any diminution in their stocks would be made up from the British stores in Portugal once a reliable transport system had been organised, he would be rebuffed on two counts. The first being that the Spaniards had hardly enough provisions to meet their own needs; the second that, even if they possessed any stores which they could draw upon in order to share with the British, there was not much sign yet that the British were capable of establishing a regular supply train between Lisbon and central Spain which would have been able to replace the Spanish stores taken; and if anyone had suggested otherwise they would have raised more Spanish eyebrows than hopes at such a prospect.

Another of the problems stemming from the lack of transport in Spain would not be long in rearing its head: that of transporting the sick and wounded, the numbers of the latter being dependent on the nature of actions fought. A general action could result in thousands of casualties, as witnessed at Talavera, and in the immediate aftermath of that contest the time to contend with such a situation was fast approaching.

In a letter to Frere of 16 July, Wellesley addressed the issues outlined above:

It is impossible for me to express to you the inconvenience and risk which we incur from the want of means of conveyance, which I cannot believe the country could not furnish if there existed any inclination to furnish them …

---

5   Wellesley to Sherbrooke, 15 July 1809, Gurwood (ed.), *Wellington's Dispatches*, vol.III, pp.357–358.

The officers, and I believe not without reason, say that the country gives unwill-
ingly the supplies of provisions we have required, and I have been obliged to promise
that they shall be replaced from our stores in Portugal; and we have not procured a
cart or a mule for the service of the army. This does not look promising; and I shall
certainly not persevere if our prospect of good treatment does not improve.[6]

The thrust of Wellesley argument was that the Spanish authorities were not complying with
what he saw as their moral responsibility to help feed his troops and procure transport
resources for his army. However, it would seem that the Spanish authorities had not been
previously consulted by their British allies as to the ways and means by which Wellesley's
army should be sustained during its operations in Spain. An egregious failure of planning
and diplomacy, it would seem. But for the next eight days Wellesley's attention was focussed
almost entirely upon what was shaping up to be a general action against Victor's army in the
neighbourhood of Talavera, as such his correspondence during that period contained little
mention of his troubles relating to transport and provisions. However, on 24 July he did
remind Frere and Castlereagh that there was much work to be done, especially with respect
to provisions, if he was to be persuaded to keep his army in Spain:

[I can] attempt no further operation till I should be made certain of my supplies, by
being furnished with proper means of transport and the requisite provisions from
the country ...
    The French army is fed well, and the soldiers who are taken are in good health,
and well supplied with bread ... In the Vera de Plasencia there are means to
supply this army for four months, as I am informed, and yet the *alcaldes* [local
mayors] have not performed their engagements with me. The Spanish army has
plenty of every thing, and we alone, upon whom everything depends, are actually
starving ...[7]

In the letter just referred to, and another to O'Donojú of 25 July, Wellesley repeated his
complaints about the lack of transport and provisions. In the case of the former, after
claiming that he might have to remain where he was or return to Portugal in order to feed
his men, he somewhat optimistically stated that, 'I have great hopes, however, that before
long I shall be supplied from Andalucía and La Mancha with the means which I require, and
I shall then resume the active operations which I have been compelled to relinquish.'[8] With
respect to the latter he told O'Donojú that:

I am doing every thing in my power to procure for the army means of transport and
provisions. I hope I have got some of the former, which may reach me in 3 or 4 days,
and in the mean time I may get something to eat. We are still in great distress for
provisions, which I don't see any very early prospect of relieving.[9]

---

6   Wellesley to Frere, 16 July 1809, Gurwood (ed.), *Wellington's Dispatches*, vol.III, p.361.
7   Wellesley to Frere, 24 July 1809, Gurwood (ed.), *Wellington's Dispatches*, vol.III, pp.366–367.
8   Wellesley to Castlereagh, 24 July 1809, Gurwood (ed.), *Wellington's Dispatches*, vol.III, pp.368–369.
9   Wellesley to O'Donojú, 25 July 1809, Gurwood (ed.), *Wellington's Dispatches*, vol.III, p.369.

Soldiers' Thoughts on the Question of Rations During July and August

In light of the fact that Wellesley would make great play of his claims that it was a lack of provisions which drove him to the decision to withdraw from Spain in the wake of Talavera, it might serve us well to examine what his men thought of the situation regarding rations during their time on Spanish soil. To do this we may turn to a few relevant passages taken from the personal accounts of some of the men who fought at Talavera. The first is by Andrew Leith Hay who, as the army retreated to the south (left) bank of the Tagus after Talavera, wrote:

> There was no possible safe line of operation now left on the right bank of the Tagus. One passage across that river alone remained open – that by the puente de Arzobispo, over which, during the 4th [August] the army passed, encamping in the woods on the left bank. At day-break, on the morning of the 5th, we marched in the direction of Mesas de Ibor, halting for the night in a ravine ... On the 6th, the army continued its route, passing over a rugged and precipitous road ... The infantry were put to the guns, who, with considerable difficulty and exertion, forced them along the mountain road.
> On this day's march, for the first time, we heard complaints from the soldiers on the subject of want of food. Toiling over these mountains, dragging the cannon, severely harassed by excessive heat, the men, conversing with each other, talked loudly of the hardships endured ...[10]

From this we may note that, just like Private George Woolgar, it was not until the first days of August that Leith Hay began to complain about a shortage of rations. By contrast Edward Costello, who arrived at Talavera with Brigadier General Robert Craufurd's light infantry regiments in the immediate aftermath of the battle, remarked that it was at about that time when the army began to suffer from want of provisions:

> On our arrival we were immediately ordered upon outpost duty: in executing which we had to throw out a line of sentinels facing the French position ...
> In consequence of the increasing weakness of the British army at this period, the ranks of which were daily thinned through the scantiness and wretched quality of the food with which they were, of necessity, supplied, as well perhaps as by the accession of strength which the French had received, Lord Wellington was induced to retire.[11]

Captain George Wood, originally of the 82nd Foot (Prince of Wales's Volunteers) was assigned to the 2nd Battalion of Detachments during the Talavera campaign. He was another of those who, immediately after the battle, felt forced to scavenge food from the

---

10   Leith Hay, *Narrative of the Peninsular War*, p.99.
11   Edward Costello, *The Peninsular and Waterloo Campaigns* (London: Longmans, 1967), p.21.

unburied dead, during the process of which he was to witness the French wounded being dispatched by vengeful Spanish soldiers:

> Whatever sensations this gory scene might have caused to a reflecting mind, I must confess my own was engrossed by thoughts of a more interested nature; for having had nothing for the last two days, except one biscuit per man, and the piece of meat I have just mentioned, hunger became the most predominate feeling. I in vain searched among the dying and the dead, in hopes of finding some food to eat; but, if they had any, it had already been taken by the men on duty and the Spaniards …
>
> This day [28 July] we were in hopes of the arrival of the Commissariat, who we expected would have stuck to us in the hour of danger, and given us our rations. If meat was wanting, they might have given us bread, or, at any rate, they might have issued out wine or spirits; but, I am sorry to say, no provisions were yet delivered to us …
>
> The day after the battle came, and we received a pint of wheat a man; the following day the same; and the next … This supply, scanty as it might have appeared to those who were partaking of the roast-beef of Old England, with us, who were partaking in its glory, it was as satisfying to the craving appetite, as mock-turtle to the pampered cit.[12]

John Spencer Cooper of the 7th Fusiliers also claimed that the food shortages first became apparent after the action at Talavera:

> Surely the French did not fight well at this battle … They had been well supplied with provisions previously. We had been half starved. They had dined on the field of battle, and liquor had been served out to them before they attacked us … On the contrary, nothing was served out to us from 2 or 3 p.m. on the 27th, until 10 a.m. on the 29th …
>
> The excitement of battle being over, we all severely felt stomach complaints. I had not tasted food for 43 hours …
>
> About 10 a.m. on the 29th, we were served with 4 ounces of bread, which was for the next 24 hours …[13]

It was not just the ordinary soldier who complained about the lack of provisions during the Battle of Talavera and its aftermath. Lieutenant Colonel Sir George Ridout Bingham, commander of the 2/53rd, wrote some four days after the battle: 'We are now without a day's provision in advance, without magazines … The whole day of the action our people were without provisions, and we have been detained here eversince for want of it …'[14]

Finally, John Aitchison, then an ensign with the 3rd Foot Guards, was highlighting the army's shortage of food and transport as early as 25 July. Writing home that day to his father in England he said:

---

12   George Wood, *The Subaltern Officer* (London: Septimus Prowett, 1825), pp.92–93.
13   John Spencer Cooper, *Rough Notes*, pp.24–26.
14   Ian Fletcher (ed.), *Voices from the Peninsula* (London: Greenhill Books, 2001), p.48.

Our prospect is now unhappy in that the enemy will either come upon us with superiority of force or, if it suits him better, he will retire (avoiding a general action) behind the Ebro – how we are to follow him, God knows, we are destitute of means of transport and already short of bread ...[15]

Numbered amongst the wounded at Talavera, Aitchison was eventually sent to Belem in Portugal to convalesce, whence he kept up his correspondence with his family. Writing on 26 September he told his father of the shortages suffered by the army in its advance to and withdrawal from Talavera:

All sorts of supplies were extremely scarce and in general very bad. The troops sometimes wanted bread for several days together. On the 27th [July] in the morning we [were] served out about ¼ lb. of bread and a pound of meat to each man and on the 28th, late in the evening, the same quantity of meat but without bread was all they received ... During the halt after the Battle of Talavera supplies were equally scanty and from the 2nd, the day before the army began to retire, until the 10th, the day on which I left, the troops used to receive about 2 ozs. of bread divided amongst eight with more than a pound of meat to each person[,] and they once received a pound of flour in addition.[16]

It is worth noting that, apart from Aitchison, none of the soldiers quoted above made any complaints about a shortage of rations until 27 July, the day on which the Battle of Talavera commenced. However, it was not only the British troops who suffered from a shortage of provisions in the aftermath of Talavera; the Spaniards too had difficulties in acquiring a sufficient quantity of rations. As we have seen, after Cuesta had been compelled to guarantee the safety of his army by following in the footsteps of Wellesley in his retreat to Portugal, he remarked that,

In that critical situation, we were in such straits due to a lack of supplies that [even] army headquarters was without rations of any sort for four or five days ... The royal treasury, passive and careless in this urgent matter, before and since the Battle of Talavera, did more to obstruct the measures taken by the divisional commanders than to facilitate the supply of necessities ... This state of affairs contributed in no small way to the misfortune of a campaign which had begun so gloriously ... Despite the severe scarcity of provisions suffered by the army, the Spanish troops displayed once more their powers of consistency and durability under the call of duty ...[17]

---

15   W.K.F. Thompson (ed.), *An Ensign in the Peninsular War. The Letters of John Aitchison* (London: Michael Joseph, 1981), p.53.

16   Thompson (ed.), *An Ensign in the Peninsular War*, p.61. Aitchison (or his publisher) probably meant to write 'lbs.' rather than 'ozs.' A pound of bread divided between eight men would give each of them a 2oz. share, whereas 2ozs divided between eight men would give each man just a quarter of an ounce (7g) of bread.

17   Cuesta, *Manifiesto*, pp.73–76.

In fact, scattered amongst his papers, Cuesta makes several references to the shortage of provisions available to his own troops, and a number of them are quoted herein. All of which tend to support Wellesley's complaints with respect to his situation.

The Plight of Wellesley's Wounded After Talavera

The Battle of Talavera was fought on 27 and 28 July 1809, and according to Wellesley's return; as well as losing 857 men killed and 653 missing, he was left with 3,913 wounded, many of whom would have to be removed from the battlefield and taken to the hospitals set up for their reception in Talavera. At some point in the future they would require conveyance to Portugal to continue their hospitalisation and recovery, all of which meant that Wellesley's need for wheeled transport had suddenly become acute. It was on 1 August that the commander in chief first made reference to the plight of his wounded in a letter to Cuesta's liaison officer, O'Donojú, asking for the release of some 40 or 50 Spanish surgeons to help with their treatment: 'We are much in want of medical assistance for the attendance of the wounded in the hospital; and I have been obliged to send there all those who ought properly to do duty with the regiments in the field.'[18] Two days later, having received intelligence that Soult had traversed the pass at Baños into Extremadura, and having decided to confront the resultant threat in his rear, his concerns for the wounded at Talavera began to grow. So certain was he that the casualties would be left to the mercy of Victor's men, should Cuesta decide to retreat, that he raised the issue with O'Donojú:

> This gives me much uneasiness. At all events, in the present state of our operations, it appears to me that the hospital is too far advanced at Talavera, and I am very desirous of moving it farther back.
>   I wish that you would mention this subject to Gen. Cuesta, and request him, from me, to make requisition in the country south of the Tagus, for carts to remove the hospital. It is impossible to hope to be able to remove it at once. Indeed, to attempt it might destroy the men whom we wish to save ...[19]

When Wellesley marched for Oropesa on 2 August he left Colonel Mackinnon in charge of the sick and wounded at the hospital, giving him orders to bring off the guard together with all of the convalescents who could either march or be carried in any carts which might be collected. Those who could not be moved were to be left behind in the care of the commissary and the medical staff under Mackinnon's orders, the British commander leaving with the latter a note for the commanding officer of the enemy troops in the hope that he: '... would insure ours such treatment as is ever shown by British troops to those who fall into their power ...'[20] Ultimately, it would appear that less than half of the British wounded were left behind at Talavera, and in a letter to Castlereagh dated 8 August, the Wellesley wrote that:

---

18   Wellesley to O'Donojú, 1 August 1809, Gurwood (ed.), *Wellington's Dispatches*, vol.III, p.386.
19   Wellesley to O'Donojú, 3 August 1809, Gurwood (ed.), *Wellington's Dispatches*, vol.III, p.390.
20   Stewart to MacKinnon, 2 August 1809, Gurwood (ed.), *Wellington's Dispatches*, vol.III, p.388.

About 2,000 of the wounded have been brought away from Talavera, the remaining 1,500 are there; and I doubt whether, under any circumstances, it would have been possible or consistent with humanity to attempt to remove any of them ... I have only to lament that a new concurrence of events, over which, from circumstances, I had and could have no control, should have placed the army in a situation to be obliged to leave any of them behind.[21]

If nothing else, the feelings here demonstrated by Wellesley strongly suggest that the transport problems he had been complaining about for several days were genuine and not, as some have ventured, just another contrived excuse for refusing to advance beyond the Alberche.

The Retreat to Portugal and Wellesley's Musings on Transport and Provisions

When Wellesley and Cuesta retreated to the south bank of the Tagus, they were moving into the territory abandoned by Victor some two months earlier because of its barrenness. So difficult were the conditions that the Spaniards who re-occupied the area as the French withdrew, were soon reduced to a miserable state themselves. Now finding himself in the same situation, Wellesley continued to bring up the subject of subsistence in Spain in his dispatches. On 8 August he wrote to Villiers from Deleitosa: 'I enclose my public and private letters to Lord Castlereagh, which will apprise you of the exact situation of affairs in this quarter. All is now safe, and I should feel no anxiety on any subject if we had provisions: but we are almost starving...'[22]

It was whilst he was at Deleitosa that the British commander found time to give some thought to future operations in Spain. In a letter to his brother, Richard, newly resident at Cádiz in his role as Ambassador to the Court of Spain, it is clear that his two main concerns regarding the practicalities of operating in Spain were the procurement and transport of provisions, and after making suggestions that the Spanish troops in the north of Spain be put in motion so as to enable those in Extremadura to take up the offensive, he went on to say:

In the mean time it is necessary that many arrangements should be adopted to enable the troops to take advantage of any success they may have in an offensive operation, or even to maintain their defensive positions. I shall endeavor to detail these in this dispatch, with my reasons for thinking them absolutely necessary.

The first of these is the formation of magazines of provisions and forage, principally biscuit, cattle and barley, at reasonable distances in the rear of the armies.

This part of Spain is but thinly inhabited, and but ill cultivated in proportion to its extent and its fertility, and it is nearly exhausted. As now equipped, the armies, amounting to not less than 60,000 mouths, and 16,000 to 18,000 horses, depend entirely for their daily supply of provisions upon the country, which does not

---

21   Wellesley to Castlereagh, 8 August 1809, Gurwood (ed.), *Wellington's Dispatches*, vol.III, pp.397–400.
22   Wellesley to Villiers, 8 August 1809, Gurwood (ed.), *Wellington's Dispatches*, vol.III, p.401.

contain a population in an extent of many square miles equal to the numbers of the army, and of course cannot produce a sufficiency for its subsistence. It is necessary, therefore, to send to great distances for supplies, which are procured with difficulty; consequently, the troops are ill fed, and not regularly; and very frequently receive no food at all.

The next arrangement to be made is to supply the armies with the means of transport, not only to move forward the magazines when that may be necessary, which means they [the transport units] should be specially attached to the magazines; but also means of transport to enable the army to communicate with the magazines, or to send to any part of the country for supplies of provisions or forage. 3,000 or 4,000 mules would effectually answer to the first object; and I should consider the British army well supplied with what it would require, if it had 1,500 mules and about 100 of the Valencian or Catalonian mule carts.

These measures are equally necessary for the Spanish and the British armies. No troops can serve to any good purpose unless they are regularly fed; and it is an error to suppose that a Spaniard or a man or animal of any country, can make an exertion without food. In fact, the Spanish troops are more clamorous for their food, and more exhausted if they do not receive it regularly, than our own are ...[23]

Wellesley is often spoken of as having a cold-hearted attitude towards his soldiers, and there are one or two phrases attributed to him which are often quoted, or sometimes misquoted, to support such claims. However, we have just seen several examples of his concerns for the basic welfare of his troops, both in relation to his worries and struggles to ensure their regular rations, and in his determination to do the best for his sick and wounded. Amongst the content of his dispatches there are sometimes listed his general orders for a particular date, one of which, for 9 August 1809, he wrote whilst at Deleitosa and it gives us an indication of his sense of concern and fair mindedness towards his men:

As the troops composing the army in Spain have not received their rations regularly since 22d July, it is not just that the full price of the ration should be stopped from the soldier's pay: from 23d July, therefore, the stoppages from the soldier's pay, on account of his rations, is to be only 3d. [pence] until the supplies are such as it will be possible to make regular deliveries of provisions ...[24]

By this, it would appear that the rations the army was supplied with as it left Plasencia on 16 July en-route to Talavera, had been more or less consumed by the 22nd. But it was not only the men of Wellesley's army that suffered from a lack of provisions during the Talavera campaign; both his cavalry mounts and draught animals were in distress, and indeed dying in substantial numbers throughout the time spent in Spain during the summer of 1809, as illustrated in another letter to his brother, Richard:

23   Wellesley to Marquess (Richard) Wellesley, 8 August 1809, Gurwood (ed.), *Wellington's Dispatches*, vol.III, pp.401–403.
24   General Order no.1 for 9 August 1809, Gurwood (ed.), *Wellington's Dispatches*, vol.III, p.405.

The horses of the British cavalry and artillery suffer much from the want of barley. We have lost many hundreds of the former, and above 200 of the latter, by the use of other grains, not having been able to procure barley (the only wholesome food for horses in this country) for the horses of the British cavalry and artillery, notwithstanding that the Spanish cavalry have been plentifully supplied.

I have also to mention to your Excellency, in order to point out the description of assistance which is given to us in this country, that having applied for a remount of cavalry of only 100 mares (which cannot be used by the Spanish cavalry, as they ride stallions) I have not got one, or even an answer from the government on the subject; and having asked Gen. Cuesta, after the Battle of Talavera, to assist me with 90 mules, to draw the British artillery, in lieu of those lost in the action, he refused to give me any, notwithstanding that there were hundreds in his army employed in drawing carts containing nothing.[25]

And so the commander in chief continued, citing further examples of Cuesta's selfishness towards him and the great difficulties he was having in purchasing draught animals and cavalry horses. On 11 August he wrote to Liuetenant General Payne from Jaraicejo telling him that he had '… just heard so melancholy a report of the state of the squadron which has been with Gen. R. Craufurd …', before asking him to relieve the unit every day; adding a note that he should, 'send them a day's forage.'[26] As the plight of his men worsened in the hot, arid province of Cáceres, Wellesley finally lost patience with Cuesta after seemingly being informed by him of instances of plundering by some of his troops. Writing from Deleitosa in a somewhat undiplomatic tone, he slammed his ally's apparent insensitivity towards the men who had done most to deliver the victory at Talavera:

I have had the honour of receiving your Excellency's letter of the 10th inst., and I am concerned that you should conceive that you should have any reason to complain of the conduct of British troops; but when troops are starving, which those under my command have been, as I have repeatedly told your excellency since I joined you on the 22d of last month, and particularly had no bread whatever from the 3d to the 8th inst., it is not astonishing that they should go to the villages, and even to the mountains, and look for food where they think they can get it. The complaints of the inhabitants, however, should not have been confined to the conduct of the British troops: in this very village I have seen the Spanish soldiers, who ought to have been elsewhere, take the doors off the houses which were locked up, in order that they might plunder the houses, and they afterwards burnt the doors. I absolutely and positively deny the assertion, that any thing going to the Spanish army has been stopped by the British troops or Commissaries.

On the 7th, when the British troops were starving in the hills, I met a convoy of 350 mules, loaded with provisions for the Spanish army. I would not allow one of them to be touched, and they all passed on. Gen. Sherbrooke, on the following day,

---

25 Wellesley to Marquess Wellesley, 10 August 1809, Gurwood (ed.), *Wellington's Dispatches*, vol.III, pp.409–410.
26 Wellesley to Payne, 11 August 1809, Gurwood (ed.), *Wellington's Dispatches*, vol.III, p.410.

the 8th, gave a written order to another convoy, addressed to all British officers, to allow them to pass through the army unmolested. Yesterday I met on the road, and passed, not less than 500 mules loaded with provisions for the Spanish army; and no later than yesterday evening, Major Campbell, my aide de camp, gave an order to another large convoy, addressed to all British officers and soldiers, not to impede its progress. I also declare to your Excellency most positively, on the honor of a gentleman, that the British army has received no provisions since it has been at Deleytosa [sic], excepting some sent from Truxillo, by Señor L. de Torres; and I can call upon the gentleman, who has informed his friend that biscuit addressed to the Spanish army has been taken by my Commissaries, to prove the truth of his assertion.

But this letter from your Excellency brings the question respecting provisions to a fair issue. I call upon your Excellency to state distinctly, whether it is understood by you that the Spanish army are to have not only all the provisions the country can afford, but all those sent from Seville, I believe, as much for the service for the one army as of the other.

I beg you let me know in reply to this letter, whether any magazines of provisions have been formed, and from whence the British troops are to draw their provisions.

I hope that I shall receive satisfactory answers to these two questions tomorrow morning. If I should not I beg that your Excellency will be prepared to occupy the post opposite Almaraz, as it will be impossible for me to remain any longer in a country in which no arrangement has been made for the supply of provisions for the troops; and in which it is understood that all the provisions which are either found in the country, or are sent from Seville, as I have been informed, for the use of the British army, are to be supplied solely and exclusively to the use of the Spanish troops.

In regard to the assertion in your Excellency's letter that the British troops sell their bread to the Spanish soldiers, it is beneath the dignity of your Excellency's situation and character to notice such things, or for me to reply to them. I must observe, however, that the British troops could not sell that which they had not, and that the reverse of the statement of your Excellency upon this subject is the fact, at the time the armies were at Talavera; as I have myself witnessed frequently in the streets of that town.[27]

It is right to sympathise with Wellesley's concern about the welfare of his own troops, but one should recall the complaints made by Cuesta about the lack of rations for his own troops in the days leading up to his resignation, before judging his apparent lack of empathy for his allies. It would have been interesting to have seen the Spaniard's reaction to the above communication but, perhaps for the sake of the alliance, we were spared its appearance. Cuesta resigned his command of the Army of Extremadura on the day after Wellesley wrote the scathing criticism of him reproduced above, which meant he probably never had an opportunity to read it. Nevertheless, the British general continued to rumble on about his

---

27   Wellesley to Cuesta, 11 August 1809, Gurwood (ed.), *Wellington's Dispatches*, vol.III, pp.411–412.

first experiences in Spain, as he loitered in the region of Trujillo, Jaraicejo and Mérida, hoping to discern the intentions of the French; especially with respect to the prospect that they might attempt a third invasion of Portugal before the summer was out. In the final paragraph of a letter to Villiers, written on 12 August from Jaraicejo, he said, 'We are starving, and are ill treated by the Spaniards in every way: but more of this hereafter. There is not a man in the army who does not wish to return to Portugal.'[28] To his brother Richard, 1st Marquess Wellesley, he wrote on the same day that:

> It is useless to complain, but we are certainly not treated as friends, much less as the only prop on which the cause of Spain can depend. But besides this want of good will, which can easily be traced to the temper and disposition of the General commanding the Spanish army, and which ought to be borne with patience if there was any hope of doing good, there is such a want of resource in the country, and so little question of bringing forward what is to be found, that if the army were to remain here much longer it would become totally useless. The daily and increasing loss of horses in the cavalry and the artillery, from a deficiency and badness of the food, is really alarming; and the Spanish cavalry having begun to intercept the small supply of food for horses which we could procure, this evil must increase.[29]

In fact, Wellesley did receive a reply to his letter of 12 August, ostensibly from Cuesta, suggesting the establishment of a magazine at Trujillo from which both the British and Spanish armies could draw their supplies, but in his response he dismissed the idea after pointing out some glaring faults in the logic of the plan, at the same time taking the opportunity to rail once more against his treatment at the hands of the Spanish:

> When the British army entered Spain I had reason to expect, and I expected, that a great effort would be made to afford us subsistence, at least for payment, and those means of transport, and other aids, without which your Excellency is well aware no army can keep the field. Your Excellency also knows how these expectations have been filled. Since I joined your army the troops have not received, upon average, half a ration, and on some days nothing at all; and the cavalry no forage or grain, excepting what they could pick up in the fields, of an unwholesome description, by the use of which hundreds of horses have died. I can procure no means of transport ...
>   Under all these circumstances, your Excellency cannot be surprised that I should think that the British army has been neglected and ill treated ... I shall march them back into Portugal, if they are not more regularly and plentifully supplied with provisions and forage, and with the means of transport, and other aids which they require ...[30]

---

28   Wellesley to Villiers, 12 August 1809, Gurwood (ed.), *Wellington's Dispatches*, vol.III, pp.414–415.
29   Wellesley to Marquess Wellesley, 12 August 1809, Gurwood (ed.), *Wellington's Dispatches*, vol.III, pp.415–416.
30   Wellesley to Cuesta, 13 August 1809, Gurwood (ed.), *Wellington's Dispatches*, vol.III, pp.416–417.

Once again, we can see in this what might be interpreted as something of a sense of entitlement from Wellesley, justifiable or not, in his demands for assistance from the Spanish.

Eguía Succeeds Cuesta as Commander in Chief of the Army of Extremadura

On 14 August, whilst he was still in the process of withdrawing his army to Portugal, Wellesley received the news that *Teniente General* Eguía had succeeded Cuesta in command of the Army of Extremadura. After congratulating him on his appointment, the British commander said, in a more concessionary tone to that adopted earlier, that he was willing to comply with Cuesta's suggestions to create a joint magazine at Trujillo, and agreed to send a delegation of officers to that place, which included Colonel Waters, whose exploits at Oporto we may recall, and William Wemyss of the Commissary General's department, all with the intention to formulate any practical arrangements they could agree upon with their allies.[31] Waters was given a shopping list to present to the Spaniards which included what would become a daily request for 25,000 rations for men and 6,000 for horses. In addition, there was a requirement for at least 1,000 beasts of burden, 100 carts each capable of carrying 600lbs of load, 100 good draught mules or horses and 300 mares as cavalry remounts. Payment to be made 'on the spot.'[32]

After having communicated with Waters, Eguía wrote to Wellesley on 17 August, listing a whole range of foodstuffs he had ordered to be set aside at the depot in Trujillo, all for use by the British army, and it was on this day that the two commanders briefly met, probably at Jaraicejo.[33] Despite this, Wellesley felt forced to write to the Spanish general on the following day: 'I am sorry to have to inform your Excellency that the British army under my command have this day no bread, instead of receiving the plentiful supply of which your Excellency announced the arrival in the conversation which I had with you yesterday'.[34] Later that day he wrote:

> I have had the honour of receiving your Excellency's letter and of its enclosures of this day's date, respecting the provisions in the magazine at Trujillo for the use of the British army; and as the soldiers have not received their provisions for this day, and there does not appear to me to be a sufficiency for the consumption of tomorrow, I shall, however unwillingly, carry in to execution the intention I announced to you yesterday. I trust, therefore, that you will have ordered troops to relieve my outposts on the Tagus ...[35]

It is almost certain that, during their meeting of the 17th, Wellesley had made it clear to Eguía that, should the question of provisions for his army not be resolved, then he would continue his retreat to Portugal.

---

31   Wellesley to Eguía, 14 August 1809, Gurwood (ed.), *Wellington's Dispatches*, vol.III, pp.421–422.
32   Wellesley to Col. Waters, 14 August 1809, Gurwood (ed.), *Wellington's Dispatches*, vol.III, p.422.
33   UoS: WP1/272/28: Eguía to Wellesley, 17 August 1809.
34   Wellesley to Eguía, 18 August 1809, Gurwood (ed.), *Wellington's Dispatches*, vol.III, pp.427.
35   Wellesley to Eguía, 18 August 1809, Gurwood (ed.), *Wellington's Dispatches*, vol.III, pp.427.

Eguía's reply was nothing other than an astonishing diplomatic disaster. Sadly, his letter, which is held amongst Southampton University's Wellington Papers, is, in some parts, difficult to decipher, despite the magnificent efforts of the conservators, but there is enough readable text to grasp the thrust of its content:

> I received Your Excellency's letter of last night, in which you informed me of your absolute determination [to return?] to Portugal, due to a lack of subsistence for the army under your command.
>
> Your Excellency will have, just as I have offered, all of the things that you need. [If not then] it will be because it is either impossible to obtain [some?] of the articles you asked for, from any of our depots, or [they are things which the Spanish army does not hold?]. [You may take it for granted that] the Spanish soldier will want for everything [rather than we fail to ensure that?] our allies have all that they need.

The following paragraph is the most difficult one to read, but Eguía begins in the somewhat brusque manner: 'In case Your Excellency did not fully understand me ...' before going on to say something like: 'In Trujillo there was a constant English presence and they had access to the keys of the depot, from where they could take all the articles stipulated, [in quantity?] according to the strength of the British army, even if it meant that my own army went without.'

The following paragraphs are much more legible, and continue as follows:

> I believe that the needs of Your Excellency have been satisfied, as demonstrated by my answer above ... [and I repeat that] I have left orders [with the garrison] at Trujillo that my wishes be met. But if Your Excellency continues to insist upon marching your troops to Portugal, then I will be left convinced that causes other than a shortage of provisions have determined Your Excellency's actions ...

From this, it may be the case that Eguía was aware of some of the rumours swirling about in certain Spanish circles regarding the British commitment, or lack of it, to the campaign on the Tagus, as well as their intrigues regarding the command of the allied armies in Spain. These themes will be discussed in full in the following chapters.

On 19 August, the British commander responded thus:

> I have had the honor of receiving your Excellency's letter ... and I feel much concerned that anything should have occurred to induce your Excellency to express a doubt of the truth of what I have written to you. As, however, your excellency entertains that doubt, any further correspondence between us appears unnecessary; and accordingly, this is the last letter I shall have the honour of addressing to you ...[36]

---

36   Wellesley to Eguía, 19 August 1809, Gurwood (ed.), *Wellington's Dispatches*, vol.III, pp.431–432.

Two days later, the activity at British army headquarters in Trujillo must have been frenetic, judging by the amount of correspondence Wellesley sent off to various parties in preparation for continuing with the next stage of his march to the Portuguese frontier, a move which began on the following day. On 22nd he was at Miajadas, the 23rd at Medellín and the 24th at Mérida, where he remained until 1 September before moving to Lobón. On the 2nd he reached Badajoz, where he would remain for several weeks, and with his men by then exhausted and malnourished after enduring the rigours of a long and trying campaign, they fell easy victims to the prevailing Guadiana fevers, a sad end to a year which for some time held out the promise of significant success. Once the final move into Portugal had been made, Wellesley would begin to map out a strategy for the war which would free him from any significant dependence upon his Spanish allies.

12

Imponderables of the Tagus Campaign

Austria Asks Britain to Support its Coming Offensive

After their defeat by Napoleonic forces in 1805, the Austrians were to remain pacified until their leaders began to stir into action once more towards the end of 1808. After taking stock of Napoleon's troublesome adventure on the Iberian Peninsula, and Britain's willingness to continue the conflict against France, they thought they could see an opportunity to take revenge upon their old adversary by opening a second front in central Europe. If the British could be persuaded to pose the French one or two additional problems, then a simultaneous offensive by Austria might well improve the chances for an allied victory. With this strategy in mind, feelers were put out during the early months of 1809 to see if there was anything the British could do that might help their cause. Moore's Spanish campaign of 1808 had been a blot on the landscape, but if Britain could be encouraged to return in strength to Spain or Portugal, and Russia be convinced either to engage in a military campaign alongside Austria, or at least remain passive, then Napoleon's resources might be stretched to breaking point.

After a series of negotiations had taken place at the start of the year, during which Tsar Alexander had given the Austrians a secret guarantee of his country's intended neutrality, a treaty of alliance was finalised between Britain and Austria on 24 April, the details of which seem never to have been fully clarified. In fact, Austria's first request of the British was that they provide the financial assistance required to sustain a sizable campaign in Germany; an approach having been made in October 1808 which was rejected by Britain's Foreign Minister, George Canning, on the grounds that the Austrian demands were far too exorbitant. A second approach was then made, in which they asked for less money, but it contained a demand for diversionary operations by British forces in southern Italy, the Iberian Peninsula and northern Germany, some or all of which they considered would be fairly straightforward for the British to accommodate. In fact, London had already made extensive preparations for an imminent reinforcement of Cradock, via the reinforcements led by Hill and Wellesley, who at that time was still at Lisbon with a force of some 11,500 men despite the failure of Moore's expedition during the latter months of 1808. There was also an opportunity to employ Sir John Stuart, who was then in Sicily with a sizeable land force and the maritime resources to project it onto the Italian mainland should the need arise. An expedition to northern Germany, it was considered, would present some significant difficulties.

Some 10 weeks after the Austrians' approach to London, on the same day that Wellesley began his march from Abrantes to join Cuesta in the Tagus valley, Canning wrote to Richard Wellesley, who was soon to become Britain's ambassador to Spain:

> ... the destination of the disposable military force of this country, at the present moment, to other objects more immediately connected with the war on the continent of Europe, and calculated to operate a diversion in favour of Austria, will probably be considered by the Spanish Government itself as of more instant necessity and more obvious advantage.
>
> Should the efforts of Austria prove unfortunately unavailing, or should they, on the other hand, so far succeed as to leave the force of this country free for more distant operations; in one or other of these cases, the necessity or temptation might arise for the employment of a large British force in Spain ...[1]

In other words, Canning seemed to be saying that the Spanish might well support the idea of disposable British forces being employed in different parts of Europe in order to support Austria's coming offensive. His reasoning apparently telling him that Spain would welcome such a diversionary offensive against the French on Spanish soil as part of the strategy. As a further inducement to the Spaniards that they help the Austrians (and allow the British army to enter Spain to assist) Canning hinted that, win or lose for the Austrians, Britain would still be able to reinforce Wellesley on the Peninsula to a significant degree.

As already mentioned, during their talks with London, the Austrians had also raised the possibility of a British expeditionary force being sent to northern Germany, ostensibly via an amphibious expedition to the Baltic coast, with the hope in mind that such an action would bring Prussia into the war. Doubting both the viability of such an expedition and the chances that it would necessarily bring the Prussians to join the Anglo-Austrian alliance, the British sidestepped the Austrian suggestion by offering to launch an operation on the Scheldt in its place. This would appear to have been a nice piece of diplomacy. If accepted by their ally, it would allow the British to carry out what had been a long-envisaged plan of theirs to neutralise a potential base of operations for the projection of French naval forces into the North Sea and English Channel, as well as a possible staging post for amphibious excursions to the English coast, if not a full sea-borne invasion. The probable truth of the matter was that a landing on Walcheren, an island lying in the Scheldt estuary, had long been a pet scheme of Castlereagh, and when British agents on the European mainland sent word of a build-up of French naval resources on the Scheldt, which included a ship building programme at the port of Flushing, Castlereagh's dreams were finally realised, if not with the eventual measure of success he was hoping for. Nevertheless, the Austrians seemed happy with the British counter-offer, thus allowing their insular allies to make a virtue of necessity; but could the necessary arrangements for such a large and complex operation be completed in time for it to be synchronised with Vienna's offensive? Unfortunately not. Ultimately, the Austrians were suing for peace before the Walcheren expedition sailed from

---

1   Canning to Marquess Wellesley, 27 June 1809, Montgomery Martin (ed.), *Despatches and Correspondence of the Marquess Wellesley during his Lordship's Mission to Spain* (London: John Murray, 1838), Appendix F, pp.190–191. See also Sañudo & Stampa, *Crisis de una Alianza*, p.126.

British shores, all of which adds weight to the suggestion that, in the minds of the British, the Walcheren adventure was more of an independent pre-emptive strike against French maritime resources, which could only have been directly deployed against Britain itself, than a planned diversionary operation in aid of Austria.

Wellesley Sails for Portugal, April 1809

Whether or not his return to Portugal and Spain was intended to deflect French attention from the Austro-Bavarian-Swiss frontier for the sake of Austria; when Wellesley sailed for Lisbon in early April 1809, the mission ostensibly assigned to him by the British government was that of expelling the French from Portuguese territory and defending its frontiers against further incursions by the common enemy. However, despite Castlereagh's initial reluctance to see British troops enter Spain, a degree of operational licence was being pondered by Wellesley himself just a few days after disembarking in Portugal. This may be seen from the letter he wrote to Frere on 24 April, in which he spoke about his wishes to cooperate with Cuesta's forces, which were then occupying Spanish Extremadura; his correspondence providing a clear hint that if an opportunity arose to attack Victor, he might well take advantage of it:

> I intend to move towards Soult and attack him ... I am not quite certain, however, that I should not do more good to the general cause by combining with Gen. Cuesta in an operation against Victor ...
>
> I think it probable, however, that Soult will not remain in Portugal when I shall pass the Mondego: if he does, I shall attack him. If he should retire I am convinced that it would be most advantageous for the common cause, that we should remain on the defensive in the north of Portugal, and act vigorously in cooperation with Cuesta against Victor ...
>
> An operation against Victor is attended by ... advantages. If successful, it effectually relieves Seville and Lisbon ...
>
> I am convinced that the French will be in serious danger in Spain only when a great force shall be assembled which will oblige them to collect their troops; and this combined operation of the force in this country [Portugal] with that under Gen. Cuesta, may be the groundwork of further measures of the same and a more extended description ...[2]

Garay and Cuesta Make Overtures to Wellesley

At this point it might appear that, once on the Iberian Peninsula, the idea of a significant British incursion into Spanish territory sprang solely from Wellesley, but both Martín de Garay and Cuesta had written to the British commander at or about the time his expedition

---

2   Wellesley to Frere, 24 April 1809, Gurwood (ed.), *Wellington's Dispatches*, vol.III, pp.187–189.

was disembarking at Lisbon. In his letter, Cuesta, true to form, was raring to unite with Wellesley and launch a combined offensive against Victor:

> Brigadier General Wilson has occupied Alcántara ... so I would much prefer it if you could detach a force of 10–12,000 men from the army under your command towards that place, uniting with Wilson and threatening Victor's rearguard in the vicinity of Cheler as well as his right flank ...That being the case, we could combine our movements and fall upon the enemy. I have no doubt that such an attack would be entirely unexpected and would force him to retire towards Madrid, from where we could pursue him to the Bidassoa [on the French frontier] ...
>
> Ignorant of the strength of forces under your command, I hope you will forgive my temerity in suggesting this plan to you, certain that I am of its successful conclusion if Your Excellency could agree to it without it being in any way detrimental to your principal attack upon Marshal Soult ...[3]

Wellesley replied:

> If I should succeed in removing Marshal Soult from the north of Portugal, I intend to go forthwith with all the troops under my command (consisting of about 25,000, of which nearly 4,000 will at that time be cavalry) to the Eastern frontier of Portugal, in the neighbourhood of Elvas; and I shall be happy to cooperate with you in any plan which may be agreed upon for the attack of [sic for on?] Marshal Victor ...
>
> In the present situation of affairs, all that we can require is time; and that we should not lose our men or any of the valuable positions which we still possess. In a short time we shall all be enabled to cooperate in a vigorous attack upon the enemy; and till that period should arrive, it is not very material whether he acquires a little more of the open country, provided we do not lose any of the men who are destined to defend the valuable points and positions which remain in our hands. [4]

The letter from Garay has so far eluded the author. Dated 21 April 1809, it does not reside amongst the Wellington Papers, which include a collection of letters written to Wellesley between 9–30 April 1809; neither does there seem to be a surviving copy of it in the Spanish archives.

According to Charles Stewart, Wellesley's Adjutant General, the British commander was at this time receiving a number of letters from Cuesta, outlining the kind of combined operations he favoured in Extremadura.[5] In response, towards the end of May, the British commander dispatched Colonel Bourke to work closely with the Spanish general, but Cuesta, perhaps having begun to sense a somewhat less than enthusiastic leaning towards his proposals emanating from British army headquarters, had already let his feelings be

---

3   UoS: WP1/254/21: Cuesta to Wellesley, 23 April 1809.
4   Wellesley to Cuesta, 29 April 1809, Gurwood (ed.), *Wellington's Dispatches*, vol.III, pp.197–198.
5   Cuesta, *Manifiesto*, p.53. See also Vane, *Story of the Peninsular War*, pp.168–169. Amongst the Wellington Papers for April 1809 held at the University of Southampton, there is only one letter from Cuesta to Wellesley, despite Vane's claim.

known in a letter to the *Junta Suprema* on 3 May as his enthusiasm for close collabora-
tion with his allies in the field began to cool. Sadly, in an act of intrigue so typical of him,
Frere, by this time employed by the *Junta Suprema*, leaked Cuesta's less than complimentary
remarks to Wellesley:

> It appears to me that the object of the English general should be to surround the
> French in Oporto or place himself between that city and the Minho in order to
> prevent [them retreating to Galicia] ... By this position [he] might also prevent the
> arrival of any succours which Soult might receive from Galicia.
>
> I know not whether the remarks I [propose] making to him upon this subject
> will have arrived in time or, even if they did, whether they will have any effect. The
> system of the British appears to be that of never exposing their troops, whence it
> happens that decisive actions by land never take place, meaning that they are then
> sacrificed in retreats and precautions, as happened to Sir John Moore from his
> not having attacked the enemy in time at Sahagún and Palencia, before they were
> reinforced ...[6]

It may be that Cuesta's apparent need to utter such thoughts about Spain's allies sprung
from his uneasiness about the rumours he is said to have heard relating to incipient plans
to appoint a British officer as an allied supremo. Despite the claims by some that he was a
somewhat irascible character, Cuesta was not without friends in high places, and it may be
that some of his acolytes in Seville were informing him of plots afoot to subordinate him to
a British general. If not, then he may well have sensed in Wellesley's reply to his letter of 23
April that the overriding priority of the British was the defence of Portugal, and that they
might be simply stringing along the Spanish to suit that purpose.[7] Either way, he let his
thoughts be known to his political masters in Seville.

With regard to Garay's missing letter of 21 April 1809, Wellesley's reply to it of the 29th
was similar to that he made to Cuesta:

> As soon as [my operation to remove Marshal Soult from the north of Portugal is
> complete] it is my intention to collect the whole of the army under my command
> on the Eastern frontier of Portugal, and to co-operate by every means in my power
> with Gen. Cuesta in an attack upon Marshal Victor. In the mean time, I cannot
> sufficiently recommend a strict defensive position in all quarters. In the present
> situation of affairs, we have every reason to hope that in a short time we shall all be
> able to co-operate in a vigorous attack upon the only remaining force of the enemy;
> in which attack we have every reasonable prospect of success, if we do not lose any
> of the valuable positions which we still possess, or the men who defend them, in
> fruitless attacks of [*sic* for on?] the enemy in the plains ...[8]

---

6   TNA: FO 72/73: Cuesta to Cornel, 3 May 1809, pp.18–19.
7   Sañudo & Stampa, *Crisis de una Alianza*, p.100.
8   Wellesley to Garay, 29 April 1809, Gurwood (ed.), *Wellington's Dispatches*, vol.III, p.199.

From this it is quite clear that Garay's letter must have been similar to that of Cuesta's of the 23rd, that is, full of urgings for Wellesley to launch operations against the French in Extremadura.

We have already seen that, as a means of laying some of the groundwork for any forthcoming Anglo-Spanish operations in Spain, Colonel Bourke was allowed to discuss plans for various missions and strategies with Cuesta, and by the first week in June, whilst Wellesley was at Abrantes, he was sending details of the Spaniard's early proposals for such cooperation to British headquarters. However, Cuesta's three alternative plans were not well received by Wellesley, which probably strengthened the former's views about what he saw as Britain's priorities in the Peninsula, as expressed in his letter to Garay of 3 May.[9] Stewart claimed that, amongst the outlines of the plans he sent to Wellesley, Cuesta included the following advice to the British general with regard to the availability of provisions in Extremadura, depending upon the route he chose to take him from Portugal to Talavera. Here is Stewart's interpretation of Cuesta's words:

> In pressing upon our consideration the first of his propositions, Cuesta strongly represented that we might expect ample supplies of every description at Badajoz; and that, should more be required than Badajoz was able to furnish, the deficiency could be promptly and sufficiently made up from [the] Alentejo. The case would be very different were we to proceed by Alcantara. The whole of that country was exhausted by the enemy, who ravished it in all directions; and we should find it extremely difficult, as well as inconvenient, to carry along with us both provisions for the men and forage for the horses.[10]

In outlining the situation with regard to the lack of provisions in the Tagus valley, had the Spanish general inadvertently presented Wellesley with the seeds of an excuse he could later use for withdrawing his army to Portugal in the wake of Talavera?

Once at Talavera, Wellesley's apparent enthusiasm for a deeper advance into Spanish territory seemed to desert him fairly quickly, but as late as 25 July he was telling the Duke of Richmond that he was thinking of manoeuvring Victor away from his position on the Alberche in order to advance on Madrid, which was a little strange to say the least, because suddenly, on or about 16 July, his enthusiasm for going beyond the Alberche had begun to cool. This abrupt change of mind on the part of the British commander was one of a number of reasons which encouraged the Spanish authors, Juan Sañudo and Leopoldo Stampa to re-visit the Tagus campaign of 1809 and attempt to discover any hitherto unknown reasons for its failure, during the course of which they gave close scrutiny to the possible reasons as to why Wellesley suddenly decided to lead his army back to Portugal after his victory at Talavera. In doing so, they constructed an argument as to what his real motivations for retiring may have been, dismissing what they regard as his publicly voiced excuses about the lack of transport and provisions for his troops, before proposing an alternative theory.[11]

9   Juan Priego López, *Guerra de la Independencia* (Madrid: Editorial Gran Capitán, 1947), vol.IV, pp.195–196.
10   Vane, *Narrative of the Peninsula War*, vol.I, p.363.
11   Sañudo & Stampa, *La Crisis de una Alianza*, pp.111–212.

The authors begin their analysis by examining Wellesley's letters to Frere and O'Donojú of 16 July, each of which are quoted in an earlier chapter. In his letter to Frere, he complained of an apparent lack of will on the part of the Spaniards to provide his army with both a means of transport and a reliable supply of provisions. In that sent to O'Donojú he made the same complaints, but then somewhat imperiously added: 'I feel that it is only fair to my army and to His Majesty that I do not set out on any new operation until I have been provided with the means of transport that my army requires …' These letters were written just six days after Wellesley's meeting with Cuesta at Miravete, and just three days after he had written to Frere on 13 July telling him that the conference with the Spanish commander had gone well and that the two men had made some outline suggestions about how they should attempt to manoeuvre Victor out of their path as they advanced on Madrid.

Of course, back in April, Wellesley's overriding priority had been the expulsion of Soult from Portugal. Whether or not he had since been given secret instructions to launch a subsequent but limited offensive across the border into Spain as a means of pinning down French resources on the Peninsula in aid of Austria, as suggested by Sañudo and Stampa, we shall examine later. But firstly, we should begin to investigate the possibility that there was a more sinister thread of thought in the mind of some of the people in London and Seville when it came to Britain's presence on the Peninsula. It was something that had been under secret discussion for several months before Wellesley's expedition set sail, and something which may have contributed to the eventual failure of the 1809 campaign on the Tagus, as we shall now see.

Was Cuesta the Intended Victim of a Plot to Appoint a Supreme Allied Commander in 1809?

The idea of appointing a supreme commander of allied forces on the Peninsula was seemingly first broached on the British side by Castlereagh in a letter to Sir Hew Dalrymple dated 20 August 1808, some three weeks after Wellesley's first disembarkation in Portugal: 'It appears to me that if there were means of making the whole Spanish force now in arms unite under a common head in the execution of a public plan, so large a body might be assembled against the French line of partition as to render it untenable.'[12] Just a few weeks later Dalrymple would be making his way home to England, having been succeeded in command of the British army in Portugal by Sir John Moore. It could have been this juxtaposition of events which led some commentators to assume that Castlereagh was lobbying for Moore to be named as supreme allied commander on the Iberian Peninsula, in overall command of British, Portuguese and Spanish troops in the war against the French. However, Castlereagh's thoughts may have been more narrowly focussed, in that he was hoping for Dalrymple to retain overall command of British and Portuguese troops, with Wellesley and Moore operating semi-independently beneath him. Of course, all of this changed when Dalrymple and Wellesley returned to England, and there is no solid evidence to suggest that Moore was ever consulted about the possibility that he be nominated supreme allied commander.

---

12   TNA: WO 1/234: Castlereagh to Dalrymple, 20 August 1808, pp.14–17.

Spanish Attempts to Appoint a Supreme Commander of Their Own Forces

On the Spanish side, there had already been an attempt to agree upon a candidate for supreme commander of their own forces, once Madrid had been retaken from the French in the aftermath of Dupont's defeat at Bailén. It was at the behest of *Capitán General* Castaños that the commanders of their somewhat disparate and quasi-autonomous collection of armies were summoned to the capital in September 1808 to discuss the matter, all of whom attended apart from Blake, who sent his apologies with his deputy, the Duque del Infantado, citing the demands of his campaign in the Cantabrian foothills as the reason for his absence. In fact, he was leading the Army of Galicia in its pursuit of the French across the north of Spain at that time. However, the actual reason for his refusal to attend may well have been the continuing rancour which existed between himself and Cuesta over the disastrous outcome of the Battle of Rioseco some two months earlier; the possibility of a face-to-face meeting with his nemesis in the presence of other high-ranking officers perhaps providing him with some second thoughts about attending. On the other hand, he may well have received pre-conference assurances from his friends in high places that Cuesta would be quietly side-lined, if and when the process for electing a Spanish supremo was set in motion, which is what actually transpired.

By the time the Madrid conference closed, its delegates had failed to agree upon the appointment of an overall commander in chief, which was a clear indication of the level of factionalism and petty jealousies dividing the Spanish high command at the time, something from which not even Castaños was exempt. As a result, the Spanish forces would soon have to face Napoleon's huge counter offensive of late autumn 1808, almost as a collection of independent armies, even though the *Junta Suprema* had nominally taken on the role of overseer of military affairs. Once the conference had concluded, all but one of the general officers present were given a set of marching orders which would take them to the Ebro front, the exception being Cuesta, at that time still in place as the commander in chief of the Army of Castilla.

Left in the lurch, and with time on his hands, it was not long before the old warrior found himself in trouble with the *Junta*, to such an extent that he was eventually placed under arrest, as explained in an earlier chapter. Such was the backdrop to the military situation in Spain as the summer of 1808 drew to a close, and it was soon to be made much worse after a series of catastrophic defeats had been inflicted upon the Spanish armies as they attempted to halt the French onslaught of the autumn. Caught up in it all, Sir John Moore's army suffered a similar fate to that experienced by the various Spanish formations, managing to escape total annihilation only when it was evacuated from La Coruña by the Royal Navy in January 1809. By the end of 1808, Napoleon's various army corps would be established deep inside Spanish territory, consolidating their hold on most of the north of the country down to the Tagus valley, where they paused to take stock as winter took its grip. Fighting would re-commence in the early spring, placing an enormous strain upon the Spanish armies once more and engendering a mutinous atmosphere amongst some of the soldiery, which in one case resulted in the murder of San Juan, as we saw in an earlier chapter. In such a situation it was not long before the relationship between the *Junta Suprema* and some of the army generals, never good at the best of times, began to deteriorate.

Wellesley returned to Portugal in April 1809 and crossed into Spain on 3 July. By that time both La Romana and Cuesta would be numbered amongst the enemies of the

Junta, whose *Secretario General*, Martín de Garay, would be willing to play the Anglo-Spanish alliance for all that he could; desperate as he was to grasp at any straw in an attempt to save his country and maintain the *Junta's de-facto* position as the supreme state authority, in the face of its detractors amongst the senior ranks of the army. With all of that in mind, it is perhaps time to present the reader with an alternative analysis of the efforts made to appoint a supreme allied commander than that put forward by Sañudo and Stampa in *La Crisis de una Alianza*, assuming, of course, that such efforts were in play at the time of Talavera.

There are uncorroborated stories of Sir John Moore having been offered the position of commander in chief of allied armies in 1808. In fact, Charles Esdaile suggested that if such a prospect was ever seriously considered, then it would probably have sprung from one of the Spanish factions opposed to the *Junta Suprema*, with a view to recruiting the British to their cause of dismantling the governing body. How fitting then, continued Esdaile, that upon discovering or anticipating such a plot, Martín de Garay decided to act quickly and turn the plotters' own scheme against them, by dangling that very same prospect before the eyes of his British allies as a means of aligning them shoulder to shoulder with the *Junta* against its home-grown adversaries. Such was the enticement set before British plenipotentiary, Frere, by Garay, in return for his help in engineering the deposition of the *Junta's* antithesis, *Capitán General* Cuesta, from his command of the Army of Extremadura, a position he had been reluctantly elevated to by the *Junta* in extremis. The fact that Frere took the bait was more a sign of credulity than astuteness as, explained Esdaile, he should have known that the legitimacy of the *Junta Suprema* had never been accepted by a sizable cadre of senior Spanish army officers, the very men who Frere, as Garay's agent, would have to help convince that Cuesta's demise was in Spain's best interests. Notwithstanding, once primed, Frere wrote to Wellesley on 9 June to inform him that many in the *Junta*, including Garay, were ready to call for Cuesta's dismissal, 'General Cuesta has recovered from the attack of the ague, but his age and his infirmities and his passion for pitched battles incline many members of the *Junta* to wish for his removal.'[13] Frere's intimation to the British commander in chief was that the Spanish government would be willing to see him in the role of supreme allied commander, no doubt hoping that the well-connected soldier would then make use of his influential contacts in Britain to set things in motion. It was, said Frere, a cause which would have been helped had Wellesley captured Soult's army at Oporto rather than allow it to escape into Galicia:

> ... there would have been a brilliancy in the event which would have enabled your friends here, among whom you may reckon Mr. Garay, to make you the same offer which it had before been proposed to hold out to Sir John Moore, that of the chief command. Any decided success on the part of the British troops against the army of Genl. Victor would probably have the same effect.[14]

---

13   Charles J. Esdaile, *The Duke of Wellington and the Command of the Spanish Army 1812-14* (London: MacMillan Press, 1990), pp.31–32. See also TNA: FO 72/73: Frere to Wellesley, 9 June 1809, pp.190–191.
14   TNA: FO 72/73: Frere to Wellesley, 9 June 1809, pp.190–191.

Ultimately, Frere's flattery failed to move Wellesley, the gist of whose reply was that, although he was aware that such a move was being contemplated at a governmental level, the thinking in London was that it would be best if the Spanish were left to call openly for it themselves, rather than the British be seen to be agitating for it.[15]

If further proof be needed of Wellesley's somewhat distanced complicity in Garay's incipient plot to make him allied supremo, then one need look no further than the content of his letter to Frere of 13 July, as the allies were preparing for a general action against Victor on the Tagus:

> I have received your letters of the 8th; and you will see in the accompanying letters an account of my endeavors to prevail on Gen. Cuesta to make a detachment upon Ávila, and eventually on Segovia. I agree with you in thinking that such a detachment would be a great advantage in a military point of view, and it might be attended by the political advantages to which you refer [the removal of Cuesta from command].
>
> In order to enable you to endeavor to attain the political advantages, I write the accompanying letter … The general sentiment of the [Spanish] army, as far as I can learn it from the British officers, appears to be contempt of the Junta and of the present form of the government; great confidence in Cuesta, and a belief that he is too powerful for the Junta, and that he will overturn that government …
>
> I acknowledge that I conceive that the Junta would gain but little by the change of the person in whose hands the command should be placed; that person, in the existing state of the government, must be formidable to them, particularly if he should be successful; and if this be true, I do not know whether there are not some advantages to be derived from the employment of Cuesta. By dividing the troops into different armies they may certainly diminish the danger; but this security must only be temporary …and they must, when together, be under one head, and this head will be an object of fear and danger to the Junta.[16]

From what he said, it is clear that Wellesley had been communicating with Frere about the means by which Cuesta might be deposed as head of the Army of Extremadura, but was he now thinking that the *Junta's* position might be safer should Cuesta be given the overall command of the Spanish army? His reckoning being that Cuesta's probable failure in the role might mean continued survival for the *Junta*?

Garay's Involvement in Proposing Wellesley as Supreme Allied Commander

A keen supporter of British intervention on the Peninsula, Don Martín de Garay, *Secretario General de Estado de la Junta Suprema*, saw the Anglo-Spanish alliance as the only means of evicting the French from Spain, his realism being based on the belief that the common enemy

---

15   UoS: WP1/265/34: Wellesley to Frere, 10 June 1809.
16   Wellesley to Frere, 13 July 1809, Gurwood (ed.), *Wellington's Dispatches*, vol.III, pp.353–354.

could be beaten only if the British maintained a significant military presence in Spain and Portugal. By early 1809, the politician in him must have allowed him to see that, if the string of recent Spanish defeats at the hands of the French was to continue, then the calls for a change in Spain's political leadership would become irresistible, thus putting his own position in some doubt. On the other hand, should the British presence begin to turn the tide on the battlefield, his government would be able to share in the laurels of victory and strengthen its grip on power. But to make the prospects of ultimate success more certain and, no doubt, to rid himself of a troublesome general, he reasoned it would be necessary to appoint a supreme military commander in the field. Wellesley's victories at Roliça and Vimeiro in 1808, and his defeat of Soult at Oporto in May 1809, would, in Garay's mind, make him the perfect choice for such a position, and in John Hookham Frere, then present in Seville, he had an enthusiastic advocate for such a plan. There was just one great stumbling block to the realisation of their desires, and that was the presence of *Capitán General* Cuesta, commander in chief of the recently formed Army of Extremadura, and no friend of the governing *Junta Suprema*, who would be bound to object.

Garay would attempt to use Frere, the erstwhile British minister plenipotentiary to Spain now in the pay of the *Junta*, in his attempt to remove Cuesta from effective command, and he would do it by placing the prospect of Wellesley as supreme allied commander before him, knowing that he would begin to tug at the strings of British diplomacy in an effort to make his plans succeed. Indeed, the old warrior had been in an increasingly antagonistic relationship with the *Junta Suprema* since his troubles with Floridablanca during the Valdés imbroglio of September and October 1808. However, his standing amongst the politicians was first compromised when, after Castaños's triumph at Bailén in July of that year, he had attempted to convince the procurer of Spain's great triumph that he should agitate for the formation of something akin to a military council, which would be responsible for all military matters with respect to the war against France, effectively bypassing if not replacing the *Junta Suprema* in the command structure.

Frere was told that the whole Valdés affair had never been forgotten by Cuesta, and that he was still itching for revenge against the *Junta*. Eager to please his new employers, the ex-plenipotentiary wasted no time in conveying these opinions to Wellesley, and so commenced a campaign to discredit Cuesta, in which Frere was to play a significant part. In fact, it was Garay and Frere who were said to have conspired to offer the role of allied supremo to Sir John Moore as he advanced towards the Ebro in 1808, though there is no firm evidence to show that such an offer was actually put to the general. When reading Garay's letter to Canning of 12 March 1809, which post-dated the evacuation of Moore's army by some two months, one can see that the Spaniard lamented the fact that Moore had not advanced as far as Vitoria, or further, during his easterly march which terminated at Sahagún, pointing out that the British commander had wasted much time in Spain whilst he languished in the region of Salamanca and Ciudad Rodrigo before commencing his thrust towards the Ebro. It was during that time, wrote Garay, that: '… requests, solicitations and a formal offer [were] made to Mr. Frere that Sir John should be invested with the command of our troops, who should act under his orders, [but] all proved fruitless …'[17] If there was any truth to

---

17   British Library (BL): Add. Mss. 37286: Garay to Canning, 12 March 1809, pp.36–44. Garay wrote to Canning during the three-month period of absence of the British army from Spain, in the wake of its evacuation from La Coruña in January 1809.

Garay's claim, then it was probably this precedent which, some four months later, and with the British (just) back in Spain, caused Canning to suggest to his correspondent that the offer of supreme command should now be made to Wellesley:

> We have already in the Peninsula an army larger than at any period last year ... led by a commander, whose talents are even greater than his reputation ...
>   To such a man I should indeed be glad to see renewed the offer, which Your Excellency informs me was about to be made last year, to another, of whose fitness for it perhaps I (individually) might not feel so confident ...[18]

However, the seeming unanimity of thought amongst the politicians with regard to the establishment of a unified command structure for the armies in Spain, as well as their preferred choice for an eventual supreme commander (Wellesley) would have to be acceptable to Cuesta, the most senior officer in the Spanish Army – if only by age – and he would have to be convinced that the path to eventual victory lay through his subordination to a foreign general. Had he been what we might these days term a progressive, open to the idea of a civilian government, albeit non-elected in this case, with supreme powers over the military, then he may have welcomed or at least accepted their suggestions, but Cuesta had been cast from a more conservative mould. As we have seen, he had taken the liberty to share his ideas for a wartime government with Castaños after his victory at Bailén, suggesting to him that the *Junta Suprema* be subordinated to a military triumvirate. Should the old warrior now catch wind of the developing conspiracy amongst the politicos, he might cause irreparable damage to Anglo-Spanish prospects for ultimate victory.[19] But were there any deeper and more subtle undercurrents running through Garay's calculations? It may be that the *Secretario General* was simply attempting to solidify or at least maintain Spain's alliance with Britain, by concocting the idea of a British allied supremo, and that he was never really serious about his vision ever materialising. In essence, goes the theory, he was simply attempting to ensure Britain's continuing presence on the Peninsula by making such an offer, knowing that Spain, on its own, could never defeat Napoleon, and that in Frere he had found the perfect conduit for his shenanigans. London may well have caught early wind of Garay's true designs, such as they were, as evidenced in their decision to replace Frere as British plenipotentiary with Wellesley's elder brother, Richard, Marquess Wellesley, who sailed to Spain in the official role of ambassador-extraordinary to Seville in April 1809, at about the same time that his brother was sailing south to take up command of British forces in Portugal. But if by this both London and the Wellesley brothers thought they had seen the last of Frere, then they were mistaken.[20] By courting the influence of his Spanish contacts he was soon employed by the *Junta Suprema* as a liaison officer, in the apparent hope that his presence would improve its communications with the British. It was whilst he held that position that Garay played him for all he was worth in his supposed cause of the

---

18   BL: Add. Mss. 37286: Canning to Garay, 20 July 1809, pp.104–115.
19   Sañudo & Stampa, *Crisis de una Alianza*, p.114.
20   Henry Wellesley, another of the brothers, took Richard's place as ambassador-extraordinary to Spain from November 1809, and was named British ambassador to Spain on 1 October 1811. He remained in Spain until March 1822.

appointment of an allied supremo; which makes it tempting to think it was the sole reason for Frere's appointment at the *Real Alcázar de Sevilla* in the first place.

As final proof that London and Seville were secretly colluding in a plot against Cuesta, and that the intrigues did not come to a halt when Frere was dismissed from his Foreign Office post, Sañudo and Stampa point to the following passage in Richard Wellesley's instructions from Canning, dated 27 June 1809, advising him that:

> ... with a view to any larger operation [on the Peninsula] (if the occasion for it should arise) it is obvious that it would be necessary to enter into previous and positive stipulations, such as might prevent the inconveniences, the complaints and recriminations which attended Sir John Moore's expedition, with this view, as well as for the purpose of a more effectual service, in the interval, the new and more perfect arrangement of the Spanish Army, and especially the delegation of the whole command to one responsible head, would be in the highest degree expedient and desirable. It was intimated some months ago, that there would be no indisposition to confide the command of the Spanish army to a British General. This cannot be required, nor while General Cuesta remains in command, does it seem likely that it should be offered; but if obtained, it would probably afford the best chance of remedying all inconveniences, and would be, above all things, likely to ensure the promptitude and unity of action by which alone any extended and important operation, such as I have above described [British operations in Spain], could be successfully carried into execution ...[21]

That all of this was going on in London and Seville for some five months before the Battle of Talavera, and in the complete ignorance of Cuesta, may be difficult to believe; after all, he did have a number of friends in high places, Seville included, but in his *Manifiesto* of 1811 he wrote:

> It is not very difficult to believe that some individuals in the *Junta Central* feared that I might take revenge for the bad treatment I had received from them at Aranjuez ... [but] what is very strange is that Frere, who should have maintained a strict impartiality in the matter, so readily sided against me without even knowing me. I knew nothing of the whole affair until the [Talavera] campaign was over and I had retired to Palma de Mallorca. I was completely ignorant of the conduct, so unfavourable towards me, that can be seen in Frere's secret correspondence with London whilst he was at Seville, both before and after the Battle of Talavera.[22]

Despite Cuesta's denial, it would seem that he may well have come to learn of the British ex-diplomat's activities at Seville in attempting to have him removed, or at least demoted, from his dominant position in the Spanish army, in order to ease Wellesley into the proposed new position of allied supremo. In fact, Frere had come to the conclusion that the best way

---

21   Canning to Marquess Wellesley, 27 June 1809, Martin (ed.), *Marquess Wellesley*, Appendix F, pp.190–191. See also Sañudo & Stampa, *Crisis de una Alianza*, p.126.
22   Cuesta, *Manifiesto*, p.82.

of going about this task was to use the connivance of some in the *Junta Suprema* to engineer Cuesta's removal from the command of the Army of Extremadura. It was to be achieved by building a case for the Duque de Alburquerque to succeed him; all of it aided and abetted directly by Frere himself, and more passively supported by London and Wellesley. In his history of the diplomacy between Spain and England during the Peninsular War, Villa-Urrutia said of this theme:

> Frere worked hard to ensure that Wellington would become the successor to Cuesta, and even went so far as to employ his favoured status when in official correspondence with the *Junta*, encouraging it to give Alburquerque the independent command they had earlier offered him but which he had refused to accept. The duke, by mere favour of the Court and without having had any opportunity to distinguish himself, had been made a brigadier at a very early age and, although yet to be displayed, possessed the great qualities of a soldier: bravery, chivalry, honour, activity and appreciable military talents. He was naturally ambitious and somewhat combative, which meant that he did not take kindly to obeying the orders of generals who he did not think were as good as they thought themselves to be. He was a great admirer of everything English and was a friend and frequent dinner guest of Frere, for which he attracted some disapproval from Cuesta, who refused to send a detachment of 10,000 men towards Ávila as proposed by Wellington [during the Talavera campaign], the command of which both the British general and Frere suggested be given to Alburquerque in order to provide him with an opportunity to prove himself.[23]

It was on the occasion of Wellesley's first meeting with Cuesta at Casas de Miravete on 10 July that the British commander suggested the flank move towards Ávila, proposing that Alburquerque should lead the operation. In response Cuesta refused to send a contingent of Spaniards on the mission, making the counter suggestion that such a move ought to be a British manned and led enterprise. His reaction to Wellesley's ideas may well have been a sign that he was either suspicious of the Englishman's motives, or was by then aware of the background manoeuvres underway to have him replaced by a figure more emollient to British hopes for eventually having Wellesley installed as allied supremo. In a letter from Frere to Wellesley dated 8 July, the erstwhile British diplomat informed him that Cuesta, still harbouring a grudge against the *Junta*, was set on getting revenge for the manner in which it treated him during the latter months of 1808, before going on to say that, in order to forestall what he thought might lead to a wider coup against the *Junta*, should Cuesta not be stopped, it might be time to weaken his grip on the command of the Army of Extremadura. Hence the suggestion to agitate for the detachment of a significant part of it under an independent commander, who might eventually acquire sufficient reputation as to gain the confidence of the troops. Once created, continued Frere, such an entity might dissuade Cuesta from making an attempt to overthrow the *Junta*:

23   W.R. Villa-Urrutia, *Relaciones entre España e Inglaterra Durante la Guerra de la Independencia. Apuntes para la Historia Diplomaática de España de 1808 a 1814* (Madrid: Librería de F. Beltrán, 1911), vol.I, p.447.

There are circumstances, however, which make the detachment of a part of the force at present united under the orders of General Cuesta exceedingly desirable under another point of view. It is a matter of general suspicion and has been for some time past, that General Cuesta meditates some serious plan of vengeance in resentment for the affronts and disgusts which he experienced about ½ a year ago on the part of the central junta … The obvious remedy seems to be to separate a detachment from [Cuesta's] army under the command of some chief who might acquire sufficient reputation and confidence amongst the troops put under his command to enable him to stand out against any violent measures on the part of [Cuesta against the *Junta*].[24]

Frere then went on to encourage Wellesley to use the first opportunity to suggest the type of tactic just outlined to him, which is exactly what he did at his conference with Cuesta on 10 July with regard to Alburquerque. It was just this kind of expression of British dislike for Cuesta which may have encouraged Juan Priego López to state that, 'The nomination of Venegas as commander in chief of the Army of La Mancha was made as a result of diplomatic pressure on the part of the English, simply because he was an enemy of Cuesta …'[25] before going on to suggest that, despite what he wrote in his *Manifiesto*, Cuesta actually was aware of the intrigues of the British and some members of the *Junta Suprema* against him:

In fact, it was inevitable that news of the machinations of Frere and his friends would eventually arrive at the ears of Cuesta's many acolytes in Seville. As such the veteran general came to understand that his confidential dispatch of 3 May to the *Secretario de Guerra*, Antonio Cornel,[26] in which he suggested that the system of war practiced by the British, whereby the defence of Portugal was seen as their top priority and therefore prejudicial to Spain, was disloyally communicated to Mr. Frere, who passed it on to Wellington, with the aim of putting him against Cuesta. By that time Cuesta had also been informed of plans to overthrow the *Junta*, plans which had been fatally attributed to him, and thereby gave rise to a proposal to have him replaced as commander in chief of the Army of Extremadura by Alburquerque, as the first step towards the nomination of the British commander in chief as Generalísimo of our armies. All of which would explain the mix of suspicion and hostility with which Cuesta awaited the visit of the British leader [at Miravete].[27]

It was not until 20 July 1809, a week before Talavera, that Canning finally replied to Martín Garay's letter of 12 March concerning the possibility of appointing a British general as supreme allied commander in Spain, informing the Spaniard that he would be happy if the offer of such a proposed post as that apparently made to Sir John Moore in 1808 but

---

24   UoS: WP1/267/28: Frere to Wellesley, 8 July 1809. Some abbreviated words have been reproduced in full to aid clarity.

25   Priego, *Guerra de la Independencia*, pp.195–196.

26   TNA: FO 72/73: Cuesta to Cornel, 3 May 1809, pp.18-19, as cited earlier.

27   Priego, *Guerra de la Independencia*, pp.195–196. Cuesta's comments to Cornel were not quite of the flavour Priego suggests, see Cuesta to Cornel, 3 May 1809, as cited earlier.

refused, was now to be made to the new commander in chief, Wellesley. See Canning's letter to Garay above.

The Extent of Wellesley's Involvement in the Plot Against Cuesta

Sañudo and Stampa surmise that London, in advance of posting Canning's letter of 20 July to Garay (see above) would have let its content be known to Frere, and they further assume, without offering any evidence to back it up, that Frere would then certainly have informed Wellesley of what was afoot. Building upon such suppositions, it is at this point that the Spanish authors begin to paint a more sinister picture of what they thought was going through the mind of the British commander during the days immediately prior to the Battle of Talavera. They do this by focussing on Charles Esdaile's analysis of Wellesley's two letters to Frere dated 24 July,[28] in which the historian suggests that the British commander may well have been hoping that Cuesta's unsupported pursuit of Victor beyond the Alberche on that very same day (Wellesley having refused to advance beyond the river) would result in a heavy defeat for the Spaniard. That being the case, his action might then have been seen by the *Junta Suprema* as having been an unjustifiably risk-strewn adventure, for which it would have been obliged, or even delighted, to censure him by perhaps removing him from his post of commander in chief of the Army of Extremadura. Such an outcome, claim Sañudo and Stampa, would have made it more or less certain that Wellesley would be nominated as supreme allied commander. Some short snippets from Wellesley's letters to Frere of 24 July have already been quoted in this work, and both are fully reproduced in Appendix II.

Some three weeks after the Battle of Talavera, *Teniente General* Eguía replaced Cuesta as commander in chief of the Army of Extremadura. At that time, both the British and Spanish armies were retreating south of the Tagus towards the Portuguese frontier, having narrowly escaped from the jaws of a trap which Victor and Soult were attempting to set for them. After initial written pleasantries had been exchanged between the two allied commanders, it did not take long for their relationship to sour, Wellesley taking umbrage at what seems to have been Eguía's reluctance to take everything he said as being examples of the purest truth, with the result that the Englishman declared never to write to him again.

As relations between the two field commanders began to deteriorate, Marquess Wellesley seemed determined to do all that he could to keep the Anglo-Spanish alliance alive; not that this prevented him from becoming involved in the scheming to remove Cuesta from his command of the Army of Extremadura, and by extension that of the army of La Mancha. In replying to a number of letters from his brother in which the British commander made several complaints about Cuesta, he wrote:

> I have read with great concern the description contained in these letters of the distress of your army and of the perverse conduct of *General* Cuesta. This govern-ment [the *Junta Suprema*] is disposed to remove *General* Cuesta from his command whenever it shall have received from you or from the British Ambassador a regular

---

28   Esdaile, *The Duke of Wellington*, pp.12–13.

and detailed statement of his misconduct. It is my intention to present to the Secretary of State [Garay] a recital of the several facts stated in your dispatches respecting *General* Cuesta, but in my judgement it would not appear to be proper that I should directly insist upon his removal …[29]

Fortunately for all, Cuesta had submitted his resignation to Cornel just 24 hours before Marquess Wellesley wrote the above, which meant that such business could now be set aside and the ambassador could begin to make more positive interventions for the sake of the teetering Anglo-Spanish alliance. In one of his first moves in this context he wrote to Wellesley on 23 August, informing him that Garay and other members of the *Junta Suprema* were sorry to hear of his decision to retreat to Portugal, the *Secretario General* stressing that his government was ready to adopt any plan for furnishing him with the transport and provisions he required, and pleading that he keep his army on the Spanish side of the border with Portugal. On 29 August, the Marquess continued with his attempts to keep Britain's Spanish allies onside by begging his brother to delay his entry into Portugal for as long as possible, as this would give him time to work on the Spanish, who were still hoping to launch further combined operations in Spain. As part of his correspondence, he provided his brother with the translation of a letter he had received from Garay outlining how the British and Spanish might launch an offensive towards the Tagus from the north bank of the Guadiana. Interestingly, the Spaniard wrote that, 'The command of the combined army shall be conferred on Sir Arthur Wellesley. It shall be composed of the whole of the British force together with 12,000 infantry, 2,000 cavalry and 12 pieces of cannon from the Spanish army.'[30] It was perhaps in preparation for this move that the *Secretario General* had, on 4 August, offered Wellesley the rank of *Capitán General* in the Spanish army, which came with an associated salary, neither of which he ever officially accepted.[31] However, the Spaniard's words above are clear confirmation that the *Junta* had, perhaps for some time, been keen to give Wellesley the overall command of British and Spanish forces.

As he continued his correspondence with Seville, Marquess Wellesley offered a final piece of encouragement to his sibling, promising him, with what appears to have been a hint of humour, that in his negotiations with the *Junta* he would refrain from repeating his earlier declaration that he did not intend to cooperate with the Spanish ever again.

Ultimately, Wellesley would become the supreme commander of British, Spanish and Portuguese troops in Spain and beyond, but not until September 1812; the careful diplomacy required to achieve their aim being accepted by those in London, once they recognised that the prize they sought would be best gained through a process of evolution, as the British commander in chief was eventually forced to tell Frere.[32] But if Cuesta had become aware of the early inter-governmental talks about displacing him for the sake of appointing Wellesley as supreme commander, then it may explain his less than fulsome embrace of Britain's apparent generosity of spirit in sending her army to assist Spain in ridding herself of the French invaders, as well as his sometimes apparent obstinance in refusing to accommodate

29   UoS: WP1/272/7: Marquess Wellesley to Wellesley, 13 August 1809.
30   UoS: WP1/272/24: Marquess Wellesley to Wellesley, 29 August 1809.
31   Wellesley to Castlereagh, 21 August 1809, Gurwood (ed.), *Wellington's Dispatches*, vol.III, p.439.
32   Sañudo & Stampa, *Crisis de una Alianza*, p.114.

some of Wellesley's requests for cooperation in the field. However, although some British writers have made much of Cuesta's intermittent contrariness during the Tagus campaign, the immediate differences which arose between him and Wellesley were neither serious nor destructive. As we have seen, the latter's major gripes were in relation to a lack of provisions and transport, and these were problems which also affected Cuesta, who was hardly in a position to remedy them. But in terms of being a willing partner to Wellesley in his confrontation with Victor, Joseph and Sebastiani, it may be said that both the *Capitán General* and his soldiers did their bit during the ultimately fruitless campaign on the Tagus of 1809.

In essence, the series of intrigues to appoint Wellesley as commander in chief of the Spanish army during 1809, came to an end when he eventually retreated into Portugal. Massena's incursion of September 1810 would initially push him back from Bussaco to the Lines of Torres Vedras, but after spending a miserable winter in front of the prepared position, the Frenchman was driven out of the country by his opponent in March 1811. Hovering around the Spanish-Portuguese frontier south of the Douro Wellesley would have to wait for the strategic situation to turn to his advantage before returning to Spain in 1812. However, if the diplomatic fumblings around the notion of Wellesley's supremacy of command had come to Cuesta's notice, it may well explain some of the accusations of real or apparent obstinacy subsequently levelled at him during the summer of 1809, although it must be stressed again that, both during and after the Battle of Talavera, he provided most of the assistance asked of him by his British counterpart.

Was the Failure of Austria's Offensive the Real Reason for Wellesley's Retreat to Portugal?

When looking at some of the salient dates relating to the Tagus campaign, there is just a hint that the claims made by Sañudo and Stampa that Wellesley's retreat to Portugal came about because of the collapse of the Austrian offensive in the north, amount to something more than a somewhat tenuous conspiracy theory. We have already seen that Castlereagh had sent instructions to Wellesley on 2 April 1809, encouraging him to extend his operations into Spain with the aim of removing Victor from the Tagus valley, and that Austria opened her offensive in central Europe just a few days later on the 9th. In the Mediterranean, Lieutenant General Sir John Stuart sailed from Milazzo on Sicily with a force of 11,000 men on 11 June, his destination being the island of Ischia situated on the western fringes of the Bay of Naples. Delayed by poor winds he did not arrive until 24 June, but once ashore he wasted no time in capturing or destroying the 30 or so French gunboats moored off the island, before taking possession of its castle on 30 June. The British were to remain in possession of Ischia until 26 July, just two weeks after Austria had signed an armistice with the French at Znaim which effectively concluded her offensive in the north. Wellesley, as we know, had seemingly determined to retreat to Portugal from Talavera by 16 July – just four days after the signing of the armistice.

After his victory at Oporto, the British commander had decided to concentrate his army at Abrantes, where he could make good some of his recent losses in personnel and material before marching for the Spanish frontier on 27 June. After crossing the border he would be at Plasencia by 8 July, allowing him to hold initial face-to-face talks with Cuesta at the village of Casas de Miravete on the south bank of the Tagus, close to Almaraz. Some days later, as the combined Anglo-Spanish army began its march on Victor, Wellesley seemed full of hope for the prospects of capturing Madrid. So what, ask Sañudo and Stampa, could have caused his enthusiasm for a move on the Spanish capital to disappear by the 16 July, the day on which he wrote to each of O'Donojú and Frere (see earlier). It was in his letter to the former that he made his first complaints about a lack of transport and other articles; in that to the latter he bemoaned the lack of transport and provisions available to his army.

The Spanish historians make the point that it was at about this time that Wellesley was expecting the arrival of considerable reinforcements from England. In fact, the units earmarked to join him were actually at Portsmouth, ready to board ship for Portugal, when it was decided that they would be required for Castlereagh's longed-for Walcheren expedition. Richard Wellesley, recently nominated as Britain's new ambassador to Spain and waiting to sail from the port along with the troops, was so upset at this decision that he resigned his post, claiming that his brother, Arthur, would not be able to achieve much with the small army then at his disposal on the Peninsula. He only withdrew his resignation when Canning intervened, promising him that the army in Spain would not be weakened as a result of the Walcheren expedition. But the bad news did not end there. The Austrian advance into Germany, for which Wellesley's incursion into Spain was said by some to be just one of three diversionary operations, had failed by the beginning of July, and during the initial peace talks between Austria and France, it was agreed that an armistice would be signed by both parties at Znaim on 12 July 1809. As such, Sañudo and Stampa maintain that the grim tidings from the north would have reached Wellesley some time between 12 and 15 July; if so, they claim, it might explain Wellesley's seemingly sudden discovery of critical shortages in his provisions and transport on or around those dates, a situation which caused him to announce that he could not advance beyond the Alberche until both issues were remedied. They make similar claims about Stuart's expedition to Ischia. But was it possible that the unwelcome news from Znaim could have reached the British camps in such distant and isolated places as Castilla-La Mancha and the Bay of Naples within four days and two weeks respectively? Almost certainly the answer to that question is, no; and the Spanish authors do not cite any sources to back up their claims that they did. Instead, they claim that Wellesley may well have received the new orders which Castlereagh referred to in his letter of 2 April 1809 (see earlier) and that these indicated the necessity to suspend his operations in Spain. But again, this would imply that the news from Znaim had reached London, before being conveyed to Wellesley in Spain, all by about 16 July 1809. That the official papers covering the period referred to provide no proof of their claim, they simply remark, '... *los bien censurados archivos que reunen la documentación wellingtoniana no dan prueba de ello.*' (...[but] the well studied archives comprising the Wellington documentation do not provide any proof of it).[33] Finally, as an example of how long it took for news to travel in 1809, it may be worth noting that the news of Austria's victory at Aspern/Esling on 22 May 1809 did not reach London until about 25 June.[34]

---

33   Sañudo & Stampa, *Crisis de una Alianza*, p.202. Note: the Spanish verb, *censurar*, used by Sañudo and Stampa, has subtly different meanings, two of which are the English, 'to study carefully' and 'to censor'. In the interests of treading carefully, I have taken it that the Spanish authors were applying the first of these in their statement.

34   A. Aspinall (ed.), *The Later Correspondence of George III* (Cambridge: Cambridge University Press, 1970), vol.V, p.304.

The 40,000 troops allocated to the Walcheren expedition would not set sail from England until 28 July, some two weeks after the treaty of Znaim had been signed, meaning that the venture would be of no assistance to Vienna, even if it was ever meant to be. Elsewhere, although the 11,000 men of Stuart's expedition to the island of Ischia had disembarked on 25 June, they would be back aboard ship and about to commence their return voyage to Milazzo on Sicily by 26 July, Stuart perhaps thinking, or having been instructed by London, that it was pointless to continue with his expedition after Austria's defeat, especially when he had received intelligence that the French were gathering forces at Toulon for what looked like a planned operation in the Mediterranean. If Wellesley's advance into the Tagus valley was ever sanctioned as a diversionary operation in aid of the Fifth Coalition's offensive of 1809, then by the middle of July he may have realised that it had served its purpose. By then, out on a limb, deep inside Spanish territory with his Iberian allies eager to push the French away from Madrid, he may have begun to feel himself dangerously exposed. That being the case, he might well have thought that his best course of action after fighting the inevitable battle at Talavera would be to return to the safety of Portugal, rather than be pulled ever further away from her frontier as he moved deeper into Spain. If so, the question was how to extricate himself from a follow-up operation in the wake of the battle, should the allies triumph. This, claim his critics, was the real reason for his complaints about a lack of transport and provisions; but were such shortages really more imagined than real, as the Spanish writers suggest? From the testimonies of some members of the British rank and file, as well as some intermittent comments from Cuesta himself – all earlier stated in the text – it would appear that both the British and Spanish armies were in want of regular and adequate provisions between mid-July and mid-August. The question is, was the level of want amongst the British army enough to justify its abandonment of their allies in mid campaign? To which a number of differing answers might arise after the study of such evidence as has been presented herein, some witnesses making much of their plight during the days just before and after the Battle of Talavera, others less so.

Initiation of Combined Operations in Spain, but to What End?

By May/June 1809 Wellesley and Cuesta were in correspondence, and we have seen that by the end of that period the British commander had been allowed a formal degree of latitude to partake in limited operations on Spanish territory in cooperation with Spanish forces. It is possible that the extension to his earlier brief that he remain close to the Portuguese frontier had come as a nod to Austria, thus signifying that the British were determined to do all that they could to support her offensive against the French in Germany (see Canning to Marquess Wellesley, 27 June 1809 above). In fact, it was Castlereagh who had communicated the news of his extended licence to Wellesley on 25 May, seemingly having gotten over his huff about the Spaniards' earlier refusal to allow British troops to land at Cádiz:

> Upon referring to my instructions to you of 3rd April, and the course that operations may take, should Victor retire upon your moving towards the Tagus, I have received his Majesty's commands, in order that you may be enabled the better to cooperate with the Spanish armies against the common enemy, to authorize you

to extend your operations in Spain beyond the provinces immediately adjacent to the Portuguese frontier, provided you shall be of the opinion that your doing so is material, in a military point of view, to the success of your operations, and not inconsistent with the safety of Portugal.[35]

At this point it may well be worth recalling that Austria launched her offensive against the French on 9 April, just six days after Castlereagh's letter to Wellesley of the 3rd in which he forbade the British commander to engage in any general operations within Spain. All well and good, but if, by 25 May, the Secretary of State for War had changed his mind and was now willing to sanction British incursions into Spain, so long as they could be seen to be in aid of Austria, then the actual determinant of the duration and scale of any British presence in Spain would appear to be the success or otherwise of the Austrian offensive in far away central Europe. If true, then none of this was ever conveyed to the Spaniards, which would seem to provide ample proof of a malfeasance by those in London towards their southern allies, to the extent that any failure on the part of the Austrians would be the signal for Wellesley to call off operations in Spain and return to Portugal – with little if any consideration for the Spaniards.[36] On the other hand, at about the time Castlereagh wrote his letter, reinforcements had just been authorized for Wellesley, which may well have been a more plausible reason for his change of mind. As we know, Austria signed an armistice with France on 12 July 1809, but it would have been unthinkable for Wellesley to have turned his army around and marched it back to Portugal directly upon hearing news of Austria's failure, assuming he had received it by the 16th, as it would have had a devastating effect on the Anglo-Spanish alliance. This is why, claim Sañudo and Stampa, he began to make such vociferous protestations about a lack of rations and transport as an opening gambit in his agitation for eventually doing so. However, it appears that, on this point, they base their supposition more upon conjecture than proven fact. What they seem to miss, or ignore, is the fact that the French and Austrians agreed only to an armistice at Znaim on 12 July 1809; the Treaty of Schönbrunn, which marked the end of the Franco-Austrian war, was not signed until 14 October. And as late as 30 August, Wellesley wrote: 'I have received no letters, excepting one from Pole, in which he informs me that it is understood in England that the Emperor did not approve of the armistice concluded by the Archduke, and that peace between Austria and France was not considered certain.'[37]

Were Wellesley's Complaints Justified?

The Question of Provisions

If we assume that the British army crossed into Spain on 3 July 1809 with provisions sufficient enough to last them for their four-day march to Plasencia, then we may say that its

---

35   Castlereagh to Wellesley, 25 May 1809, Charles William Vane, *Correspondence, Despatches, and Other Papers of Viscount Castlereagh* (London: William Shoberl, 1851), p.71.
36   Sañudo & Stampa, *Crisis de una Alianza*, pp.118–119.
37   Wellesley to Marquess Wellesley, 30 August 1809, Gurwood (ed.), *Wellington's Dispatches*, vol.III, p.461.

dependence on the Spanish authorities for rations and forage began on 7 July, their first full day of rest in the provincial town. Sañudo and Stampa provide us with substantial evidence that, during their 10-day stay there, Wellesley's men were amply supplied with food before being seen off with generous provisions for their march towards the Tagus and their union with Cuesta's army. Both Don Ventura Delgado, *Presidente de la Junta de Plasencia*, and Don Lozano de Torres, a state-appointed quartermaster assigned to assist the British troops in procuring provisions whilst in Spain, are quoted by the Spanish historians, the former as saying that after their 10-day stay, '...they left Plasencia with enough "mouth ammunition" for five days,' the latter maintaining that the *Junta de Plasencia* had supplied the army '... not for three days, nor with the number of rations that they asked for, but for eight or ten days and with double or triple the rations requested ...,' which may have been something of an exaggeration.

It may be worth pointing out that Wellesley was at Plasencia between 6 and 16 July, and he is quoted by Sañudo and Stampa as having said, 'When I entered Spain I certainly expected to be provided with the provisions and other necessaries required by an army stationed in the country, more so when one considers that we had come to assist her. My hopes of receiving the necessary provisions and supplies have not been deceived, and I am therefore very grateful for all the efforts the *Junta [de Plasencia]* has made to that effect ...'[38] The Spanish authors next invite their readers to compare those sentiments with the ones expressed by the British commander in chief when he wrote to O'Donojú on 16 July (see above) the day he left Plasencia, claiming that his army was short of many 'necessary articles,' due to a lack of means to convey them. Then, in the last of three successive quotes used in an attempt to discredit Wellesley, the authors again point to his letter to Frere of 16 July, in which he went on to inform the diplomat that he would not persevere in Spain unless the prospect of 'good treatment' for his army improved.

These are points cleverly made by the Spanish pair, but in none of the three quotes does Wellesley explicitly complain that there was any hunger or even any shortage of food amongst his men by 16 July; it was only the scarcity of 'articles' and 'transport' he was complaining about. Indeed, few if any of the soldiers, whose memoires the author has already quoted, make complaints about a lack of provisions during their first 20 days in Spain, such protests only began to appear in the days immediately before, during and after the Battle of Talavera. However, a commander gifted with the foresight of Wellesley must surely have been focussed upon any looming situation which might become the cause of a lack of provisions, before his troops were actually feeling the pangs of hunger in their bellies. After leaving Plasencia with what would seem to have been at least a week's worth of provisions, he would have become all too aware of the apparent scarcities of both transport, provisions and 'other articles' in the surrounding country as he approached the Tagus. Since leaving Portugal his troops had been adequately fed, but he could not simply assume that this would continue to be the case

---

38   Sañudo & Stampa, *Crisis de una Alianza*, p.160. The source reference provided for Wellesley's quote is a document entitled, 'Plasencia Durante la Invasión Napoleónica', which is listed in 'A Summary of [the contents of] Archives, Libraries and Museums compiled by, J. Martinez de Quesada, Doc. 18, p.81, Copy of two answers from General Arthur Wellesley, chief of the armies of His Britanic Majesty, to the Junta Suprema, [mis-dated] Plasencia, 26 February 1812', which is held at the Archivo Historico de Cáceres.

as he moved deeper into Spanish territory, especially so in the knowledge that the French would have stripped the country bare whilst in occupation of it, and as they retreated before the allied advance. All of which gave him every right to raise the issue with his allies.

The Question of Transport
We saw earlier how Wellesley first began to complain about the scarcity of waggons and draught animals once he reached Plasencia, the whole issue blowing up when his deputy paymaster general failed to bring up the military chest from Abrantes to headquarters, giving the excuse that it had been impossible to procure the required means of transport in Portugal. All of which prompted the British commander to write to Villiers, British Minister Plenipotentiary to the Portuguese Court, instructing him to complain to the Portuguese government about their failure to purchase carts and mules for his army. The reason for the deputy paymaster's difficulties may well be explained by the fact that many draught and pack animals had been lost in Portugal during the previous year's campaign, subsequent efforts made to purchase mules and donkeys in North Africa having been met with little success.[39]

Sañudo and Stampa explore this theme to provide support to their argument that scarcities in transport resources did not suddenly appear in mid-July 1809, and even if they had, the Spanish authorities had never been under any formal obligation to make up for the rate of attrition suffered in Portugal, nor indeed any initial shortages in draught animals experienced by Wellesley's army at the outset of its Spanish sojourn.

> ... the British had failed to foresee the necessity of providing themselves with a sufficient number [of draught and pack animals] despite the lessons of the experience suffered during Moore's campaign just six months earlier. Perhaps they had imagined, mistakenly, that they would easily find all they needed as they moved through the country. It did not turn out that way. And it may also have been their bad luck, or their inexperience, which contributed to the loss of many of the waggons they had brought with them, as they made the successive marches which defined the campaign in Portugal.
> ... one cannot deny that one of the first measures to be considered when assembling an expeditionary army, is that of providing it with all of its foreseeable needs.[40]

In making these claims, Sañudo and Stampa seem to be unaware of the way in which the British Commissariat operated when it came to furnishing the transport needs of an expeditionary force, in terms of wheeled transport, draught animals and pack animals. Such items were invariably hired or purchased by the army in the host countries, in order to reduce the demand upon the shipping resources required to launch overseas campaigns. In fact, Wellesley's difficulties in Portugal arose because of the attrition rates applying to draught and pack animals, as well as vehicles, during the turmoil of the 1808 campaigns. It was a problem the British commander was already aware of, having written to Castlereagh

---

39   Gabriel Espirito Santo Pedro de Brito, *An Introduction to the Anglo-Portuguese Army Logistics in the Peninsular War* (Coimbra: Gráfica de Coimbra, 2012), p.48.
40   Sañudo & Stampa, *Crisis de una Alianza*, pp.160–161.

in the wake of his victory at Oporto complaining about the difficulties of procuring conveyance which, he said, was partly responsible for a shortage of ammunition for the army in the
field.[41] Such a scarcity of carts may also have been responsible for the loss of several artillery
horses during the Oporto campaign, causing Wellesley to write to his Commissary General,
Dalrymple, demanding to know, '…why the artillery horses are dying of want due to irregular forage deliveries …,' adding that, 'The officers of the commissariat will be responsible
in an eminent degree, if owing to their want of capacity and management, I should lose the
use of the British artillery.'[42] And so things rumbled on, Quartermaster General Murray
writing to Wellesley on 1 July asking that carts earlier sent to Castelo Branco be returned in
order to maintain his efforts to keep supplies moving.[43] By that time the artillery was also
complaining of a lack of mules to transport their cannon shot. These and other examples
concerning a lack of waggons and animals abound amongst the Wellington Papers, many
of them raised well before he led his army into Spain.

Quoting their own research, Sañudo and Stampa go on to point out a letter from Brigadier
General Howorth to Wellesley, in which he said that he had seen a letter between two assis-
tant commissaries general, Ogilvie, and Dalrymple, dated 3 July, pointing out the impos-
sibilities of procuring more than 17 or 18 carts from the neighbourhood of Abrantes. An
earlier letter (30 April) from Lieutenant Colonel Fisher to Howorth, containing an audit of
the horses brought from England, was also cited by the latter in a communique to Wellesley
dated 10 July, when he wrote of 'the bad condition of the 300 horses landed at Lisbon
from England in April,' before going on to say that, 'this supply of horses is now nearly
exhausted'.[44] The Spanish authors claim that all of three examples provide clear evidence
that the British expedition's shortages in its means of transport stemmed, in a significant
part, from deficiencies in the quality and quantity of the animals disembarked at Lisbon on
30 April:

Fisher's audit:
Serviceable horses: 215
Sick, lame or unserviceable horses: 57
Suspected sick horses: 4

A footnote to Fisher's audit added that there were also many 'very old' horses amongst the
shipment.[45] In response to this information, Wellesley was forced to request a shipment of
300 horses from Ireland. However, the two letters involving Howorth refer only to artillery
horses, and artillery horses, unlike those of the commissariat, were shipped directly from
Britain (or Ireland) to the Peninsula. They were not used by the commissariat, and therefore their number and/or condition should not have been taken into consideration when
analysing the performance of Wellesley's transport system, something which Sañudo and

41   UoS: WP1/263/ 3/56: Wellesley to Castlereagh, 31 May 1809.
42   UoS: WP1/265/ 2/12: Wellesley to Dalrymple, 5 June 1809.
43   UoS: WP1/267/2/2: Murray to Wellesley, 1 July 1809.
44   UoS: WP1/267/1/37: Howorth to Wellesley, 10 July 1809.
45   UoS: WP1/267/1/37: Fisher to Howorth, 30 April 1809, as cited in Howorth's letter to Wellesley of 10
     July.

Stampa did not seem to appreciate. In fact, if, by dint of their reference to artillery horses being shipped from Britain, the Spanish authors simply assumed that all, or many, of the draught animals destined for use by the commissariat were also shipped from England, then it might explain their attempt to claim that Wellesley's expedition was not properly equipped before sailing for Portugal.

Exhausted though the supply of draught animals accompanying the expedition was by the end of Wellesley's 10-week campaign in Portugal, it seems that the number of non-draught equines had not been so diminished, which may explain why, just six days after Howorth's letter, with the British army beyond the Tiétar and Wellesley having met with Cuesta, the British commander in chief was able to write to O'Donojú with regard to his needs for horses and state, 'The British Army does not require much assistance in this direction; none for the baggage for the individuals, and what is wanted is to be applied solely to the transport of provisions, ammunition, money & medical stores.'[46] Here Wellesley was clearly distinguishing between different types of horses – cavalry horses, artillery horses and riding horses for the officers, of which there seemed to have been a sufficient number, having been shipped from England, as opposed to the mules and draught animals as used by the commissariat and therefore sourced locally, of which he implies there was a shortage. In attempting to make a point, Sañudo and Stampa then claim that the shortage of transport facilities for the army's medical stores, for instance, declared once it had crossed into Spain, arose from the fact that the animals brought from England specifically for that purpose had been left behind at Abrantes. However, the source of the letter, William Fergusson, Deputy Inspector of Hospitals, then at Plasencia, simply stated that '... the apothecaries stores have not arrived from Abrantes'.[47]

So, was Wellesley really so poorly off as he claimed he was for such resources? Not surprisingly, the Spanish authors claim he was overstating his actual position, and provide some evidence to support their assertions when they point to the order of march for the British army on beginning its movement from Oropesa towards Talavera on 21 July quoting: 'The existence of a battery of 6-pounders together with the artillery of the Lusitanian Legion amongst the vanguard ...' before citing a description of the main column as consisting of: 'The batteries of artillery marching in front of the divisions of infantry to which they were assigned; all followed up by the reserve artillery and munitions. The baggage of the army was with the rearguard together with the reserve artillery, all followed by the teams of mules hauling the field kitchens, sappers tools, pharmacy waggons and the carts assigned to collect stragglers.'[48] All of which, claim Sañudo and Stampa, makes it difficult to understand Wellesley's simultaneous and disproportionate claims of want, and his accompanying decision to retreat to Portugal in the face of having to suffer the absence of just a few carts, plus a shortage of rations, for a period amounting to no more than a couple of days or so. But here again, the Spanish authors are confusing British-sourced resources for the artillery with locally-sourced commissariat resources.

---

46   Wellesley to O'Donojú, 16 July 1809, Gurwood (ed.), *Wellington's Dispatches*, vol.III, p.360.
47   UoS: WP1/267/1/37: William Fergusson, Deputy Inspector of Hospitals, to Lieutenant Colonel James Bathurst, Military Secretary to Wellesley, 12 July 1809.
48   Sañudo & Stampa, *Crisis de una Alianza*, p.203. Sadly, the Spanish authors did not cite a reference for the order of march document they quoted.

The point that the Spanish historians were attempting to make was that, yes, Wellesley's transport resources may not have been fully adequate, but neither were they scarce to the point that the army would not be able to move beyond the Alberche until they had been increased, and even if his claims were true, the British commander could hardly place the blame for his predicament upon the Spanish authorities. The fault, they claim, lay with the British themselves for not furnishing the army with enough transport for its requirements, and they sense a modicum of exaggeration in Wellesley's complaints as he began to look for a way out of his commitment to partake fully in Cuesta's planned offensive beyond the Alberche:

> The *Junta* may have displayed a lack of foresight [in some instances] but the blame for Wellesley's transport problems must be shared by the British Government, its representative in Spain, Frere, and those in the Quartermaster General's department responsible for equipping the expedition, as well as its commander in chief, who did nothing to prepare, organise and coordinate with the *Junta Suprema* in order to come up with a system which would have guaranteed the supply of enough provisions and transport ... for both armies.
>
> In our judgement ... there were some underlying and transcendental reasons for Wellington's attitude [in not wanting to move beyond the Alberche]: the news that the British general was receiving from family and political circles in London; the poor impression he had gained of *General* Cuesta and his army, as well as his difficulty to understand and come to agreements with him, and the constant efforts by Frere to induce him to undermine Cuesta who, claimed the former, was disliked by the *Junta*. All of this in the hope that Seville would offer the British overall command of the allied armies. These were all elements which Wellington had to evaluate in two senses: firstly, how they affected his commitment to attack Victor in concert with Cuesta, in view of the changes to the strategic situation in the rest of Europe, especially with respect to Austria; and secondly how his constant lashing out at Cuesta, criticising him and possibly agitating for his removal from command, might play out. In this context, the existence of shortages or difficulties, such as those in the realm of transport and provisions, were deliberately exaggerated in their importance and effect, thus converting them into an instrument to be put to use at an opportune moment.[49]

Once again, it would seem that Sañudo and Stampa were of the impression that all of Wellesley's transport resources should have been shipped together with with his army, and their misunderstanding, or ignorance, of the difference between the roles of the Quartermaster General and the Commissariat is reinforced when they state:

> ... when London decided to send Sir John Moore to Spain with his expeditionary force, they could not find sufficient [naval] transports to ship its horses. Few were

---

49   Sañudo & Stampa, *Crisis de una Alianza*, pp.160–164.

the animals for the mounted regiments, the artillery and the transport that the British brought with them in 1808.[50]

Response of the Spanish Authorities to Wellesley's Complaints

Wellesley's insistence that the Spanish do something to alleviate his situation began to percolate through the ranks of the *Junta Suprema* after Frere had, on 27 July, passed on the content of his letter from Wellesley of 16 July, but it generated what seems to have been only a semblance of activity; Garay writing to Wellesley on 27 July, as the fighting commenced at Talavera:

> Mr. Frere has passed a note to the *Junta Suprema* indicating that, because of a shortage of provisions and transport, the auxiliary [British] army has determined to suspend its march, leaving the army of *General* Cuesta to pursue the enemy alone. Such news has come as a great surprise to His Majesty, as it is the first time he has received notice that the [British] army was in need of those articles necessary for it to continue with its operations.
>
> Once I was made aware that there was no great abundance of transport, I commissioned various army units to procure all that they could and send it to the [British] troops as soon as possible. I would have done the same with the other articles had I been provided with the necessary information beforehand ... and it hurts me to say that the first inkling I had of the situation was when I heard news of the extraordinary resolution contained in Mr. Frere's communication. Should such a resolution come into effect it would, without doubt, be the cause of the destruction of the combined plans which, with such happiness, we have begun to execute ...[51]

For good measure, Garay included in his communication to Wellesley a copy of a letter sent by the *Junta Suprema* to the *Junta de Plasencia*, and a copy of his own letter to Cuesta; both of which were written in the hope of energising the local efforts to supply Wellesley with the transport and provisions he claimed he was lacking:

> The *Junta Suprema* ... has discovered that various *juntas* of the *Partido de Plasencia* have received orders from the quartermaster commissioned to accompany the British army, to the effect that they supply it with provisions and draught animals, and that they have failed to comply with those orders, despite the negative effect it will have upon the salvation of the Motherland ... In response, His Majesty has agreed to send to you two of his deputies, the first with instructions to arrest those persons who, through their indolence, are responsible for the troubles besetting our allies; the second is to remain with the *partido* and be at the disposition of the quartermaster in his task to obtain all of the wine, meat, vegetables, bread,

50   Sañudo & Stampa, *Crisis de una Alianza*, pp.162–163.
51   UoS: WP1/268/46: Garay to Wellesley, 27 July 1809.

flour and whatever other provisions he requires, as well as the draught animals he requires ...[52]

Because the Justices of the Vera de Plasencia have failed to comply with orders earlier communicated [see above], [the British troops] now find themselves short of many articles, and these shortages have now reached such an extent that it is having a prejudicial effect upon their efforts to save the Motherland. It is therefore the expressed will of the *Junta* that the British troops be supplied in preference to our own with regard to provisions and draught animals, to the point that their needs are fully satisfied. As a consequence, it has been agreed that *General* Cuesta will summons the quartermaster currently commissioned to accompany the allied army, and inform him that he [Cuesta] will provide him with all the help he needs in order to fulfil the urgent role he has been assigned ...[53]

On 28 July, Garay wrote to Frere, informing him that he had passed on Wellesley's complaints to Cuesta, before going on to detail the reply he had received from the Spanish general:

Cuesta was sent a copy of Wellesley's complaints, and in response he claimed that on 21 July four cavalry officers were sent out from Santa Olalla with orders to take 2/3 of the horses they found, plus any of the articles Wellesley claimed he was short of (provisions, munitions, hospitals and medicines). The quartermaster was also ordered to embargo 1/3 of the mules found in the towns around Santa Olalla ...[54]

All of these commandeered items, it seems, were to have been handed over to the British.

In fairness to the *Junta de Plasencia* we should note that, after hearing of Wellesley's complaints, they wrote to him explaining that they had done their best to collect all that they could and all that they were asked for – if not more – but added that many of the provisions they had collected for the British troops were ruined as they were being delivered to them, due to the soldiers stampeding to grab what they could, before going on to remind him that they did ask him to help establish some order amongst his men so that the supplies could be properly distributed.

If any of the efforts claimed to have been made by the Spaniards ever resulted in an improvement to Wellesley's situation then he said little if anything about it, other than to continue with his complaints more or less to the end of the campaign. In fact, *General* Eguía, writing to the British commander as late as 21 August, asked him to read an enclosed copy of a letter he had recently received from the *Junta de Plasencia*, ensuring him that they were doing all they could to supply the British army with provisions:

I have the honour of sending to Your Excellency a copy of the secret report which I have just received from the *Junta de Plasencia*, [now] established at Talavera. You

52   UoS: WP1/268/46: Copy of a letter from the *Junta Suprema* to the *Junta de Plasencia*, enclosed in Garay's letter to Wellesley of 27 July 1809.
53   UoS: WP1/268/46: Copy of a letter from Garay to Cuesta, enclosed in Garay's letter to Wellesley of 27 July 1809.
54   UoS: WP1/268/50: Garay to Frere, 28 July 1809.

will be able to judge for yourself its content, especially the level of security they claim to be able to offer you for the supply of provisions to the British army, and decide if you wish to alter your determination to march for Portugal ...

Eguía, making every effort to keep the British in the fight for Spain, then continued with an increasing air of desperation:

> The situation in which we find ourselves is interesting and very critical, and there is an urgent need for Your Excellency's army to help us distract the enemy. All of the bread we can supply you with, all the barley and everything, everything we can acquire will be handed over to the British army as I have assured Your Excellency, whom I beg, in the name of my government, to take part in our intended movement for the sake of avoiding the serious consequences which may result in not doing so ... I have given orders that my troops be ready to move at first notice ...[55]

Wellesley, true to his word in an earlier dispatch that he would never write to Eguía again, refused to acknowledge Spanish general's correspondence. By this time the British army was at Trujillo, en-route to Badajoz via Mérida, with little appetite to unite with the Spaniards, as may be seen when reading the content of the British commander's long letter to Marquess Wellesley of 24 August. For example:

> The question then comes before me to be decided as a new one, whether I shall join in cooperation with the Spanish army again ... Upon every ground... of objects, means and risks, it is my opinion that I ought to avoid to enter into any farther cooperation with the Spanish armies, and that at all events Your Excellency should avoid to hold out to the government any hope that I would consent to remain within the Spanish frontier with any intention of cooperating with the Spanish troops in future ... At the present moment, however, I have been compelled to separate from the Spanish army; and the question now is, whether I will place myself in cooperation with them again ...[56]

Once at Mérida, Wellesley wrote to his brother again, justifying his decision to separate his army from that of Eguía by informing him that none of the provisions promised by the Spaniards had materialised:

> Having been able to separate the army, the troops have received their regular rations since the 25th instant ... I have to inform Your Excellency, however, that none of the supplies, either of provisions or means of transport which Monsieur De Calvo informed me and the Spanish ministers informed Your Excellency were so near the army, have yet reached Mérida ...[57]

---

55   UoS: WP1/273/8: Eguía to Wellesley, 21 August 1809.
56   UoS: WP1/275/27: Wellesley to Marquess Wellesley, 24 August 1809.
57   Wellesley to Marquess Wellesley, 28 August 1809, Gurwood (ed.), *Wellington's Dispatches*, vol.III, p.456.

After all that has been said above, especially in the context of Wellesley's complaint about a lack of provisions, and the suggestion that his Tagus excursion was sanctioned by London at the behest of Austria, it might be interesting to add a couple of footnotes. Firstly, Major Philip Keating Roche, then serving in the rank of colonel in the Portuguese army, under which he was attached to the Spanish army, wrote to Wellesley regarding what he saw as the *Junta de Plasencia's* attempts to foil his intention to cite a lack of provisions as the reason for his retreat to Portugal:

> I see one thing very clearly, that they are taking advantage of every possible means to put it out of your power to attribute your falling back to the want of provisions, and are most anxious if any public investigation should hereafter arrive to make it appear that not this but some other motive was the real cause of your retreat.[58]

Secondly, Villiers, somewhat cryptically:

> Pole has desired me to forward to you the letter which accompanies this note, and I take for granted that he tells you whatever is to be told from England. The Austrian truce will probably enable Bonaparte to send his nearest troops to reinforce his armies in the peninsula, which will only prove still more the prudence of your movement …[59]

We should note that Villiers' letter was dated 31 August 1809, roughly at the time that Wellesley was beginning to receive news of the Austrians' difficulties, and almost four weeks after he had fallen back after Talavera. Final proof that Wellesley's first Spanish adventure was somehow linked to the success or failure of the Austrian offensive on the Danube? Probably not. In fact, Villiers would seem to be suggesting that Austria's offensive in the north had been keeping the heat off Wellesley in Spain.

By 3 September Wellesley was at Badajoz, just a stone's throw from the Portuguese frontier, which becomes delineated by the Guadiana for a distance of some 40 miles along its southerly course, just a little to the west of the city. It was in this region where the army was to remain for almost exactly three months as the politics of the Anglo-Spanish alliance came to the fore; Marquess Wellesley and others putting significant pressure on the British commander to remain on Spanish soil in order to shore up bilateral cooperation. The offering up of this sop to Seville resulted in the army falling victim to what was termed the Guadiana fever, probably a species of malarial sickness which swept through its ranks during the period of its stay on the banks of the river. Weakened by a long and arduous campaign which saw its ranks thinned, in both interpretations of the phrase, by irregular and short rations, especially during the latter weeks, the men were in no condition to avoid the worst of its ravages, losing 979, 1269, 900, and 650 men to it during the months of October, November, December 1809 and January 1810, respectively.[60] It was a heavy price

---

58   UoS: WP1/273/17: Roche to Wellesley, 24 August 1809.
59   UoS: WP1/273/21: Villiers to Wellesley, 31 August 1809.
60   Andrew Bamford, 'The Guadiana Fever Epidemic', *The Napoleon Series*, <https://www.napoleon-series.org/military-info/battles/1809/Peninsula/c_Guadiana1.html>, accessed October 2022.

to pay for the Marquess's policy of appeasement towards Britain's Spanish allies, and to no detectable benefit; Wellesley eventually marching his army into Portugal without protest from Seville. It was a cruel ending to a campaign which achieved much and promised even more, before ending in near disaster as in-fighting and intrigue spread amongst and betwixt the army commanders and some senior political figures in both London and Seville.

13

Summary of the Main Issues Affecting the Tagus Campaign

Transport and Provisions

To sum up on the question of transport and provisions made available to the British army during its short incursion into Spain of 1809, it may be fair to say that, because the primary aim of Wellesley's campaign on the Peninsula had been that of removing the French from Portugal, it was neither properly supplied with locally sourced transport resources whilst in Portugal, such as waggons and draught animals, nor given advanced notice to communicate with the Spanish authorities to acquire such resources upon entering Spain, in order for it to carry out operations beyond the Portuguese frontier.

With the defence of Portugal being uppermost in their minds, Wellesley's political masters seem to have assumed that his requirements for transport would be comfortably met by the Portuguese authorities. With his main base at Lisbon, where regular supplies could be safely delivered by naval transports, anything destined for the interior could be shipped as far as Santarem, where a large depot was established. From there, wheeled transport or mule trains would take supplies towards the east and north of Portugal as required, with auxiliary depots set up at strategic points on the Portuguese transport network. Although his transport needs were barely covered whilst in Portugal, it was when his brief was extended to allow him to operate inside Spanish territory that his troubles in this sphere really became acute.

But what of Wellesley's complaints about a lack of provisions for his army? Sañudo and Stampa point to the fact that he first announced such shortages in his letter to Frere of 24 July (see Appendix) implying that they began to appear on or about the 23rd of the month. As such, the Spanish authors point to the fact that the British army had marched from Plasencia on 16 July, by all accounts having been well fed and watered during their 10-day stay in the city, with the authorities of the town claiming that it had also been provided with five days' generous rations when it set off for Talavera. That being the case, Wellesley's complaint of the 23rd would have been made just two days or so after his mens' rations had begun to run out. After allowing for the probability that the British troops had consumed their marching rations by 21 July, the Spanish authors make the point that, even if the British had not managed to obtain any further provisions whilst on the march from Plasencia, for Wellesley to have made such vociferous complaints after his men had gone just two days on short rations, was unreasonable.

In defence of the British commander, one might point out that by then he would have become aware of the growing signs of a scarcity of livestock and agricultural produce the closer he came to the banks of the Tagus. July 24 would have marked the beginning of the third week since his first meeting with Cuesta, and one must assume that, in his communications with the Spanish general's *aides de camp* and other Spanish officers, there must have been some mention of the severe food shortages which both they and their French adversaries had suffered during their respective operations on the south bank of the Tagus during the spring. In fact, Cuesta himself had earlier advised Wellesley of the dire situation on both banks of the river. So, on the question of provisions, we may say that, yes, they were becoming scarce by the time the Battle of Talavera was fought, and that the shortages soon became exaggerated once the fighting was over. If any proof of this were needed, it is to be found in the personal accounts of the British soldiers included earlier in this work, and from several comments made by Cuesta himself with regard to his own problems when it came to feeding the Spanish army during its eventual retreat towards the Portuguese frontier in Wellesley's wake. To claim that Wellesley over-reacted to the situation on the Alberche by simply feigning the levels of hunger he claimed existed amongst his troops, in order to have an excuse to halt his march at Talavera, is to doubt his abilities as a commander in chief. Having witnessed the dwindling of his men's daily rations as he approached Talavera, he must surely have been anticipating the prospects for his army should it have to make a forced retreat in the face of a worsening situation regarding provisions. In this context the expression of his concerns to his Spanish allies was fully justified. As to the claim that his complaints were nothing other than a cover for his retreat to Portugal after having received secret orders from London to withdraw from Spain, it would be fair to say that Sañudo and Stampa have fallen somewhat short of the mark when it comes to the submission of hard evidence to back up their hypothesis.

Did Austria's Failure on the Danube Signal the End of Wellesley's Tagus Campaign?

When it comes to asking why the Tagus campaign ended in failure, Sañudo and Stampa make a mistaken interpretation of Wellesley's claims with respect to a lack of provisions and transport. Their misconceptions are then reinforced when they subsequently stray into the sphere of conjecture with their assertions relating to the Austrian offensive on the Danube of 1809. To begin with, they quote the following passage from Castlereagh's instructions to Wellesley of 2 April 1809: 'Until you receive further orders your operations must necessarily be conducted with a special reference to the protection of [Portugal] …' (see earlier). Fixing upon the first five words of this, the Spanish authors make the assumption that, after the issue of his orders on 2 April, Wellesley may well have received further, secret instructions from Castlereagh, to the effect that he should synchronise his operations in Spain to coincide with the projected Walcheren expedition. Their implication being that the raid on the Scheldt was to be just one of three diversionary operations by the British in aid of Austria's 1809 offensive on the Danube against Napoleonic forces. However it was not until 28 July that the Earl of Chatham finally sailed for the Dutch coast with his well-equipped force, which was some 25 days after Wellesley had crossed from Portugal into Spain and, more significantly, exactly two weeks after the Austrians had sued for peace with the French. In other words, the Spanish writers would seem to be off the mark with their assumptions in this particular case.

As to their claims of an 'Austrian effect' on Wellesley's Spanish adventure, it would seem that, here too, there is a lack of substantiating documentation for their insinuations. Taking it almost as fact that Wellesley's move into Spain was a diversionary move to assist Austria, they go on to point out that the British commander effectually called a halt to his operation on 16 July (see his letter to Frere of that date) which, they claim, would have been at or about the time he would have learned of Austria's surrender on the Danube. Stretching their point, they also point out that Sir John Stuart called a halt to his operations in the Bay of Naples on 26 July, claiming that Stuart's expedition, like Wellesley's, was synchronised and sanctioned by London as a diversionary affair in aid of Austria. In an attempt to add perhaps a little more substance to their claims, the Spanish authors endeavour to link the two operations just mentioned, by asserting that it was barely credible that both Stuart and Wellesley had been endowed with a level of autonomy which would allow them to take such strategic decisions as calling a halt to expeditions which had been instigated and authorised by London, thus implying that they had been the recipients of 'further instructions' from their political masters to abandon their offensives after Austria had sued for peace. Accounts of the culminating confrontation on the Danube, the Battle of Aspern-Essling, fought on 21 and 22 May 1809, did not begin to appear in the British press until 16–21 July. Whether or not the news became known in the Tagus valley by 16 July, the date on which Wellesley began to voice doubts about continuing in Spain, is difficult to say, but it may well have reached Stuart by the 26th, the date on which he ceased operations, which makes it feasible that his expedition actually was linked to the Austrian offensive on the Danube. After all, in their negotiations with the British regarding their planned re-entry into the war with France, the Austrians did specifically mention that such an operation in the south of Italy might be of great value as a diversionary move. However, the suggestion by Sañudo and Stampa that the British expedition to Spain and Portugal was just another diversionary operation in favour of the Austrians, seems to be based on what was almost certainly the coincidental materialisation of Wellesley's appearance in Portugal in April 1809 with that of the launch of the Austrian offensive. In fact, with Cradock occupying Lisbon in the wake of Moore's failure in Spain, it was always Britain's intention to return to the Iberian Peninsula in the spring of 1809. As to their contention that Wellesley did not have the authority to call off his Spanish sojourn and return to Portugal, Sañudo and Stampa are probably misinterpreting his brief and, indeed, underestimating his will when at the head of an army in face of the enemy, a moment when the niceties of national strategy and governmental interference count for less than the *actualité* on the ground. In other words, their presumptions that both Stuart's and Wellesley's offensives were two sides of the same coin would seem to be somewhat tenuous.

A further claim made by Sañudo and Stampa was that, from the content of Wellesley's letters to Frere of 24 July, it is easy to discern that the real reasons for the British commander's decision to diverge from the plan of operations agreed upon by himself and Cuesta, were that, in the grand scheme of things, he knew that any success he might meet with in Spain would be only fleeting in the context of a failure by the Austrians in Germany. Which is why, they continue, that after being in Spain for just 20 days, and having suffered losses amounting to just 11 horses by the time he would have been hearing that the Austrians' advance had stalled, the British commander made the claim that it was time for him to return to Portugal on the premise that he had by then honoured the engagement he had entered into with Cuesta.[1]

But what about the possibility that Wellesley never received any 'secret' instructions from London to withdraw to Portugal in the light of Austria's failure? After all, not a shred of evidence that such orders were ever issued has emerged in the 210 years or so since the end of the Peninsular War. Sañudo and Stampa address this point when they focus upon the legitimacy of Wellesley's decision to withdraw to Portugal, a decision he seemed to have made some days before the Battle of Talavera, even if he did not act upon it until 3 August, a full six days after the battle had taken place. And they do eventually concede that, on the key question of the timing of a British withdrawal from Spain, Wellesley was within his rights in acting autonomously when invoking the move, pointing out that Castlereagh's original instructions prioritised the defence of Portugal above all else. After all, the leeway the British commander had been given to advance into Spain and cooperate with Spanish forces in their operations against the French, rested on the condition that such actions would ultimately lend themselves to his primary mission of defending Portugal. When and how he might choose to enter Spain, and indeed when he might withdraw, were thus questions left to his own discretion in the absence of instructions from a higher authority, but the overriding factor in all of his decisions had to be the integrity of Portugal. Accepting this, the Spanish authors seem to imply, almost grudgingly, that, in extremis, Wellesley would not have required further orders from London before ordering a withdrawal towards the Portuguese frontier, ultimately claiming that all he needed to justify his doing so, as far as his Spanish allies were concerned, was ample excuse, which he presented to Frere in the form of his claims that his troops were ill-supplied and on the verge of starvation, knowing that, via Frere, the route for his thoughts would lead to the latter's new masters in Seville. Whether Wellesley was gilding the lily or not by issuing such claims, he was well within his rights when deciding to return to Portugal, and it hardly needs mentioning that he did not require confirmation from London before acting tactically in the field, as the associated correspondence for such an arrangement would not complete its return journey for two or three weeks at least. It is this point that the authors seemingly dismiss when they talk of the possibility that secret, tactical orders were being been sent to Wellesley from London.

As a final point on the question of the supposed link between Austria's and Wellesley's offensives, we turn to Canning's letter to Garay of 20 July:

> ... we have found the way to Austria, with such aid as there was a possibility of conveying: and Austria in return will, I trust, open the continent to us by the success of her arms.

---

1   Sañudo & Stampa, *Crisis de una Alianza*, p.199.

At all events, a most powerful diversion, the very object of Your Excellency's most valued wishes, has been effected in favour of Spain, and I trust and hope that Spain will have taken full advantage of the interval thus afforded to her ...[2]

In other words, far from seeing Wellesley's expedition as a diversion in favour of Austria, Canning regarded Austria's offensive as a diversion of French resources from Spain, as did Villiers (see earlier).

Was Wellesley's Delay at Plasencia the Cause of the Failure on the Tagus?

When analysing Wellesley's aborted venture into Spain of 1809, it is all well and good to speculate about an 'Austrian effect' and any secret orders he may have received from London, once the business on the Danube had been settled in France's favour. However, it may be more rewarding to look at some fairly well documented reasons as to why the allied campaign of 1809 eventually failed, and why, in light of that failure, Wellesley decided to retreat to Portugal, leaving his Spanish allies to decide their own fate for themselves.

As we have seen, the major tenet of the allies' plan to push the French away from Madrid during the summer of 1809 was that they would launch a coordinated, twin-pronged attack towards the capital. Venegas, whose Army of La Mancha was subordinated to Cuesta in preparation for the offensive, was to act as a lure to French forces based within the city under the command of King Joseph, as well as Sebastiani's IV Corps lying to the south of the capital. Should Venegas be successful, his presence in La Mancha would prevent Joseph and Sebastiani from uniting with Victor's I Corps, which was stationed to the west of Madrid in anticipation of an advance by Cuesta and Wellesley from the region of Talavera. Of course, the key to any allied success in such a widespread field of operations would be coordination, cooperation and, *sine qua non*, communications, the three Cs. Unfortunately, by the time the allies were ready to move, none of those elements were present in any appreciable measure within their command structure. As such, during the latter two weeks of June 1809, whilst Wellesley waited at Abrantes in Portugal for the funds he required to finance his Spanish adventure, and Cuesta advanced along the south bank of the Tagus in pursuit of Victor as he retreated towards Madrid, Venegas, apparently on his own initiative, decided to advance from his safe haven in the Sierra Morena towards the Guadiana. It was a fool-hardy move; firstly, because neither Wellesley nor Cuesta were in any position to offer him support, and secondly because he was fully aware that the Army of La Mancha was no match for Sebastiani's IV Corps which, reinforced by Joseph's Guard, soon descended into La Mancha in search of an easy victory. On that occasion Venegas had the sense to retreat to the Sierra Morena, thus saving his army for the fight to come.

Eventually, the specie which Wellesley was pleading with Castlereagh to send him duly arrived, thus allowing him to advance into Spain, but the delay had set back allied plans by some 14 days. Had money not been a problem, he could have united with Cuesta on Victor's front at about the same time as Joseph and Sebastiani arrived on the Guadiana to confront

---

2   BL: Add. Mss. 37286: Canning to Garay, 20 July 1809, pp.104–115.

Venegas. With the French forces being thus separated by a distance of some 200 miles – just what the allied plan envisaged – a great Anglo-Spanish victory at Madrid would have been within reach. Viewed from this perspective, it could be argued that, for the sake of £100,000, the amount of money eventually delivered to Wellesley at Abrantes, the Tagus campaign was lost. Fortescue points out that the funds were placed ashore in Lisbon on 15 June 1809 but were not taken up to Abrantes until 25 June, which in itself may have been down to the very shortages in transport that Wellesley railed about.[3] Even so, with London's growing acquiescence to a projected campaign in Spain after the removal of Soult from Portugal, perhaps the wheels of Wellesley's coming offensive should have been oiled a month or so earlier. That said, perhaps it was lucre, filthy lucre; not Cuesta's obstinacy, not Spanish failings, not a lack of transport and provisions, just London's apparent tardiness, or even paltriness, in failing to fund the extended terms of Wellesley's expedition once he had expelled the French from Portugal, which could be said to have been the cause of the near-disaster that followed. Unless, that is, it was a genuine scarcity of specie, rather than Treasury dilatoriness, that retarded the arrival of Wellesley's purse.

Why Did Beresford Fail to Notice the Reinforcement and Movements of Soult?

In the above section we talked only of the French forces commanded by Victor, Sebastiani and Joseph, but there was a fourth enemy force for the allies to contend with during the Tagus campaign: Soult's amalgam of his own II Corps, Mortier's V Corps and Ney's VI Corps, some 50,000 men in total, all of which had been concentrated in the region of Zamora and Salamanca during the weeks following the French defeat at Oporto. Unaware of Soult's reinforcement, Wellesley had dismissed the idea of a resurgent II Corps appearing in his rear as he prepared to fight Victor, apparently comforting himself in the notion that, even if Soult's army had recovered from its recent beating in Portugal, at a strength of some 12,000 men it was still too small to trouble him. This, and the fact that Beresford's reconstituted Portuguese force was just across the frontier from him and well within striking distance, would mean that his corps would be pinned to its ground, unable to go to Victor's aid. But, incredibly, not only did Beresford seem to fail to notice the arrival of Mortier and Ney, he seemed also to have taken only rudimentary interest when Soult's combined force set off on its march south towards Béjar and the puerto de Baños, en-route to Plasencia, where it would be within easy reach of the bridge at Almaraz in Wellesley's rear, thus endangering what was probably his only escape route back to Portugal. Still convinced of Soult's weakness in the immediate aftermath of Talavera, the British commander, on hearing of the *Maréchal's* stirrings, decided to act, inviting Cuesta to send one of his divisions to take control of the mountain pass at Baños. The Spaniard, also dismissive of the idea that Soult offered a credible threat, somewhat reluctantly sent Bassecourt's 5th Division to do the job, only for it to arrive too late to prevent Soult from traversing the pass, thus allowing him to occupy Plasencia and establish a presence in the allied rear.

---

3   J.W. Fortescue, *A History of the British Army* (London: MacMillan & Co., 1912), vol.7, p.202.

Between them, Beresford's apparent ignorance of Soult's whereabouts, combined with Cuesta's surliness, could easily have spelt the end for Wellesley's army when, with increasing uneasiness about the Frenchman's approach, the British commander decided to go in search of him, only to discover that he was about to offer battle to a force at least double the size of his own. Left with no choice other than to make a dash for the south bank of the Tagus via the bridge at Arzobispo, the British could easily have discovered Soult in their path as they headed for Portugal, had not the Marqués de la Reyna dismantled the pontoon bridge at Almaraz, thus confining the French to the north bank of the river until they could effect the necessary repairs to the crossing.

Beresford's inaction has been seemingly downplayed or ignored in the historiography of the Tagus campaign, but the truth of the matter is that, on 31 July, he crossed the Spanish frontier and occupied San Felices near Ciudad Rodrigo. It was there where he heard of Soult's march from Salamanca towards Plasencia, but it seems he did not inform Wellesley that the French were on the move in his rear. Nevertheless, in following Wellesley's earlier instruction on how to react to such a move, he marched his army south, parallel to Soult's movement, and was at Moraleja near Coria on the north bank of the Alagón, some 25 miles west of Plasencia, before Soult arrived at his destination. According to Oman, Wellesley was unconvinced by the rumours of Soult's approach at the head of a large army. But such information was arriving at his headquarters up to and including 1 August, all of it origi-nating from secret agents operating in the region of Salamanca.[4] Fortescue claimed that, even as Wellesley was hearing that the French advanced guard had reached Navalmoral on 3 August, he was still ignorant of their true strength. Just two hours later a second letter arrived from O'Donojú, telling him that the whole of the French troops in northern Spain, some 50,000 men, were descending upon him.[5] The Spanish intelligence did not arrive a moment too soon, as he was on the point of marching to meet Soult when it was shared with him. Why Beresford did not keep his commander in chief fully informed of the situation as he shadowed the Frenchman is difficult to understand, and the consequences of his seeming lack of thoroughness could have been disastrous.

Was Cuesta More Sinned Against than Sinner?

Despite Venegas's abortive first advance from the Sierra Morena in late June, he was ready to stir once more by 4 July. This time there would be several attempts to ensure that his move-ments were coordinated with those of Wellesley and Cuesta, albeit via extremely long lines of communication; but throughout the remainder of the campaign, he absolutely refused to offer any measure of cooperation to his superior. This attitude, and Cornel's acquiescence to it, would be a determining factor, not only in the overall failure on the Tagus, but in the defeat and destruction of his own Army of La Mancha at Almonacid. Wilful treachery may not be too strong a description for Venegas's behaviour during the month of July 1809.

---

4   Oman, *History of the Peninsular War*, vol.2, p.571.
5   Fortescue *A History of the British Army*, vol.7, p.268.

As well as Venegas's contrariness, the treatment of Cuesta by the senior members of the *Junta Suprema*, almost from the day it was formed, was questionable to say the least. On the other hand, Cuesta himself had little if any respect for that self-appointed body, and was at one point discussing with a number of other senior officers the possibility of stripping it of its influence over the army. Venegas was not involved in the plot and, having little respect for Cuesta, was happy to play a prejudicial role to his plans for the 1809 campaign, often giving vent to his feelings about his direct superior in his communications with Seville.

Wellesley too had some choice words to say about Cuesta during their short working partnership of 1809. He saw his Spanish ally as being unduly obstinate and obstructive, words whose Spanish equivalents Cuesta might probably have been happy to use to describe his English ally in turn. However, despite these mutually held assessments of each other's character, the short but active relationship between the two during the three or four weeks surrounding the Battle of Talavera seems to have borne some fruit, Cuesta seemingly happy to take on the minor role during the two days of battle, as the French singled out the British troops holding the Cerro de Medellín for their special attention.

By the time the British and Spanish troops took the field at Talavera, there had been some background rumblings about the possibility of appointing Wellesley as supreme allied commander, the idea of creating such a post having surfaced in late 1808 as Sir John Moore led his expeditionary force towards the Ebro valley. Such plans were shelved when the British were forced to evacuate Spain in January 1809, but by the time they had returned to Iberia in April 1809, the notion of appointing a British allied supremo was again in play. As the related intrigues took root in London and Seville, many of them fuelled by an innate dislike of Cuesta held by a number of deputies in the *Junta*, it is difficult to believe his claims that he did not come to know of them until some time after illness had put an end to his military career. Should the old warrior's assertions in this vein fall a little short of the truth, then it might explain some of the uncooperative behaviour attributed to him by some in his dealings with Wellesley during the days leading up to the clash of arms at Talavera, but in no way should he be blamed for the eventual failure on the Tagus during the summer of 1809.

Final Words

In the final analysis, it must be said that there would not have been a campaign in the Tagus valley during the summer of 1809, had Cuesta not challenged Victor on the south bank of the river during the early months of the year. Even after his defeat at Medellín, the mere fact that he regrouped and began to reconstruct his army in the region of Monesterio and Llerena, both before and after Wellesley's return to the Peninsula in April, meant that Victor was wary about setting foot into Portugal. Had he done so, Wellesley would not have been able to march upon Soult, and may even have been forced to re-embark at Lisbon had Soult and Victor united around the Portuguese capital. With his scratch armies, and we should recall that he put two such structures together between December 1808 and April 1809, Cuesta kept up the pressure on his adversary, distracting Victor from his ambition either to drive south into Andalucía or to enter Portugal; all of which allowed Wellesley the time and opportunity to disembark at Lisbon without opposition. Still very much in the fight by the time the British commander had dealt with Soult at Oporto, the old warrior would provide a platform for the Englishman's subsequent incursion into Spain.

With regard to the persistent claims that he was unjustifiably antagonistic towards the *Junta Suprema*, his supporters would argue that, in the original flashpoint issue between the contending parties, Cuesta had a legitimate case against Valdés, as well as the *Junta*, during the period when Garay, Cornel and Floridablanca *et al* were declaring themselves the rightful holders of national authority in Spain. Nevertheless, once in their self-appointed position as arbiters of justice, they found in favour of the *Capitán General's* adversary and confined Cuesta to a form of house arrest whilst thinking about what next to do with him. However, after their inglorious flight from Aranjuez to the safety of Seville, as Napoleon's legions surged across northern Spain, the *Junta's* leaders were more than happy to support the old warrior in his attempts to keep the French at bay, releasing him from the dubiously legitimate incarceration they had imposed upon him and allowing him to take command of the Army of Extremadura. Unfortunately, business as usual returned at Seville once Wellesley had re-appeared in Portugal, allowing them to install their man, Venegas, at the head of the Army of La Mancha. It was then that the *Junta's* machinations and intrigues against Cuesta resurfaced, with the British being drawn into the affair by promises to offer them command over the Spanish armies in the field once the old warrior had been side-lined. Whether or not Cuesta knew of these plans at the time of the Tagus campaign is debatable, but what should not be in any doubt was the level of commitment and cooperation shown to Wellesley by Cuesta during the months of July and August 1809, when the allies were in direct confrontation with the French. Sadly, in their analysis of the events of 1809, many commentators focus upon Wellesley's accusations of obstinacy and worse against the Spaniard, and after compounding these with the British commander's complaints about the lack of provisions and transport made available to his army, something which had nothing to do with Cuesta, they have tended to cast him as the villain of the piece when lamenting the lack of overall success of the Tagus campaign. The truth of the matter is that, although sometimes lacking in the level of zeal expected by Wellesley, the Spaniard did all that was asked of him during the crucial 48 hours of fighting at Talavera, effectively, and it would seem willingly, playing second fiddle to the British commander.

It should also be remembered that Cuesta was the first of the allied commanders to discover the true strength of Soult's army as it marched to take the allies in the rear at Talavera, Spanish intelligence alerting him to the danger as Wellesley counter-marched to confront his recent adversary once more. And it was the Spaniard's analysis of the information presented to him that convinced him to abandon his own holding position at Talavera and march to both warn his ally of the danger in his front, and to help him confront Soult if he could not be avoided. That the old warrior had to contend with all of this whilst being undermined by Venegas and Cornel, to say nothing of the continuing British intrigues against him, tells us more about the failings of those around him than it does about Cuesta's apparent obduracy. That his battles were seen as being expensive in terms of the lives of the men who fought under him, should come as no surprise. Most of his troops were simply raw, peasant recruits plucked from their agricultural surroundings; the vast majority of them entirely bereft of military preparedness, but it was almost certainly better for the allied cause that he fought those battles than not, especially that of Medellín.

In the final analysis, it could even be said that the Tagus campaign was Cuesta's campaign. Who else in Spain was willing to place themselves in the path of the seemingly unstoppable French counter-offensive of 1808–1809? His confrontation with Victor at Medellín was costly – to both sides, and at one point it looked as though his usual tactic of all-out attack might succeed, until his cavalry let him down. Undaunted by his eventual defeat on the Guadiana he retired to the western foothills of the Sierra Morena to regroup and recover, ready to take the fight to the enemy once more. Victor took the hint. To march south into a sparse wilderness in pursuit of his adversary would risk a fate similar to that suffered by Dupont at Bailén during the previous year; and to advance along the Tagus into Portugal might lead to entrapment within its territory, with Wellesley newly arrived at Lisbon and Cuesta once again stirring on the south bank of the great river in Spanish Extremadura.

Later, whilst Wellesley was dealing with Soult in the north of Portugal, Cuesta was harassing Victor from his bases south of the Tagus, eventually succeeding in forcing him to retreat towards Talavera. And it was only after Wellesley's decision to operate in Spain that the old warrior perhaps began to sense that there was collusion between London and Seville, the aim of which was to depose him in favour of establishing a unified command under a single head – Wellesley himself. Both this and the insubordination of Venegas, again with the collusion of Cornel in Seville, may account for Cuesta's somewhat less than sanguine attitude towards his British allies once his army had united with that of Sir Arthur.

If Spain needed a hero around whom to rally in 1809, then perhaps Cuesta could be said to be such a figure. Always willing to take the fight to the enemy, he should have been afforded all the support that could have been mustered from the highest ranks in the Anglo-Spanish alliance. Instead, he sometimes found himself fighting on three fronts: against the French on the ground; against Wellesley and his masters in London; and against his enemies in the *Junta Suprema* at Seville and their favourite, Francisco Venegas.

Appendix

Letter 1, Wellesley to Frere, 24 July 1809

I conclude that *General* Cuesta apprised the government of the success of the first operation of the combined armies. We intended to attack the enemy this morning at daylight in his position on the Alberche, and all the arrangements were made and the columns formed for that purpose; but the enemy retired to Sta Olalla in the course of the night. Gen. Cuesta has since marched to Cevolla; and I do not know if he intends to halt there, or what are to be his future operations.

I have been obliged to intimate to him, since my arrival here, that I should consider that I had performed the engagement that I had made with him as soon as I should have removed the enemy from the Alberche, and should thereby have given him possession of the course of the Tagus, and should have laid open to him the communication with La Mancha and Gen. Venegas' corps, and that I could attempt no further operation till I should be made certain of my supplies, by being furnished with proper means of transport and the requisite provisions from the country.

This intimation has become still more necessary within the last 2 days, in which I am concerned to say that, although my troops have been on forced marches, engaged in operations with the enemy, the success of which I must say depended on them, they have had nothing to eat, while the Spanish army have had plenty; notwithstanding that I have returns of engagements made by the *alcaldes* of villages in the Vera de Plasencia to furnish this army before the 24th of this month with 250,000 rations.

I certainly lament the necessity which obliges me to halt at present, and will oblige me to withdraw from Spain, if it should continue. There is no man that does not acknowledge, even Gen. Cuesta acknowledges, the justice and propriety of my conduct in halting now, or in eventually withdrawing; and I can only say, that I have never seen an army so ill-treated in any country, or, considering that all depends upon its operations, one which deserved good treatment so much.

It is ridiculous to pretend that the country cannot supply our wants. The French army is well fed, and the soldiers who are taken in good health, and well supplied with bread, of which indeed they left a small magazine behind them. This is a rich country in corn, in comparison with Portugal, and yet, during the whole of my operations in that country, we never wanted bread but on one day on the frontiers of Galicia. In the Vera de Plasencia there are means to supply this army for four months, as I am informed, and yet the *alcaldes* have not performed their engagements with me. The Spanish army has plenty of everything, and we alone, upon whom everything depends, are actually starving.

Index

People

General Index

From Reason to Revolution – Warfare 1721-1815

http://www.helion.co.uk/series/from-reason-to-revolution-1721-1815.php

The 'From Reason to Revolution' series covers the period of military history 1721–1815, an era in which fortress-based strategy and linear battles gave way to the nation-in-arms and the beginnings of total war.

This era saw the evolution and growth of light troops of all arms, and of increasingly flexible command systems to cope with the growing armies fielded by nations able to mobilise far greater proportions of their manpower than ever before. Many of these developments were fired by the great political upheavals of the era, with revolutions in America and France bringing about social change which in turn fed back into the military sphere as whole nations readied themselves for war. Only in the closing years of the period, as the reactionary powers began to regain the upper hand, did a military synthesis of the best of the old and the new become possible.

The series will examine the military and naval history of the period in a greater degree of detail than has hitherto been attempted, and has a very wide brief, with the intention of covering all aspects from the battles, campaigns, logistics, and tactics, to the personalities, armies, uniforms, and equipment.

Submissions

The publishers would be pleased to receive submissions for this series. Please contact series editor Andrew Bamford via email (andrewbamford@helion.co.uk), or in writing to Helion & Company Limited, Unit 8 Amherst Business Centre, Budbrooke Road, Warwick, CV34 5WE

Titles

1   *Lobositz to Leuthen: Horace St Paul and the Campaigns of the Austrian Army in the Seven Years War 1756-57* (Neil Cogswell)

2   *Glories to Useless Heroism: The Seven Years War in North America from the French journals of Comte Maurés de Malartic, 1755-1760* (William Raffle (ed.))

3   *Reminiscences 1808-1815 Under Wellington: The Peninsular and Waterloo Memoirs of William Hay* (Andrew Bamford (ed.))

4   *Far Distant Ships: The Royal Navy and the Blockade of Brest 1793-1815* (Quintin Barry)

5   *Godoy's Army: Spanish Regiments and Uniforms from the Estado Militar of 1800* (Charles Esdaile and Alan Perry)

6   *On Gladsmuir Shall the Battle Be! The Battle of Prestonpans 1745* (Arran Johnston)

7   *The French Army of the Orient 1798-1801: Napoleon's Beloved 'Egyptians'* (Yves Martin)

8   *The Autobiography, or Narrative of a Soldier: The Peninsular War Memoirs of William Brown of the 45th Foot* (Steve Brown (ed.))

9   *Recollections from the Ranks: Three Russian Soldiers' Autobiographies from the Napoleonic Wars* (Darrin Boland)

10   *By Fire and Bayonet: Grey's West Indies Campaign of 1794* (Steve Brown)

11   *Olmütz to Torgau: Horace St Paul and the Campaigns of the Austrian Army in the Seven Years War 1758-60* (Neil Cogswell)

12   *Murat's Army: The Army of the Kingdom of Naples 1806-1815* (Digby Smith)

13   *The Veteran or 40 Years' Service in the British Army: The Scurrilous Recollections of Paymaster John Harley 47th Foot – 1798-1838* (Gareth Glover (ed.))

14   *Narrative of the Eventful Life of Thomas Jackson: Militiaman and Coldstream Sergeant, 1803-15* (Eamonn O'Keeffe (ed.))

No.15   *For Orange and the States: The Army of the Dutch Republic 1713-1772 Part I: Infantry* (Marc Geerdinck-Schaftenaar)

16   *Men Who Are Determined to be Free: The American Assault on Stony Point, 15 July 1779* (David C. Bonk)